RADIANT

TONY VALENTE

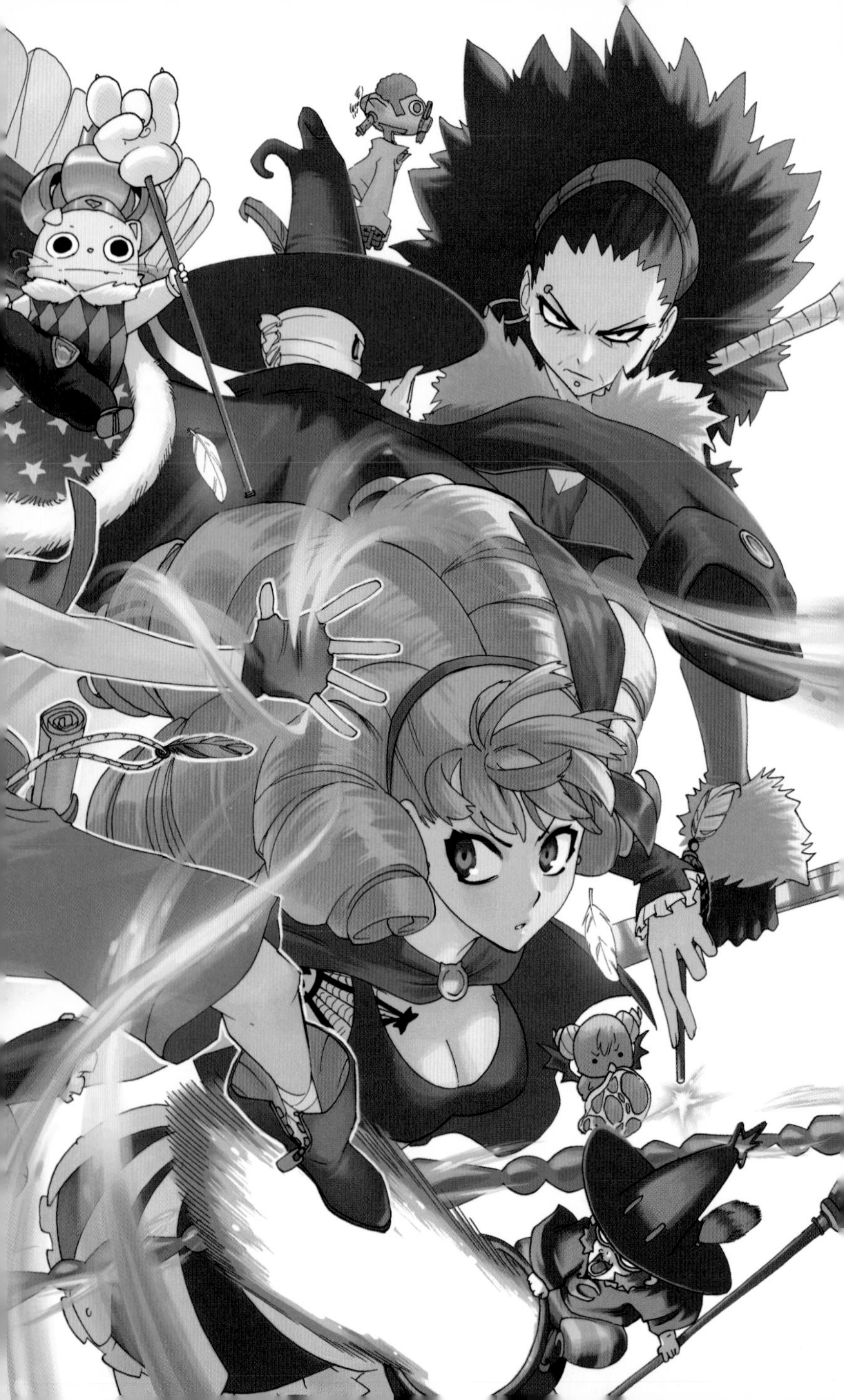

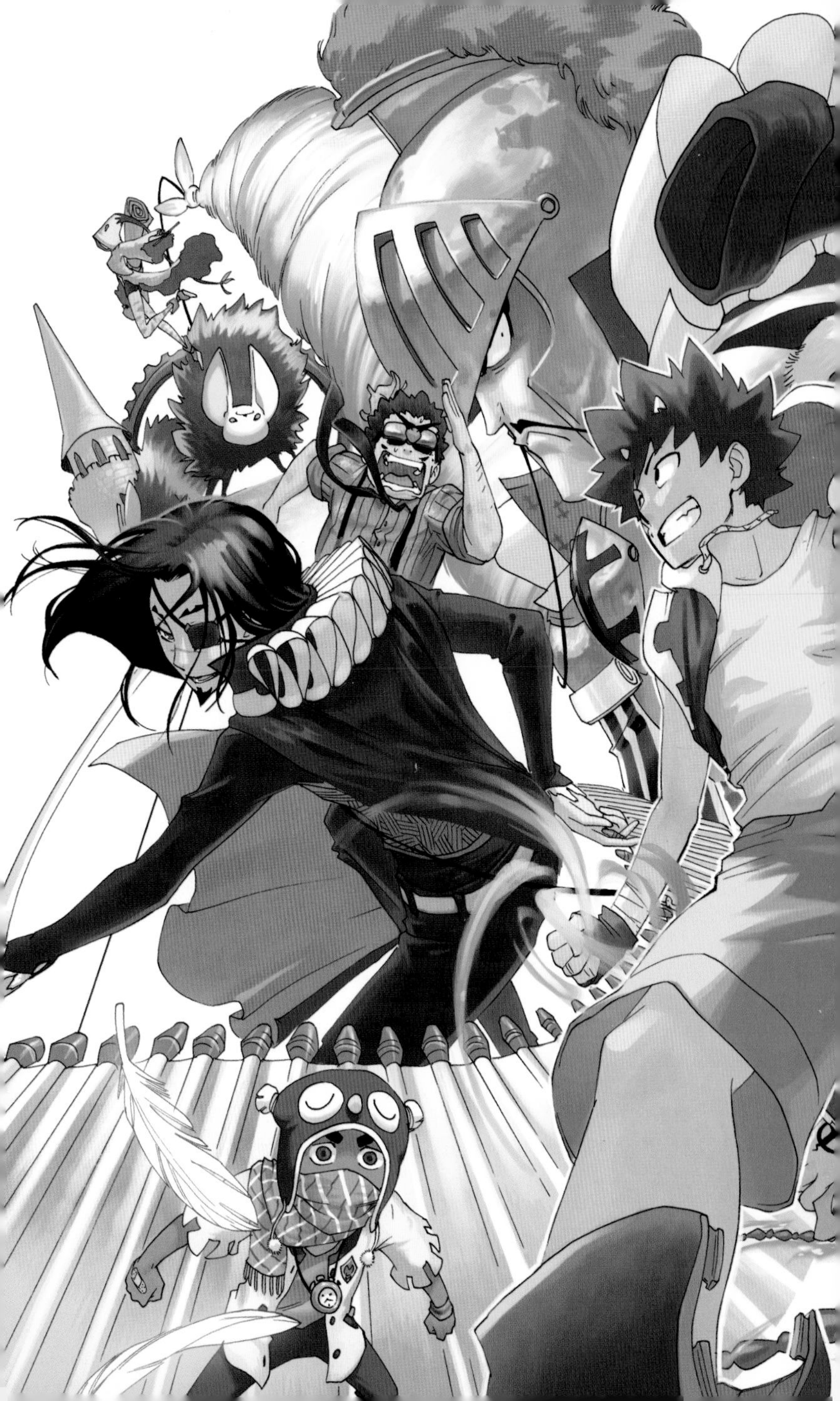

CONTENTS

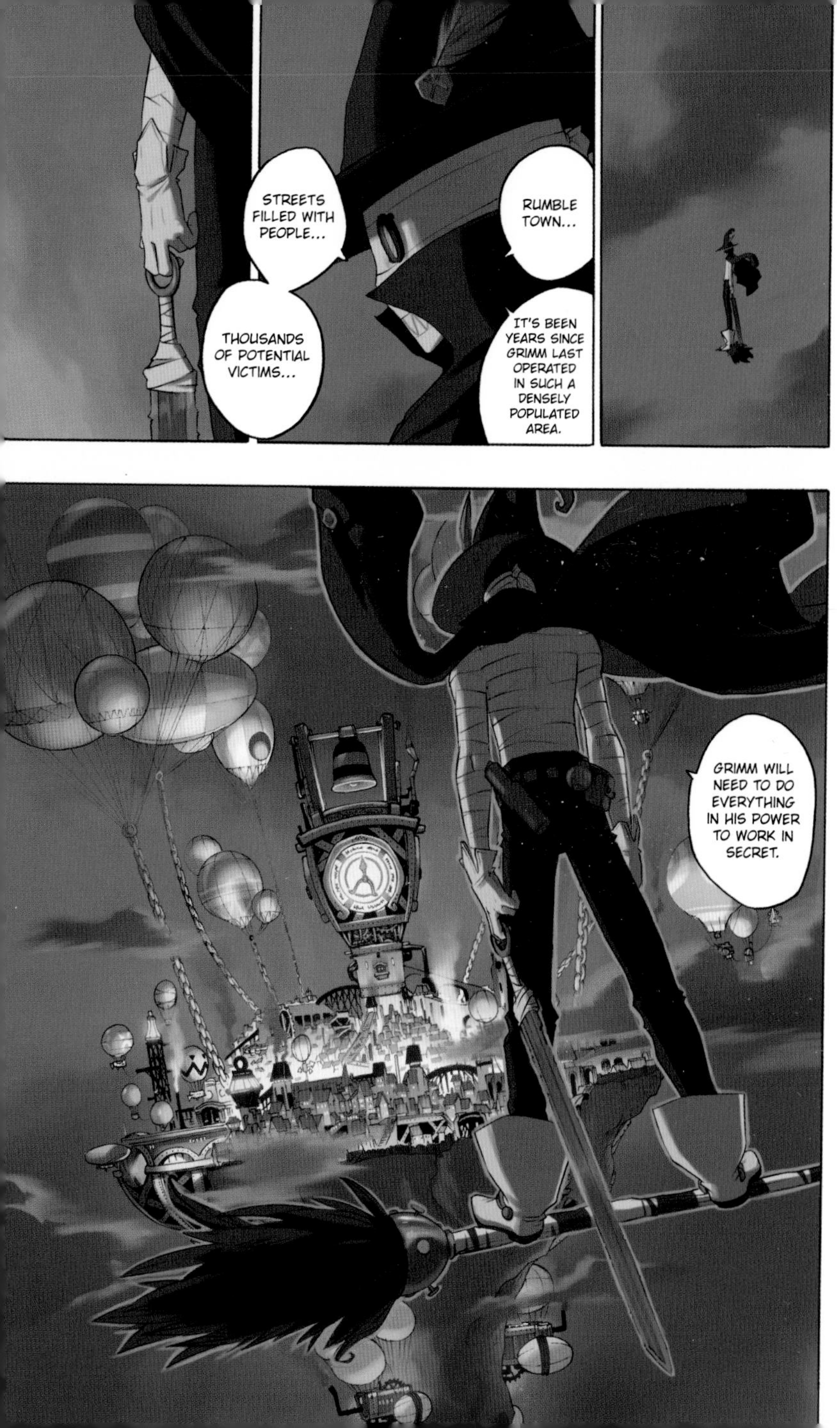
RUMBLE TOWN...
IT'S BEEN YEARS SINCE GRIMM LAST OPERATED IN SUCH A DENSELY POPULATED AREA.
STREETS FILLED WITH PEOPLE...
THOUSANDS OF POTENTIAL VICTIMS...
GRIMM WILL NEED TO DO EVERYTHING IN HIS POWER TO WORK IN SECRET.

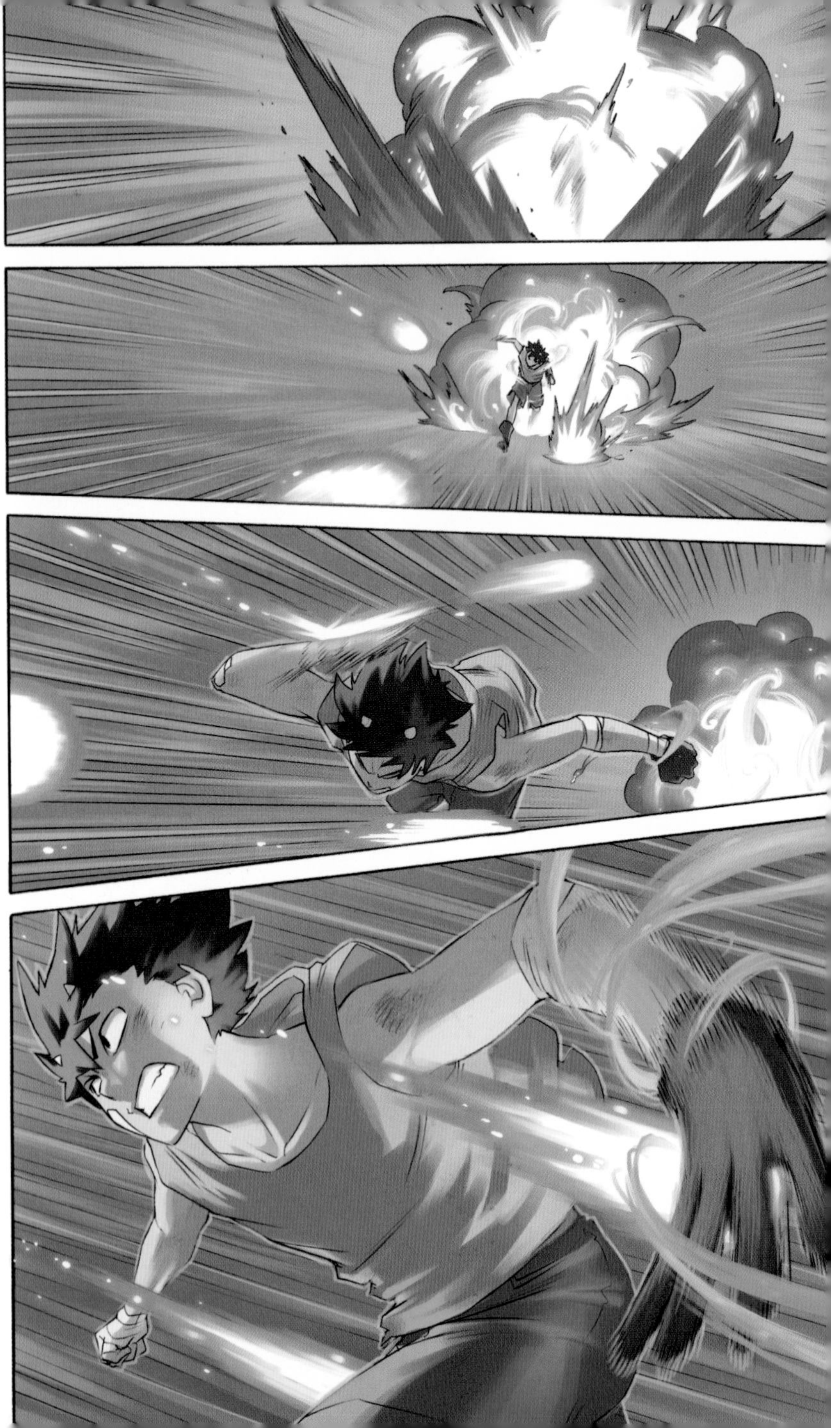

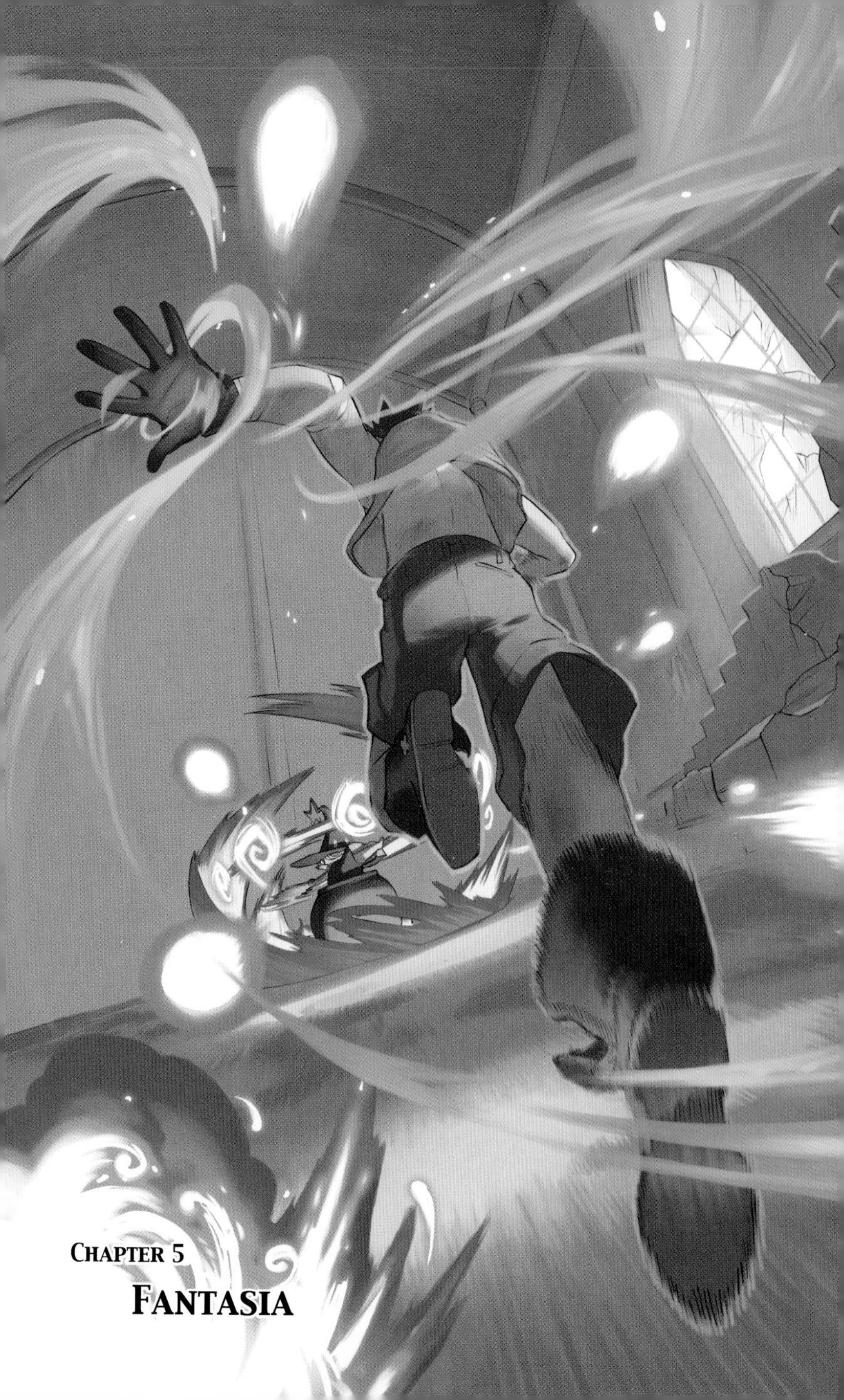

Chapter 5
Fantasia

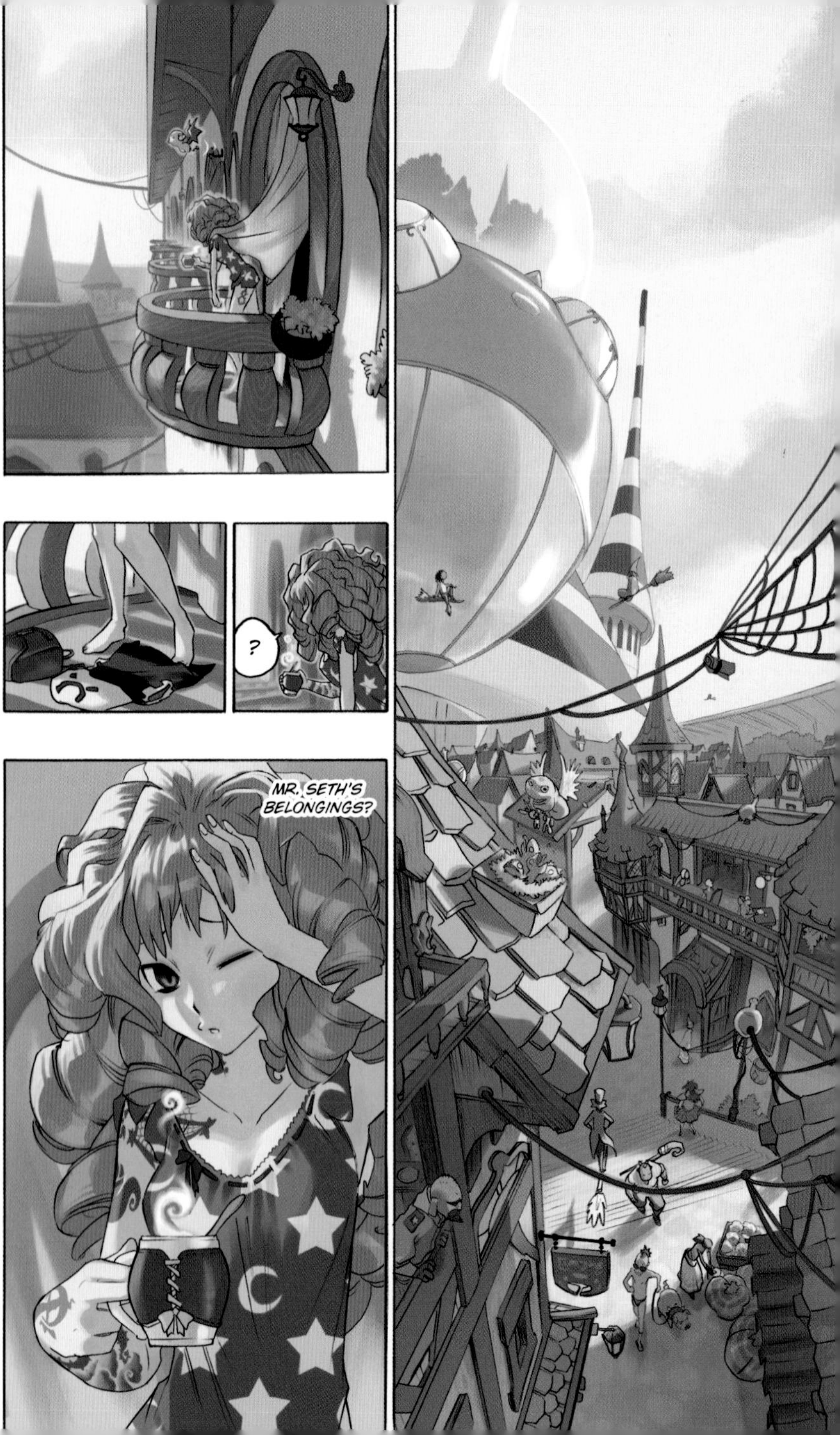
?
MR. SETH'S BELONGINGS?

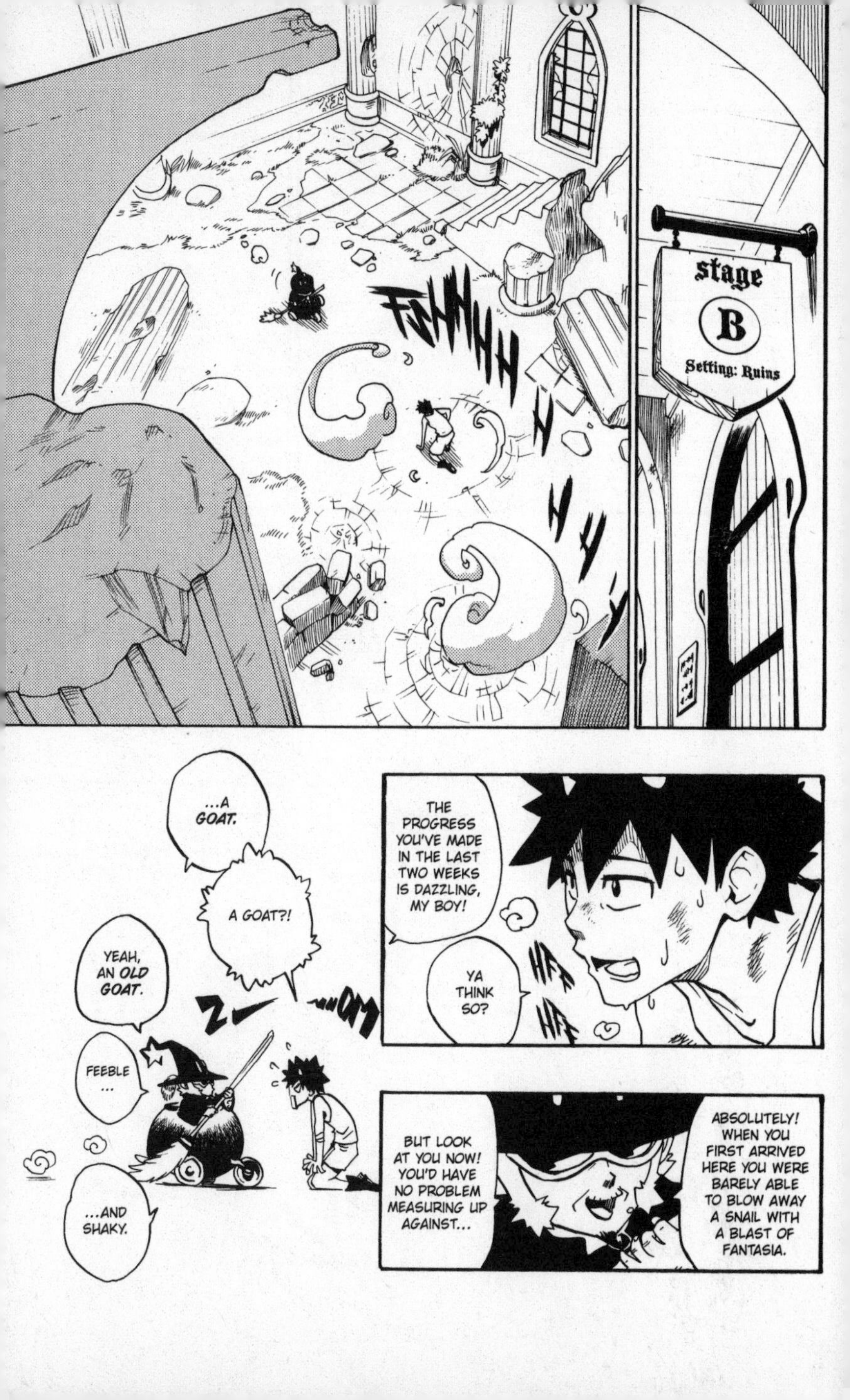
stage
B
Setting: Ruins
FSHHHHH
THE PROGRESS YOU'VE MADE IN THE LAST TWO WEEKS IS DAZZLING, MY BOY!
YA THINK SO?
HFF
HFF
ABSOLUTELY! WHEN YOU FIRST ARRIVED HERE YOU WERE BARELY ABLE TO BLOW AWAY A SNAIL WITH A BLAST OF FANTASIA.
BUT LOOK AT YOU NOW! YOU'D HAVE NO PROBLEM MEASURING UP AGAINST...
...A GOAT.
A GOAT?!
YEAH, AN OLD GOAT.
FEEBLE...
...AND SHAKY.

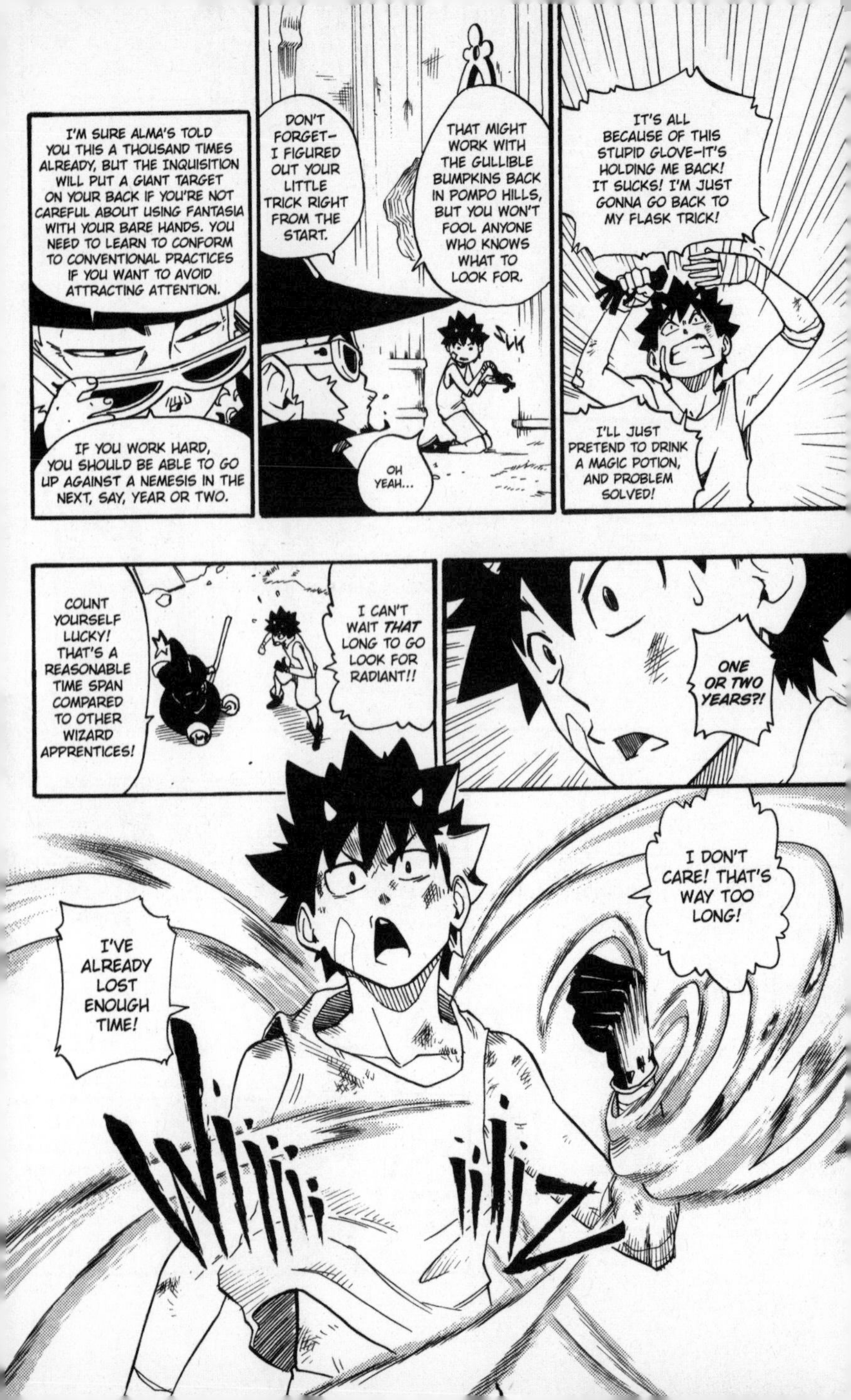
IT'S ALL BECAUSE OF THIS STUPID GLOVE—IT'S HOLDING ME BACK! IT SUCKS! I'M JUST GONNA GO BACK TO MY FLASK TRICK!
I'LL JUST PRETEND TO DRINK A MAGIC POTION, AND PROBLEM SOLVED!
SLK
THAT MIGHT WORK WITH THE GULLIBLE BUMPKINS BACK IN POMPO HILLS, BUT YOU WON'T FOOL ANYONE WHO KNOWS WHAT TO LOOK FOR.
DON'T FORGET— I FIGURED OUT YOUR LITTLE TRICK RIGHT FROM THE START.
OH YEAH...
I'M SURE ALMA'S TOLD YOU THIS A THOUSAND TIMES ALREADY, BUT THE INQUISITION WILL PUT A GIANT TARGET ON YOUR BACK IF YOU'RE NOT CAREFUL ABOUT USING FANTASIA WITH YOUR BARE HANDS. YOU NEED TO LEARN TO CONFORM TO CONVENTIONAL PRACTICES IF YOU WANT TO AVOID ATTRACTING ATTENTION.
IF YOU WORK HARD, YOU SHOULD BE ABLE TO GO UP AGAINST A NEMESIS IN THE NEXT, SAY, YEAR OR TWO.
ONE OR TWO YEARS?!
I CAN'T WAIT *THAT* LONG TO GO LOOK FOR RADIANT!!
COUNT YOURSELF LUCKY! THAT'S A REASONABLE TIME SPAN COMPARED TO OTHER WIZARD APPRENTICES!
I DON'T CARE! THAT'S WAY TOO LONG!
I'VE ALREADY LOST ENOUGH TIME!
WHIIIIIIZ

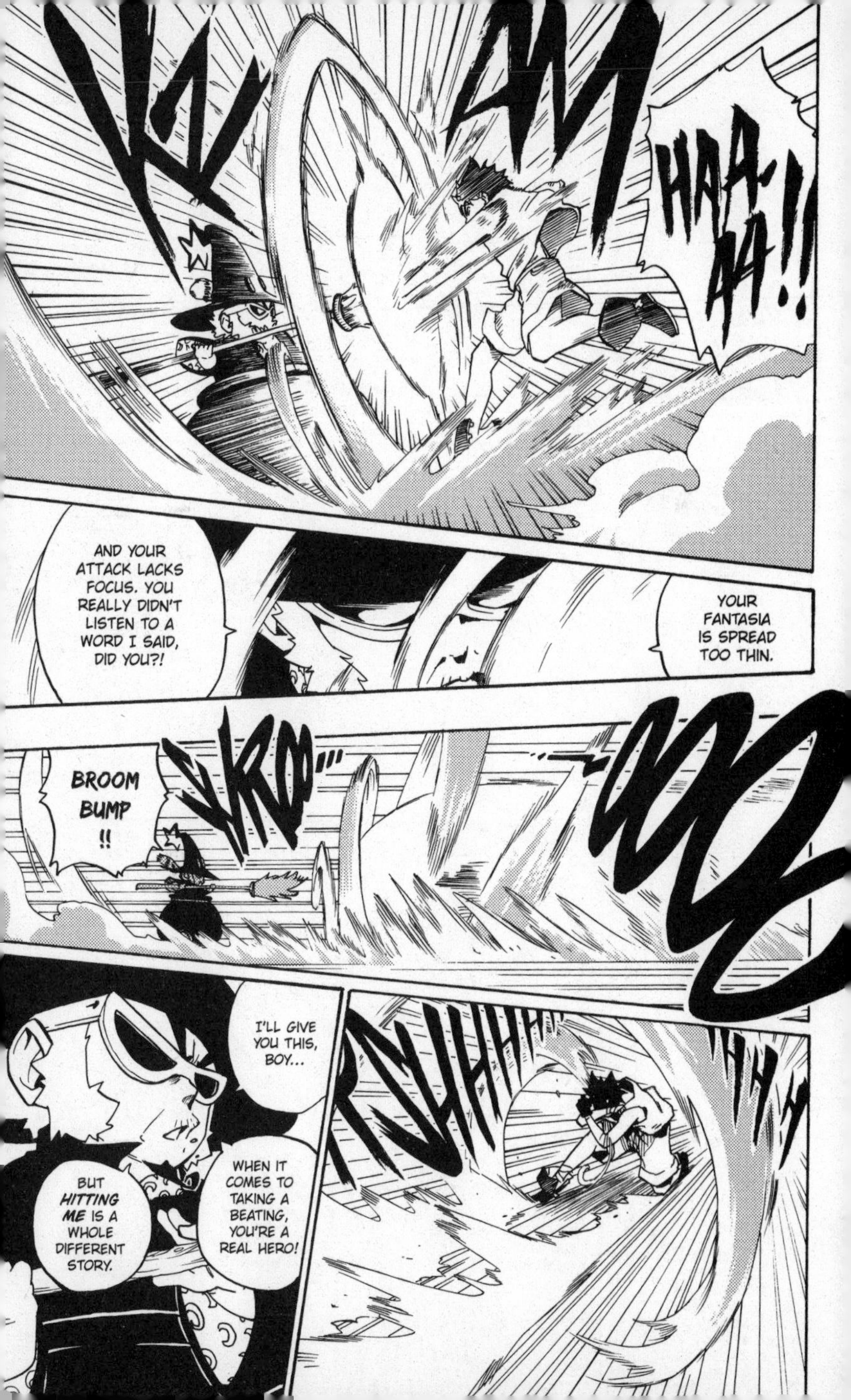
HAA-AA!!
YOUR FANTASIA IS SPREAD TOO THIN.
AND YOUR ATTACK LACKS FOCUS. YOU REALLY DIDN'T LISTEN TO A WORD I SAID, DID YOU?!
BROOM BUMP !!
I'LL GIVE YOU THIS, BOY...
WHEN IT COMES TO TAKING A BEATING, YOU'RE A REAL HERO!
BUT *HITTING ME* IS A WHOLE DIFFERENT STORY.

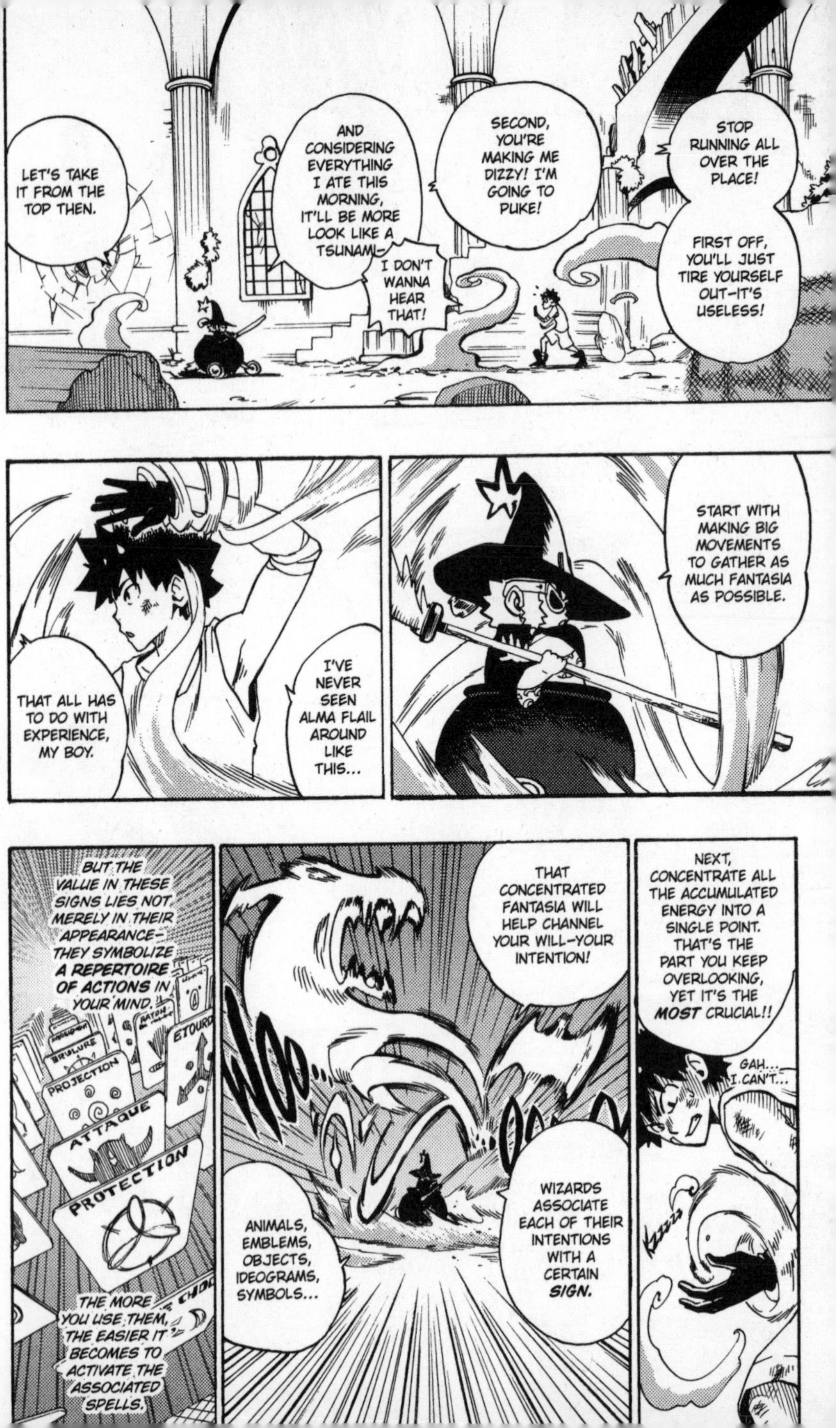
STOP RUNNING ALL OVER THE PLACE!
FIRST OFF, YOU'LL JUST TIRE YOURSELF OUT–IT'S USELESS!
SECOND, YOU'RE MAKING ME DIZZY! I'M GOING TO PUKE!
AND CONSIDERING EVERYTHING I ATE THIS MORNING, IT'LL BE MORE LOOK LIKE A TSUNAMI–
I DON'T WANNA HEAR THAT!
LET'S TAKE IT FROM THE TOP THEN.
START WITH MAKING BIG MOVEMENTS TO GATHER AS MUCH FANTASIA AS POSSIBLE.
I'VE NEVER SEEN ALMA FLAIL AROUND LIKE THIS...
THAT ALL HAS TO DO WITH EXPERIENCE, MY BOY.
NEXT, CONCENTRATE ALL THE ACCUMULATED ENERGY INTO A SINGLE POINT. THAT'S THE PART YOU KEEP OVERLOOKING, YET IT'S THE **MOST** CRUCIAL!!
GAH... I CAN'T...
THAT CONCENTRATED FANTASIA WILL HELP CHANNEL YOUR WILL–YOUR INTENTION!
WOO...
WIZARDS ASSOCIATE EACH OF THEIR INTENTIONS WITH A CERTAIN **SIGN.**
ANIMALS, EMBLEMS, OBJECTS, IDEOGRAMS, SYMBOLS...
BUT THE VALUE IN THESE SIGNS LIES NOT MERELY IN THEIR APPEARANCE–THEY SYMBOLIZE **A REPERTOIRE OF ACTIONS** IN YOUR MIND.
BRULURE
ETOURD
PROJECTION
ATTAQUE
PROTECTION
THE MORE YOU USE THEM, THE EASIER IT BECOMES TO ACTIVATE THE ASSOCIATED SPELLS.

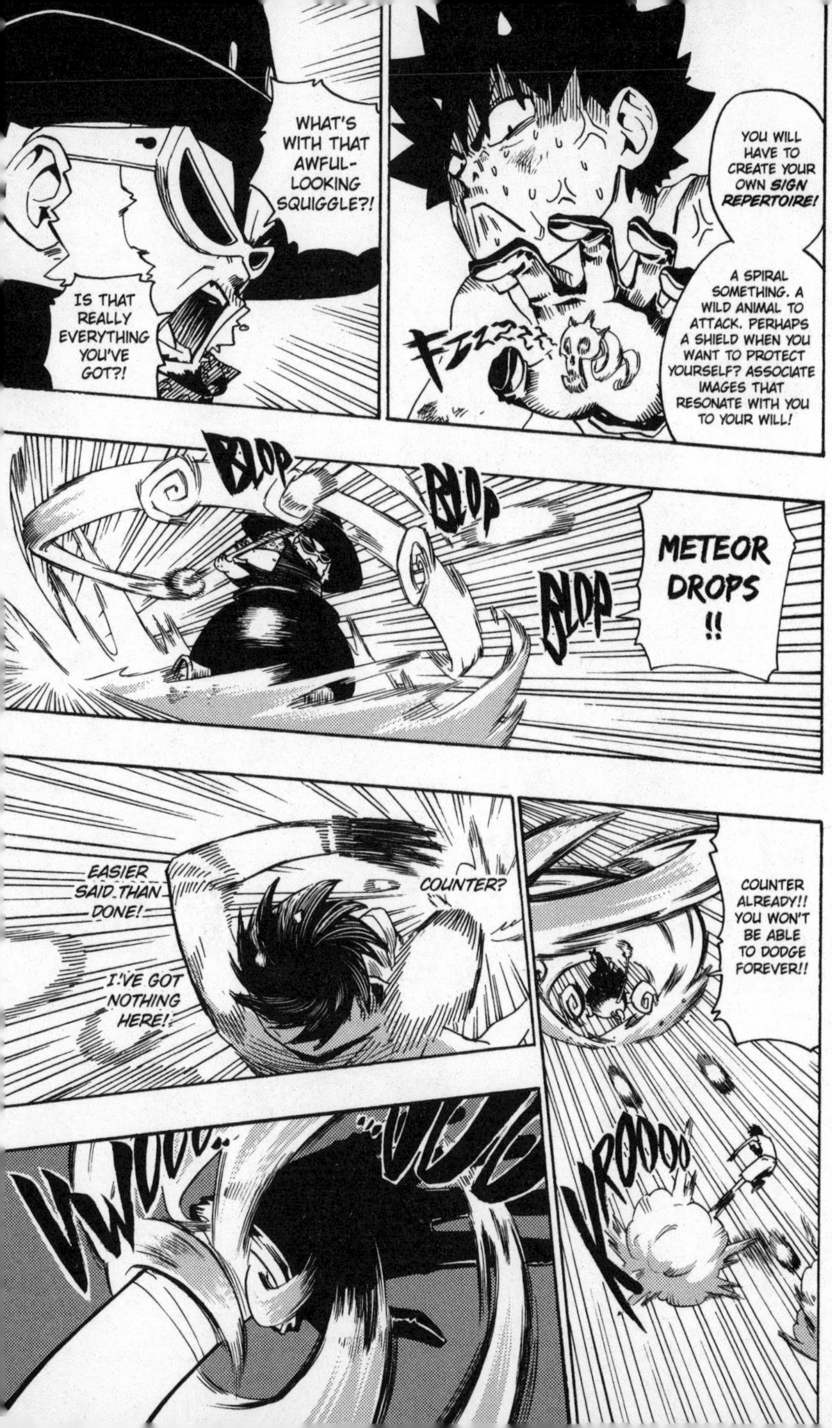

YOU WILL HAVE TO CREATE YOUR OWN SIGN REPERTOIRE!
A SPIRAL SOMETHING. A WILD ANIMAL TO ATTACK. PERHAPS A SHIELD WHEN YOU WANT TO PROTECT YOURSELF? ASSOCIATE IMAGES THAT RESONATE WITH YOU TO YOUR WILL!
FZZZZZ
WHAT'S WITH THAT AWFUL-LOOKING SQUIGGLE?!
IS THAT REALLY EVERYTHING YOU'VE GOT?!
METEOR DROPS !!
BLOP
BLOP
BLOP
COUNTER ALREADY!! YOU WON'T BE ABLE TO DODGE FOREVER!!
COUNTER?
EASIER SAID THAN DONE!
I'VE GOT NOTHING HERE!
KROOOO
VWOOO...OOO

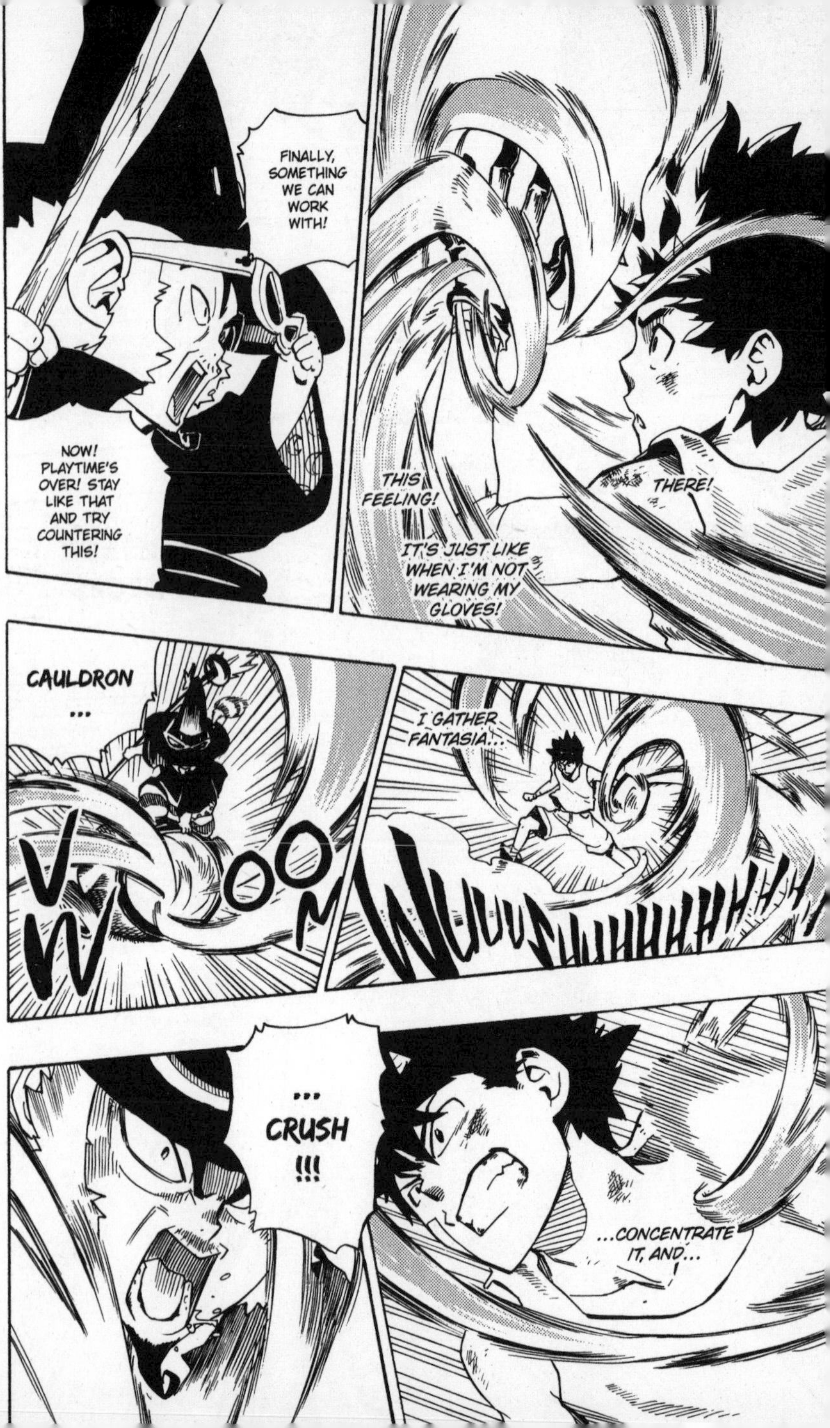
THERE!
THIS FEELING!
IT'S JUST LIKE WHEN I'M NOT WEARING MY GLOVES!
FINALLY, SOMETHING WE CAN WORK WITH!
NOW! PLAYTIME'S OVER! STAY LIKE THAT AND TRY COUNTERING THIS!
I GATHER FANTASIA...
WHUUUSHHHHHHHH
CAULDRON...
VWOOOM
...CONCENTRATE IT, AND...!
...CRUSH!!!

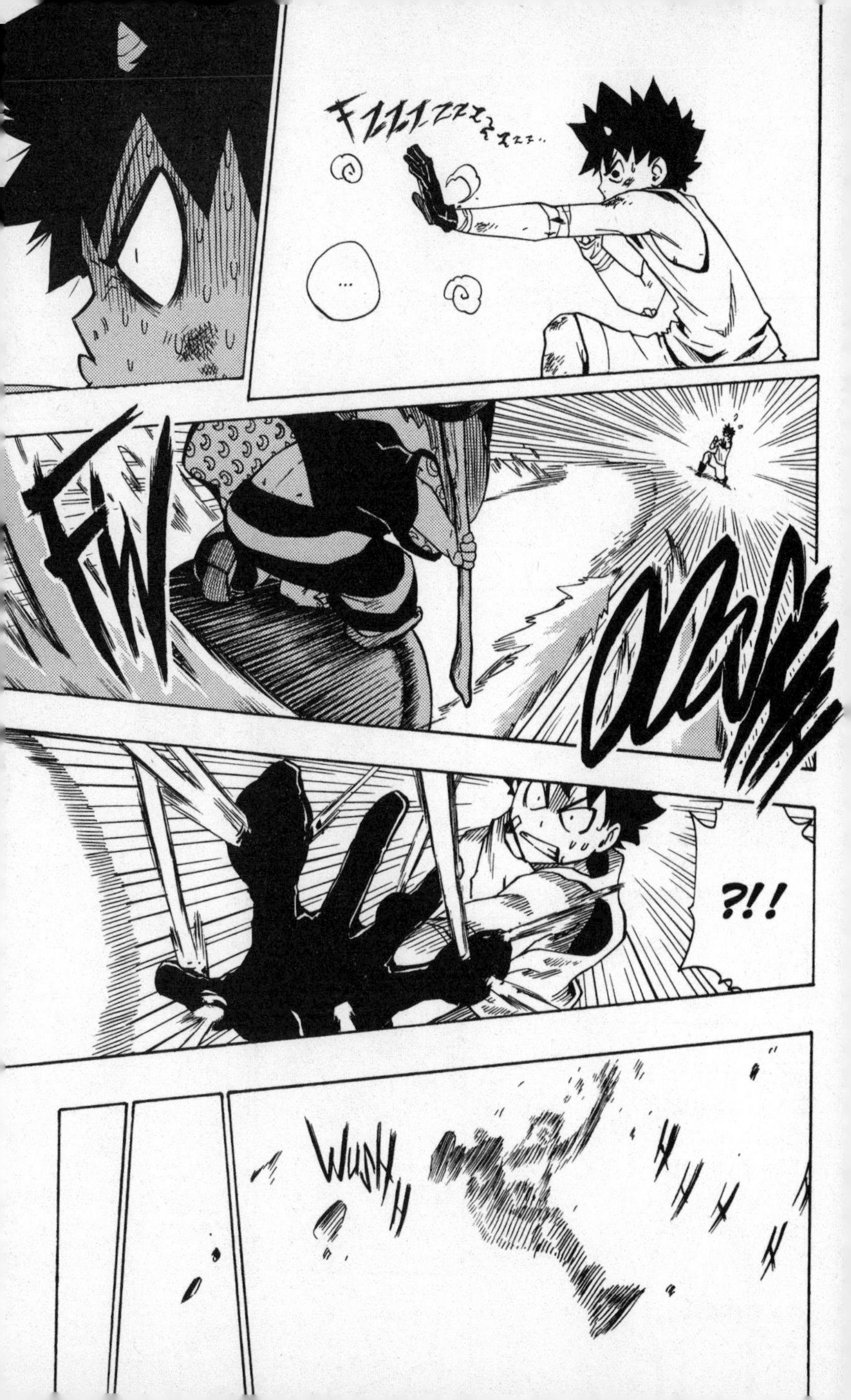
FZZZZZZZZZZ..
...
FW
?!!
WUSHHH

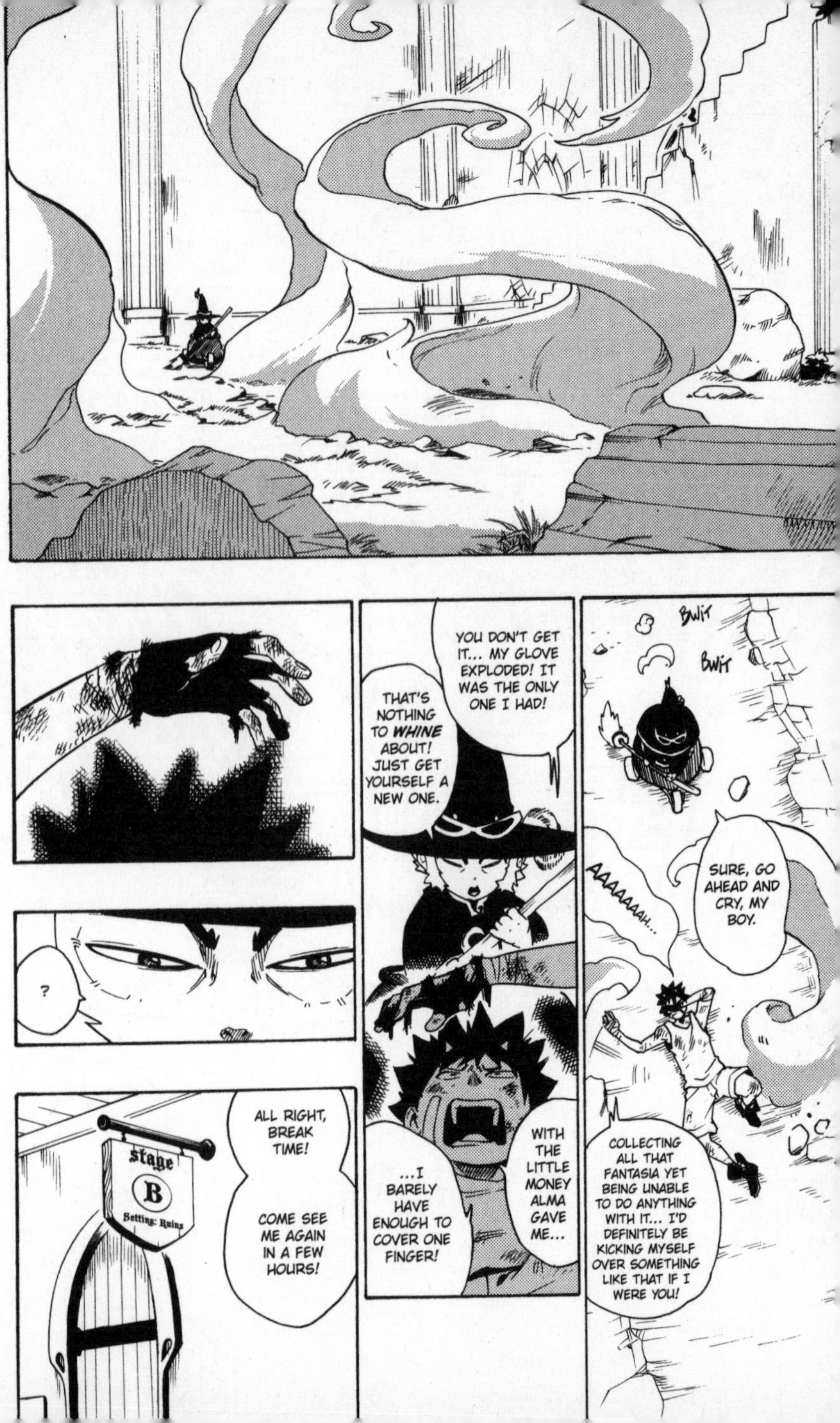
BWIT
BWIT
SURE, GO AHEAD AND CRY, MY BOY.
AAAAAAAH...
COLLECTING ALL THAT FANTASIA YET BEING UNABLE TO DO ANYTHING WITH IT... I'D DEFINITELY BE KICKING MYSELF OVER SOMETHING LIKE THAT IF I WERE YOU!
YOU DON'T GET IT... MY GLOVE EXPLODED! IT WAS THE ONLY ONE I HAD!
THAT'S NOTHING TO *WHINE* ABOUT! JUST GET YOURSELF A NEW ONE.
WITH THE LITTLE MONEY ALMA GAVE ME...
...I BARELY HAVE ENOUGH TO COVER ONE FINGER!
?
stage
B
Setting: Ruins
ALL RIGHT, BREAK TIME!
COME SEE ME AGAIN IN A FEW HOURS!

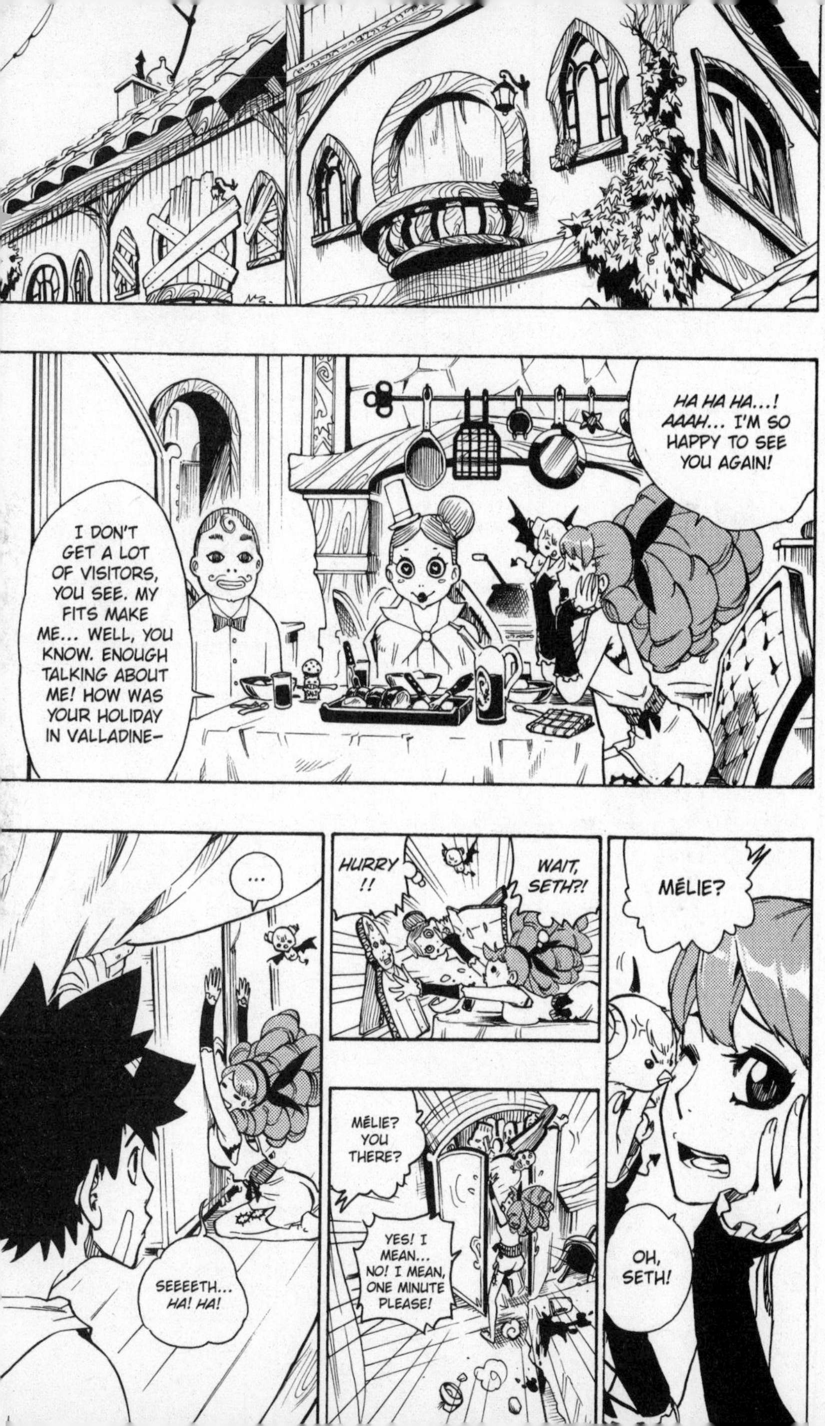
HA HA HA...! AAAH... I'M SO HAPPY TO SEE YOU AGAIN!
I DON'T GET A LOT OF VISITORS, YOU SEE. MY FITS MAKE ME... WELL, YOU KNOW. ENOUGH TALKING ABOUT ME! HOW WAS YOUR HOLIDAY IN VALLADINE-
MÉLIE?
OH, SETH!
WAIT, SETH?!
HURRY !!
MÉLIE? YOU THERE?
YES! I MEAN... NO! I MEAN, ONE MINUTE PLEASE!
...
SEEEETH... HA! HA!

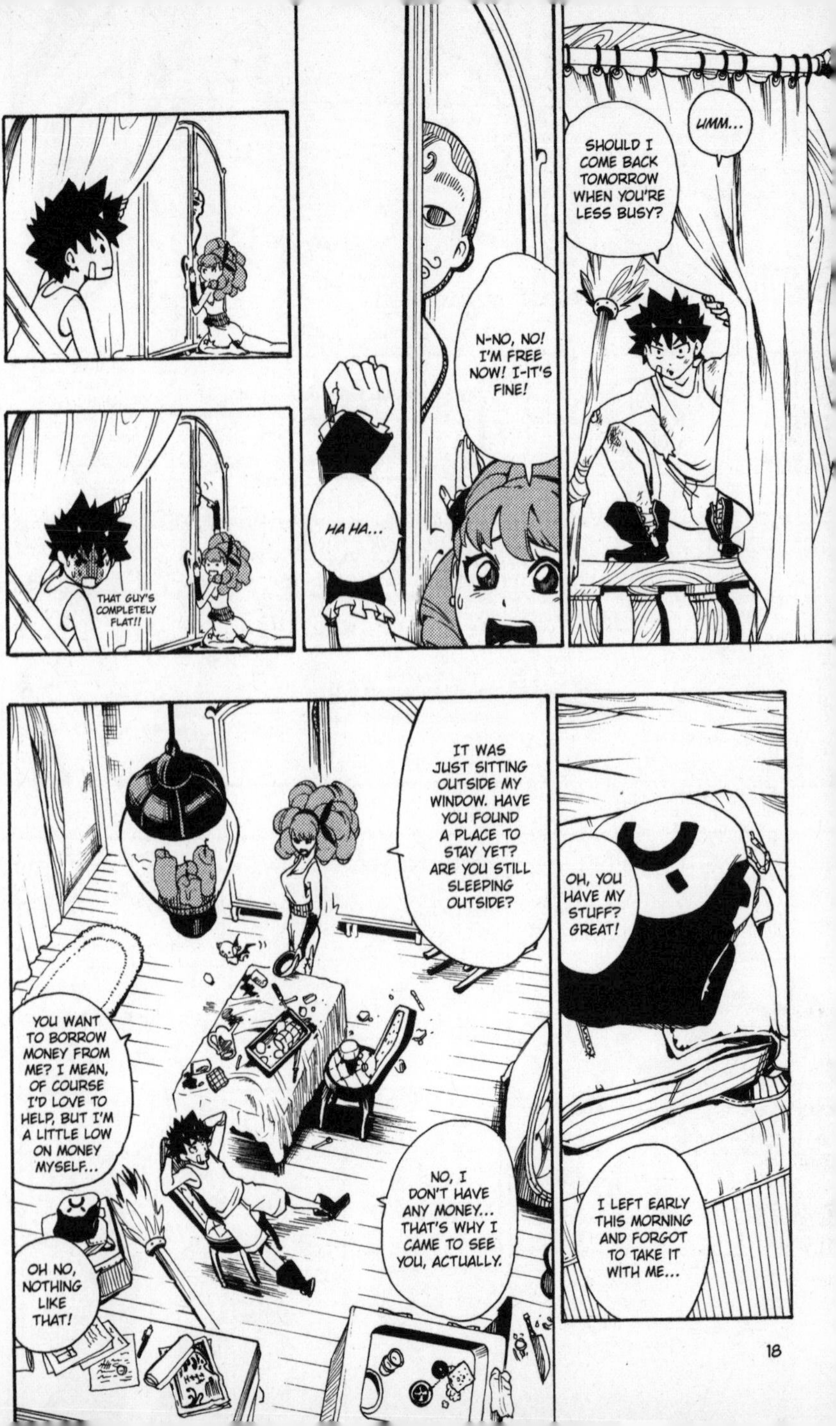
UMM...
SHOULD I COME BACK TOMORROW WHEN YOU'RE LESS BUSY?
N-NO, NO! I'M FREE NOW! I-IT'S FINE!
HA HA...
THAT GUY'S COMPLETELY FLAT!!
OH, YOU HAVE MY STUFF? GREAT!
I LEFT EARLY THIS MORNING AND FORGOT TO TAKE IT WITH ME...
IT WAS JUST SITTING OUTSIDE MY WINDOW. HAVE YOU FOUND A PLACE TO STAY YET? ARE YOU STILL SLEEPING OUTSIDE?
NO, I DON'T HAVE ANY MONEY... THAT'S WHY I CAME TO SEE YOU, ACTUALLY.
YOU WANT TO BORROW MONEY FROM ME? I MEAN, OF COURSE I'D LOVE TO HELP, BUT I'M A LITTLE LOW ON MONEY MYSELF...
OH NO, NOTHING LIKE THAT!

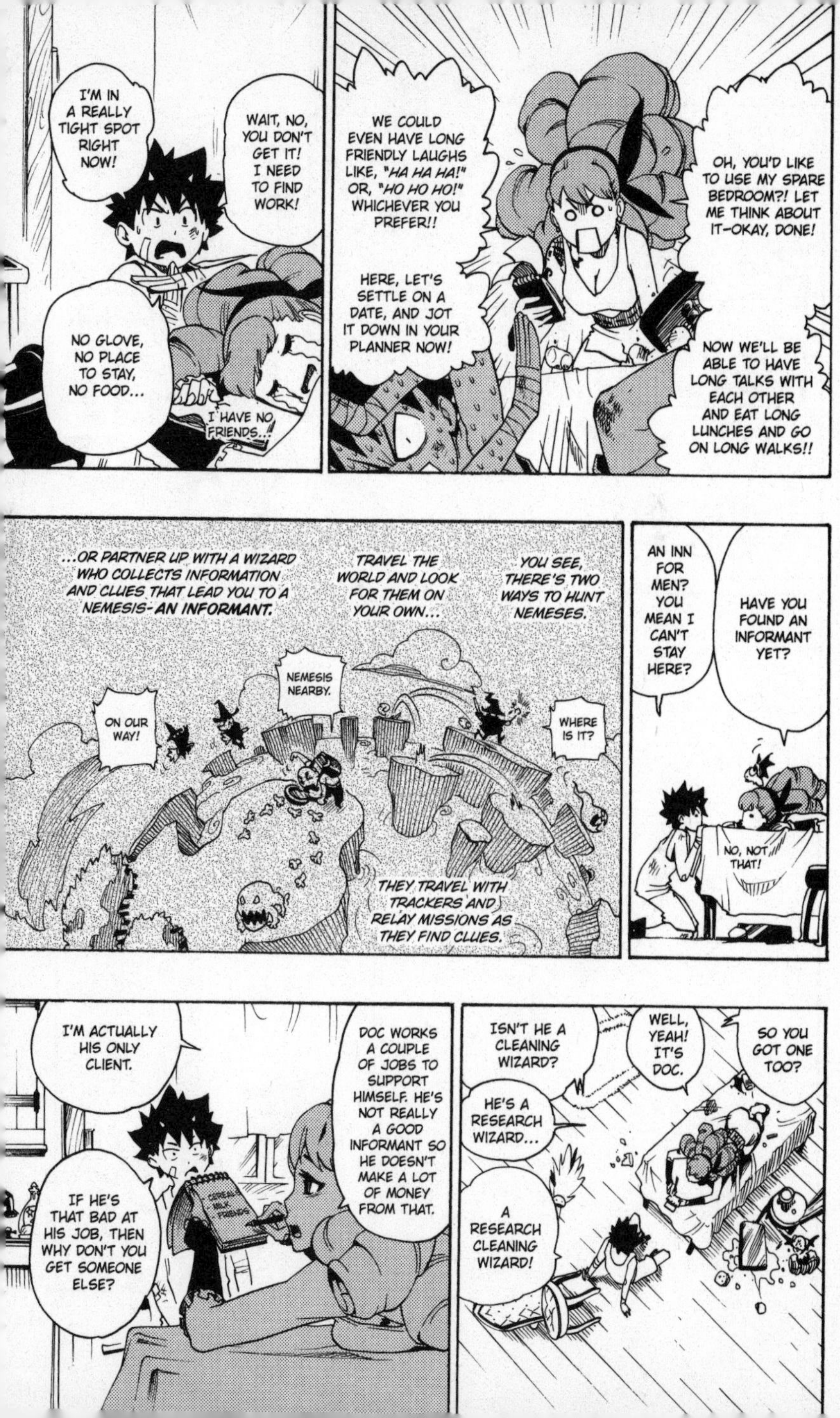
OH, YOU'D LIKE TO USE MY SPARE BEDROOM?! LET ME THINK ABOUT IT–OKAY, DONE!
NOW WE'LL BE ABLE TO HAVE LONG TALKS WITH EACH OTHER AND EAT LONG LUNCHES AND GO ON LONG WALKS!!
WE COULD EVEN HAVE LONG FRIENDLY LAUGHS LIKE, "HA HA HA!" OR, "HO HO HO!" WHICHEVER YOU PREFER!!
HERE, LET'S SETTLE ON A DATE, AND JOT IT DOWN IN YOUR PLANNER NOW!
WAIT, NO, YOU DON'T GET IT! I NEED TO FIND WORK!
I'M IN A REALLY TIGHT SPOT RIGHT NOW!
NO GLOVE, NO PLACE TO STAY, NO FOOD...
I HAVE NO FRIENDS...
HAVE YOU FOUND AN INFORMANT YET?
AN INN FOR MEN? YOU MEAN I CAN'T STAY HERE?
NO, NOT THAT!
YOU SEE, THERE'S TWO WAYS TO HUNT NEMESES.
TRAVEL THE WORLD AND LOOK FOR THEM ON YOUR OWN...
...OR PARTNER UP WITH A WIZARD WHO COLLECTS INFORMATION AND CLUES THAT LEAD YOU TO A NEMESIS- AN INFORMANT.
WHERE IS IT?
NEMESIS NEARBY.
ON OUR WAY!
THEY TRAVEL WITH TRACKERS AND RELAY MISSIONS AS THEY FIND CLUES.
SO YOU GOT ONE TOO?
WELL, YEAH! IT'S DOC.
ISN'T HE A CLEANING WIZARD?
HE'S A RESEARCH WIZARD...
A RESEARCH CLEANING WIZARD!
DOC WORKS A COUPLE OF JOBS TO SUPPORT HIMSELF. HE'S NOT REALLY A GOOD INFORMANT SO HE DOESN'T MAKE A LOT OF MONEY FROM THAT.
I'M ACTUALLY HIS ONLY CLIENT.
CEREAL MILK FRIENDS
IF HE'S THAT BAD AT HIS JOB, THEN WHY DON'T YOU GET SOMEONE ELSE?

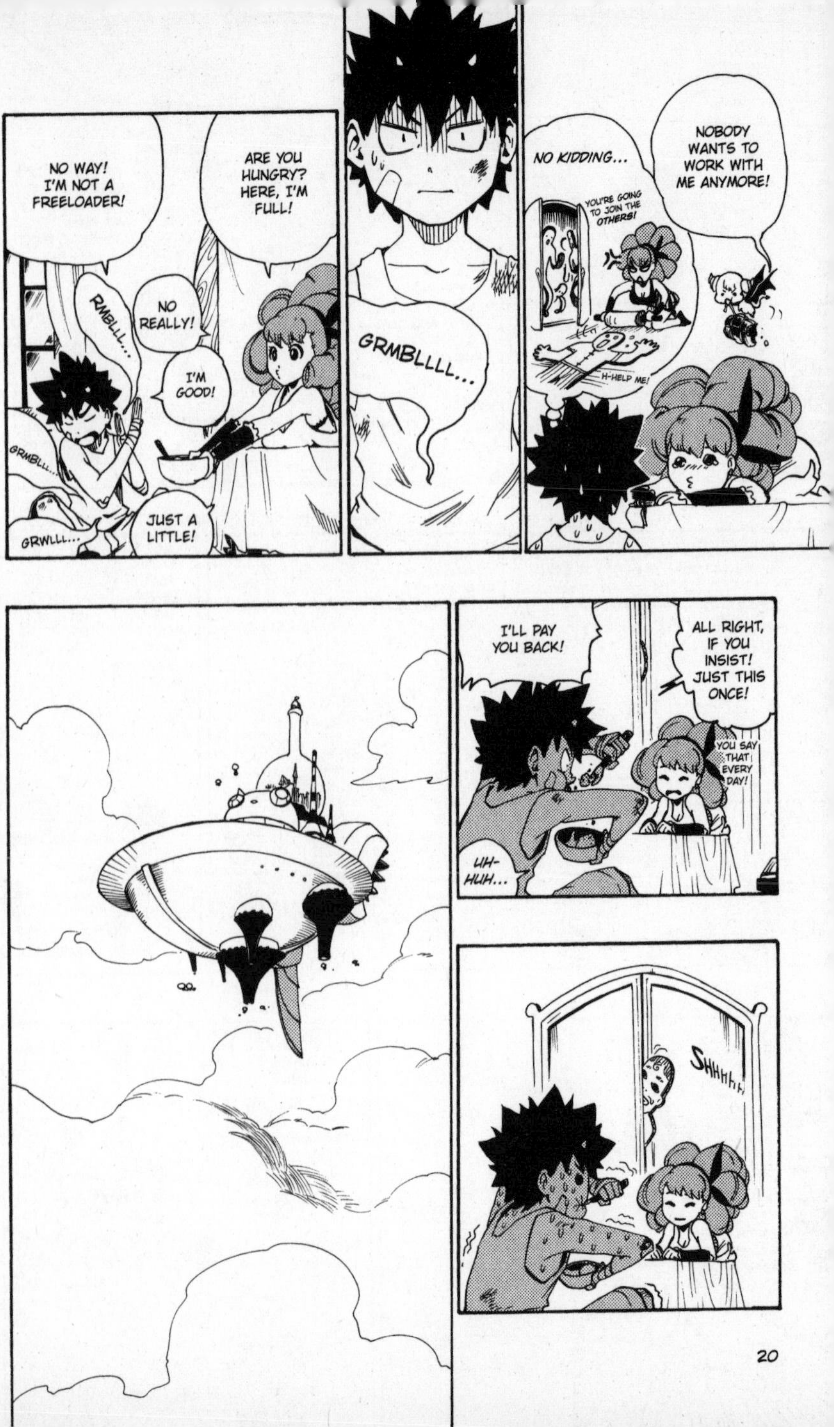

NOBODY WANTS TO WORK WITH ME ANYMORE!
NO KIDDING...
YOU'RE GOING TO JOIN THE OTHERS!
H-HELP ME!
GRMBLLLL...
ARE YOU HUNGRY? HERE, I'M FULL!
NO WAY! I'M NOT A FREELOADER!
NO REALLY!
RMBLLL...
I'M GOOD!
GRMBLLL...
JUST A LITTLE!
GRWLLL...
ALL RIGHT, IF YOU INSIST! JUST THIS ONCE!
I'LL PAY YOU BACK!
YOU SAY THAT EVERY DAY!
UH-HUH...
SHHhhh

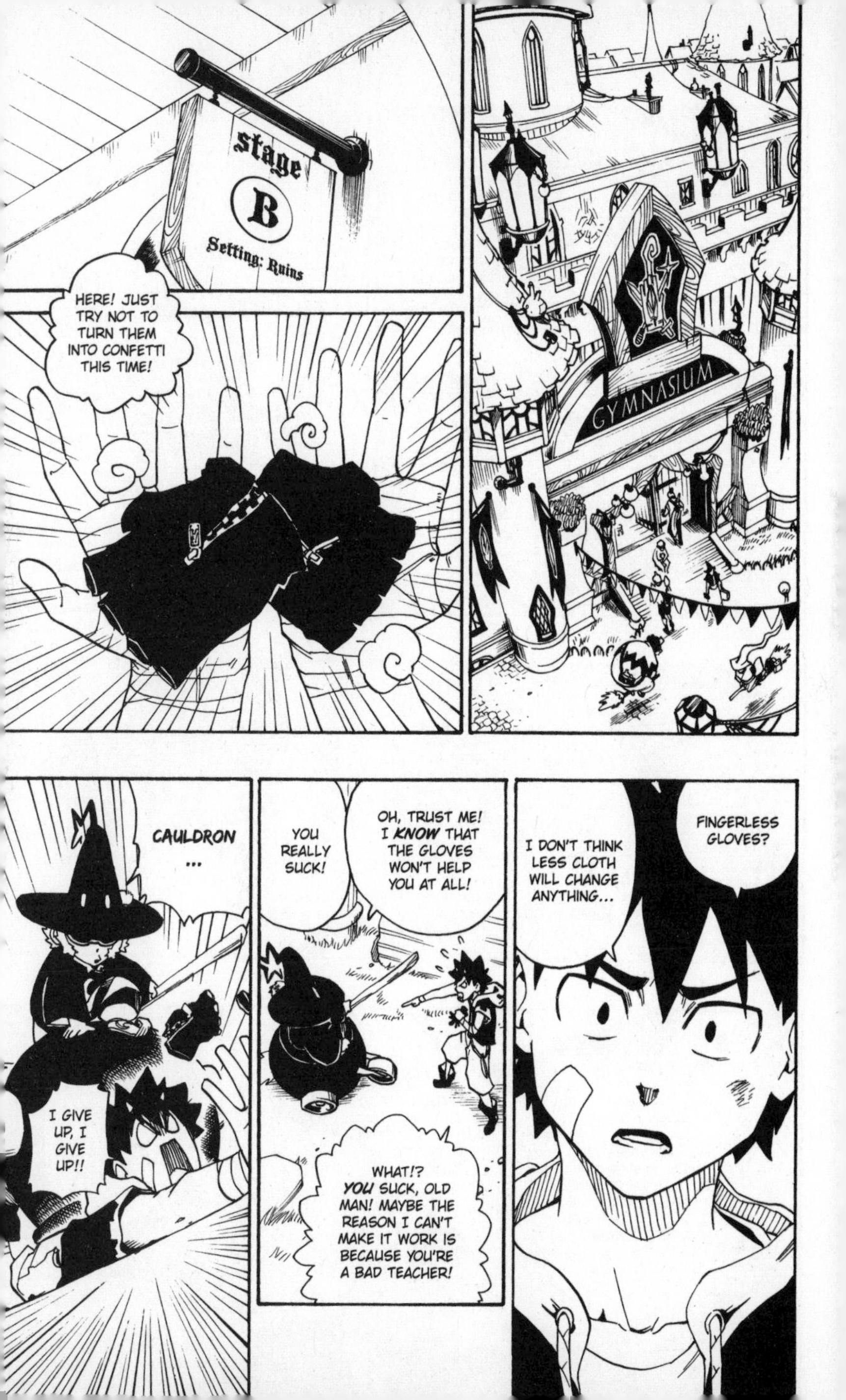
GYMNASIUM
stage B Setting: Ruins
HERE! JUST TRY NOT TO TURN THEM INTO CONFETTI THIS TIME!
FINGERLESS GLOVES?
I DON'T THINK LESS CLOTH WILL CHANGE ANYTHING...
OH, TRUST ME! I KNOW THAT THE GLOVES WON'T HELP YOU AT ALL!
YOU REALLY SUCK!
WHAT!? YOU SUCK, OLD MAN! MAYBE THE REASON I CAN'T MAKE IT WORK IS BECAUSE YOU'RE A BAD TEACHER!
CAULDRON ...
I GIVE UP, I GIVE UP!!

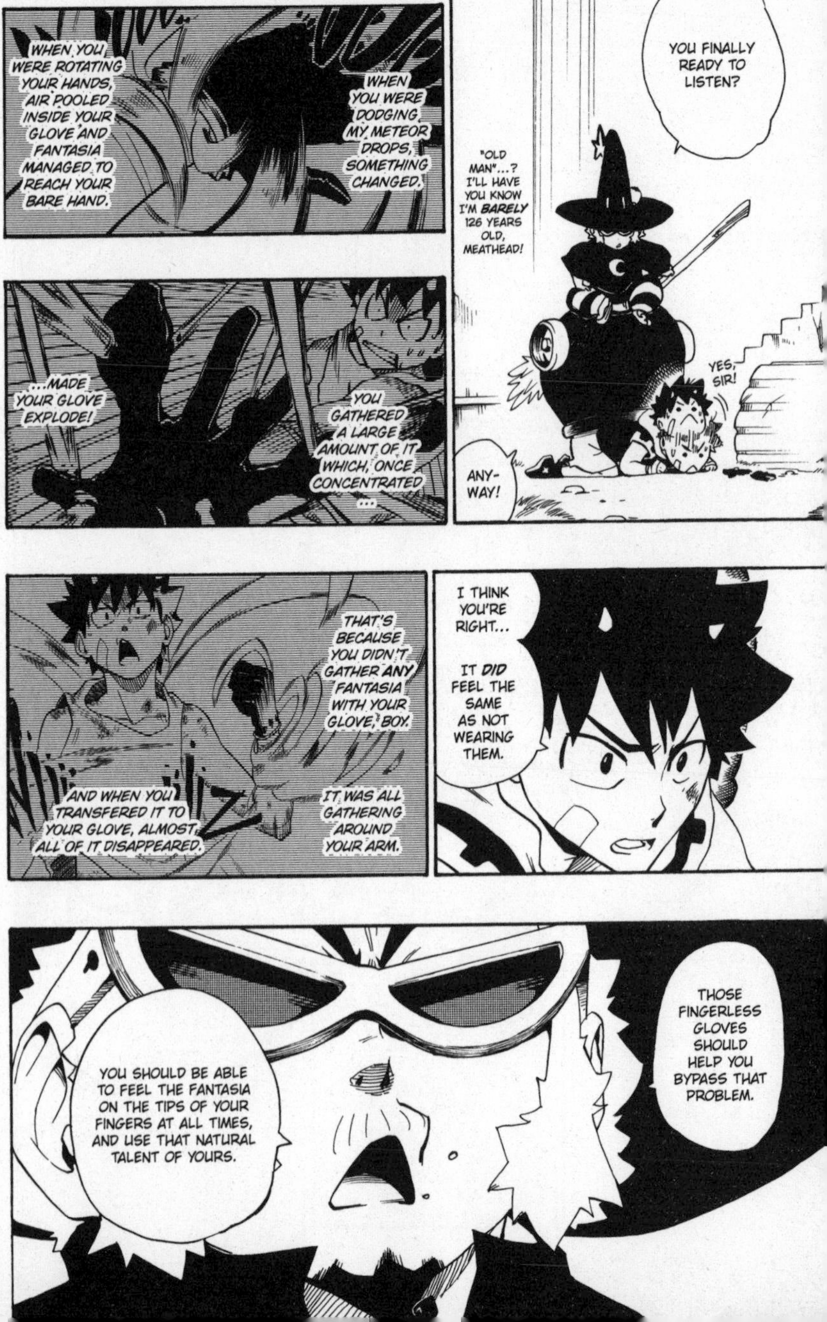
YOU FINALLY READY TO LISTEN?
"OLD MAN"...? I'LL HAVE YOU KNOW I'M BARELY 126 YEARS OLD, MEATHEAD!
YES, SIR!
ANY-WAY!
WHEN YOU WERE DODGING MY METEOR DROPS, SOMETHING CHANGED.
WHEN YOU WERE ROTATING YOUR HANDS, AIR POOLED INSIDE YOUR GLOVE AND FANTASIA MANAGED TO REACH YOUR BARE HAND.
YOU GATHERED A LARGE AMOUNT OF IT WHICH, ONCE CONCENTRATED ...
...MADE YOUR GLOVE EXPLODE!
I THINK YOU'RE RIGHT...
IT DID FEEL THE SAME AS NOT WEARING THEM.
THAT'S BECAUSE YOU DIDN'T GATHER ANY FANTASIA WITH YOUR GLOVE, BOY.
IT WAS ALL GATHERING AROUND YOUR ARM.
AND WHEN YOU TRANSFERED IT TO YOUR GLOVE, ALMOST ALL OF IT DISAPPEARED.
THOSE FINGERLESS GLOVES SHOULD HELP YOU BYPASS THAT PROBLEM.
YOU SHOULD BE ABLE TO FEEL THE FANTASIA ON THE TIPS OF YOUR FINGERS AT ALL TIMES, AND USE THAT NATURAL TALENT OF YOURS.

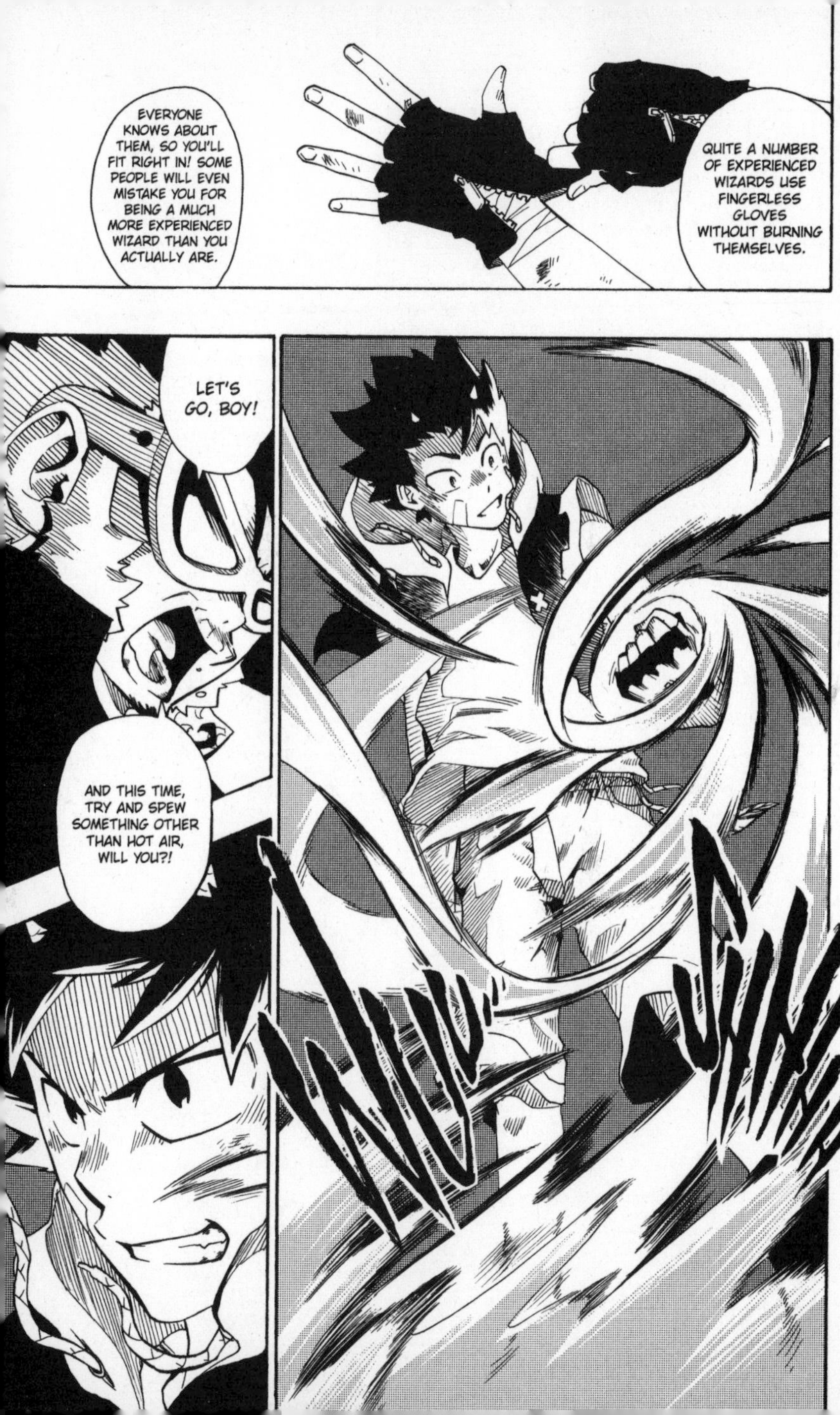
QUITE A NUMBER OF EXPERIENCED WIZARDS USE FINGERLESS GLOVES WITHOUT BURNING THEMSELVES.
EVERYONE KNOWS ABOUT THEM, SO YOU'LL FIT RIGHT IN! SOME PEOPLE WILL EVEN MISTAKE YOU FOR BEING A MUCH MORE EXPERIENCED WIZARD THAN YOU ACTUALLY ARE.
LET'S GO, BOY!
AND THIS TIME, TRY AND SPEW SOMETHING OTHER THAN HOT AIR, WILL YOU?!

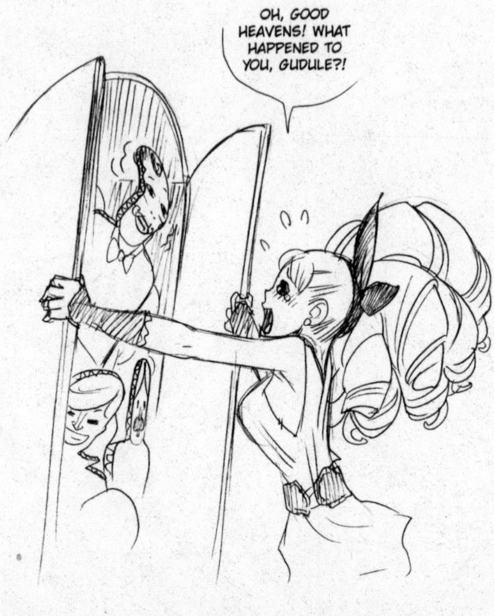
OH, GOOD HEAVENS! WHAT HAPPENED TO YOU, GUDULE?!

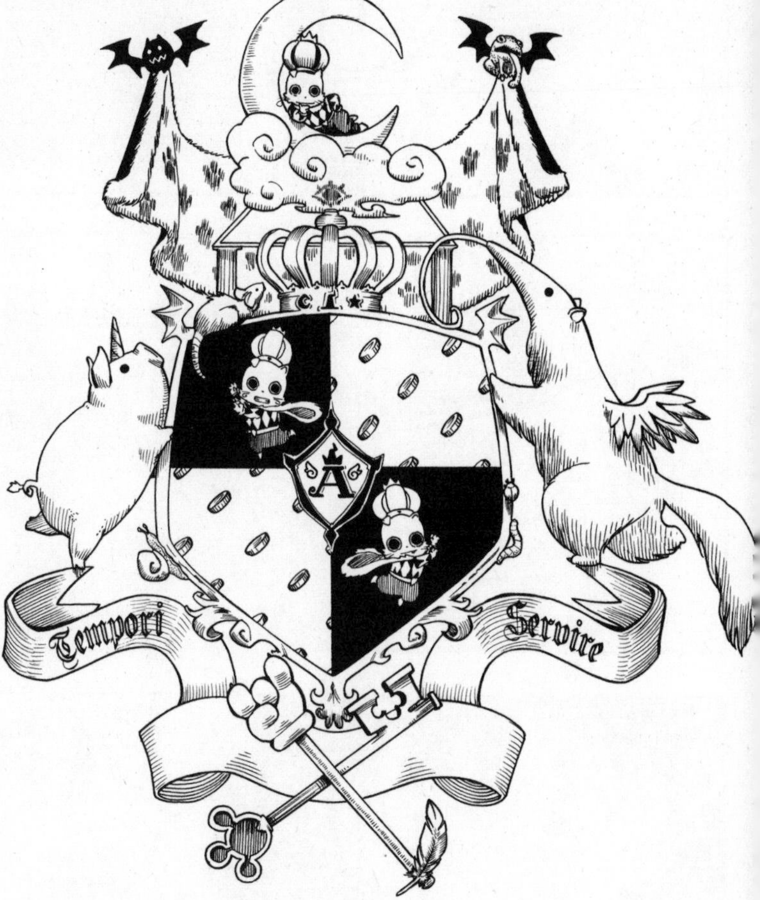
Tempori
Servire

Chapter 6

Jean Pedrovitch of Noche Salomon Grispépin Wondersmith

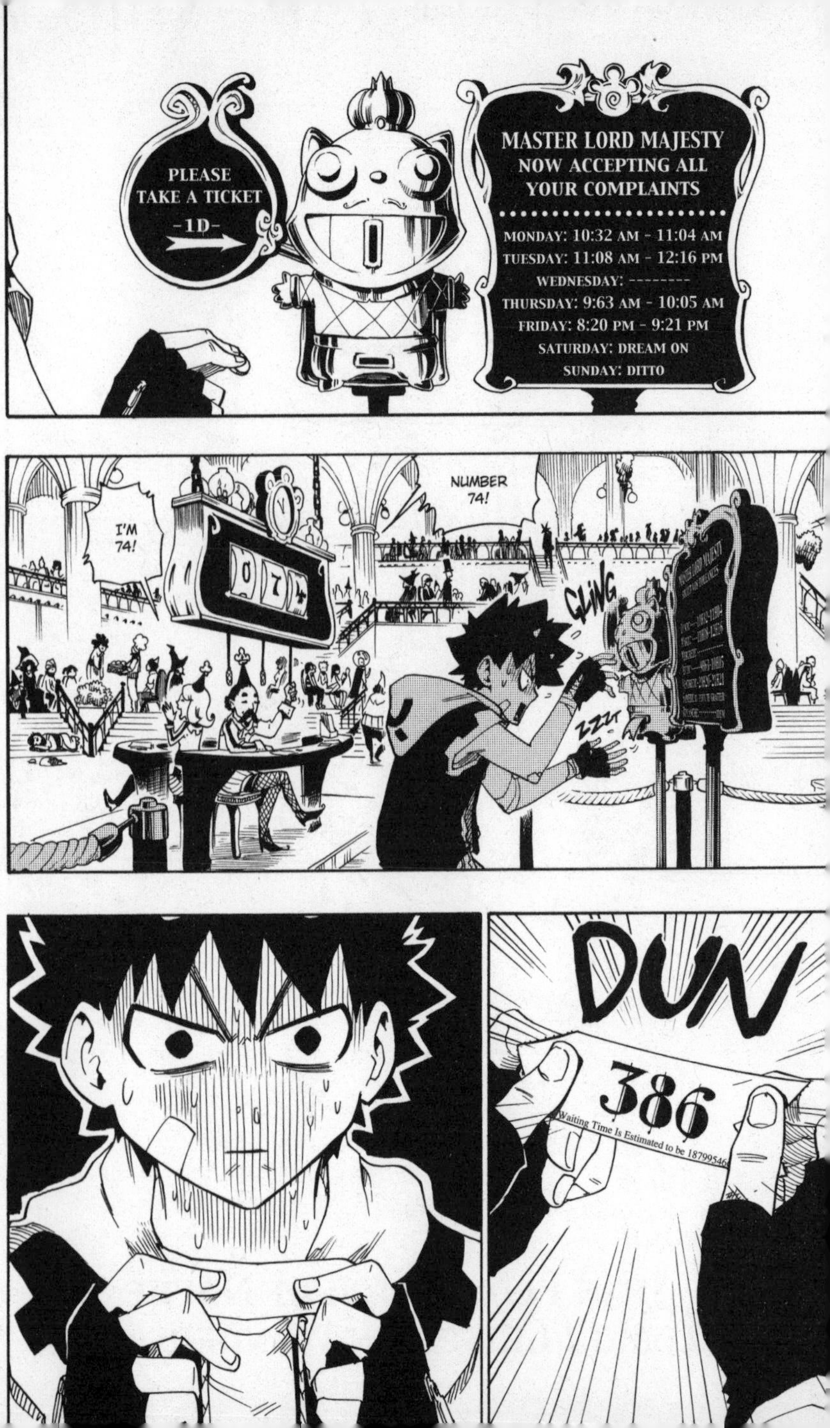

MASTER LORD MAJESTY
NOW ACCEPTING ALL
YOUR COMPLAINTS
MONDAY: 10:32 AM - 11:04 AM
TUESDAY: 11:08 AM - 12:16 PM
WEDNESDAY: --------
THURSDAY: 9:63 AM - 10:05 AM
FRIDAY: 8:20 PM - 9:21 PM
SATURDAY: DREAM ON
SUNDAY: DITTO
PLEASE
TAKE A TICKET
-1D-
GLING
ZZZT
NUMBER 74!
074
I'M 74!
DUN
386
Waiting Time Is Estimated to be 18799546

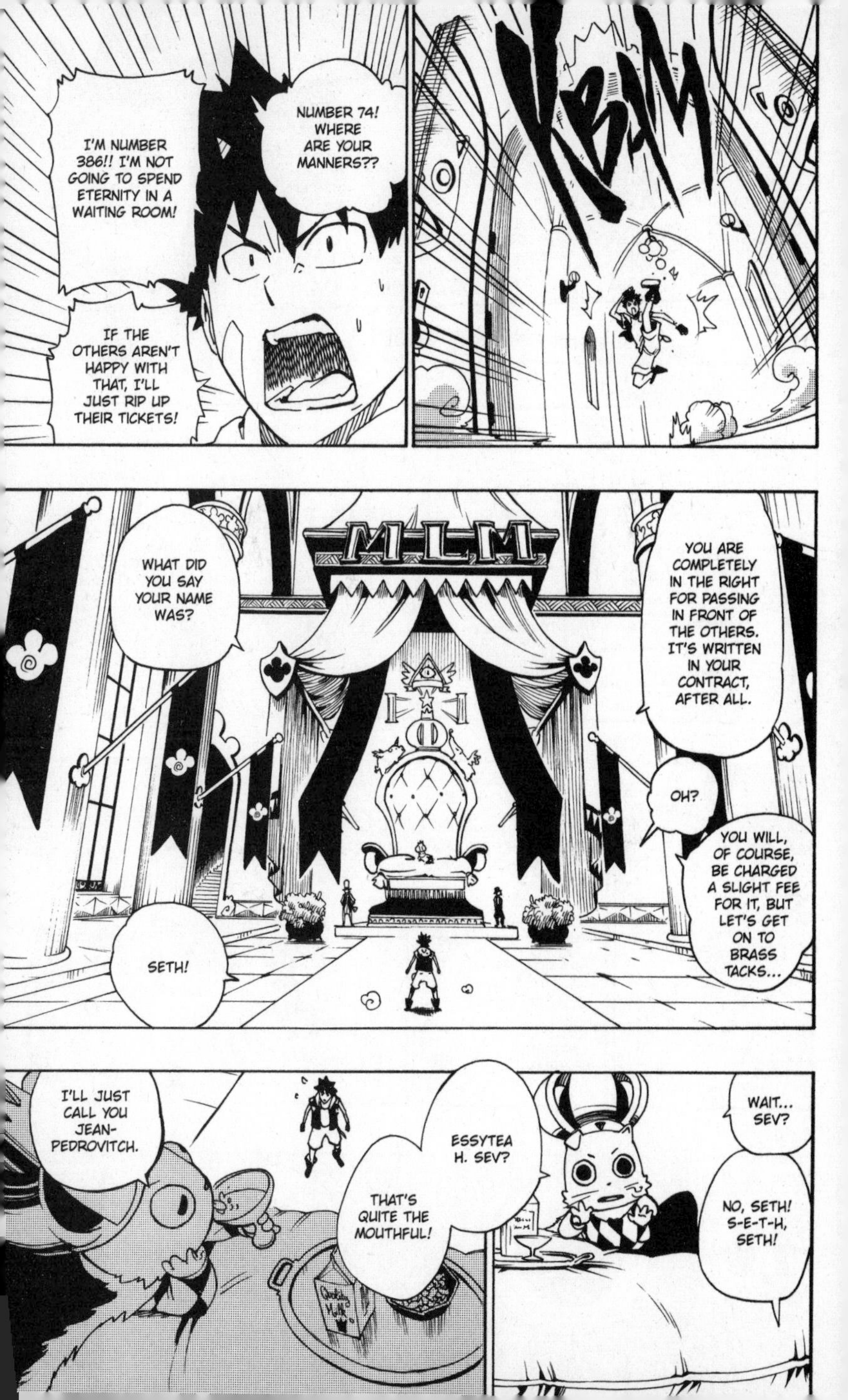
KBAM
NUMBER 74! WHERE ARE YOUR MANNERS??
I'M NUMBER 386!! I'M NOT GOING TO SPEND ETERNITY IN A WAITING ROOM!
IF THE OTHERS AREN'T HAPPY WITH THAT, I'LL JUST RIP UP THEIR TICKETS!
YOU ARE COMPLETELY IN THE RIGHT FOR PASSING IN FRONT OF THE OTHERS. IT'S WRITTEN IN YOUR CONTRACT, AFTER ALL.
OH?
YOU WILL, OF COURSE, BE CHARGED A SLIGHT FEE FOR IT, BUT LET'S GET ON TO BRASS TACKS...
WHAT DID YOU SAY YOUR NAME WAS?
SETH!
M.L.M.
WAIT... SEV?
NO, SETH! S-E-T-H, SETH!
ESSYTEA H. SEV?
THAT'S QUITE THE MOUTHFUL!
I'LL JUST CALL YOU JEAN-PEDROVITCH.

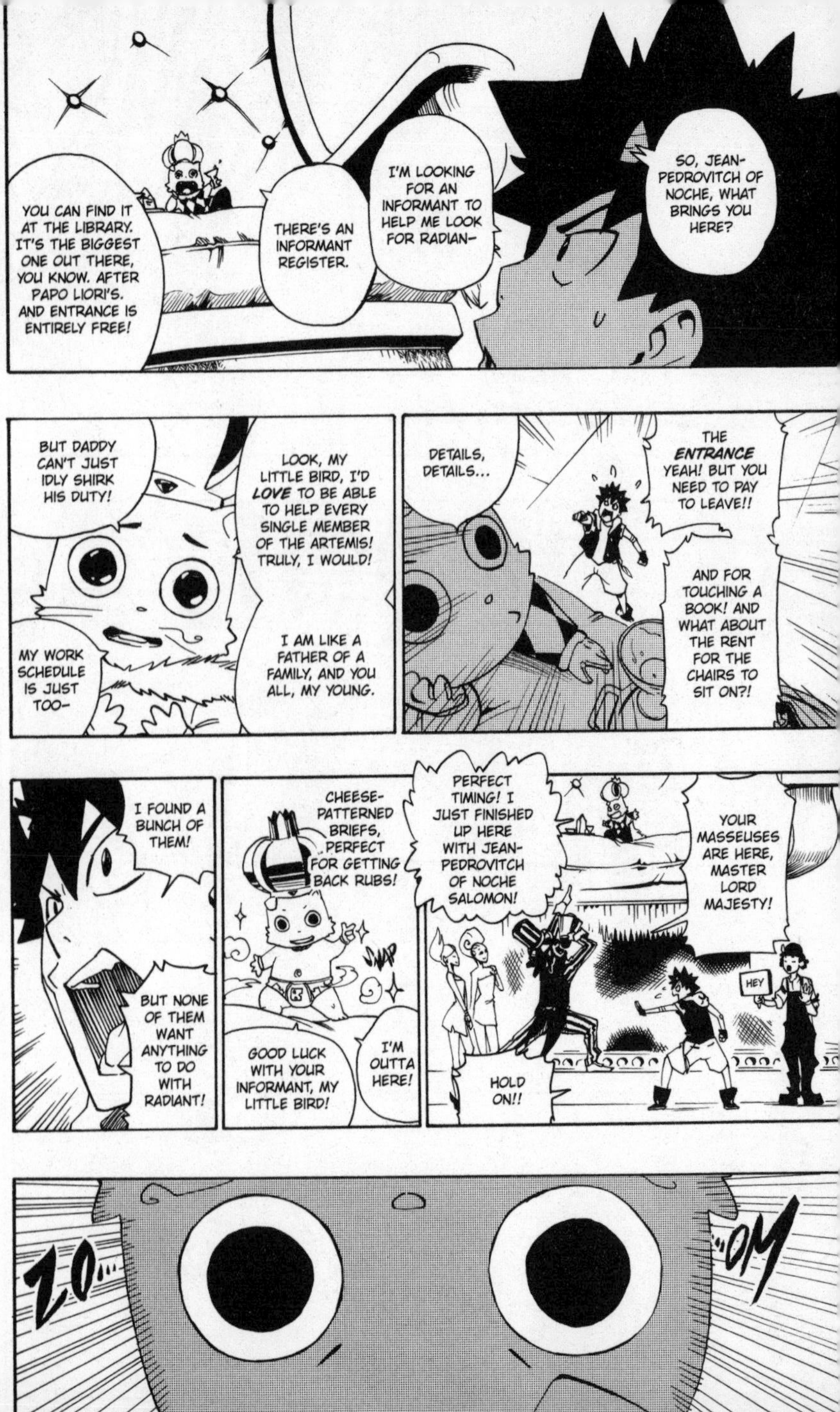

SO, JEAN-PEDROVITCH OF NOCHE, WHAT BRINGS YOU HERE?
I'M LOOKING FOR AN INFORMANT TO HELP ME LOOK FOR RADIAN-
THERE'S AN INFORMANT REGISTER.
YOU CAN FIND IT AT THE LIBRARY. IT'S THE BIGGEST ONE OUT THERE, YOU KNOW. AFTER PAPO LIORI'S. AND ENTRANCE IS ENTIRELY FREE!
THE ***ENTRANCE*** YEAH! BUT YOU NEED TO PAY TO LEAVE!!
DETAILS, DETAILS...
AND FOR TOUCHING A BOOK! AND WHAT ABOUT THE RENT FOR THE CHAIRS TO SIT ON?!
LOOK, MY LITTLE BIRD, I'D ***LOVE*** TO BE ABLE TO HELP EVERY SINGLE MEMBER OF THE ARTEMIS! TRULY, I WOULD!
BUT DADDY CAN'T JUST IDLY SHIRK HIS DUTY!
I AM LIKE A FATHER OF A FAMILY, AND YOU ALL, MY YOUNG.
MY WORK SCHEDULE IS JUST TOO-
YOUR MASSEUSES ARE HERE, MASTER LORD MAJESTY!
PERFECT TIMING! I JUST FINISHED UP HERE WITH JEAN-PEDROVITCH OF NOCHE SALOMON!
HEY
HOLD ON!!
CHEESE-PATTERNED BRIEFS, PERFECT FOR GETTING BACK RUBS!
SNAP
I'M OUTTA HERE!
GOOD LUCK WITH YOUR INFORMANT, MY LITTLE BIRD!
I FOUND A BUNCH OF THEM!
BUT NONE OF THEM WANT ANYTHING TO DO WITH RADIANT!
ZO...
...OM

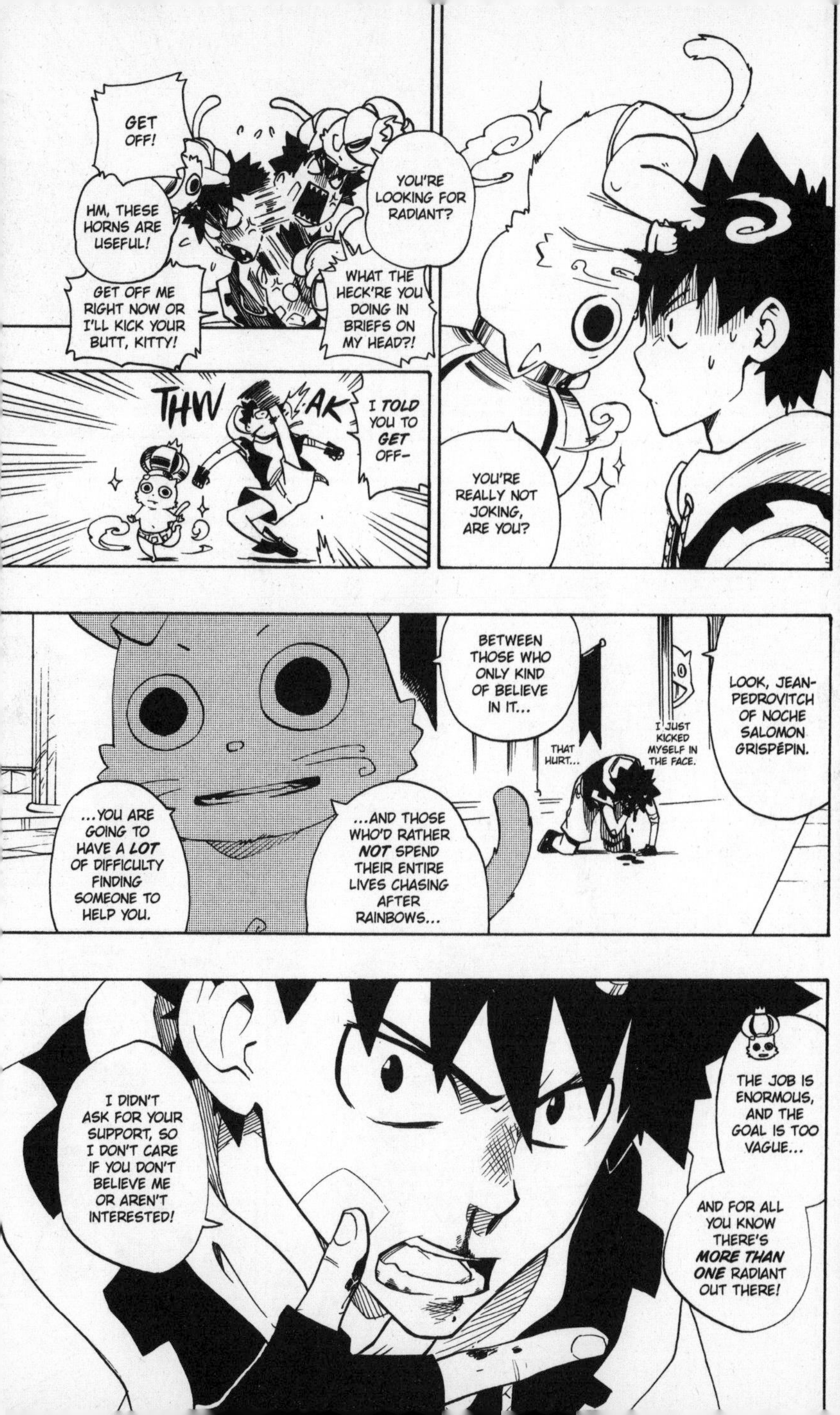
YOU'RE LOOKING FOR RADIANT?
YOU'RE REALLY NOT JOKING, ARE YOU?
WHAT THE HECK'RE YOU DOING IN BRIEFS ON MY HEAD?!
GET OFF!
HM, THESE HORNS ARE USEFUL!
GET OFF ME RIGHT NOW OR I'LL KICK YOUR BUTT, KITTY!
I TOLD YOU TO GET OFF-
THWAK
LOOK, JEAN-PEDROVITCH OF NOCHE SALOMON GRISPÉPIN.
I JUST KICKED MYSELF IN THE FACE.
THAT HURT...
BETWEEN THOSE WHO ONLY KIND OF BELIEVE IN IT...
...AND THOSE WHO'D RATHER NOT SPEND THEIR ENTIRE LIVES CHASING AFTER RAINBOWS...
...YOU ARE GOING TO HAVE A LOT OF DIFFICULTY FINDING SOMEONE TO HELP YOU.
THE JOB IS ENORMOUS, AND THE GOAL IS TOO VAGUE...
AND FOR ALL YOU KNOW THERE'S MORE THAN ONE RADIANT OUT THERE!
I DIDN'T ASK FOR YOUR SUPPORT, SO I DON'T CARE IF YOU DON'T BELIEVE ME OR AREN'T INTERESTED!

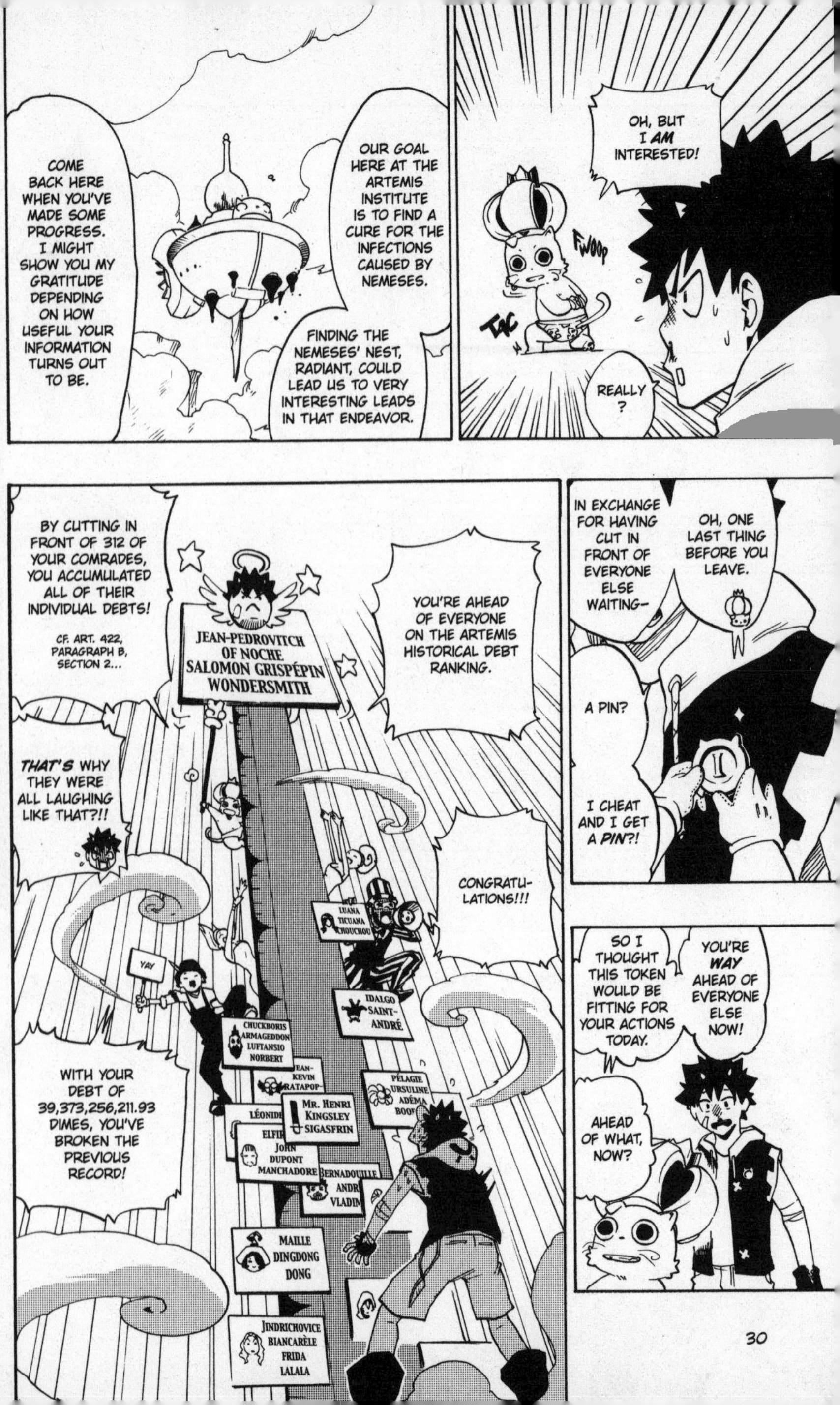

OH, BUT I AM INTERESTED!
FWOOP
TAC
REALLY?
OUR GOAL HERE AT THE ARTEMIS INSTITUTE IS TO FIND A CURE FOR THE INFECTIONS CAUSED BY NEMESES.
FINDING THE NEMESES' NEST, RADIANT, COULD LEAD US TO VERY INTERESTING LEADS IN THAT ENDEAVOR.
COME BACK HERE WHEN YOU'VE MADE SOME PROGRESS. I MIGHT SHOW YOU MY GRATITUDE DEPENDING ON HOW USEFUL YOUR INFORMATION TURNS OUT TO BE.
OH, ONE LAST THING BEFORE YOU LEAVE.
IN EXCHANGE FOR HAVING CUT IN FRONT OF EVERYONE ELSE WAITING–
A PIN?
I CHEAT AND I GET A PIN?!
YOU'RE WAY AHEAD OF EVERYONE ELSE NOW!
SO I THOUGHT THIS TOKEN WOULD BE FITTING FOR YOUR ACTIONS TODAY.
AHEAD OF WHAT, NOW?
YOU'RE AHEAD OF EVERYONE ON THE ARTEMIS HISTORICAL DEBT RANKING.
BY CUTTING IN FRONT OF 312 OF YOUR COMRADES, YOU ACCUMULATED ALL OF THEIR INDIVIDUAL DEBTS!
CF. ART. 422, PARAGRAPH B, SECTION 2...
JEAN-PEDROVITCH OF NOCHE SALOMON GRISPÉPIN WONDERSMITH
CONGRATULATIONS!!!
THAT'S WHY THEY WERE ALL LAUGHING LIKE THAT?!!
LUANA TICUANA CHOUCHOU
YAY
IDALGO SAINT-ANDRÉ
CHUCKBORIS ARMAGEDDON LUFTANSIO NORBERT
PÉLAGIE URSULINE ADÉMA BOOF
MR. HENRI KINGSLEY SIGASFRIN
JOHN DUPONT MANCHADORE
WITH YOUR DEBT OF 39,373,256,211.93 DIMES, YOU'VE BROKEN THE PREVIOUS RECORD!
MAILLE DINGDONG DONG
JINDRICHOVICE BIANCARÈLE FRIDA LALALA

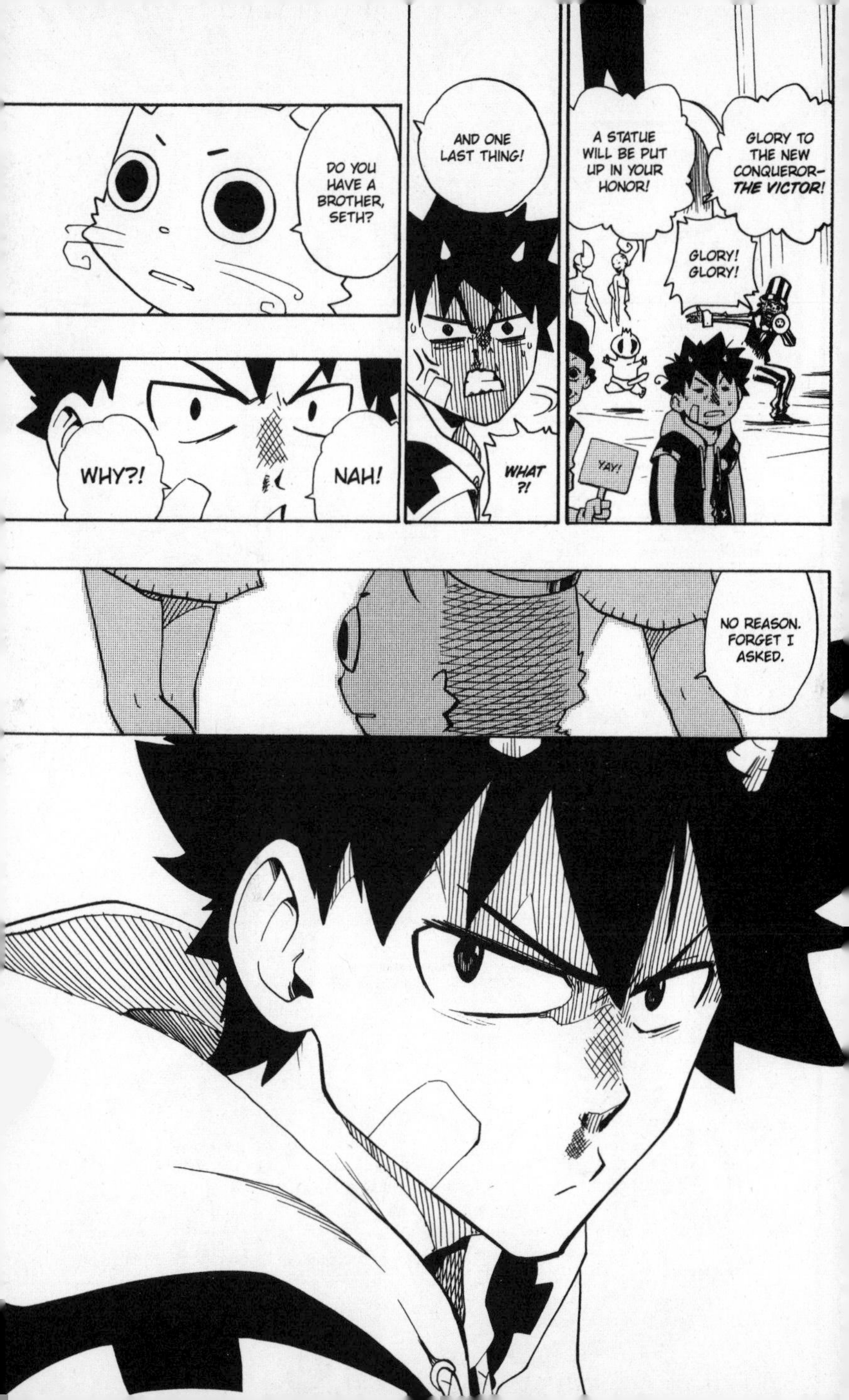
GLORY TO THE NEW CONQUEROR—THE VICTOR!
A STATUE WILL BE PUT UP IN YOUR HONOR!
GLORY! GLORY!
YAY!
AND ONE LAST THING!
WHAT?!
DO YOU HAVE A BROTHER, SETH?
NAH!
WHY?!
NO REASON. FORGET I ASKED.

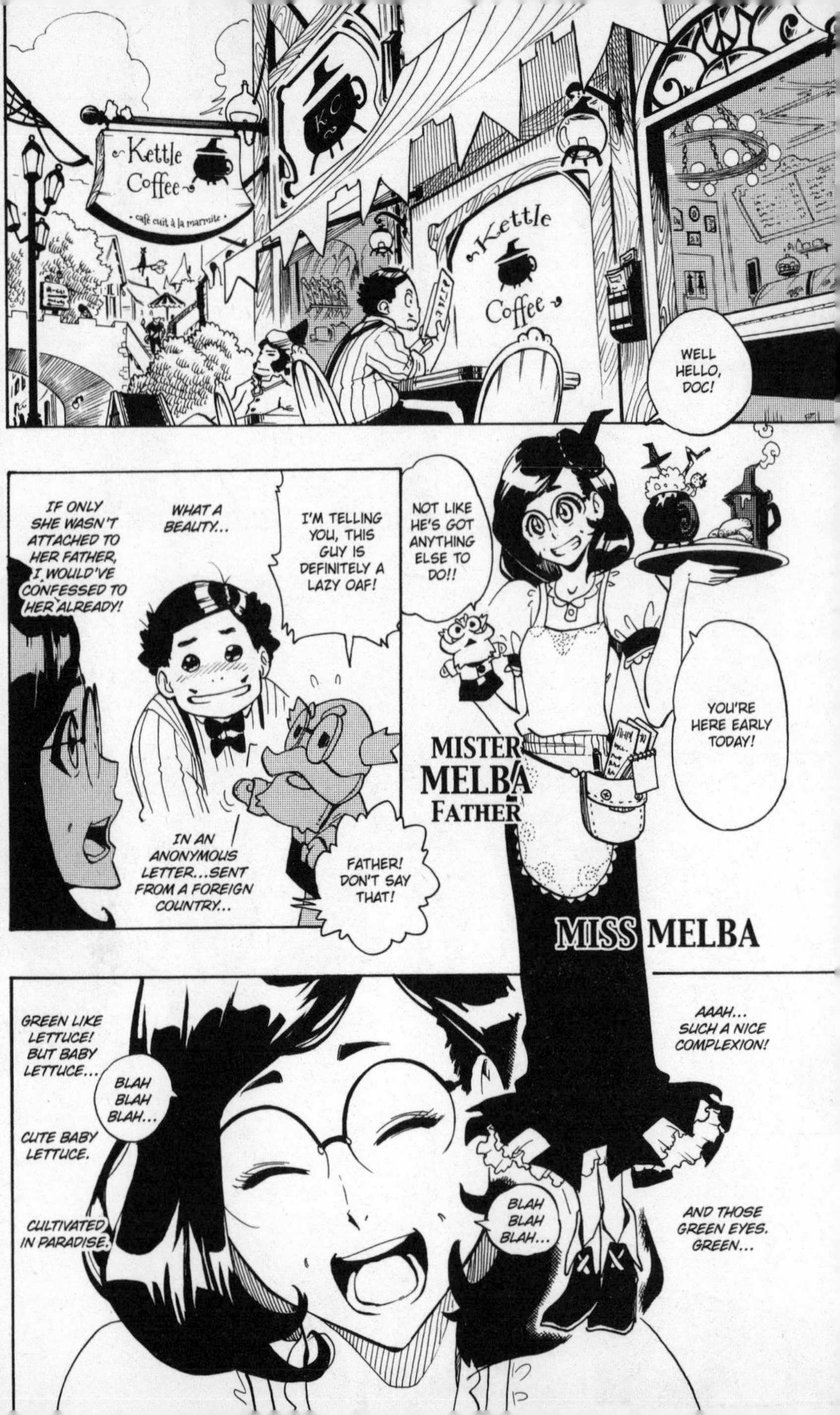
Kettle Coffee
café cuit à la marmite
Kettle Coffee
WELL HELLO, DOC!
YOU'RE HERE EARLY TODAY!
NOT LIKE HE'S GOT ANYTHING ELSE TO DO!!
MISTER MELBA FATHER
MISS MELBA
I'M TELLING YOU, THIS GUY IS DEFINITELY A LAZY OAF!
WHAT A BEAUTY...
IF ONLY SHE WASN'T ATTACHED TO HER FATHER, I WOULD'VE CONFESSED TO HER ALREADY!
IN AN ANONYMOUS LETTER...SENT FROM A FOREIGN COUNTRY...
FATHER! DON'T SAY THAT!
AAAH... SUCH A NICE COMPLEXION!
AND THOSE GREEN EYES. GREEN...
BLAH BLAH BLAH...
GREEN LIKE LETTUCE! BUT BABY LETTUCE...
BLAH BLAH BLAH...
CUTE BABY LETTUCE.
CULTIVATED IN PARADISE.

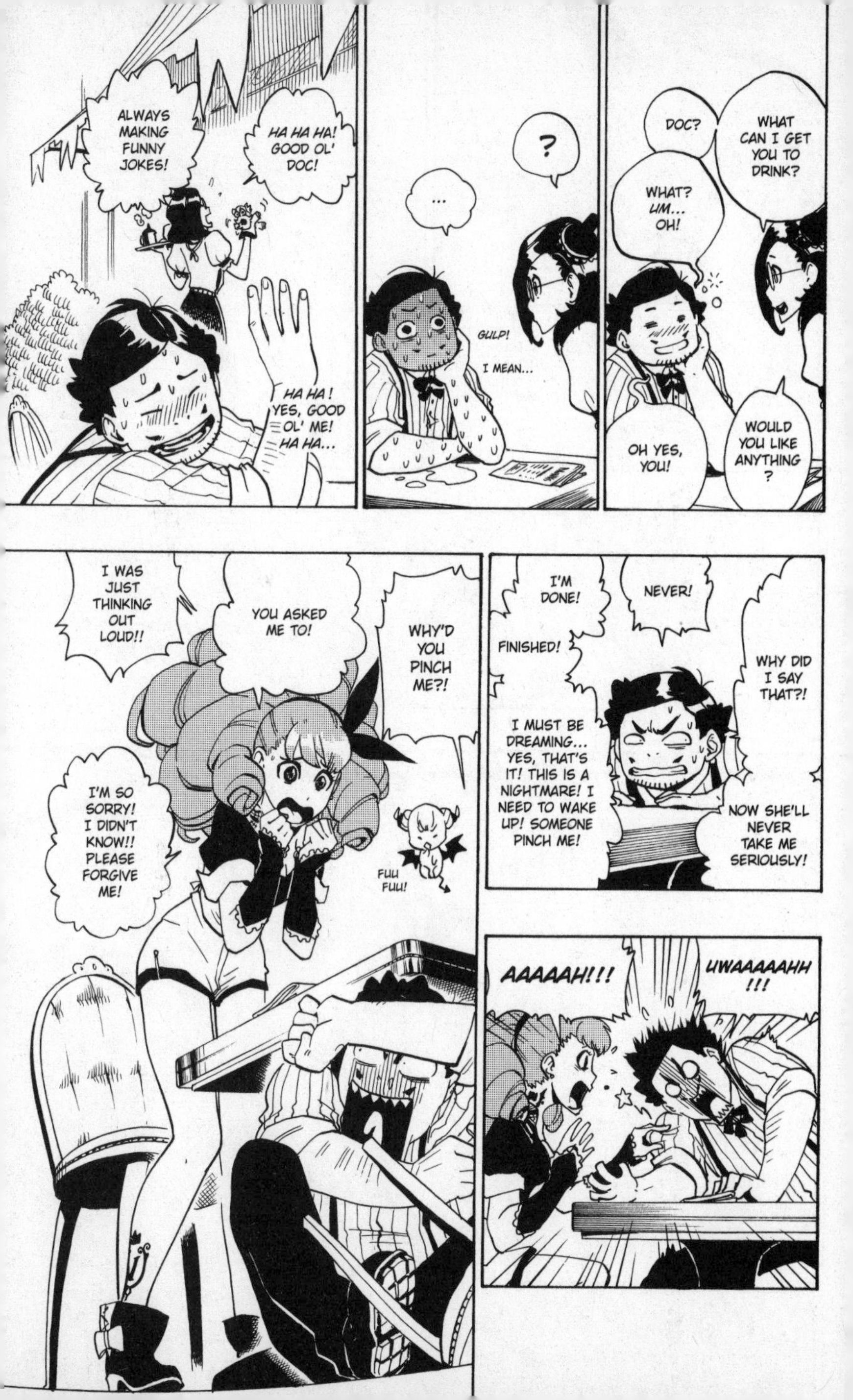

WHAT CAN I GET YOU TO DRINK?
DOC?
WHAT? UM... OH!
WOULD YOU LIKE ANYTHING?
OH YES, YOU!
?
...
GULP!
I MEAN...
HA HA HA! GOOD OL' DOC!
ALWAYS MAKING FUNNY JOKES!
HA HA! YES, GOOD OL' ME! HA HA...
NEVER!
I'M DONE!
FINISHED!
WHY DID I SAY THAT?!
I MUST BE DREAMING... YES, THAT'S IT! THIS IS A NIGHTMARE! I NEED TO WAKE UP! SOMEONE PINCH ME!
NOW SHE'LL NEVER TAKE ME SERIOUSLY!
UWAAAAAHH!!!
AAAAAH!!!
WHY'D YOU PINCH ME?!
YOU ASKED ME TO!
I WAS JUST THINKING OUT LOUD!!
FUU FUU!
I'M SO SORRY! I DIDN'T KNOW!! PLEASE FORGIVE ME!

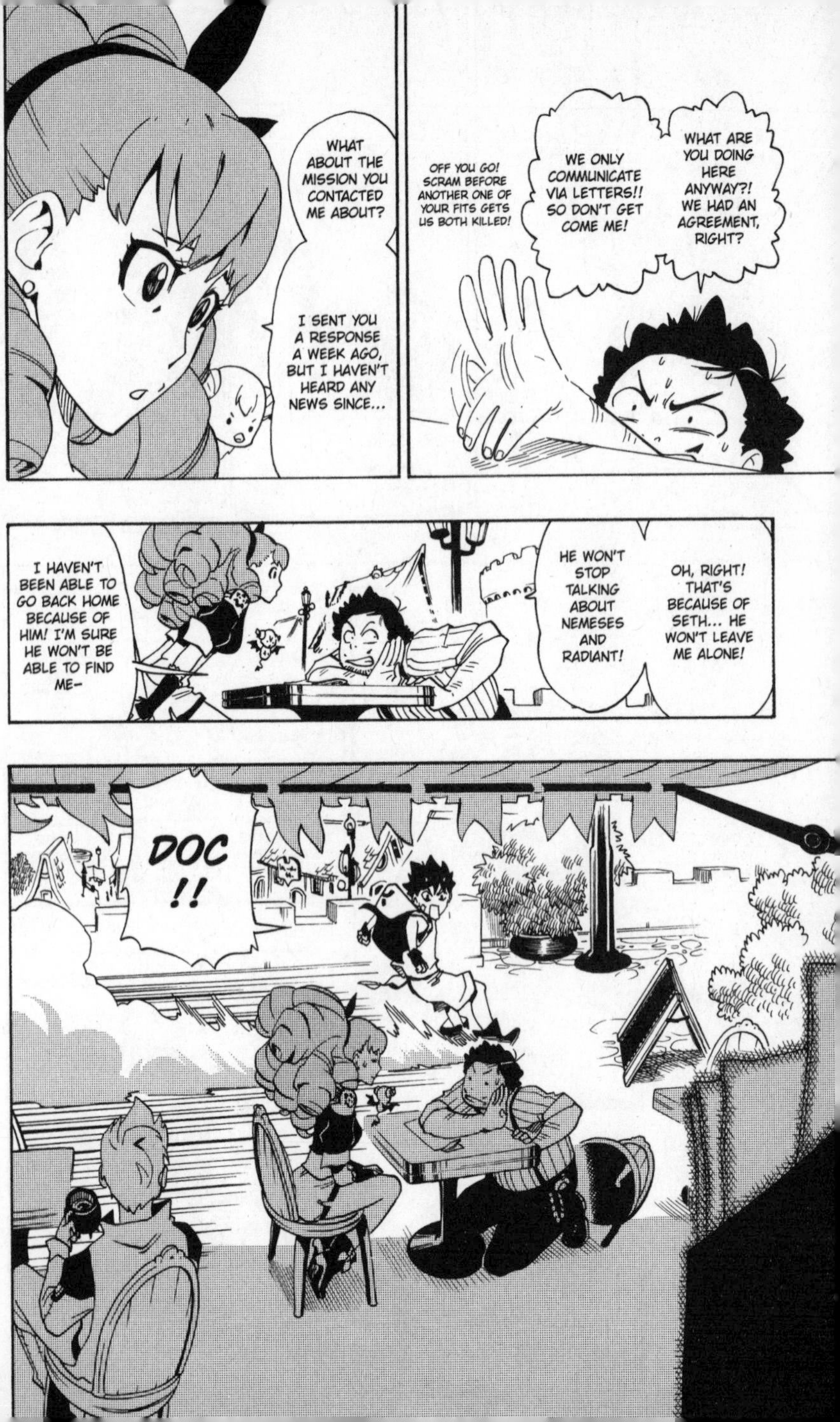
WHAT ARE YOU DOING HERE ANYWAY?! WE HAD AN AGREEMENT, RIGHT?
WE ONLY COMMUNICATE VIA LETTERS!! SO DON'T GET COME ME!
OFF YOU GO! SCRAM BEFORE ANOTHER ONE OF YOUR FITS GETS US BOTH KILLED!
WHAT ABOUT THE MISSION YOU CONTACTED ME ABOUT?
I SENT YOU A RESPONSE A WEEK AGO, BUT I HAVEN'T HEARD ANY NEWS SINCE...
OH, RIGHT! THAT'S BECAUSE OF SETH... HE WON'T LEAVE ME ALONE!
HE WON'T STOP TALKING ABOUT NEMESES AND RADIANT!
I HAVEN'T BEEN ABLE TO GO BACK HOME BECAUSE OF HIM! I'M SURE HE WON'T BE ABLE TO FIND ME-
DOC !!

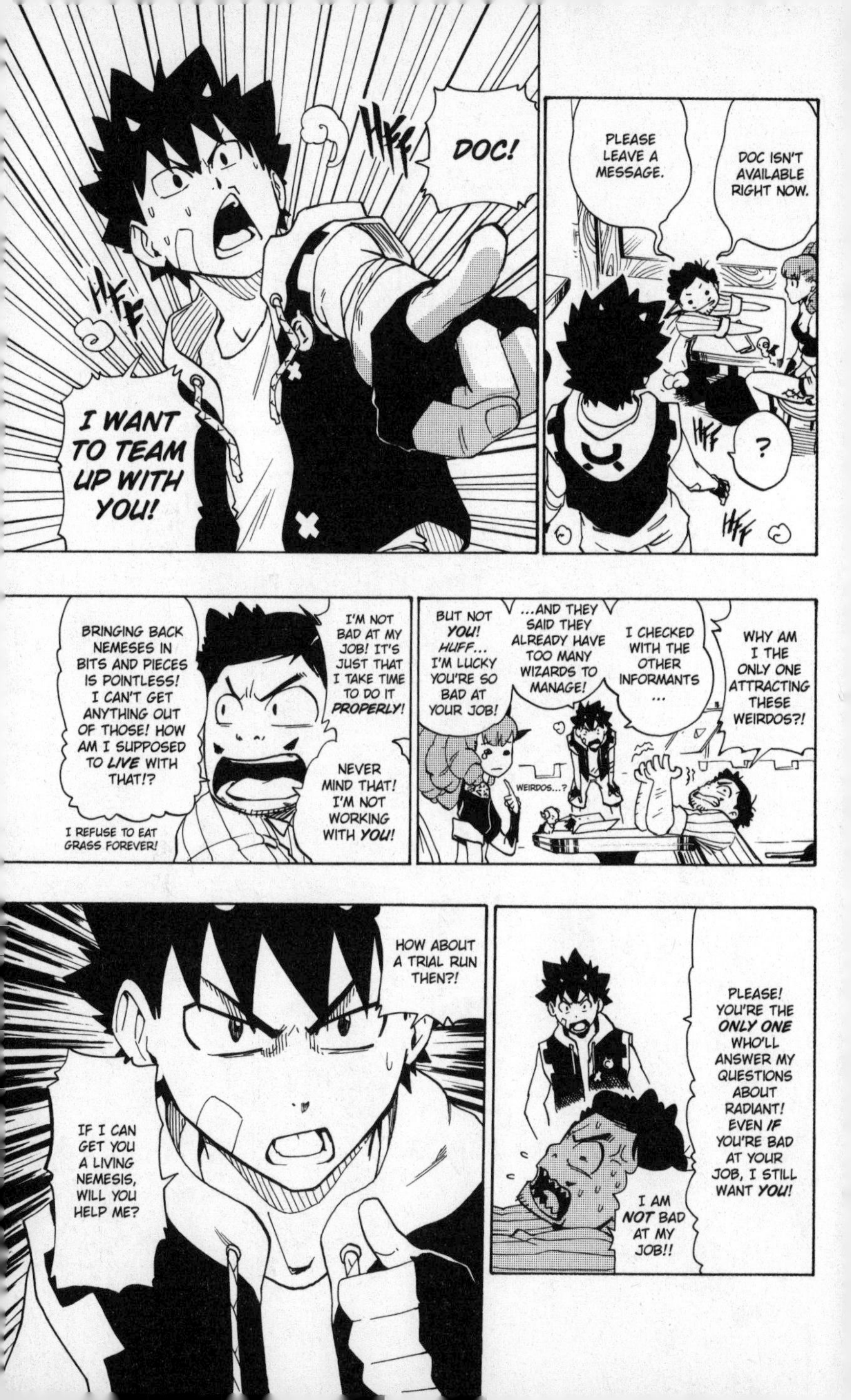
DOC ISN'T AVAILABLE RIGHT NOW.
PLEASE LEAVE A MESSAGE.
?
HFF
HFF
HFF
DOC!
HFF
I WANT TO TEAM UP WITH YOU!
WHY AM I THE ONLY ONE ATTRACTING THESE WEIRDOS?!
I CHECKED WITH THE OTHER INFORMANTS...
...AND THEY SAID THEY ALREADY HAVE TOO MANY WIZARDS TO MANAGE!
BUT NOT YOU! HUFF... I'M LUCKY YOU'RE SO BAD AT YOUR JOB!
WEIRDOS...?
I'M NOT BAD AT MY JOB! IT'S JUST THAT I TAKE TIME TO DO IT PROPERLY!
BRINGING BACK NEMESES IN BITS AND PIECES IS POINTLESS! I CAN'T GET ANYTHING OUT OF THOSE! HOW AM I SUPPOSED TO LIVE WITH THAT!?
NEVER MIND THAT! I'M NOT WORKING WITH YOU!
I REFUSE TO EAT GRASS FOREVER!
PLEASE! YOU'RE THE ONLY ONE WHO'LL ANSWER MY QUESTIONS ABOUT RADIANT! EVEN IF YOU'RE BAD AT YOUR JOB, I STILL WANT YOU!
I AM NOT BAD AT MY JOB!!
HOW ABOUT A TRIAL RUN THEN?!
IF I CAN GET YOU A LIVING NEMESIS, WILL YOU HELP ME?

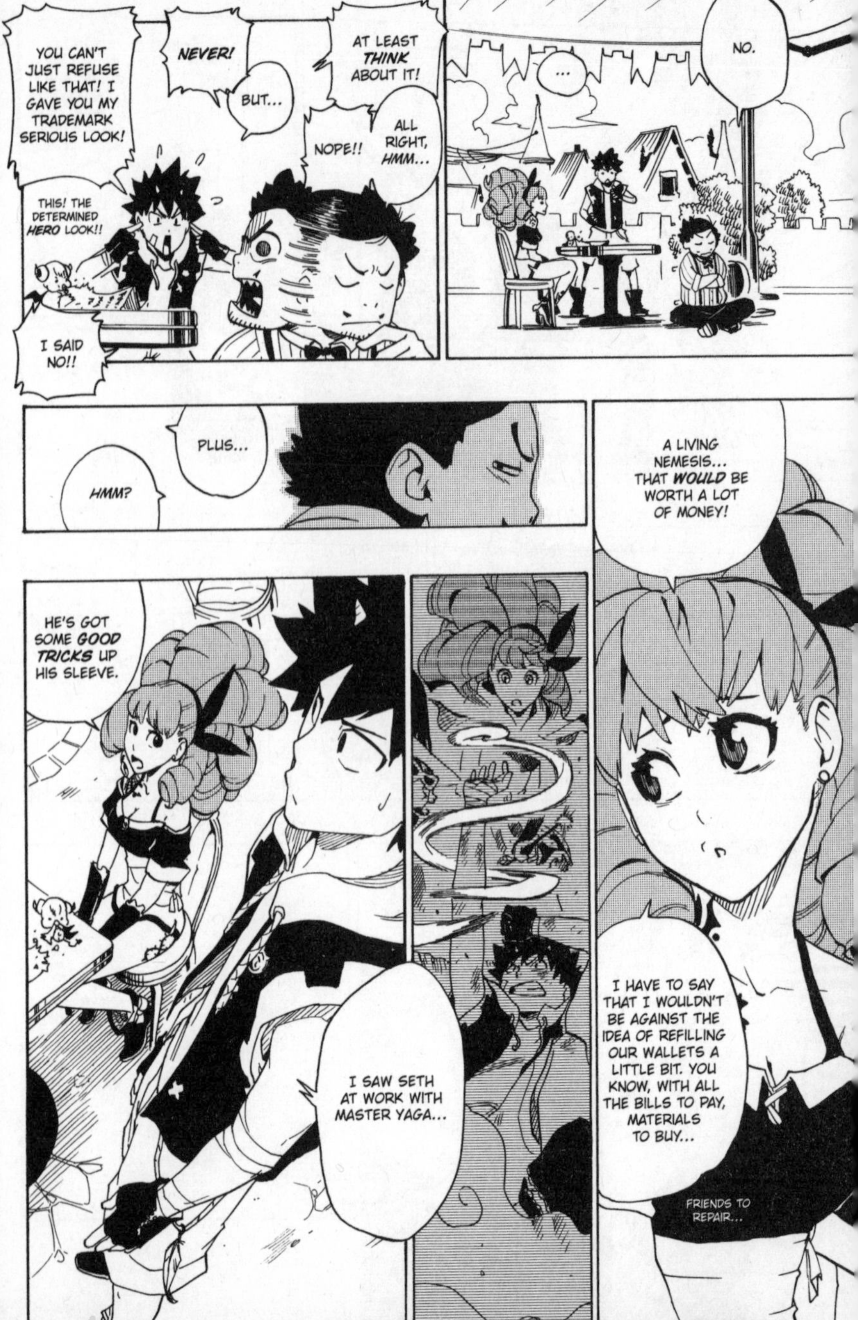
NO.
...
AT LEAST **THINK** ABOUT IT!
ALL RIGHT, *HMM...*
NEVER!
BUT...
NOPE!!
YOU CAN'T JUST REFUSE LIKE THAT! I GAVE YOU MY TRADEMARK SERIOUS LOOK!
THIS! THE DETERMINED ***HERO*** LOOK!!
I SAID NO!!
A LIVING NEMESIS... THAT ***WOULD*** BE WORTH A LOT OF MONEY!
I HAVE TO SAY THAT I WOULDN'T BE AGAINST THE IDEA OF REFILLING OUR WALLETS A LITTLE BIT. YOU KNOW, WITH ALL THE BILLS TO PAY, MATERIALS TO BUY...
FRIENDS TO REPAIR...
PLUS...
HMM?
HE'S GOT SOME ***GOOD TRICKS*** UP HIS SLEEVE.
I SAW SETH AT WORK WITH MASTER YAGA...

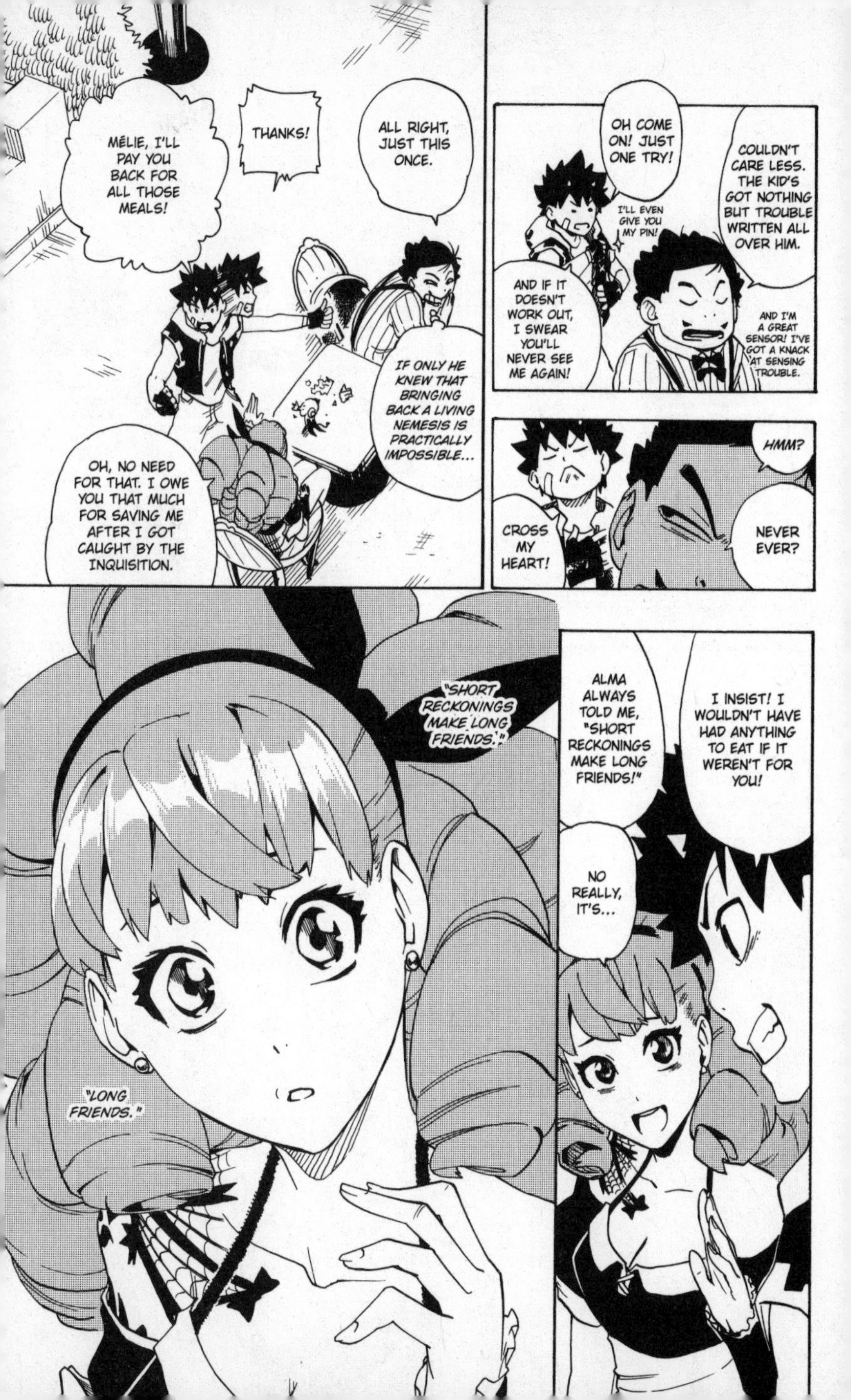
COULDN'T CARE LESS. THE KID'S GOT NOTHING BUT TROUBLE WRITTEN ALL OVER HIM.
OH COME ON! JUST ONE TRY!
I'LL EVEN GIVE YOU MY PIN!
AND I'M A GREAT SENSOR! I'VE GOT A KNACK AT SENSING TROUBLE.
AND IF IT DOESN'T WORK OUT, I SWEAR YOU'LL NEVER SEE ME AGAIN!
HMM?
NEVER EVER?
CROSS MY HEART!
ALL RIGHT, JUST THIS ONCE.
THANKS!
MÉLIE, I'LL PAY YOU BACK FOR ALL THOSE MEALS!
IF ONLY HE KNEW THAT BRINGING BACK A LIVING NEMESIS IS PRACTICALLY IMPOSSIBLE...
OH, NO NEED FOR THAT. I OWE YOU THAT MUCH FOR SAVING ME AFTER I GOT CAUGHT BY THE INQUISITION.
I INSIST! I WOULDN'T HAVE HAD ANYTHING TO EAT IF IT WEREN'T FOR YOU!
ALMA ALWAYS TOLD ME, "SHORT RECKONINGS MAKE LONG FRIENDS!"
NO REALLY, IT'S...
"SHORT RECKONINGS MAKE LONG FRIENDS."
"LONG FRIENDS."

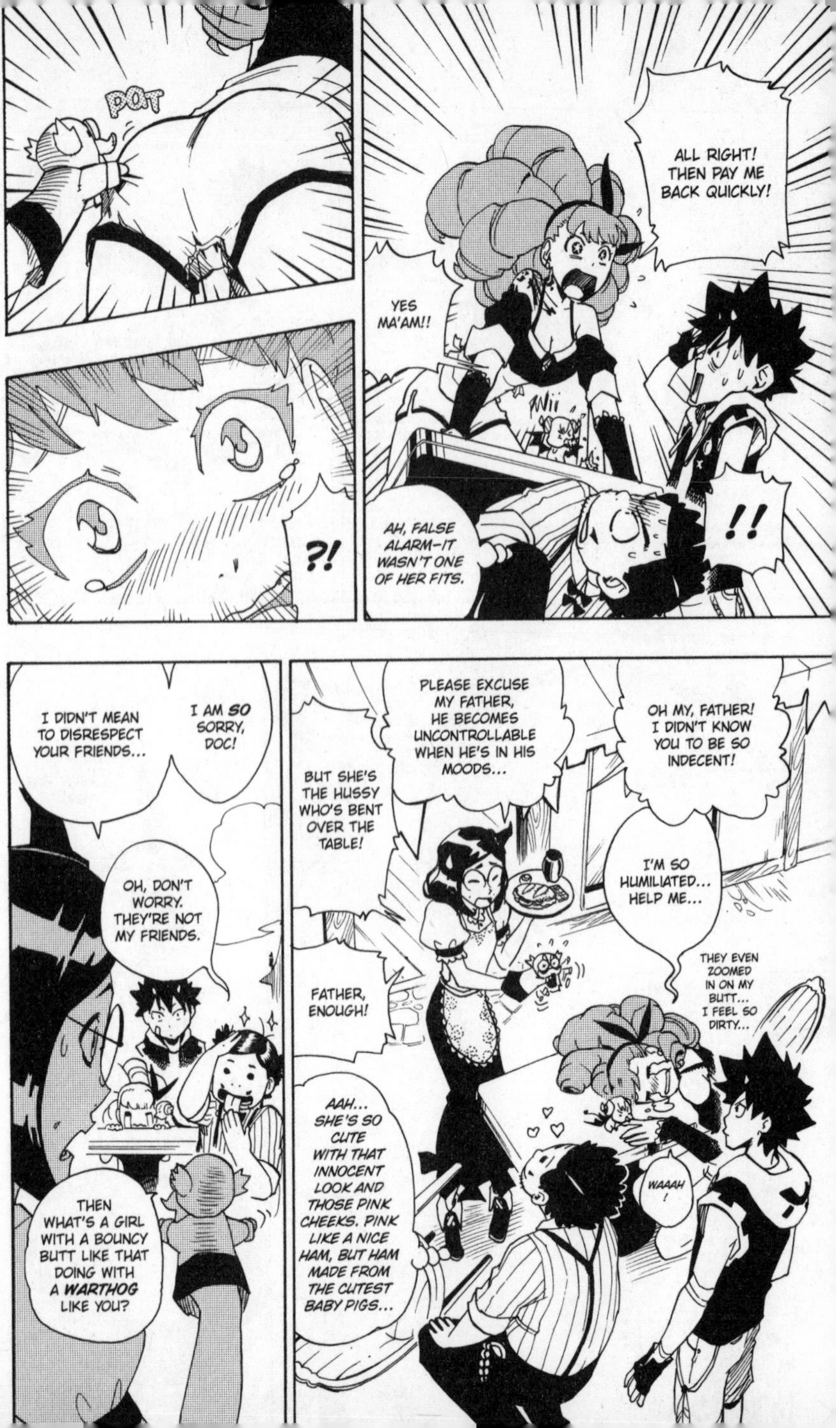
ALL RIGHT! THEN PAY ME BACK QUICKLY!
YES MA'AM!!
!!
AH, FALSE ALARM—IT WASN'T ONE OF HER FITS.
POT
?!
OH MY, FATHER! I DIDN'T KNOW YOU TO BE SO INDECENT!
PLEASE EXCUSE MY FATHER, HE BECOMES UNCONTROLLABLE WHEN HE'S IN HIS MOODS...
BUT SHE'S THE HUSSY WHO'S BENT OVER THE TABLE!
I'M SO HUMILIATED... HELP ME...
THEY EVEN ZOOMED IN ON MY BUTT... I FEEL SO DIRTY...
FATHER, ENOUGH!
AAH... SHE'S SO CUTE WITH THAT INNOCENT LOOK AND THOSE PINK CHEEKS. PINK LIKE A NICE HAM, BUT HAM MADE FROM THE CUTEST BABY PIGS...
WAAAH!
I AM SO SORRY, DOC!
I DIDN'T MEAN TO DISRESPECT YOUR FRIENDS...
OH, DON'T WORRY. THEY'RE NOT MY FRIENDS.
THEN WHAT'S A GIRL WITH A BOUNCY BUTT LIKE THAT DOING WITH A WARTHOG LIKE YOU?

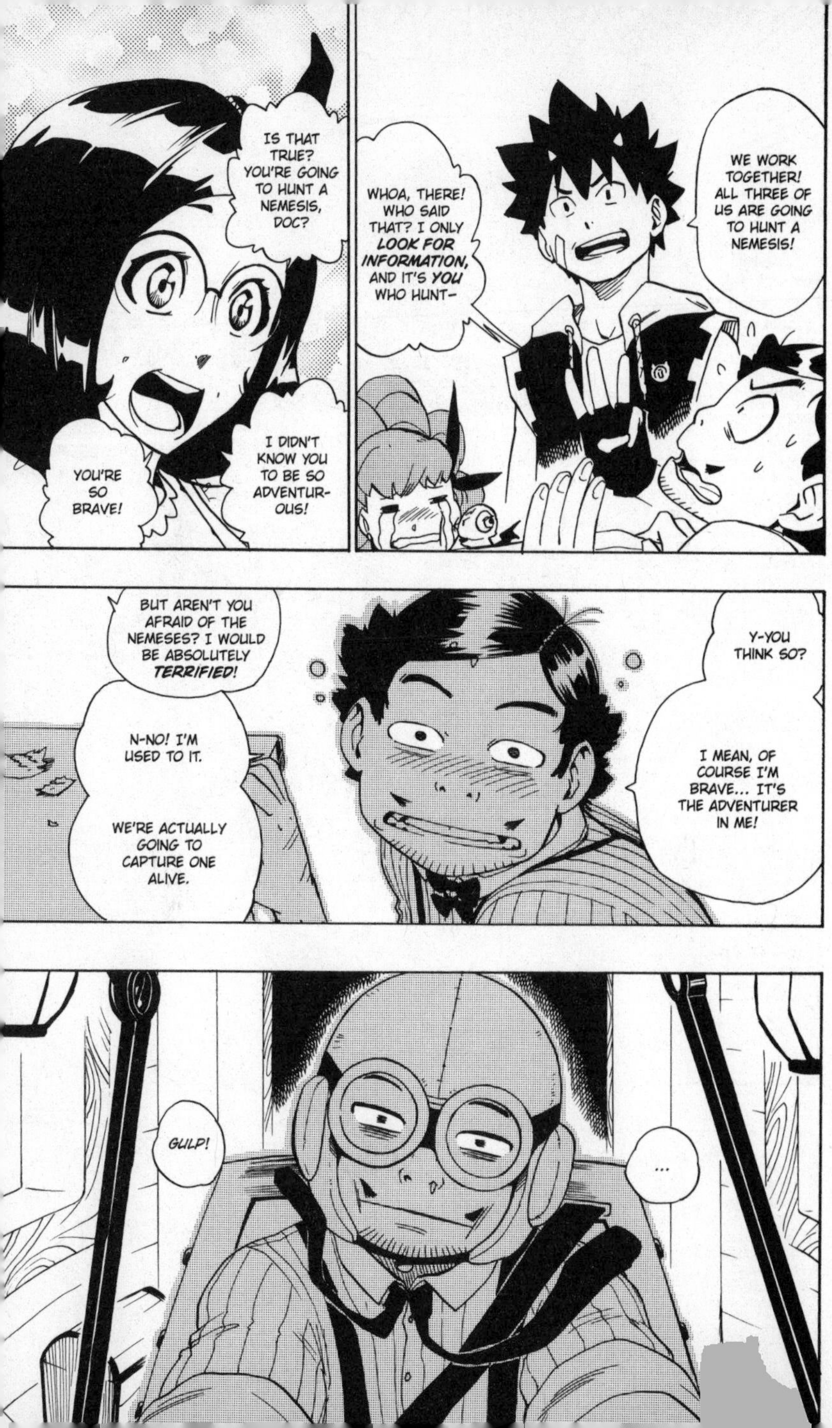
WE WORK TOGETHER! ALL THREE OF US ARE GOING TO HUNT A NEMESIS!
WHOA, THERE! WHO SAID THAT? I ONLY LOOK FOR INFORMATION, AND IT'S YOU WHO HUNT-
IS THAT TRUE? YOU'RE GOING TO HUNT A NEMESIS, DOC?
I DIDN'T KNOW YOU TO BE SO ADVENTUR-OUS!
YOU'RE SO BRAVE!
Y-YOU THINK SO?
I MEAN, OF COURSE I'M BRAVE... IT'S THE ADVENTURER IN ME!
BUT AREN'T YOU AFRAID OF THE NEMESES? I WOULD BE ABSOLUTELY TERRIFIED!
N-NO! I'M USED TO IT.
WE'RE ACTUALLY GOING TO CAPTURE ONE ALIVE.
...
GULP!

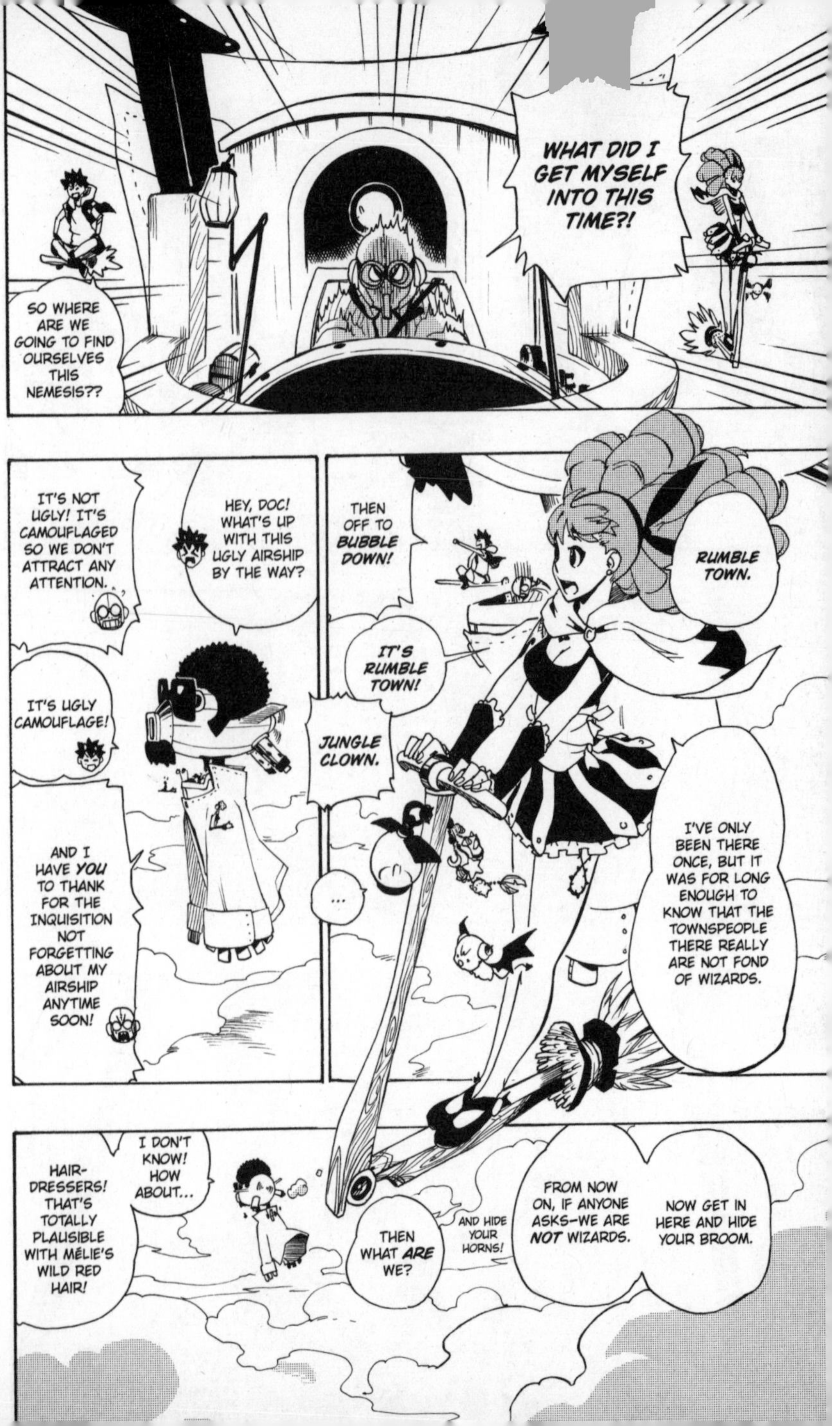
WHAT DID I GET MYSELF INTO THIS TIME?!
SO WHERE ARE WE GOING TO FIND OURSELVES THIS NEMESIS??
RUMBLE TOWN.
THEN OFF TO BUBBLE DOWN!
IT'S RUMBLE TOWN!
JUNGLE CLOWN.
I'VE ONLY BEEN THERE ONCE, BUT IT WAS FOR LONG ENOUGH TO KNOW THAT THE TOWNSPEOPLE THERE REALLY ARE NOT FOND OF WIZARDS.
...
HEY, DOC! WHAT'S UP WITH THIS UGLY AIRSHIP BY THE WAY?
IT'S NOT UGLY! IT'S CAMOUFLAGED SO WE DON'T ATTRACT ANY ATTENTION.
IT'S UGLY CAMOUFLAGE!
AND I HAVE YOU TO THANK FOR THE INQUISITION NOT FORGETTING ABOUT MY AIRSHIP ANYTIME SOON!
NOW GET IN HERE AND HIDE YOUR BROOM.
FROM NOW ON, IF ANYONE ASKS—WE ARE NOT WIZARDS.
AND HIDE YOUR HORNS!
THEN WHAT ARE WE?
I DON'T KNOW! HOW ABOUT...
HAIR-DRESSERS! THAT'S TOTALLY PLAUSIBLE WITH MÉLIE'S WILD RED HAIR!

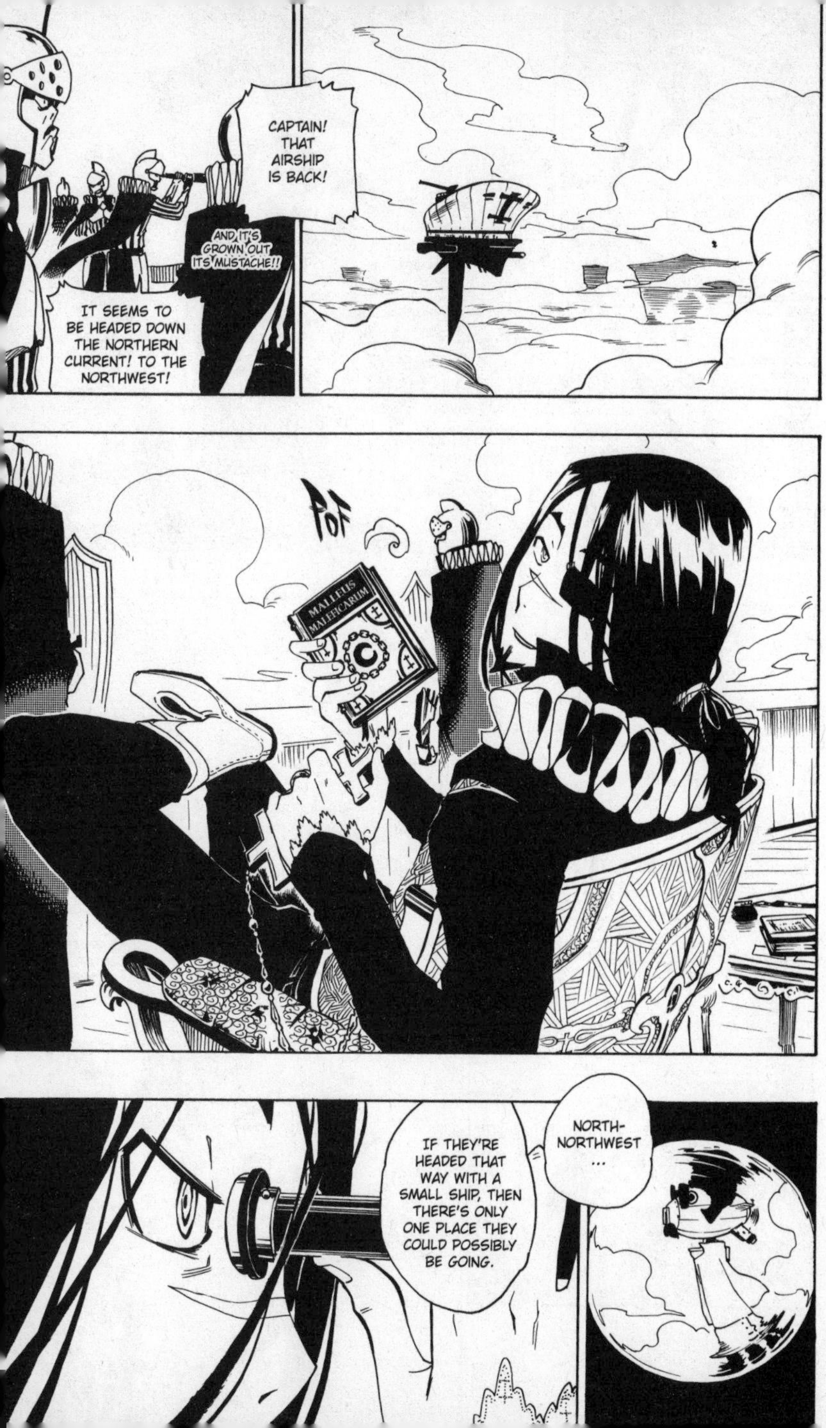
CAPTAIN! THAT AIRSHIP IS BACK!
AND IT'S GROWN OUT ITS MUSTACHE!!
IT SEEMS TO BE HEADED DOWN THE NORTHERN CURRENT! TO THE NORTHWEST!
POF
MALLEUS MALEFICARUM
NORTH-NORTHWEST ...
IF THEY'RE HEADED THAT WAY WITH A SMALL SHIP, THEN THERE'S ONLY ONE PLACE THEY COULD POSSIBLY BE GOING.

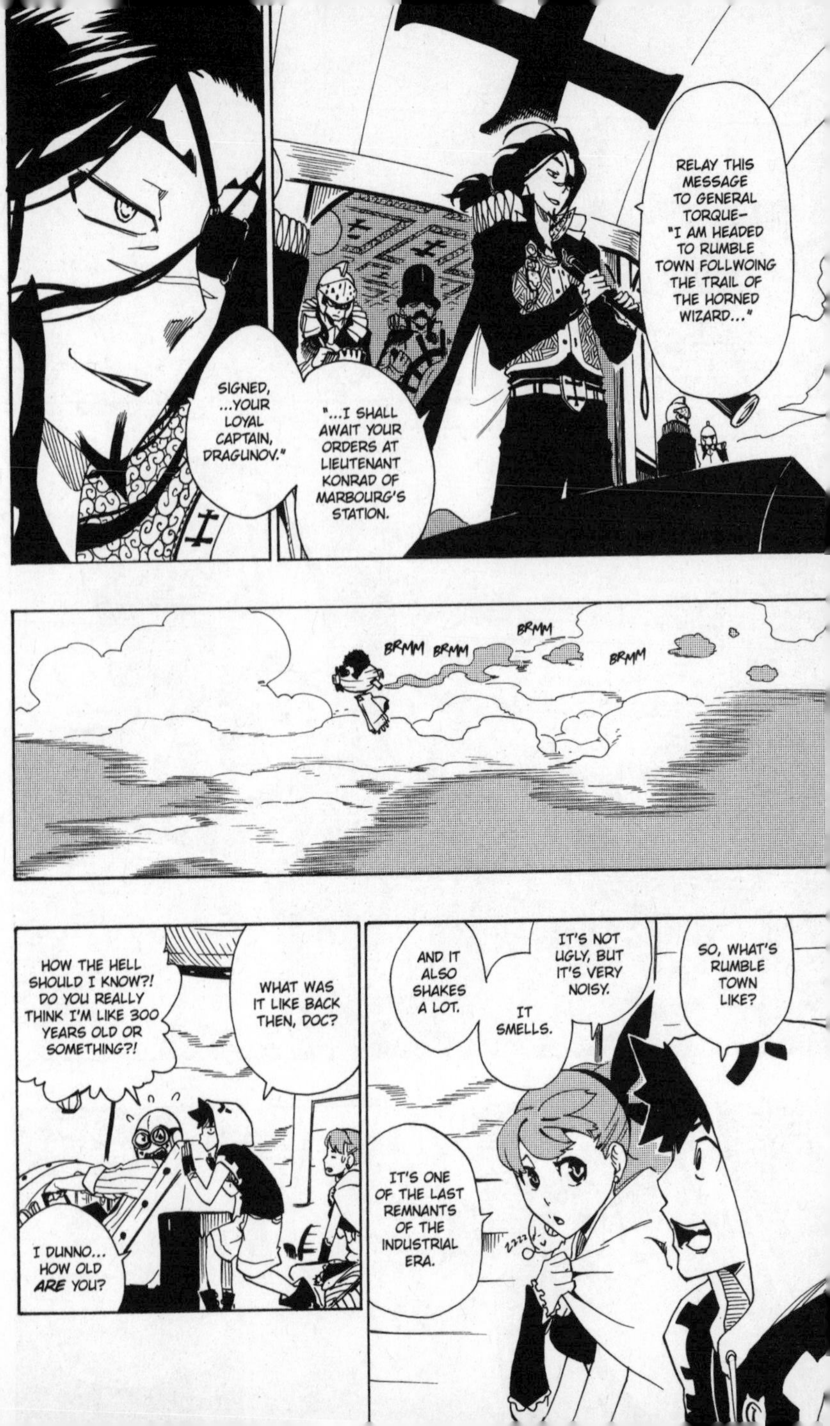
RELAY THIS MESSAGE TO GENERAL TORQUE– "I AM HEADED TO RUMBLE TOWN FOLLWOING THE TRAIL OF THE HORNED WIZARD..."
"...I SHALL AWAIT YOUR ORDERS AT LIEUTENANT KONRAD OF MARBOURG'S STATION.
SIGNED, ...YOUR LOYAL CAPTAIN, DRAGUNOV."
BRMM
BRMM
BRMM BRMM
SO, WHAT'S RUMBLE TOWN LIKE?
IT'S NOT UGLY, BUT IT'S VERY NOISY.
IT SMELLS.
AND IT ALSO SHAKES A LOT.
IT'S ONE OF THE LAST REMNANTS OF THE INDUSTRIAL ERA.
WHAT WAS IT LIKE BACK THEN, DOC?
HOW THE HELL SHOULD I KNOW?! DO YOU REALLY THINK I'M LIKE 300 YEARS OLD OR SOMETHING?!
I DUNNO... HOW OLD *ARE* YOU?

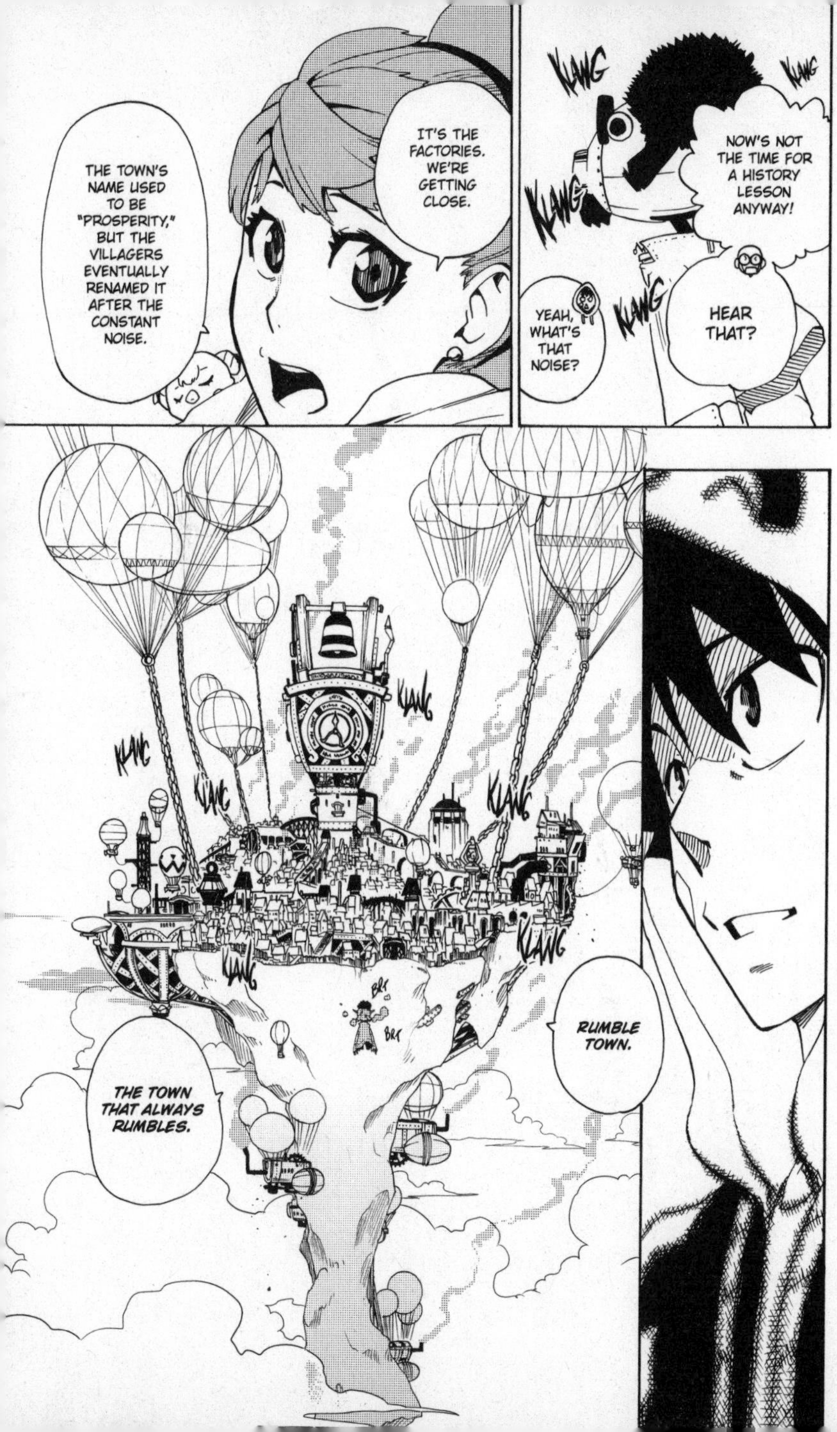
KLANG
NOW'S NOT THE TIME FOR A HISTORY LESSON ANYWAY!
KLANG
HEAR THAT?
YEAH, WHAT'S THAT NOISE?
IT'S THE FACTORIES. WE'RE GETTING CLOSE.
THE TOWN'S NAME USED TO BE "PROSPERITY," BUT THE VILLAGERS EVENTUALLY RENAMED IT AFTER THE CONSTANT NOISE.
KLANG
BRT
RUMBLE TOWN.
THE TOWN THAT ALWAYS RUMBLES.

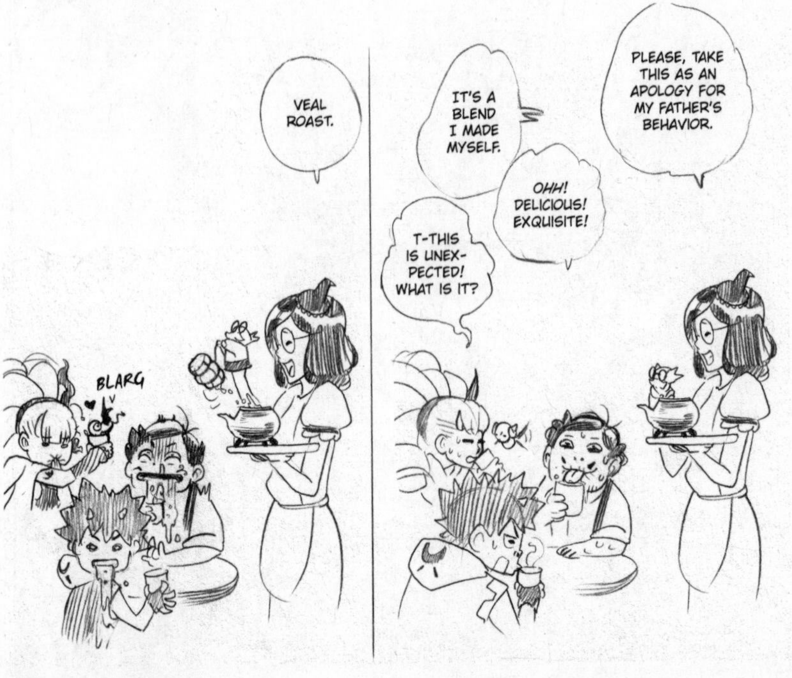
PLEASE, TAKE THIS AS AN APOLOGY FOR MY FATHER'S BEHAVIOR.
IT'S A BLEND I MADE MYSELF.
OHH! DELICIOUS! EXQUISITE!
T-THIS IS UNEX-PECTED! WHAT IS IT?
VEAL ROAST.
BLARG

Chapter 7
Welcome to Rumble Town

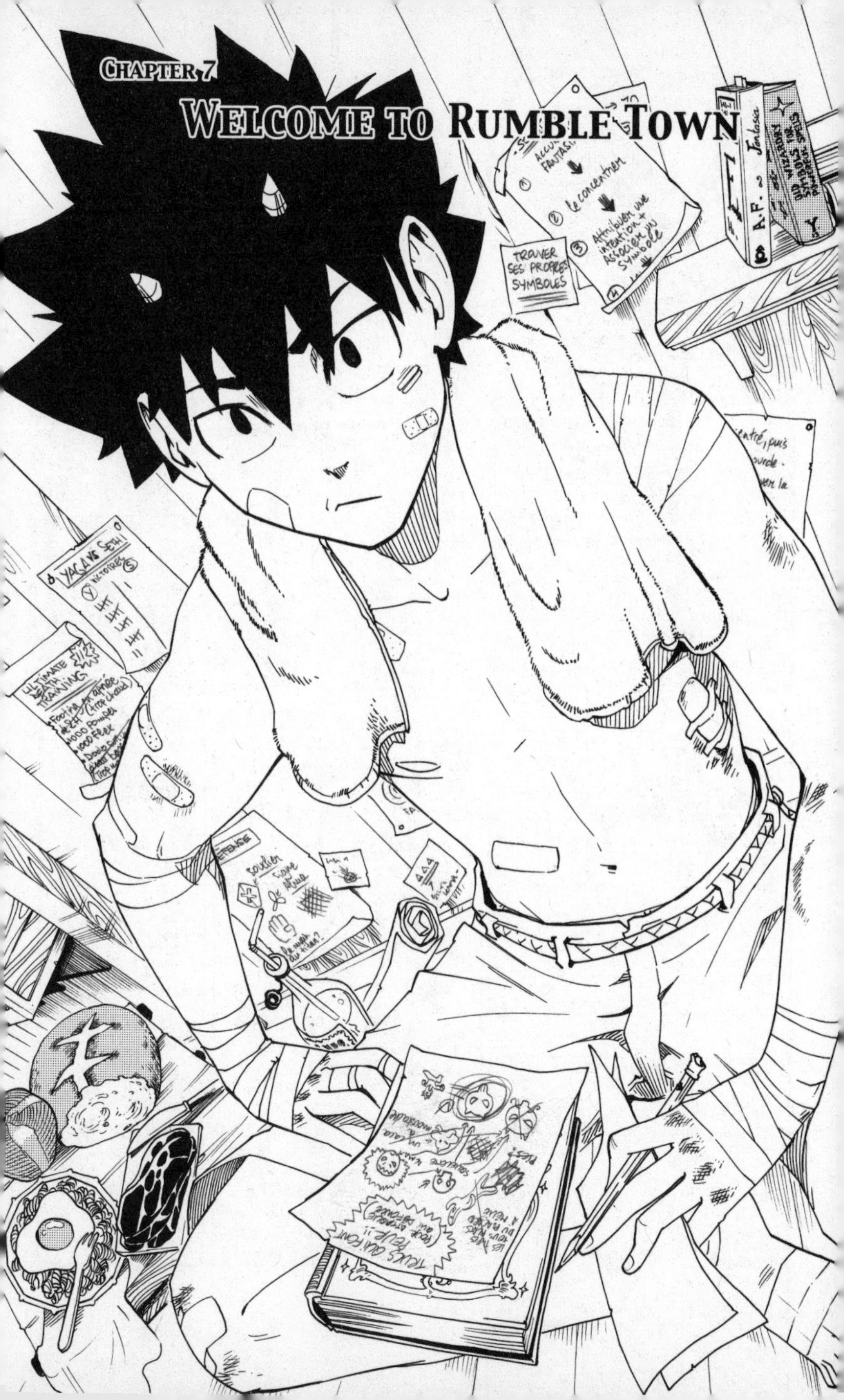

TROUVER SES PROPRES SYMBOLES
le concentrer
YAGA VS SETHI
ULTIMATE DEATH TRAINING
A.F.
Fantasia

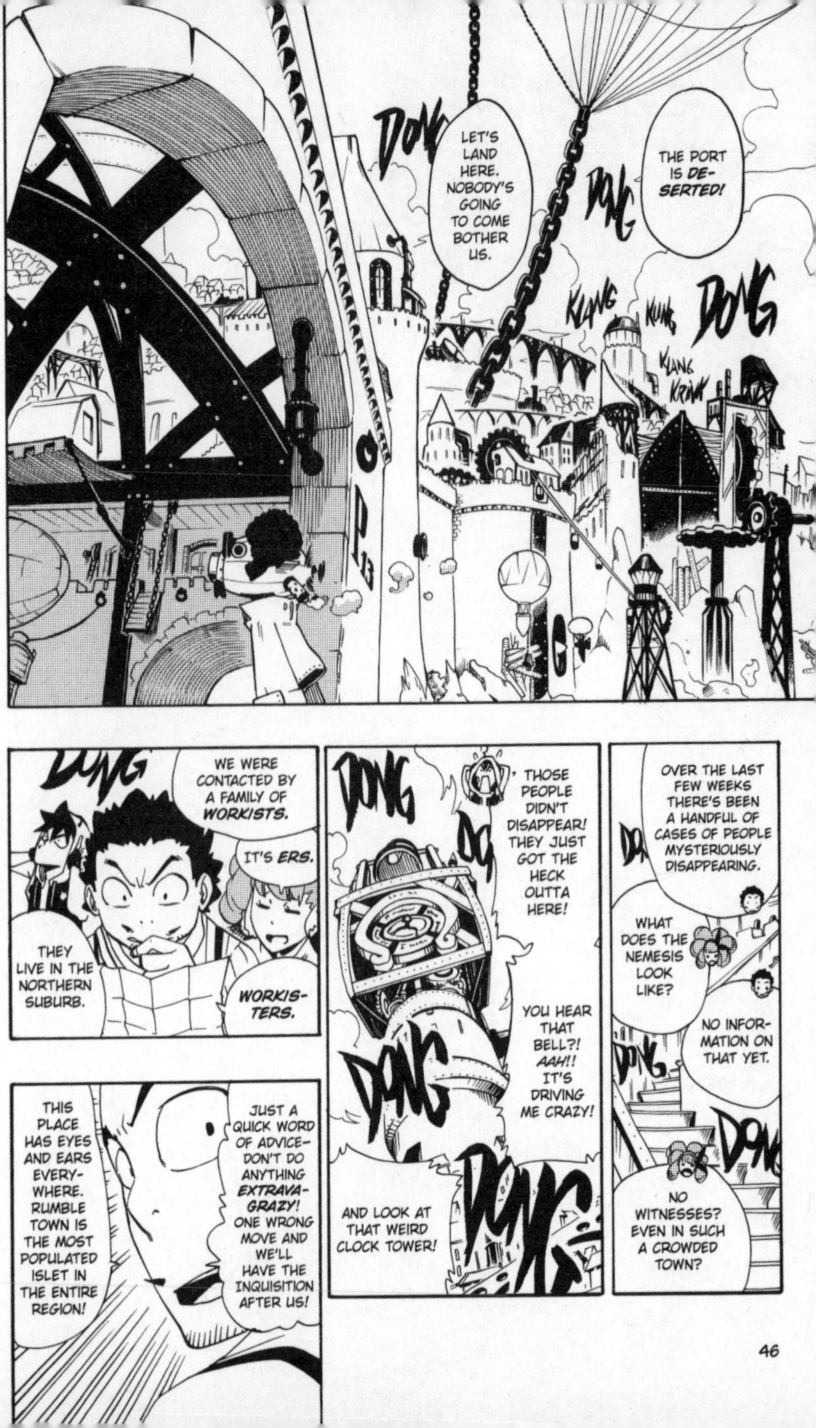
THE PORT IS DE-SERTED!
DONG
LET'S LAND HERE. NOBODY'S GOING TO COME BOTHER US.
DONG
DONG
KLANG
KLANG
KLANG
KRINK
OVER THE LAST FEW WEEKS THERE'S BEEN A HANDFUL OF CASES OF PEOPLE MYSTERIOUSLY DISAPPEARING.
WHAT DOES THE NEMESIS LOOK LIKE?
NO INFOR-MATION ON THAT YET.
NO WITNESSES? EVEN IN SUCH A CROWDED TOWN?
THOSE PEOPLE DIDN'T DISAPPEAR! THEY JUST GOT THE HECK OUTTA HERE!
YOU HEAR THAT BELL?! AAH!! IT'S DRIVING ME CRAZY!
AND LOOK AT THAT WEIRD CLOCK TOWER!
WE WERE CONTACTED BY A FAMILY OF WORKISTS.
IT'S ERS.
WORKIS-TERS.
THEY LIVE IN THE NORTHERN SUBURB.
JUST A QUICK WORD OF ADVICE- DON'T DO ANYTHING EXTRAVA-GRAZY! ONE WRONG MOVE AND WE'LL HAVE THE INQUISITION AFTER US!
THIS PLACE HAS EYES AND EARS EVERY-WHERE. RUMBLE TOWN IS THE MOST POPULATED ISLET IN THE ENTIRE REGION!

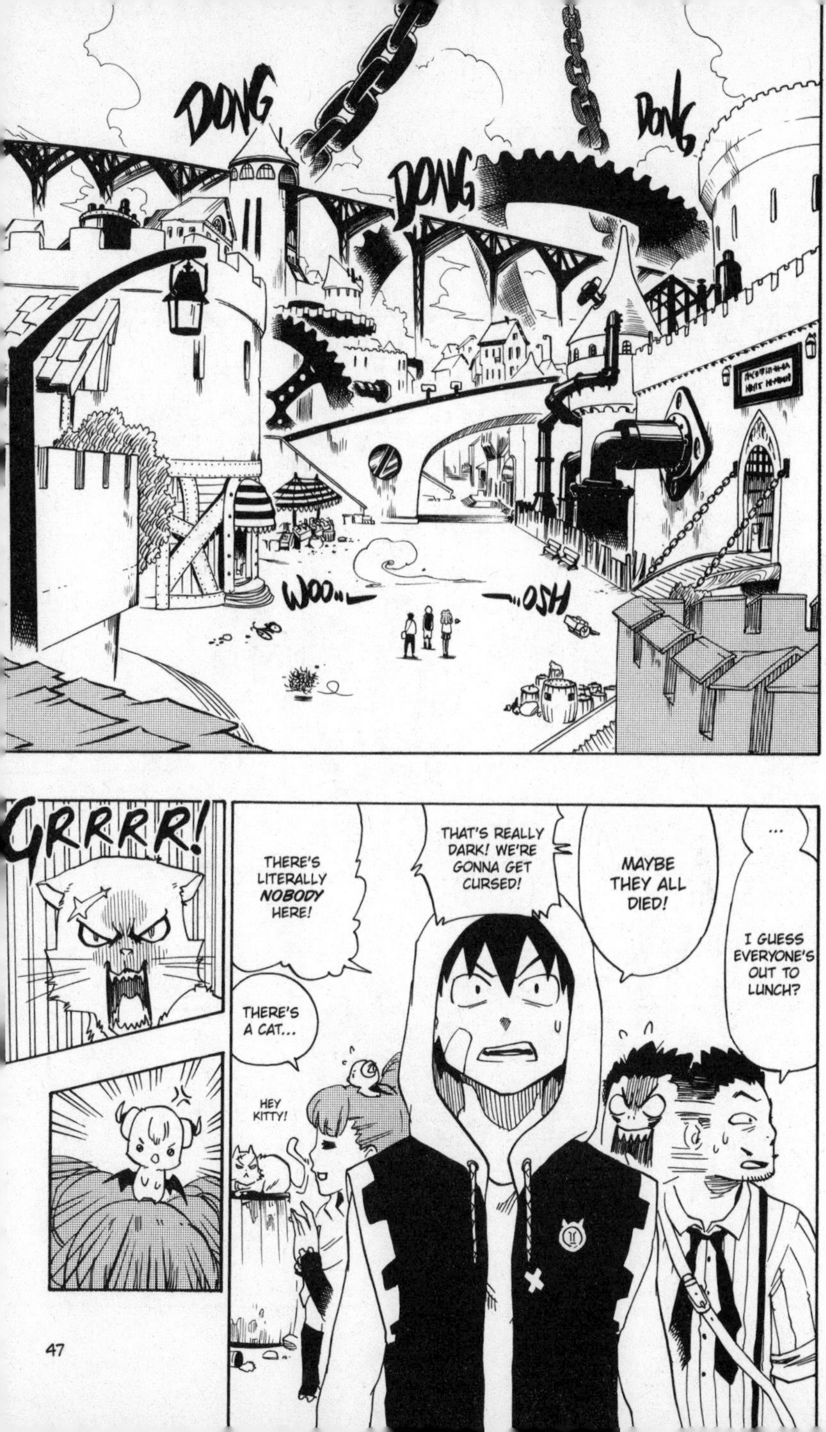
DONG
DONG
DONG
WOO... —...OSH
...
I GUESS EVERYONE'S OUT TO LUNCH?
MAYBE THEY ALL DIED!
THAT'S REALLY DARK! WE'RE GONNA GET CURSED!
THERE'S LITERALLY *NOBODY* HERE!
THERE'S A CAT...
HEY KITTY!
GRRRR!

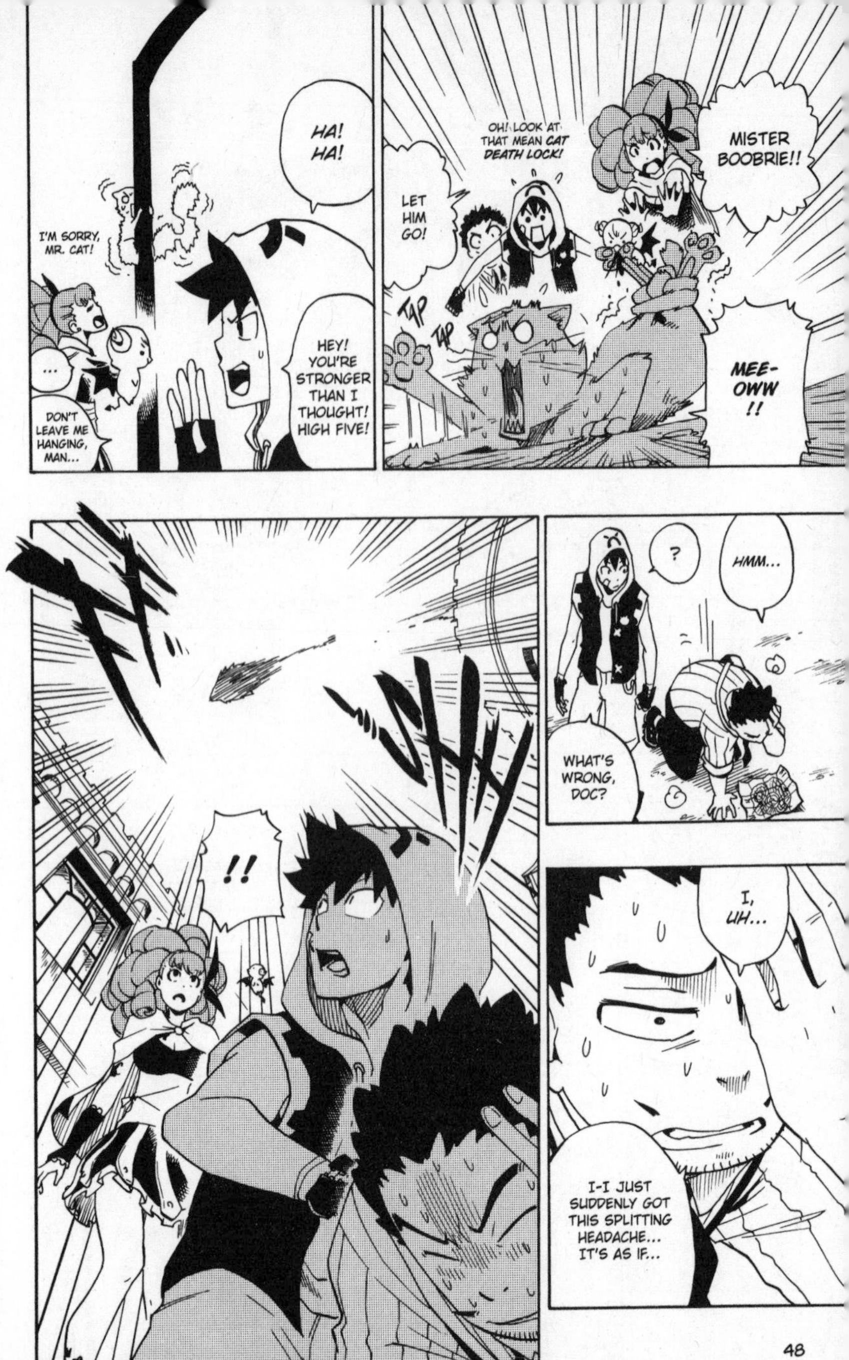
MISTER BOOBRIE!!
OH! LOOK AT THAT MEAN CAT DEATH LOCK!
LET HIM GO!
MEE-OWW!!
TAP
TAP
HA! HA!
HEY! YOU'RE STRONGER THAN I THOUGHT! HIGH FIVE!
I'M SORRY, MR. CAT!
...
DON'T LEAVE ME HANGING, MAN...
HMM...
?
WHAT'S WRONG, DOC?
I, UH...
I-I JUST SUDDENLY GOT THIS SPLITTING HEADACHE... IT'S AS IF...
SHH
!!

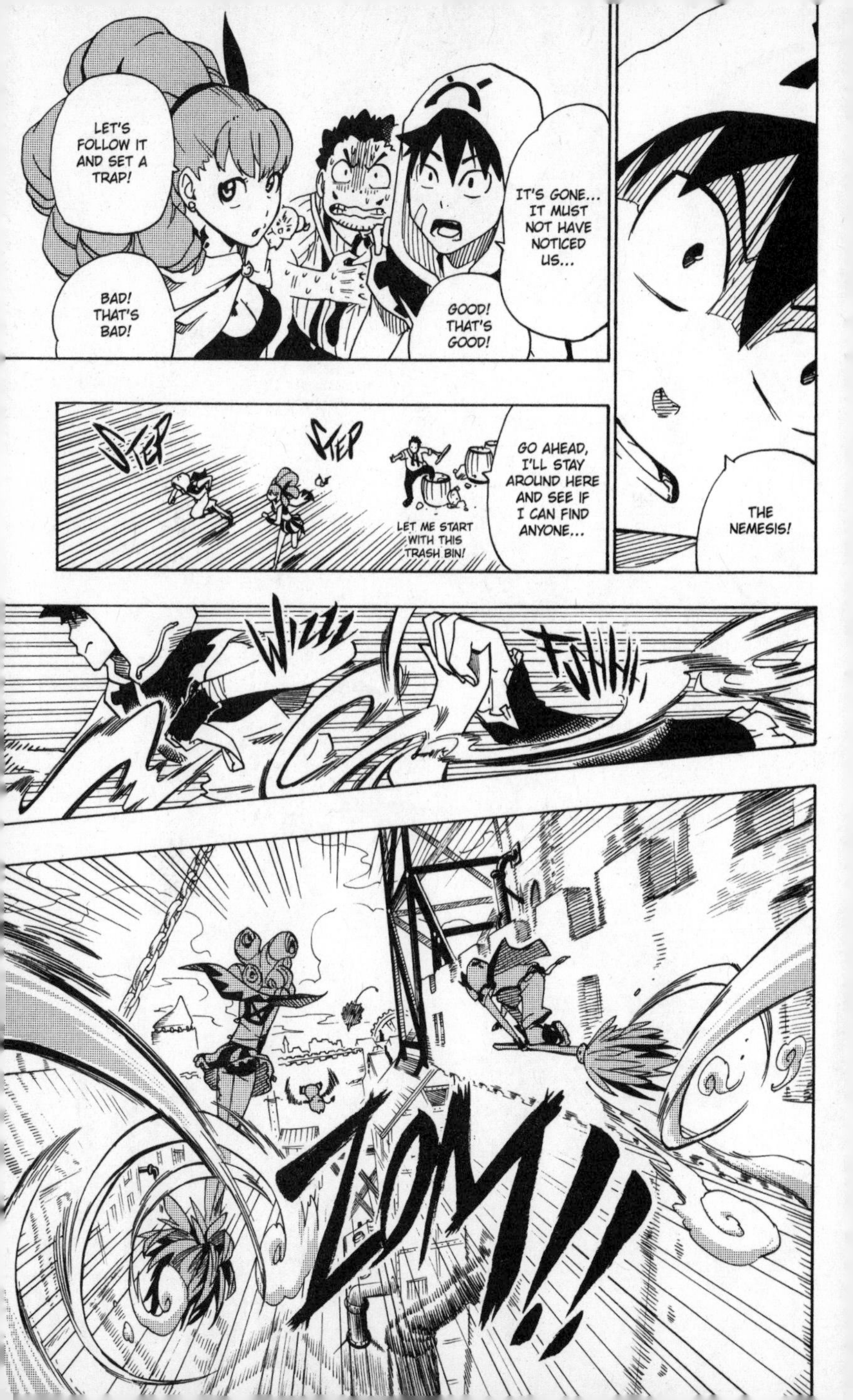
THE NEMESIS!
IT'S GONE... IT MUST NOT HAVE NOTICED US...
GOOD! THAT'S GOOD!
LET'S FOLLOW IT AND SET A TRAP!
BAD! THAT'S BAD!
GO AHEAD, I'LL STAY AROUND HERE AND SEE IF I CAN FIND ANYONE...
LET ME START WITH THIS TRASH BIN!
STEP
STEP
FSHHH
WIZZZ
ZOM!!

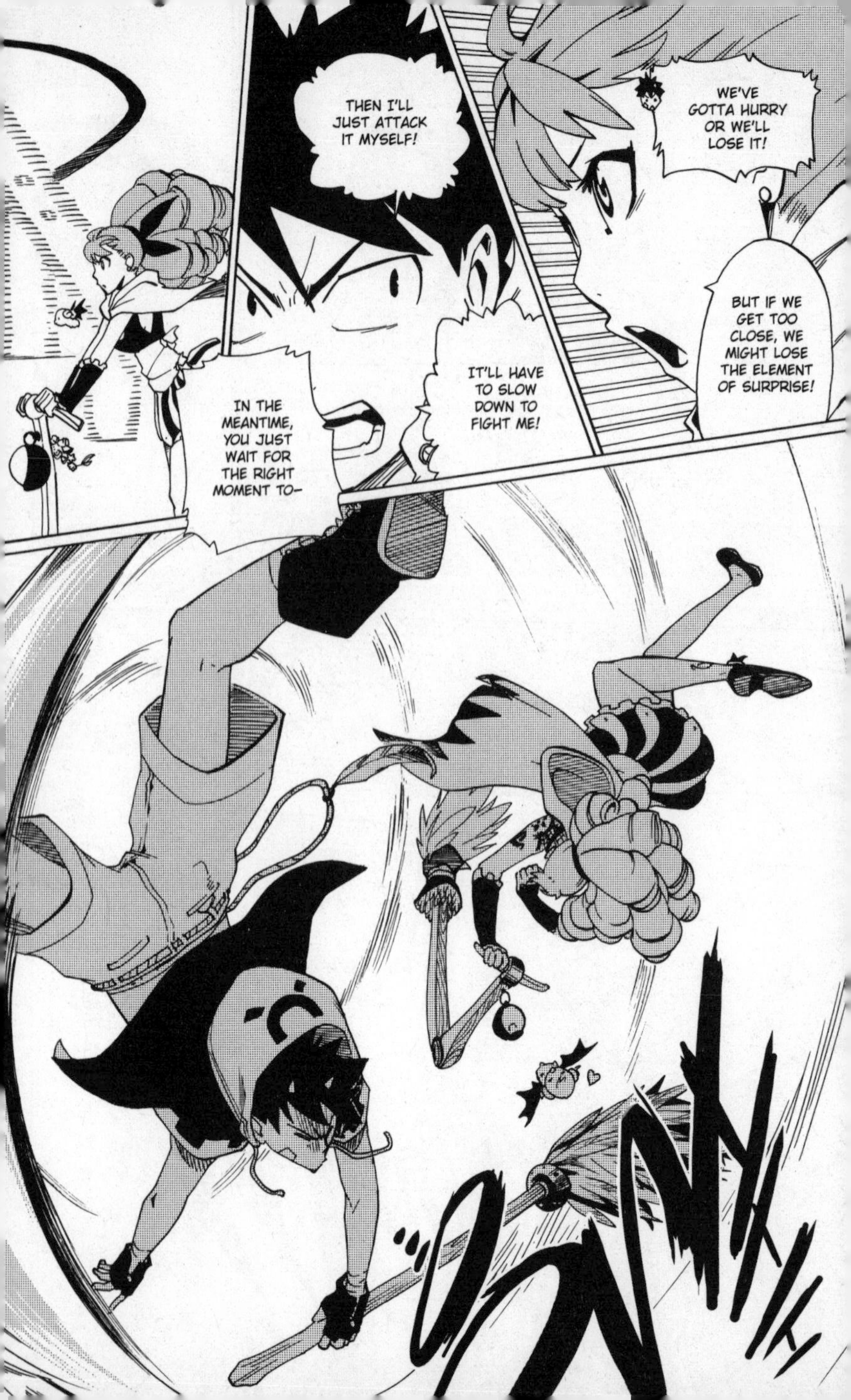
WE'VE GOTTA HURRY OR WE'LL LOSE IT!
BUT IF WE GET TOO CLOSE, WE MIGHT LOSE THE ELEMENT OF SURPRISE!
THEN I'LL JUST ATTACK IT MYSELF!
IT'LL HAVE TO SLOW DOWN TO FIGHT ME!
IN THE MEANTIME, YOU JUST WAIT FOR THE RIGHT MOMENT TO-

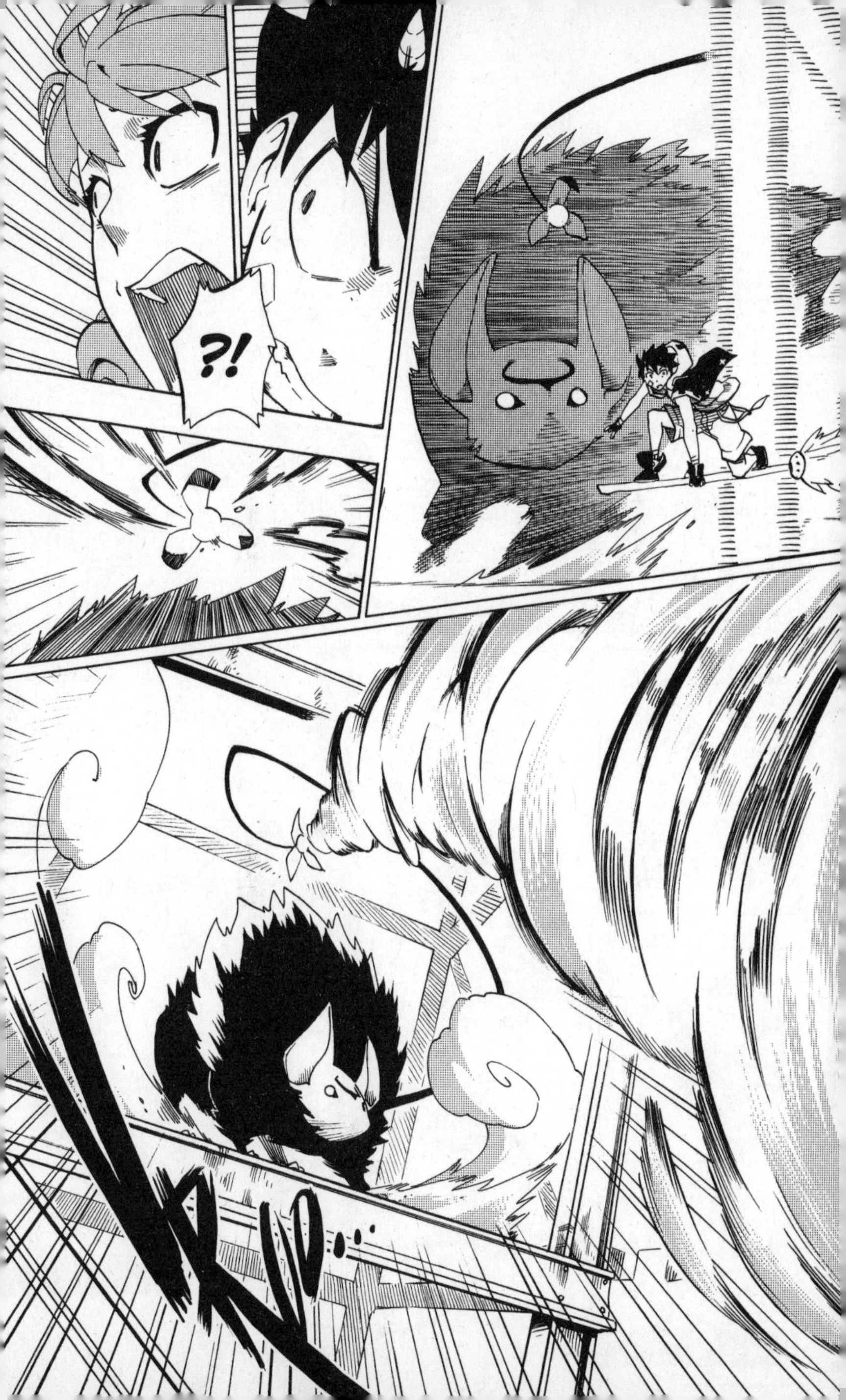
?!

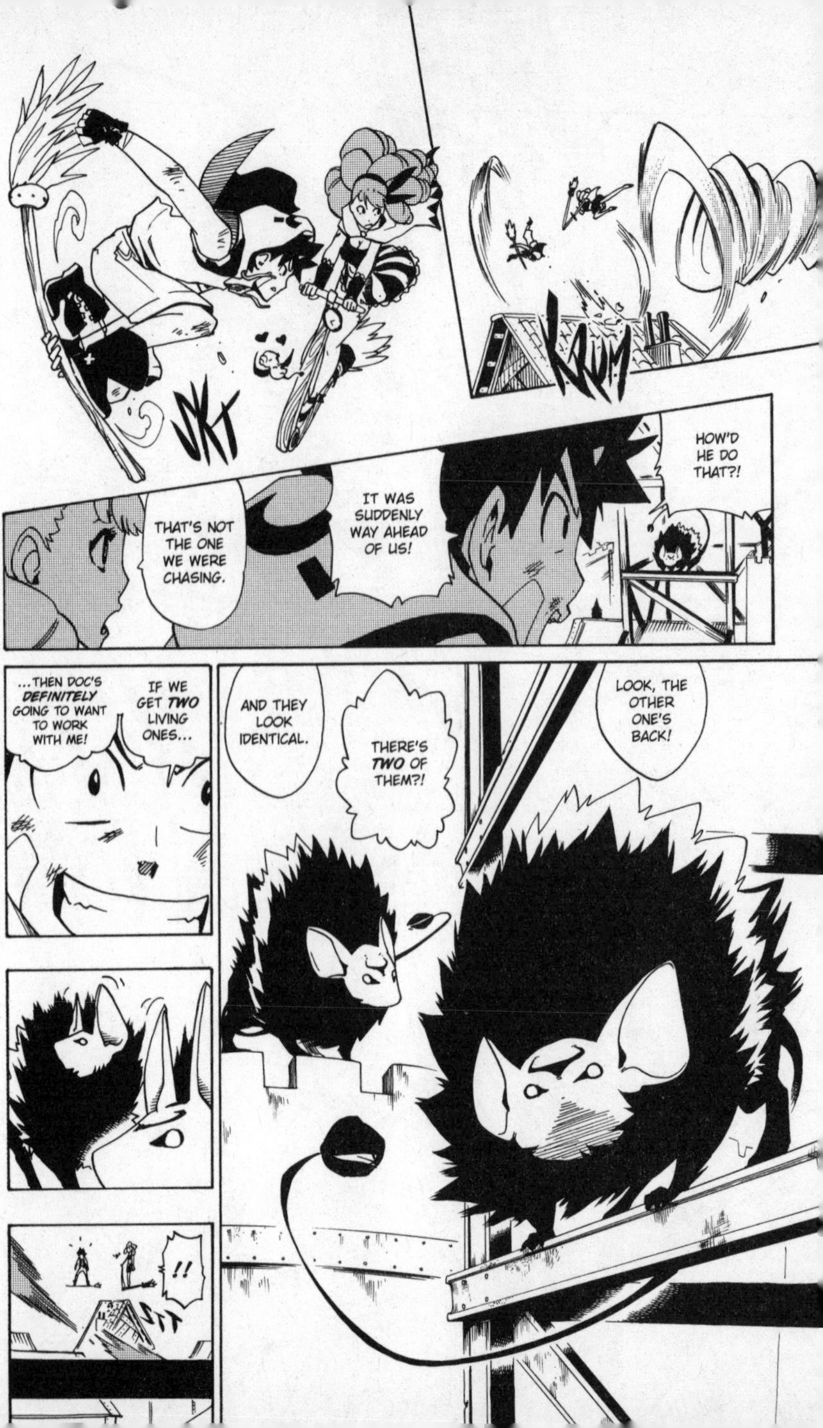
KRUM
SKT
HOW'D HE DO THAT?!
IT WAS SUDDENLY WAY AHEAD OF US!
THAT'S NOT THE ONE WE WERE CHASING.
LOOK, THE OTHER ONE'S BACK!
THERE'S **TWO** OF THEM?!
AND THEY LOOK IDENTICAL.
IF WE GET **TWO** LIVING ONES...
...THEN DOC'S **DEFINITELY** GOING TO WANT TO WORK WITH ME!
!!
STT

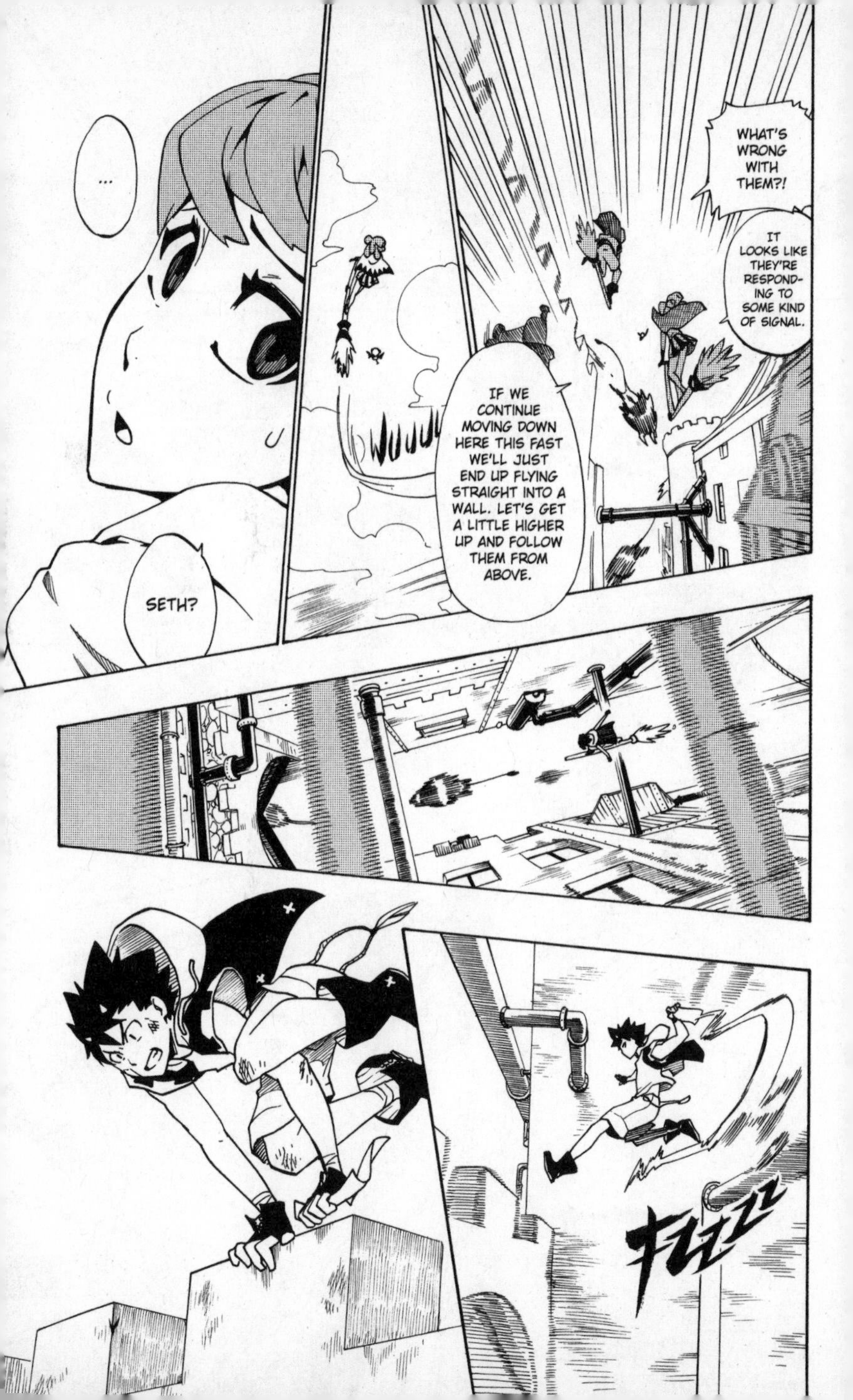
WHAT'S WRONG WITH THEM?!
IT LOOKS LIKE THEY'RE RESPONDING TO SOME KIND OF SIGNAL.
IF WE CONTINUE MOVING DOWN HERE THIS FAST WE'LL JUST END UP FLYING STRAIGHT INTO A WALL. LET'S GET A LITTLE HIGHER UP AND FOLLOW THEM FROM ABOVE.
...
SETH?
FZZZZ

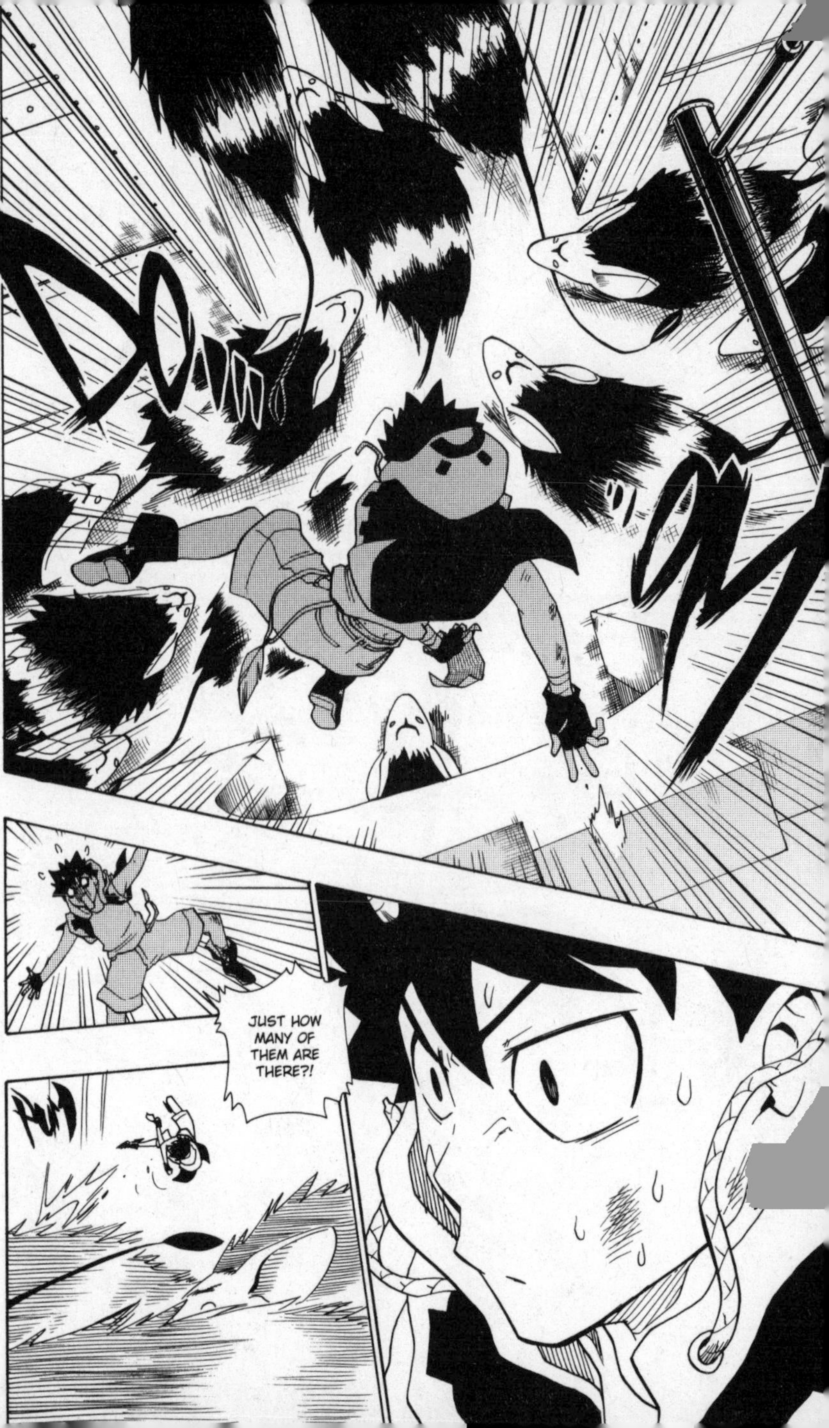
DOOM
JUST HOW MANY OF THEM ARE THERE?!

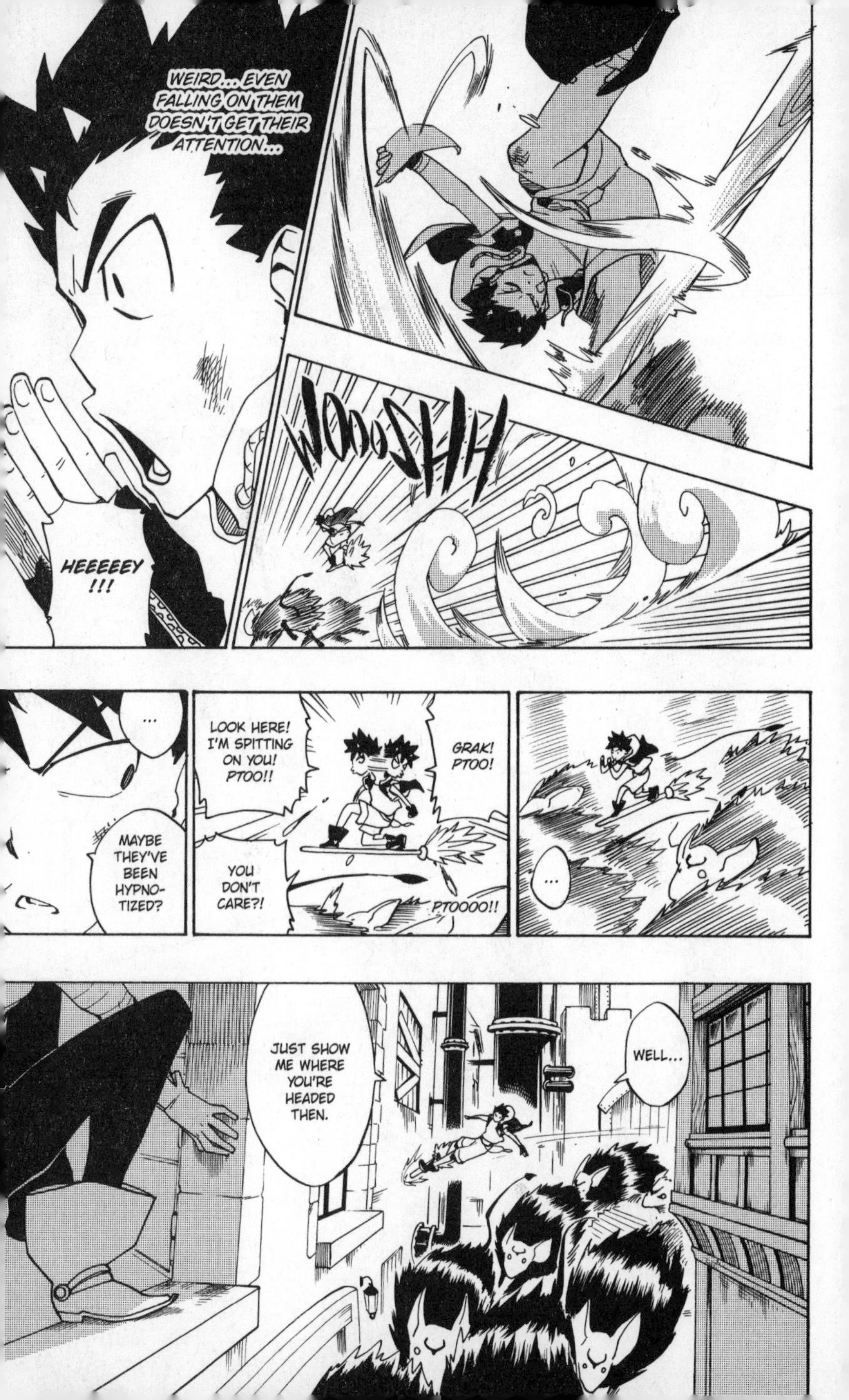
WHOOSH
WEIRD... EVEN FALLING ON THEM DOESN'T GET THEIR ATTENTION...
HEEEEEY!!!
...
GRAK! PTOO!
LOOK HERE! I'M SPITTING ON YOU! PTOO!!
YOU DON'T CARE?!
PTOOOO!!
...
MAYBE THEY'VE BEEN HYPNO-TIZED?
WELL...
JUST SHOW ME WHERE YOU'RE HEADED THEN.

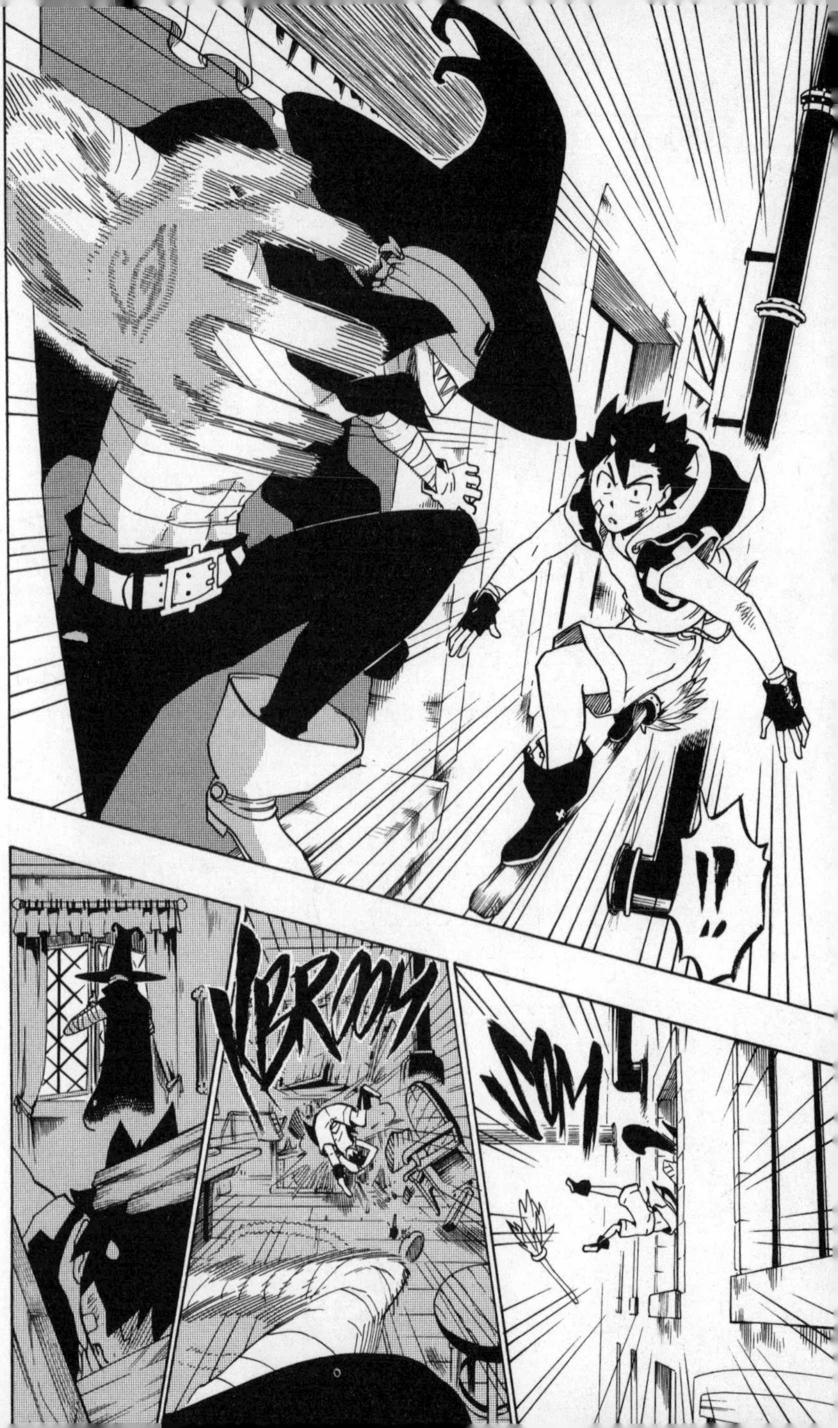
!!

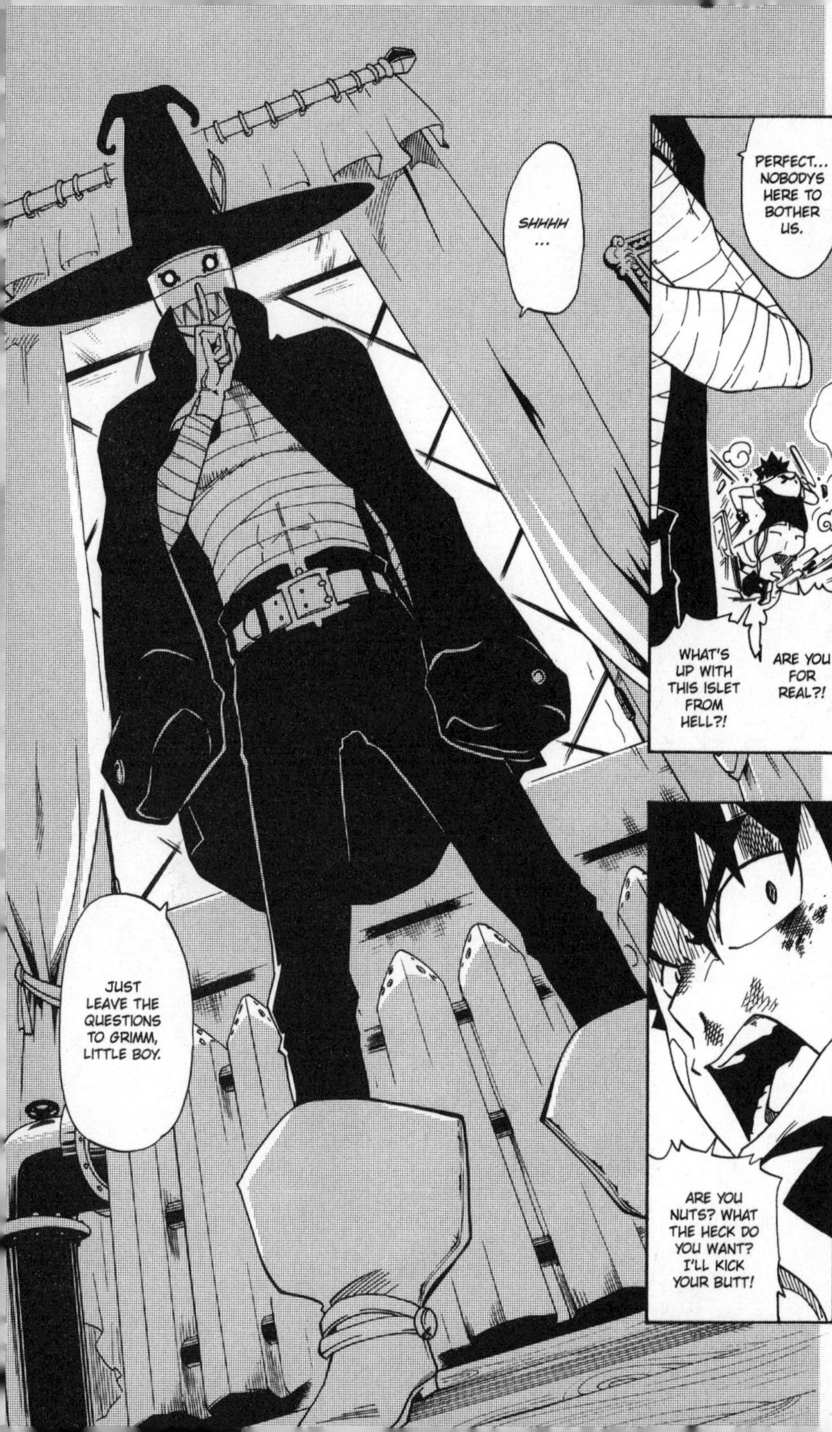
PERFECT... NOBODYS HERE TO BOTHER US.
ARE YOU FOR REAL?!
WHAT'S UP WITH THIS ISLET FROM HELL?!
ARE YOU NUTS? WHAT THE HECK DO YOU WANT? I'LL KICK YOUR BUTT!
SHHHH ...
JUST LEAVE THE QUESTIONS TO GRIMM, LITTLE BOY.

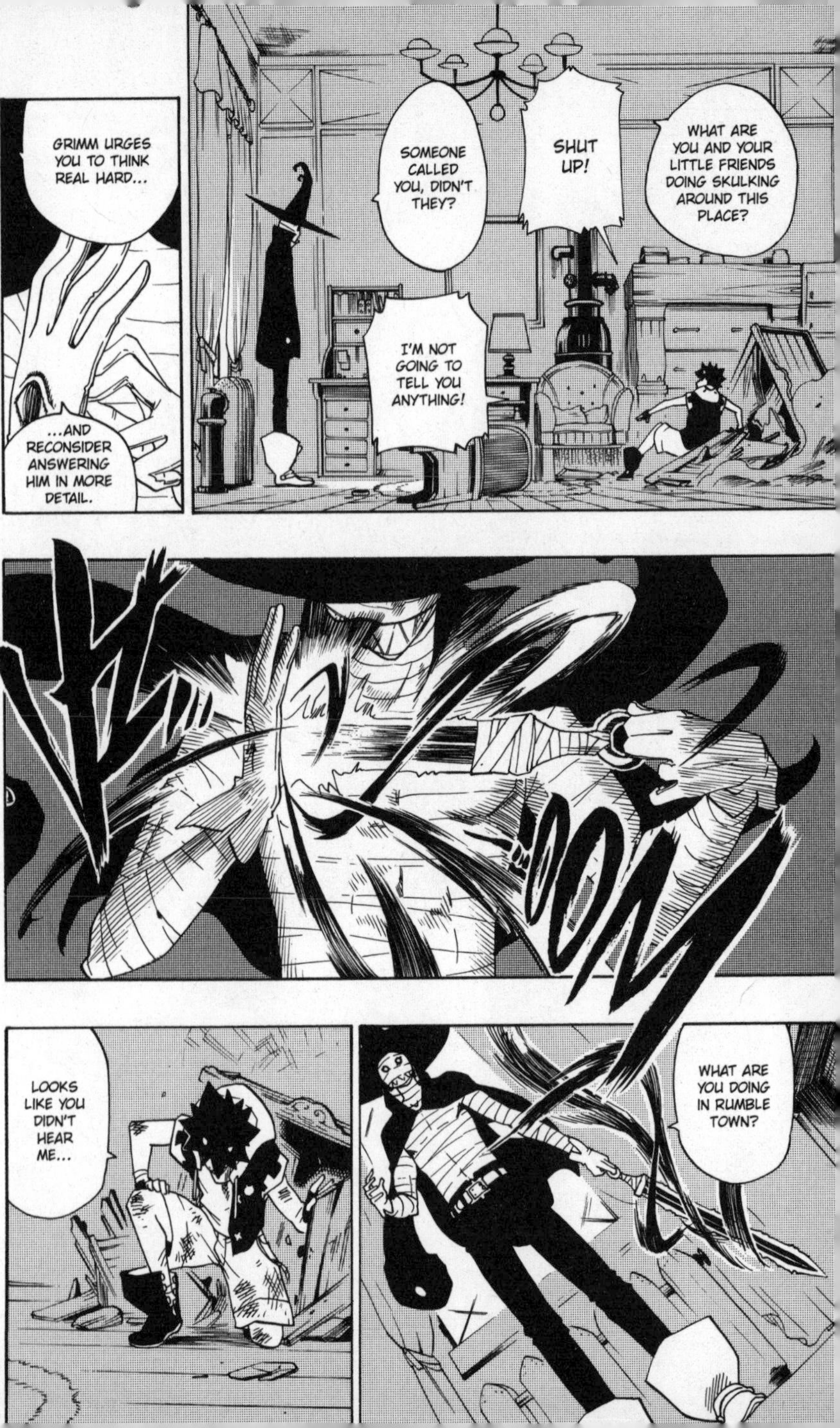
WHAT ARE YOU AND YOUR LITTLE FRIENDS DOING SKULKING AROUND THIS PLACE?
SHUT UP!
SOMEONE CALLED YOU, DIDN'T THEY?
I'M NOT GOING TO TELL YOU ANYTHING!
GRIMM URGES YOU TO THINK REAL HARD...
...AND RECONSIDER ANSWERING HIM IN MORE DETAIL.
WHAT ARE YOU DOING IN RUMBLE TOWN?
LOOKS LIKE YOU DIDN'T HEAR ME...

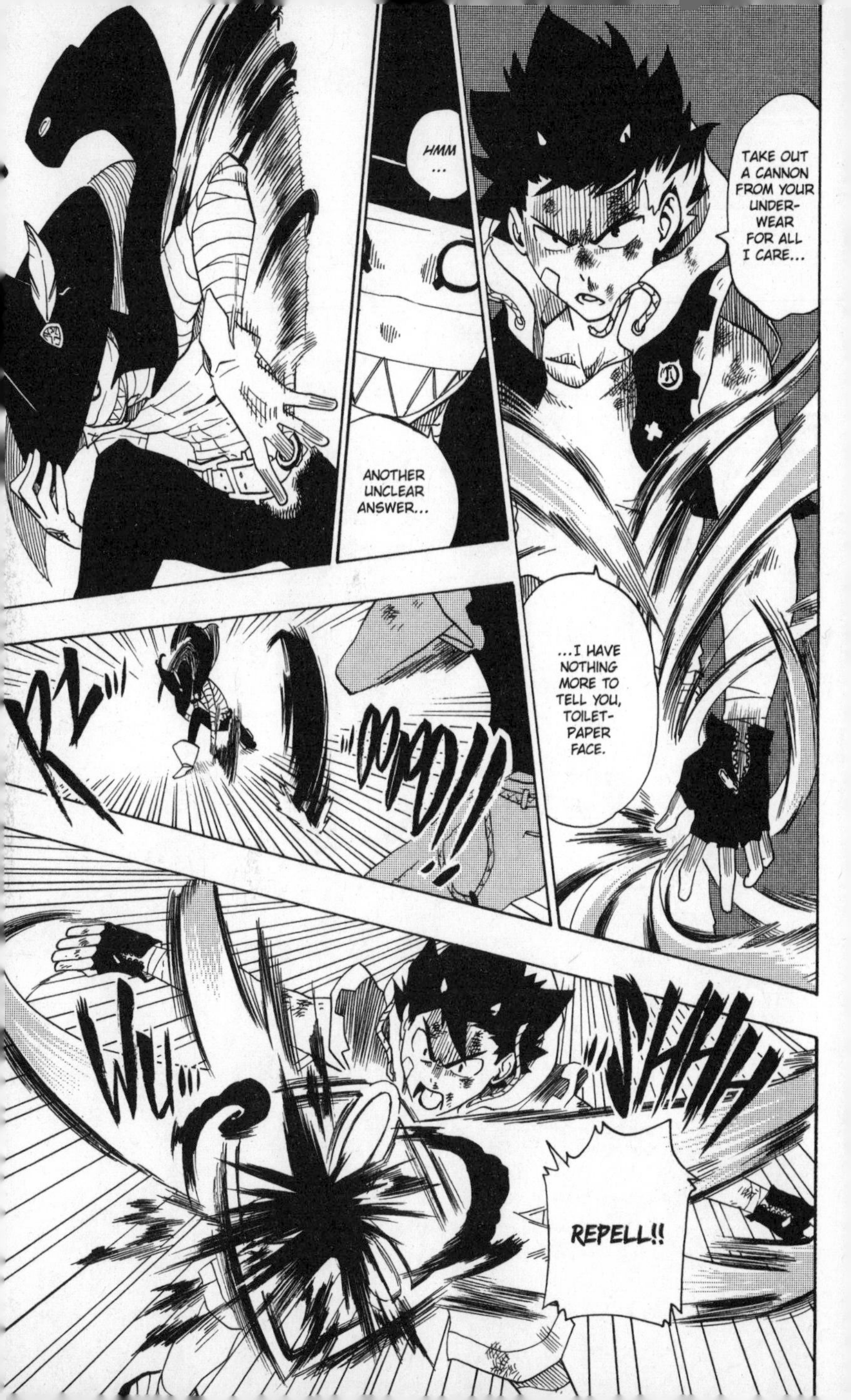
TAKE OUT A CANNON FROM YOUR UNDER-WEAR FOR ALL I CARE...
...I HAVE NOTHING MORE TO TELL YOU, TOILET-PAPER FACE.
HMM...
ANOTHER UNCLEAR ANSWER...
REPELL!!

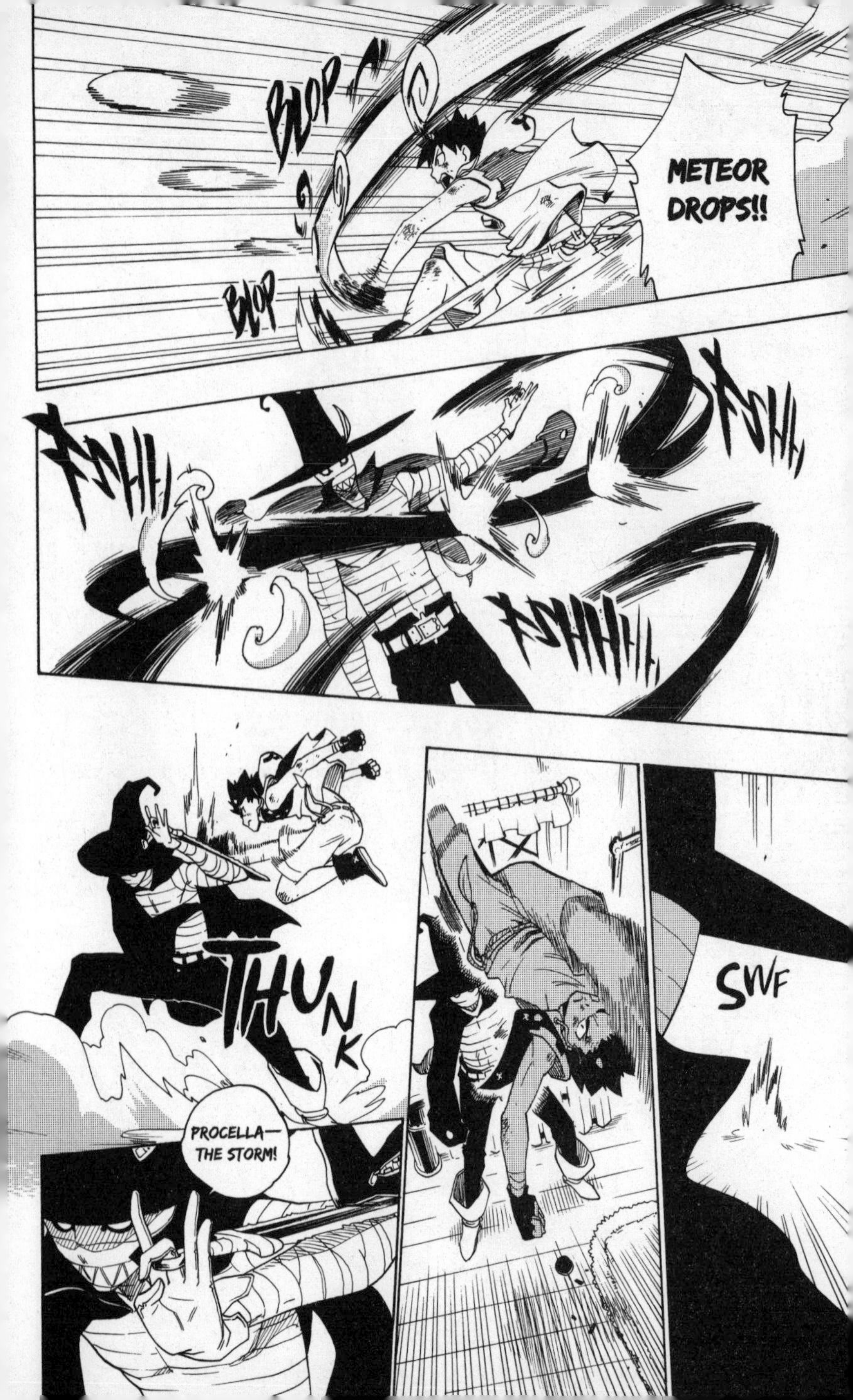

METEOR DROPS!!
BLOP
BLOP
FSHH
FSHH
FSHHH
SWF
THUNK
PROCELLA—THE STORM!

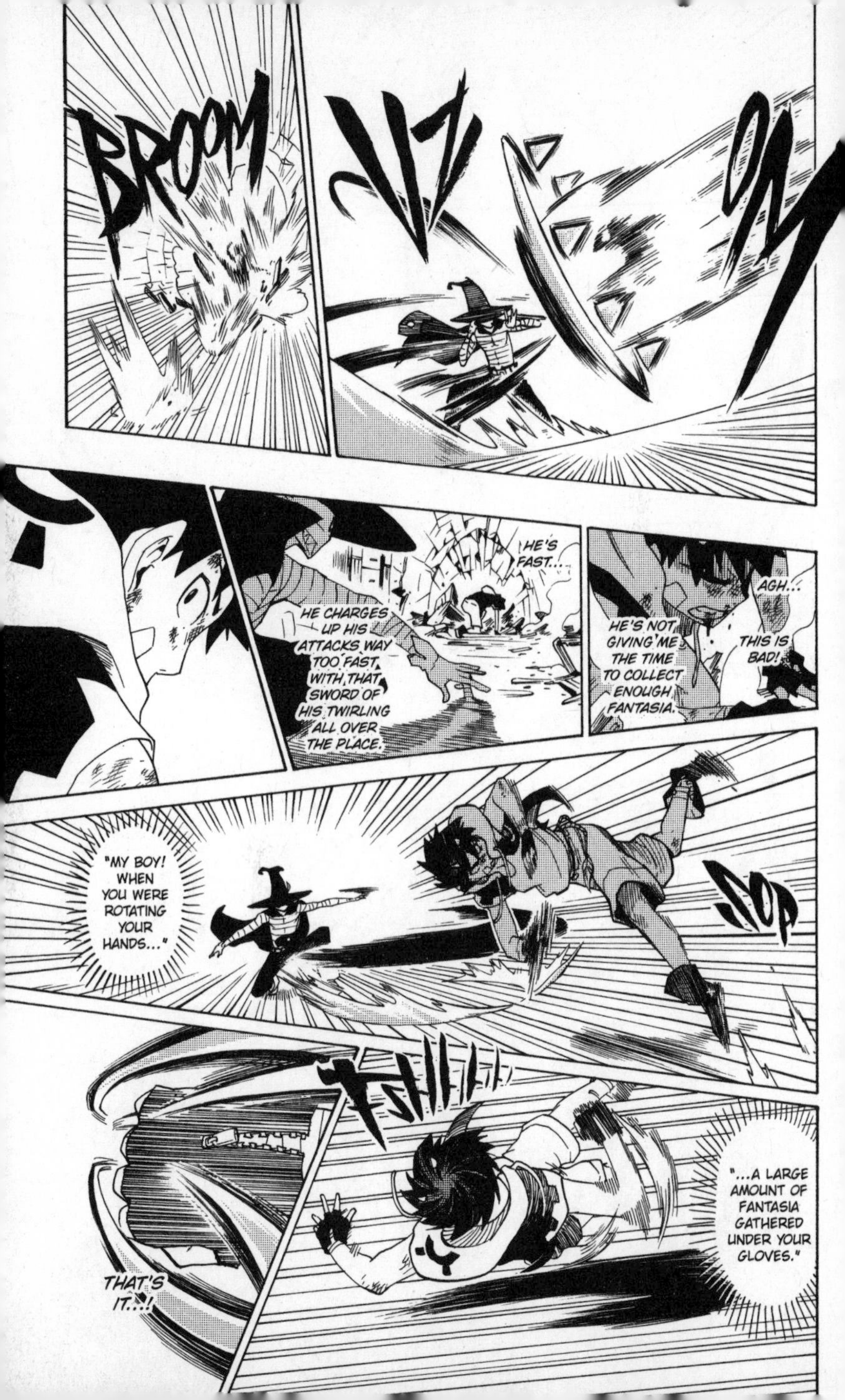
BROOM
AGH... THIS IS BAD!
HE'S NOT GIVING ME THE TIME TO COLLECT ENOUGH FANTASIA.
HE'S FAST...
HE CHARGES UP HIS ATTACKS WAY TOO FAST, WITH THAT SWORD OF HIS TWIRLING ALL OVER THE PLACE.
"MY BOY! WHEN YOU WERE ROTATING YOUR HANDS..."
"...A LARGE AMOUNT OF FANTASIA GATHERED UNDER YOUR GLOVES."
THAT'S IT...!

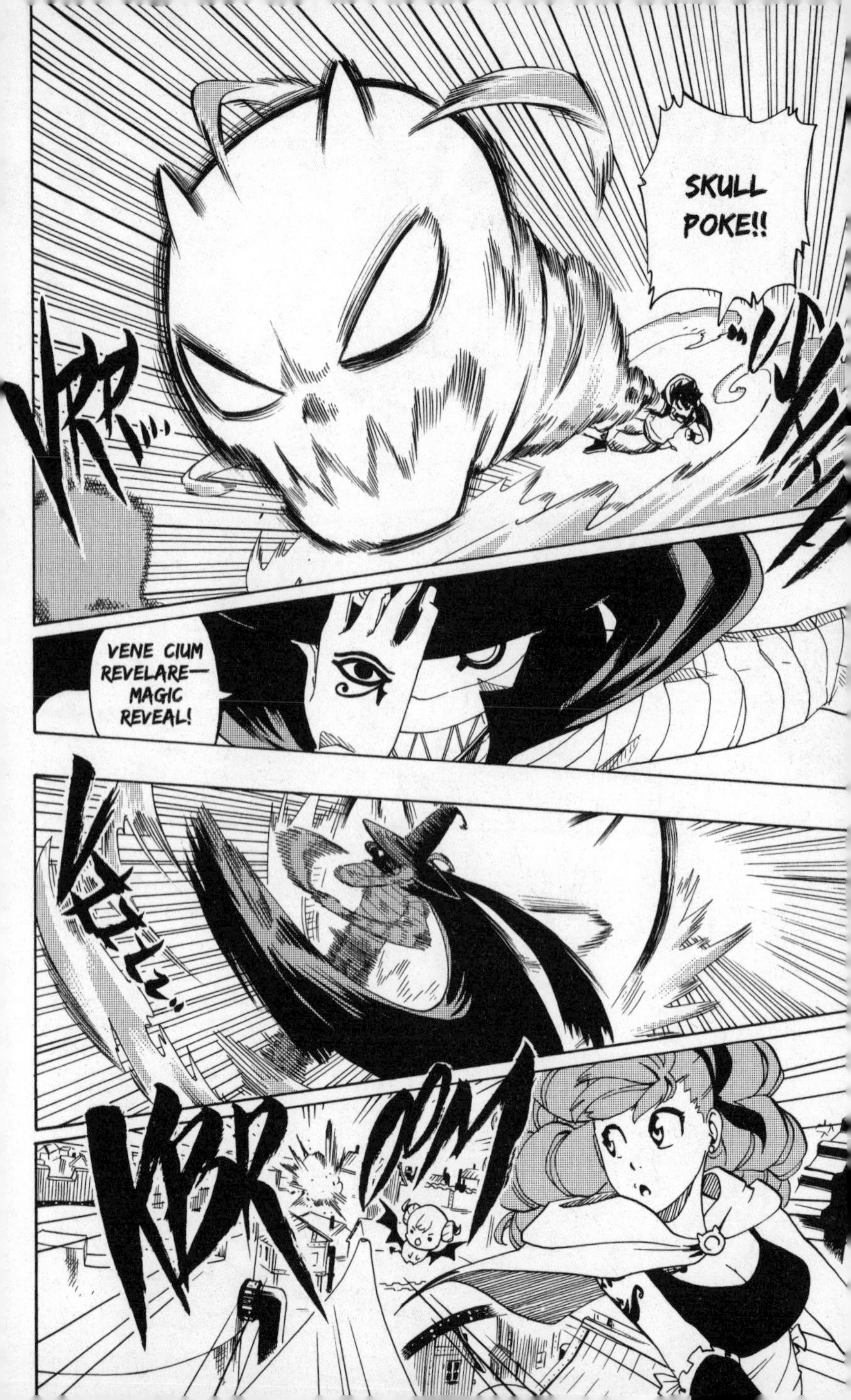
SKULL POKE!!
VENE CIUM REVELARE— MAGIC REVEAL!

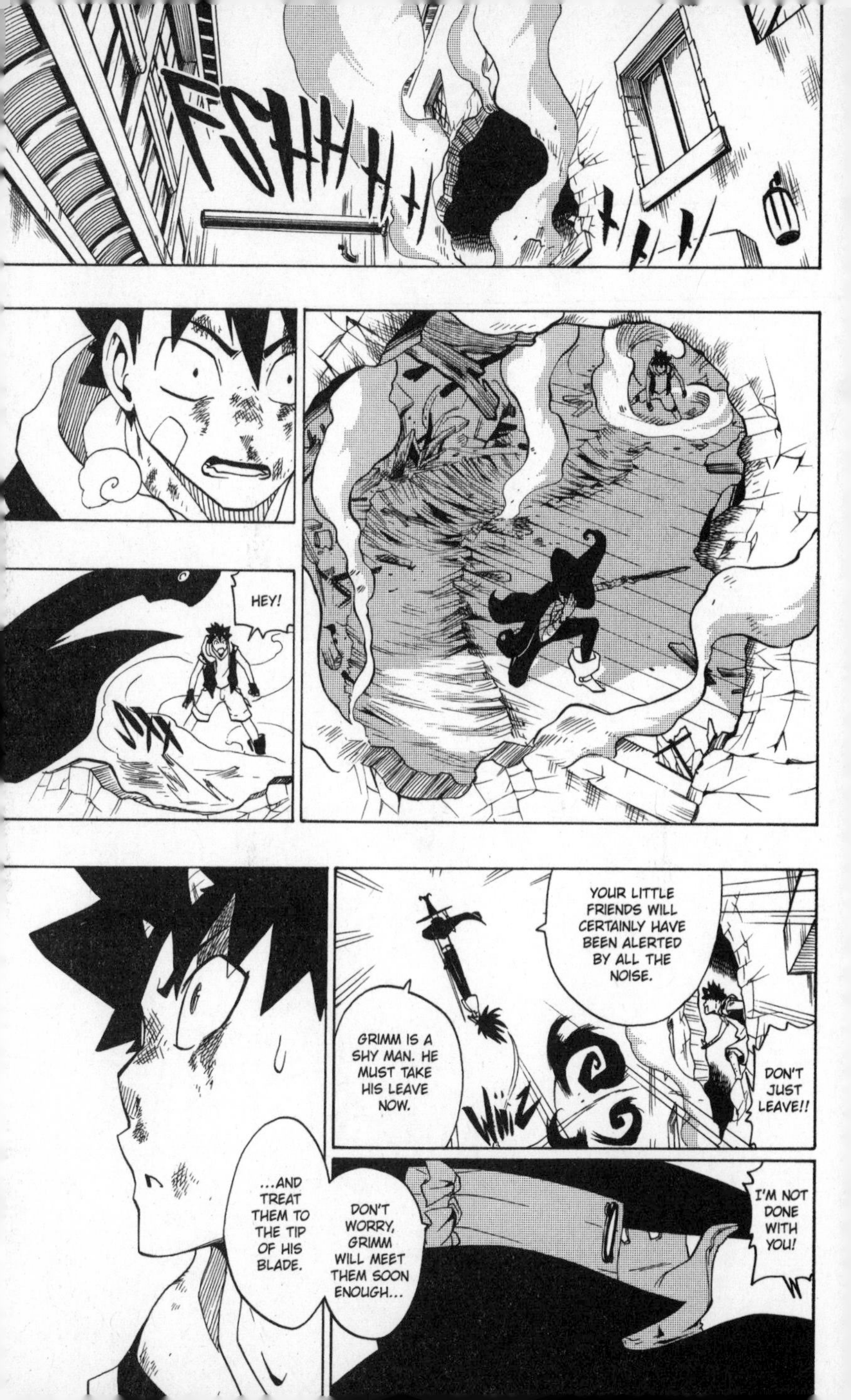
FSHHH
HEY!
YOUR LITTLE FRIENDS WILL CERTAINLY HAVE BEEN ALERTED BY ALL THE NOISE.
DON'T JUST LEAVE!!
GRIMM IS A SHY MAN. HE MUST TAKE HIS LEAVE NOW.
I'M NOT DONE WITH YOU!
DON'T WORRY, GRIMM WILL MEET THEM SOON ENOUGH...
...AND TREAT THEM TO THE TIP OF HIS BLADE.

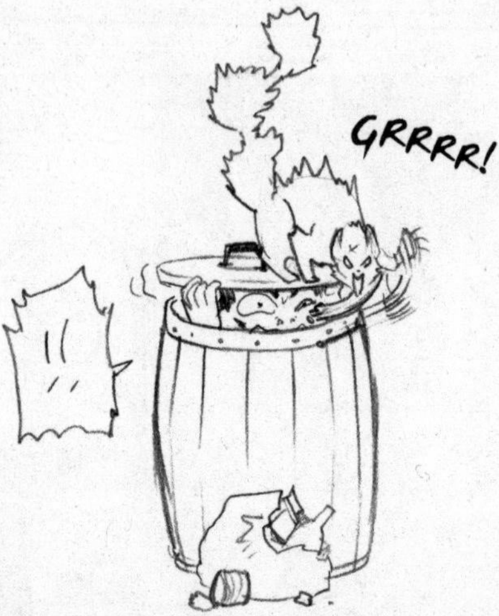
GRRRR!

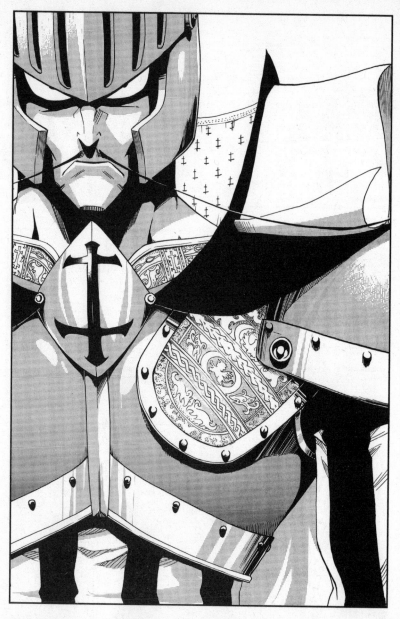

CHAPTER 8

NORTHERN SUBURB

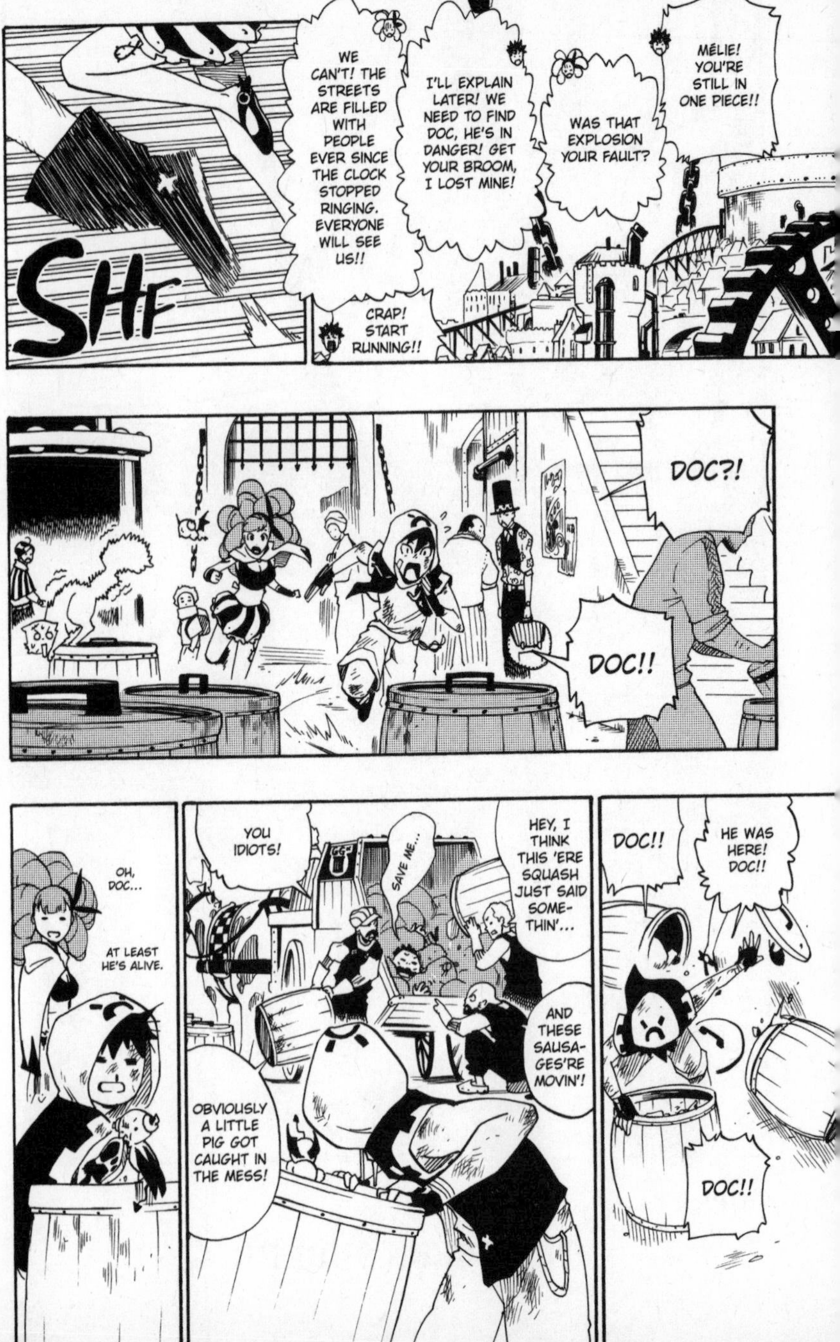
MÉLIE! YOU'RE STILL IN ONE PIECE!!
WAS THAT EXPLOSION YOUR FAULT?
I'LL EXPLAIN LATER! WE NEED TO FIND DOC, HE'S IN DANGER! GET YOUR BROOM, I LOST MINE!
WE CAN'T! THE STREETS ARE FILLED WITH PEOPLE EVER SINCE THE CLOCK STOPPED RINGING. EVERYONE WILL SEE US!!
CRAP! START RUNNING!!
SHF
DOC?!
DOC!!
HE WAS HERE! DOC!!
DOC!!
DOC!!
HEY, I THINK THIS 'ERE SQUASH JUST SAID SOME-THIN'...
AND THESE SAUSA-GES'RE MOVIN'!
SAVE ME...
YOU IDIOTS!
OBVIOUSLY A LITTLE PIG GOT CAUGHT IN THE MESS!
OH, DOC...
AT LEAST HE'S ALIVE.

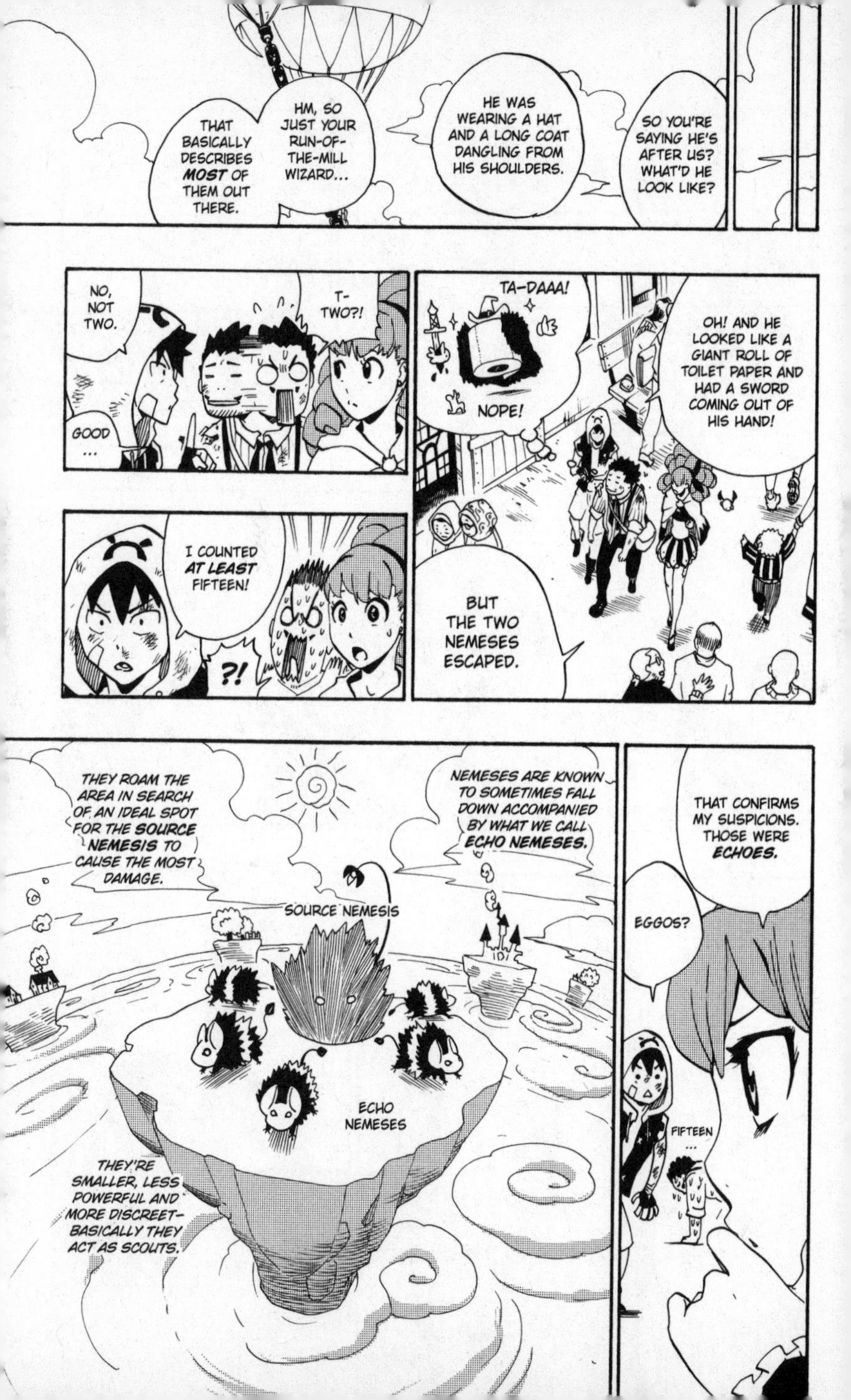
SO YOU'RE SAYING HE'S AFTER US? WHAT'D HE LOOK LIKE?
HE WAS WEARING A HAT AND A LONG COAT DANGLING FROM HIS SHOULDERS.
HM, SO JUST YOUR RUN-OF-THE-MILL WIZARD...
THAT BASICALLY DESCRIBES **MOST** OF THEM OUT THERE.
OH! AND HE LOOKED LIKE A GIANT ROLL OF TOILET PAPER AND HAD A SWORD COMING OUT OF HIS HAND!
TA-DAAA!
NOPE!
BUT THE TWO NEMESES ESCAPED.
T-TWO?!
NO, NOT TWO.
GOOD ...
I COUNTED **AT LEAST** FIFTEEN!
?!
THAT CONFIRMS MY SUSPICIONS. THOSE WERE **ECHOES.**
EGGOS?
FIFTEEN ...
NEMESES ARE KNOWN TO SOMETIMES FALL DOWN ACCOMPANIED BY WHAT WE CALL **ECHO NEMESES.**
THEY ROAM THE AREA IN SEARCH OF AN IDEAL SPOT FOR THE **SOURCE NEMESIS** TO CAUSE THE MOST DAMAGE.
SOURCE NEMESIS
ECHO NEMESES
THEY'RE SMALLER, LESS POWERFUL AND MORE DISCREET-BASICALLY THEY ACT AS SCOUTS.

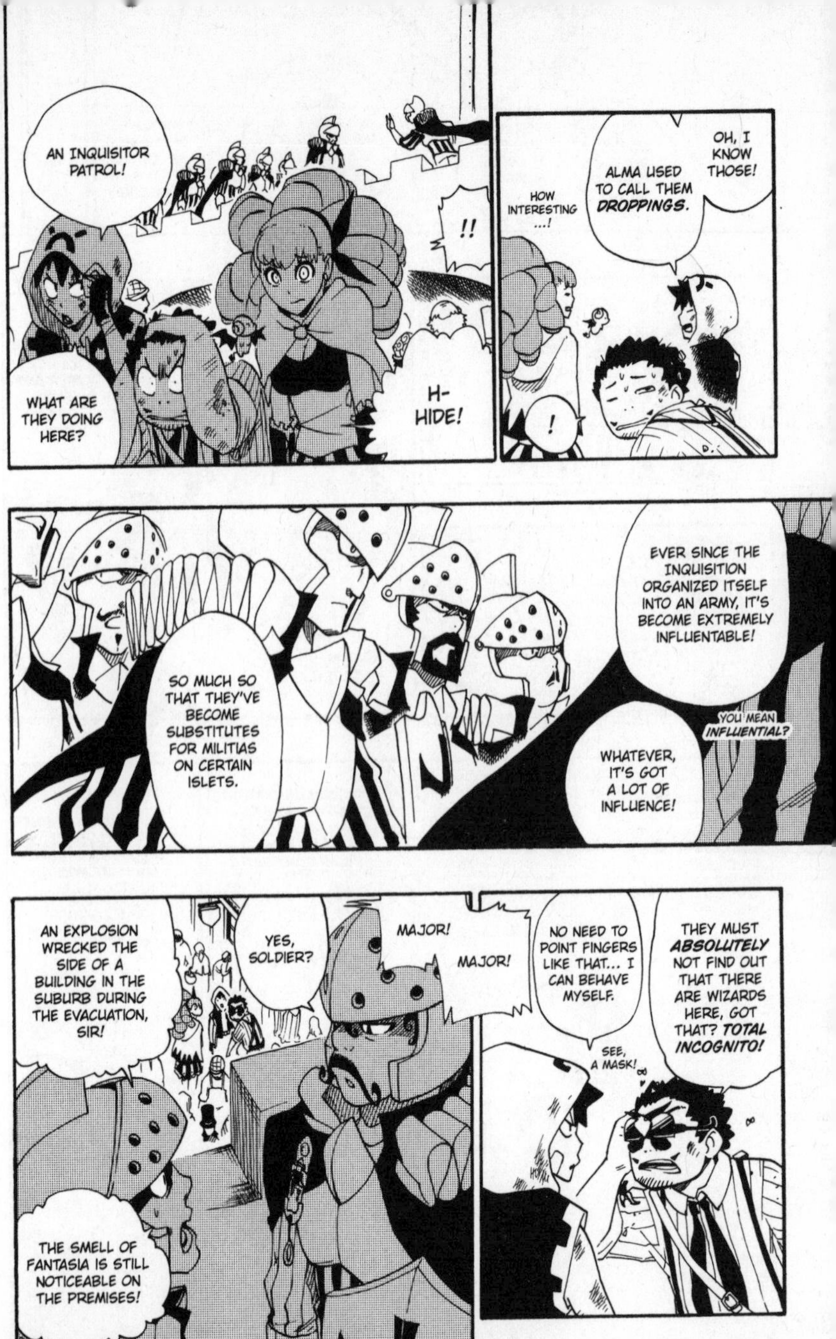

OH, I KNOW THOSE!
ALMA USED TO CALL THEM DROPPINGS.
HOW INTERESTING ...!
!
!!
AN INQUISITOR PATROL!
H-HIDE!
WHAT ARE THEY DOING HERE?
EVER SINCE THE INQUISITION ORGANIZED ITSELF INTO AN ARMY, IT'S BECOME EXTREMELY INFLUENTABLE!
YOU MEAN INFLUENTIAL?
WHATEVER, IT'S GOT A LOT OF INFLUENCE!
SO MUCH SO THAT THEY'VE BECOME SUBSTITUTES FOR MILITIAS ON CERTAIN ISLETS.
THEY MUST ABSOLUTELY NOT FIND OUT THAT THERE ARE WIZARDS HERE, GOT THAT? TOTAL INCOGNITO!
NO NEED TO POINT FINGERS LIKE THAT... I CAN BEHAVE MYSELF.
SEE, A MASK!
MAJOR!
MAJOR!
YES, SOLDIER?
AN EXPLOSION WRECKED THE SIDE OF A BUILDING IN THE SUBURB DURING THE EVACUATION, SIR!
THE SMELL OF FANTASIA IS STILL NOTICEABLE ON THE PREMISES!

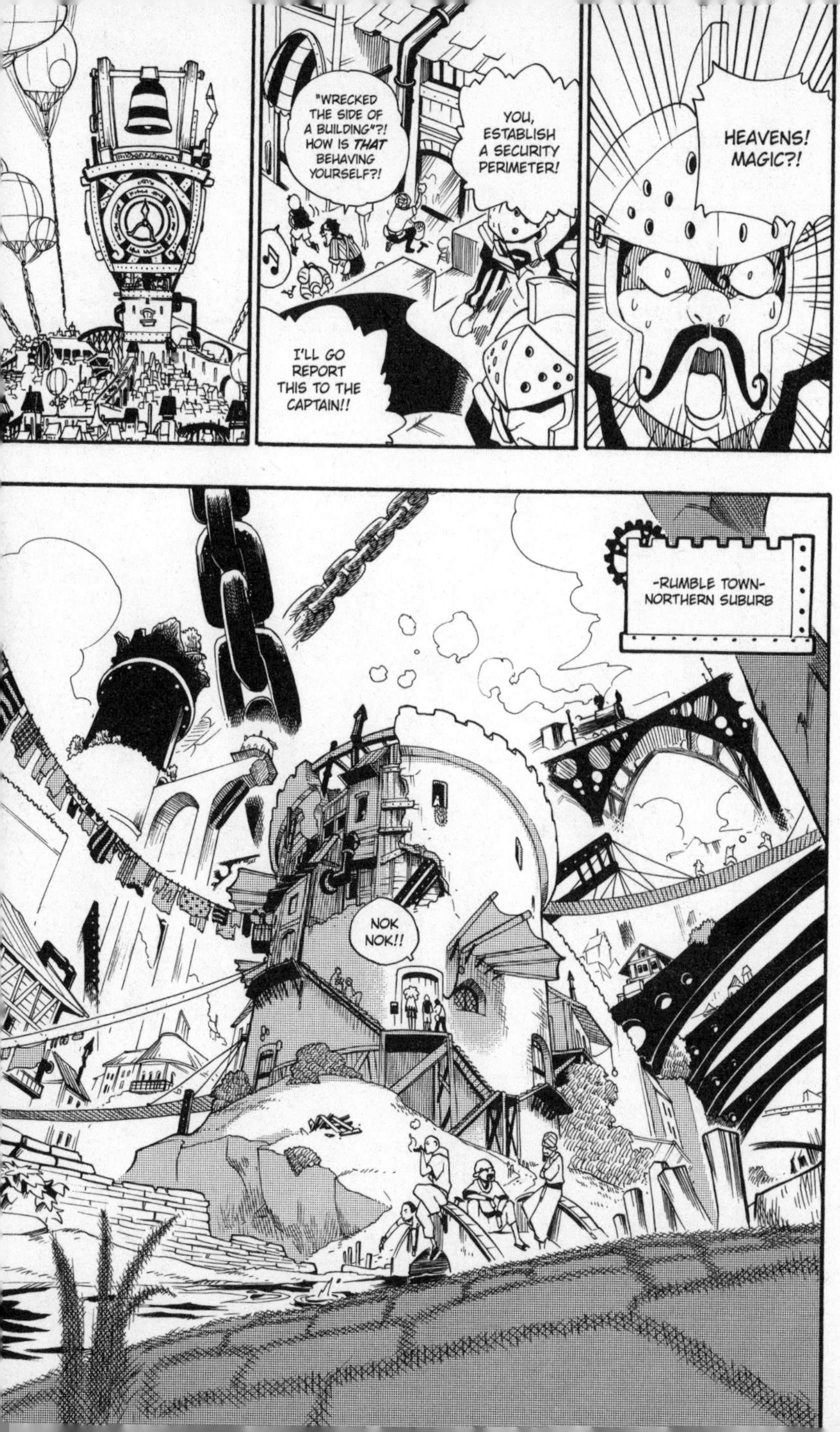
HEAVENS! MAGIC?!
YOU, ESTABLISH A SECURITY PERIMETER!
"WRECKED THE SIDE OF A BUILDING"?! HOW IS *THAT* BEHAVING YOURSELF?!
I'LL GO REPORT THIS TO THE CAPTAIN!!
-RUMBLE TOWN-
NORTHERN SUBURB
NOK NOK!!

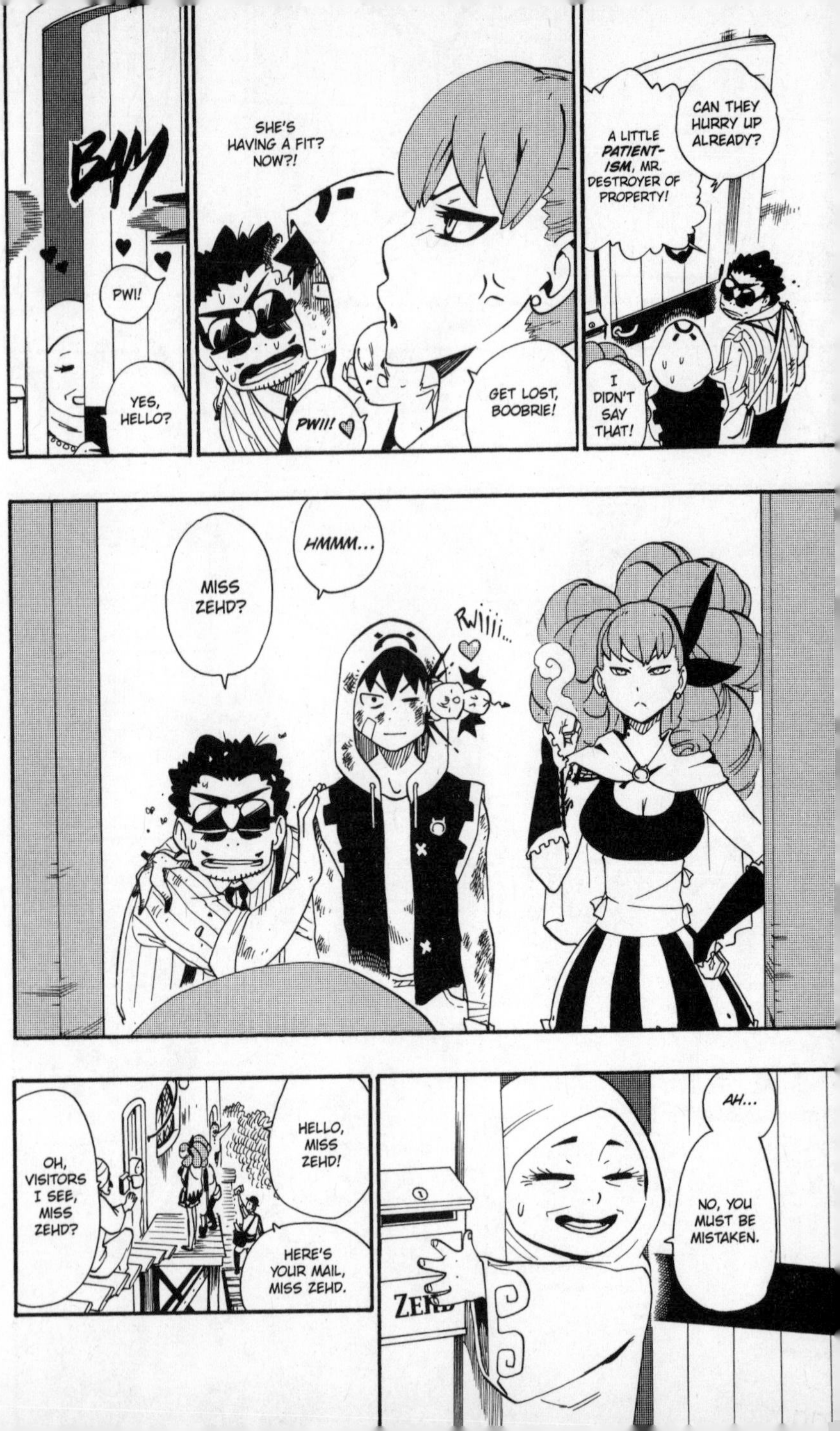
CAN THEY HURRY UP ALREADY?
A LITTLE PATIENT-ISM, MR. DESTROYER OF PROPERTY!
I DIDN'T SAY THAT!
SHE'S HAVING A FIT? NOW?!
GET LOST, BOOBRIE!
PWII! ♡
BAM
PWI!
YES, HELLO?
HMMM...
MISS ZEHD?
AH...
NO, YOU MUST BE MISTAKEN.
ZEHD
HELLO, MISS ZEHD!
HERE'S YOUR MAIL, MISS ZEHD.
OH, VISITORS I SEE, MISS ZEHD?

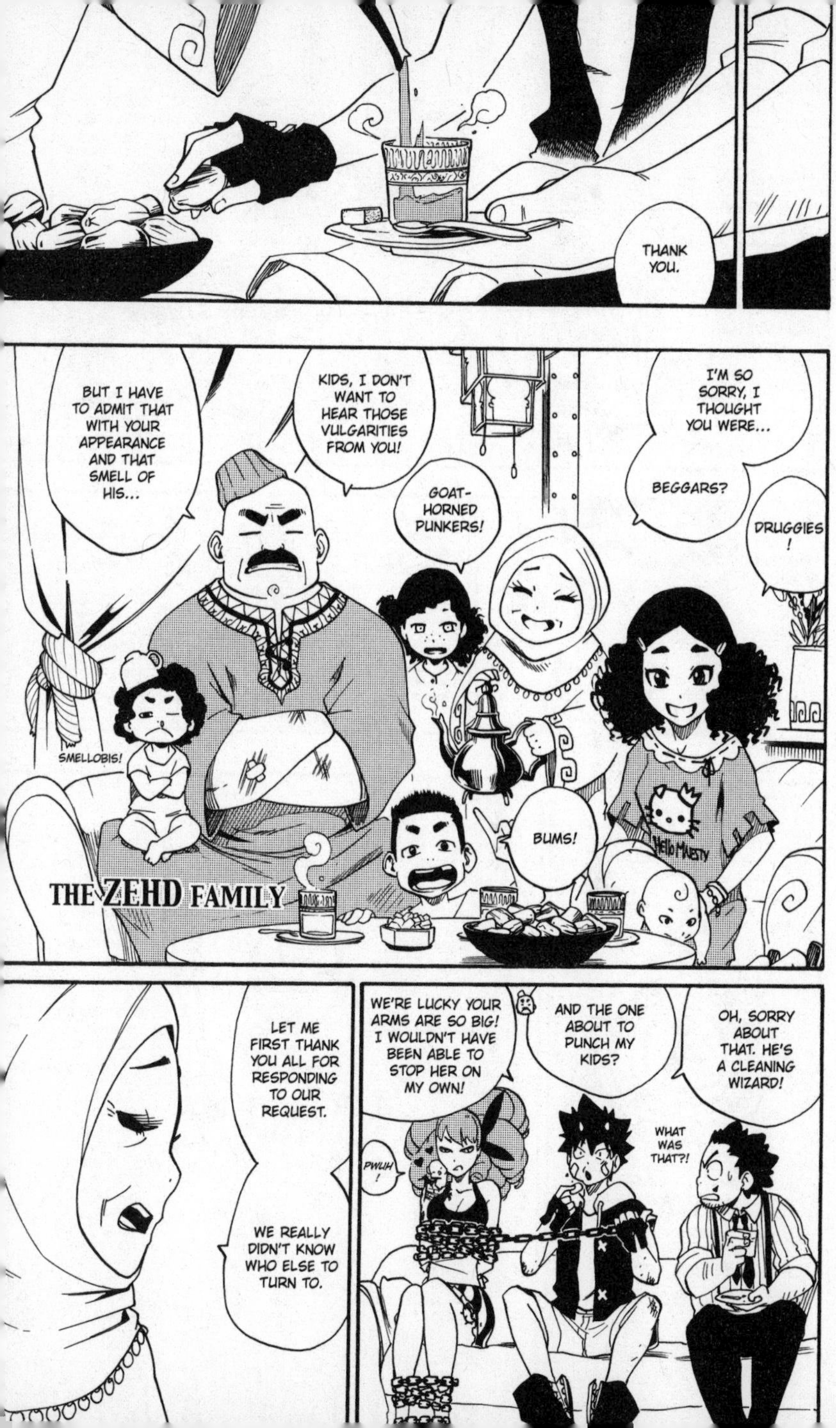
THANK YOU.
I'M SO SORRY, I THOUGHT YOU WERE...
BEGGARS?
DRUGGIES!
GOAT-HORNED PUNKERS!
BUMS!
HELLO MAJESTY
KIDS, I DON'T WANT TO HEAR THOSE VULGARITIES FROM YOU!
SMELLOBIS!
BUT I HAVE TO ADMIT THAT WITH YOUR APPEARANCE AND THAT SMELL OF HIS...
THE ZEHD FAMILY
OH, SORRY ABOUT THAT. HE'S A CLEANING WIZARD!
AND THE ONE ABOUT TO PUNCH MY KIDS?
WHAT WAS THAT?!
WE'RE LUCKY YOUR ARMS ARE SO BIG! I WOULDN'T HAVE BEEN ABLE TO STOP HER ON MY OWN!
PWUH!
LET ME FIRST THANK YOU ALL FOR RESPONDING TO OUR REQUEST.
WE REALLY DIDN'T KNOW WHO ELSE TO TURN TO.

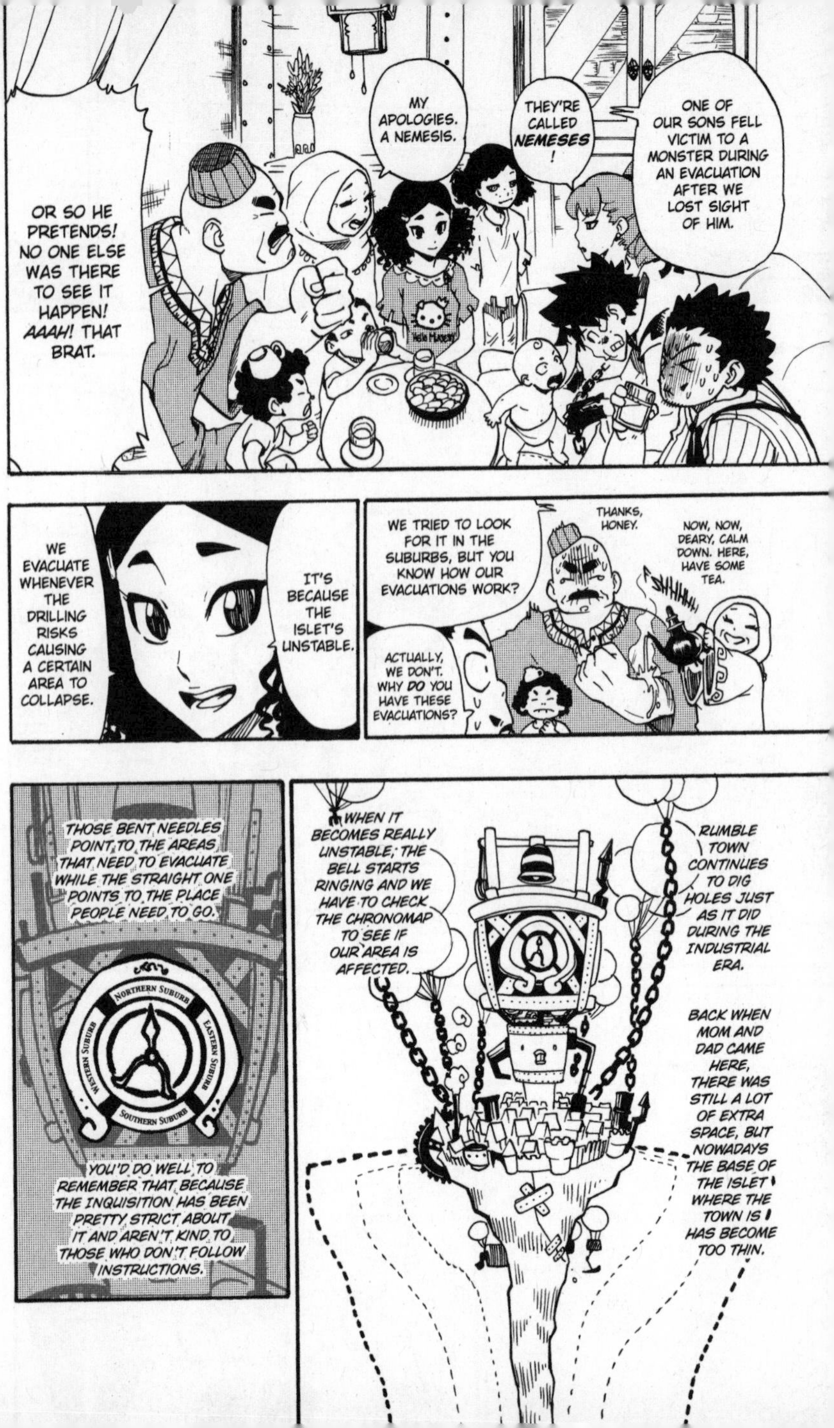
ONE OF OUR SONS FELL VICTIM TO A MONSTER DURING AN EVACUATION AFTER WE LOST SIGHT OF HIM.
THEY'RE CALLED *NEMESES*!
MY APOLOGIES. A NEMESIS.
OR SO HE PRETENDS! NO ONE ELSE WAS THERE TO SEE IT HAPPEN! *AAAH!* THAT BRAT.
NOW, NOW, DEARY, CALM DOWN. HERE, HAVE SOME TEA.
FSHHHHH
THANKS, HONEY.
WE TRIED TO LOOK FOR IT IN THE SUBURBS, BUT YOU KNOW HOW OUR EVACUATIONS WORK?
ACTUALLY, WE DON'T. WHY *DO* YOU HAVE THESE EVACUATIONS?
IT'S BECAUSE THE ISLET'S UNSTABLE.
WE EVACUATE WHENEVER THE DRILLING RISKS CAUSING A CERTAIN AREA TO COLLAPSE.
RUMBLE TOWN CONTINUES TO DIG HOLES JUST AS IT DID DURING THE INDUSTRIAL ERA.
WHEN IT BECOMES REALLY UNSTABLE, THE BELL STARTS RINGING AND WE HAVE TO CHECK THE CHRONOMAP TO SEE IF OUR AREA IS AFFECTED.
BACK WHEN MOM AND DAD CAME HERE, THERE WAS STILL A LOT OF EXTRA SPACE, BUT NOWADAYS THE BASE OF THE ISLET WHERE THE TOWN IS HAS BECOME TOO THIN.
THOSE BENT NEEDLES POINT TO THE AREAS THAT NEED TO EVACUATE WHILE THE STRAIGHT ONE POINTS TO THE PLACE PEOPLE NEED TO GO.
NORTHERN SUBURB
EASTERN SUBURB
SOUTHERN SUBURB
WESTERN SUBURB
YOU'D DO WELL TO REMEMBER THAT BECAUSE THE INQUISITION HAS BEEN PRETTY STRICT ABOUT IT AND AREN'T KIND TO THOSE WHO DON'T FOLLOW INSTRUCTIONS.

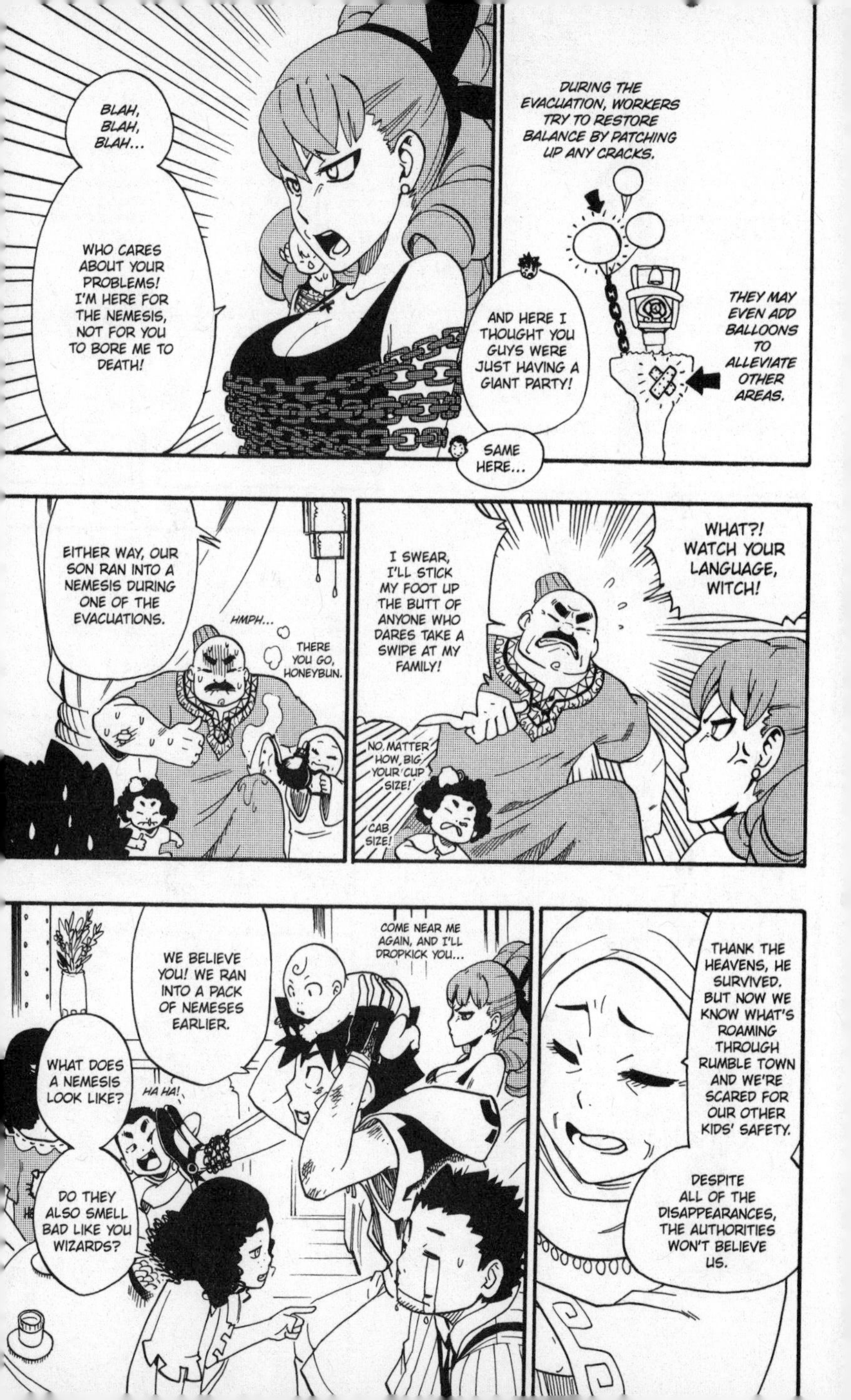

DURING THE EVACUATION, WORKERS TRY TO RESTORE BALANCE BY PATCHING UP ANY CRACKS.
THEY MAY EVEN ADD BALLOONS TO ALLEVIATE OTHER AREAS.
BLAH, BLAH, BLAH...
WHO CARES ABOUT YOUR PROBLEMS! I'M HERE FOR THE NEMESIS, NOT FOR YOU TO BORE ME TO DEATH!
AND HERE I THOUGHT YOU GUYS WERE JUST HAVING A GIANT PARTY!
SAME HERE...
WHAT?! WATCH YOUR LANGUAGE, WITCH!
I SWEAR, I'LL STICK MY FOOT UP THE BUTT OF ANYONE WHO DARES TAKE A SWIPE AT MY FAMILY!
NO MATTER HOW BIG YOUR CUP SIZE!
CAB SIZE!
EITHER WAY, OUR SON RAN INTO A NEMESIS DURING ONE OF THE EVACUATIONS.
HMPH...
THERE YOU GO, HONEYBUN.
THANK THE HEAVENS, HE SURVIVED. BUT NOW WE KNOW WHAT'S ROAMING THROUGH RUMBLE TOWN AND WE'RE SCARED FOR OUR OTHER KIDS' SAFETY.
DESPITE ALL OF THE DISAPPEARANCES, THE AUTHORITIES WON'T BELIEVE US.
COME NEAR ME AGAIN, AND I'LL DROPKICK YOU...
WE BELIEVE YOU! WE RAN INTO A PACK OF NEMESES EARLIER.
WHAT DOES A NEMESIS LOOK LIKE?
HA HA!
DO THEY ALSO SMELL BAD LIKE YOU WIZARDS?

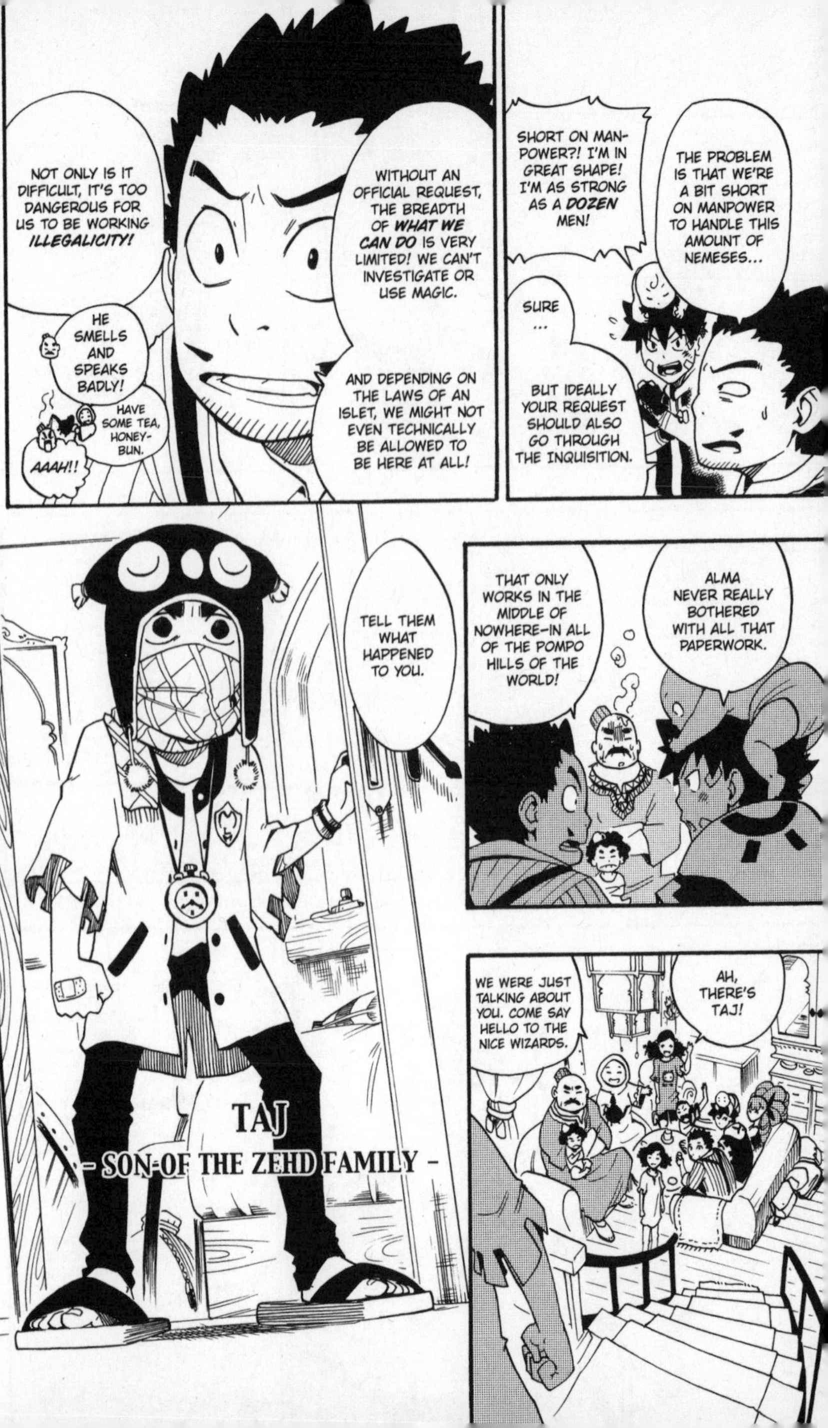
THE PROBLEM IS THAT WE'RE A BIT SHORT ON MANPOWER TO HANDLE THIS AMOUNT OF NEMESES...
SHORT ON MAN-POWER?! I'M IN GREAT SHAPE! I'M AS STRONG AS A *DOZEN* MEN!
SURE ...
BUT IDEALLY YOUR REQUEST SHOULD ALSO GO THROUGH THE INQUISITION.
WITHOUT AN OFFICIAL REQUEST, THE BREADTH OF *WHAT WE CAN DO* IS VERY LIMITED! WE CAN'T INVESTIGATE OR USE MAGIC.
NOT ONLY IS IT DIFFICULT, IT'S TOO DANGEROUS FOR US TO BE WORKING *ILLEGALICITY!*
AND DEPENDING ON THE LAWS OF AN ISLET, WE MIGHT NOT EVEN TECHNICALLY BE ALLOWED TO BE HERE AT ALL!
HE SMELLS AND SPEAKS BADLY!
HAVE SOME TEA, HONEY-BUN.
AAAH!!
ALMA NEVER REALLY BOTHERED WITH ALL THAT PAPERWORK.
THAT ONLY WORKS IN THE MIDDLE OF NOWHERE—IN ALL OF THE POMPO HILLS OF THE WORLD!
AH, THERE'S TAJ!
WE WERE JUST TALKING ABOUT YOU. COME SAY HELLO TO THE NICE WIZARDS.
TELL THEM WHAT HAPPENED TO YOU.
TAJ
- SON OF THE ZEHD FAMILY -

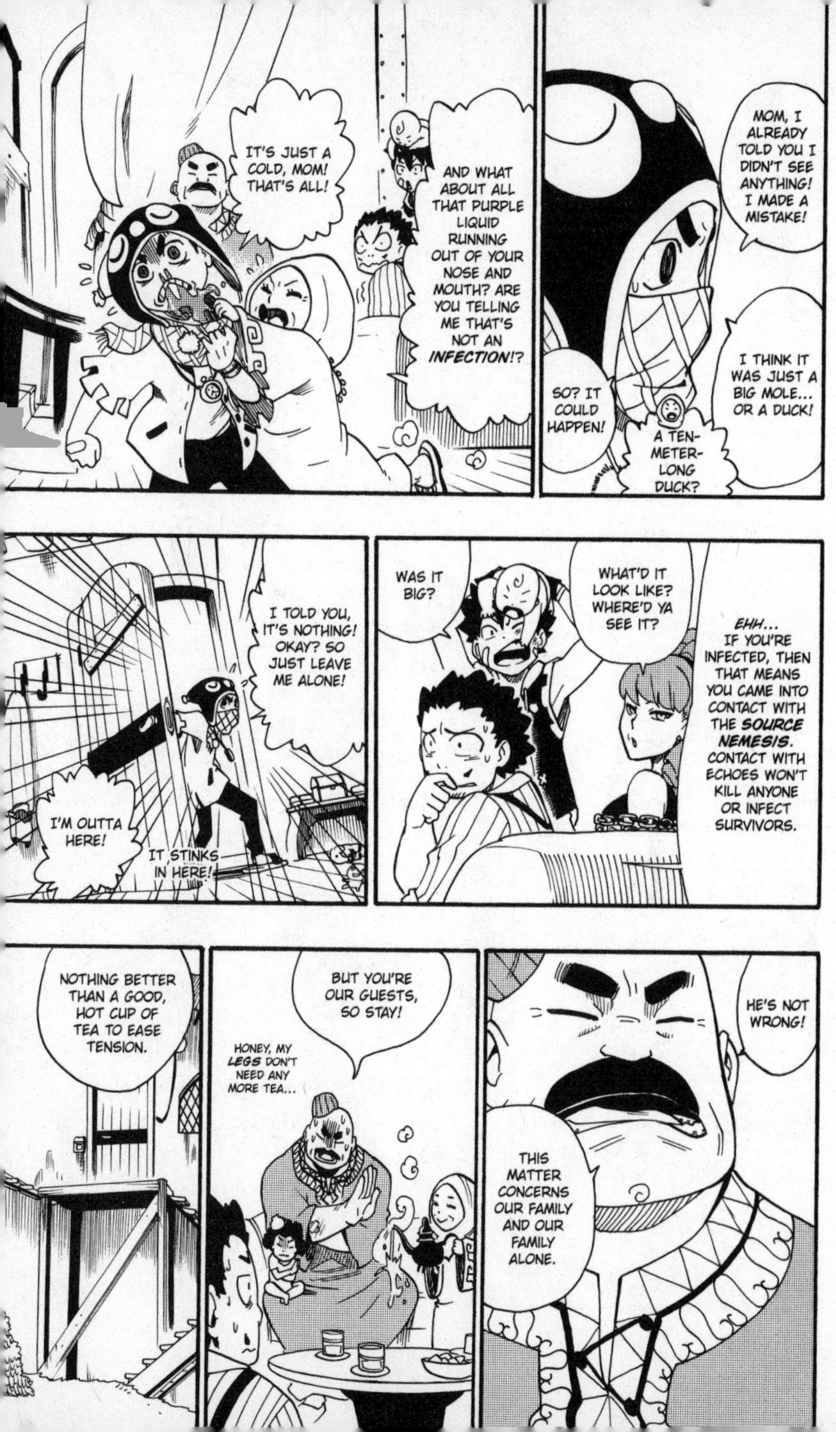
MOM, I ALREADY TOLD YOU I DIDN'T SEE ANYTHING! I MADE A MISTAKE!
I THINK IT WAS JUST A BIG MOLE... OR A DUCK!
A TEN-METER-LONG DUCK?
SO? IT COULD HAPPEN!
AND WHAT ABOUT ALL THAT PURPLE LIQUID RUNNING OUT OF YOUR NOSE AND MOUTH? ARE YOU TELLING ME THAT'S NOT AN INFECTION!?
IT'S JUST A COLD, MOM! THAT'S ALL!
EHH... IF YOU'RE INFECTED, THEN THAT MEANS YOU CAME INTO CONTACT WITH THE SOURCE NEMESIS. CONTACT WITH ECHOES WON'T KILL ANYONE OR INFECT SURVIVORS.
WHAT'D IT LOOK LIKE? WHERE'D YA SEE IT?
WAS IT BIG?
I TOLD YOU, IT'S NOTHING! OKAY? SO JUST LEAVE ME ALONE!
I'M OUTTA HERE!
IT STINKS IN HERE!
HE'S NOT WRONG!
THIS MATTER CONCERNS OUR FAMILY AND OUR FAMILY ALONE.
BUT YOU'RE OUR GUESTS, SO STAY!
HONEY, MY LEGS DON'T NEED ANY MORE TEA...
NOTHING BETTER THAN A GOOD, HOT CUP OF TEA TO EASE TENSION.

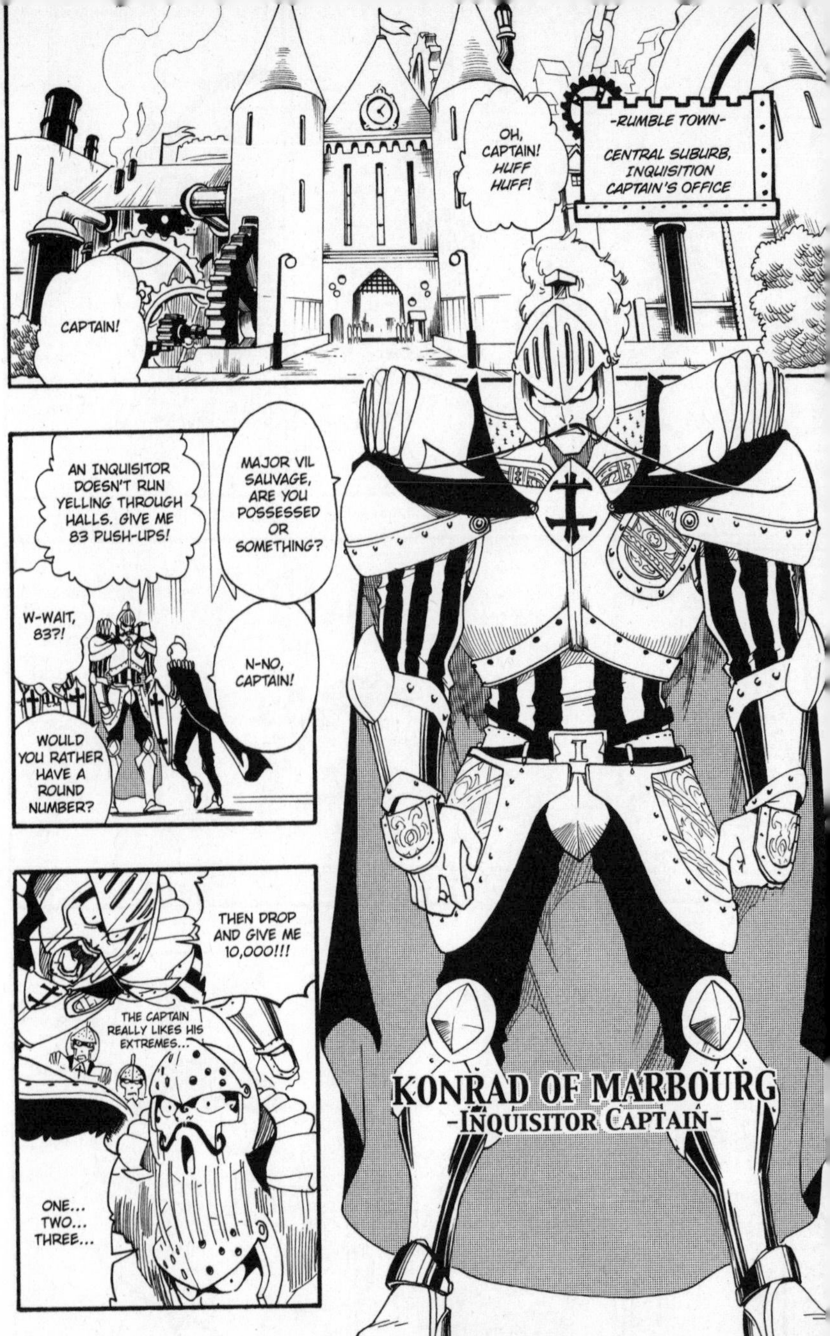
-RUMBLE TOWN-
CENTRAL SUBURB, INQUISITION CAPTAIN'S OFFICE
OH, CAPTAIN! HUFF HUFF!
CAPTAIN!
KONRAD OF MARBOURG
-INQUISITOR CAPTAIN-
MAJOR VIL SAUVAGE, ARE YOU POSSESSED OR SOMETHING?
AN INQUISITOR DOESN'T RUN YELLING THROUGH HALLS. GIVE ME 83 PUSH-UPS!
W-WAIT, 83?!
WOULD YOU RATHER HAVE A ROUND NUMBER?
N-NO, CAPTAIN!
THEN DROP AND GIVE ME 10,000!!!
THE CAPTAIN REALLY LIKES HIS EXTREMES...
ONE... TWO... THREE...

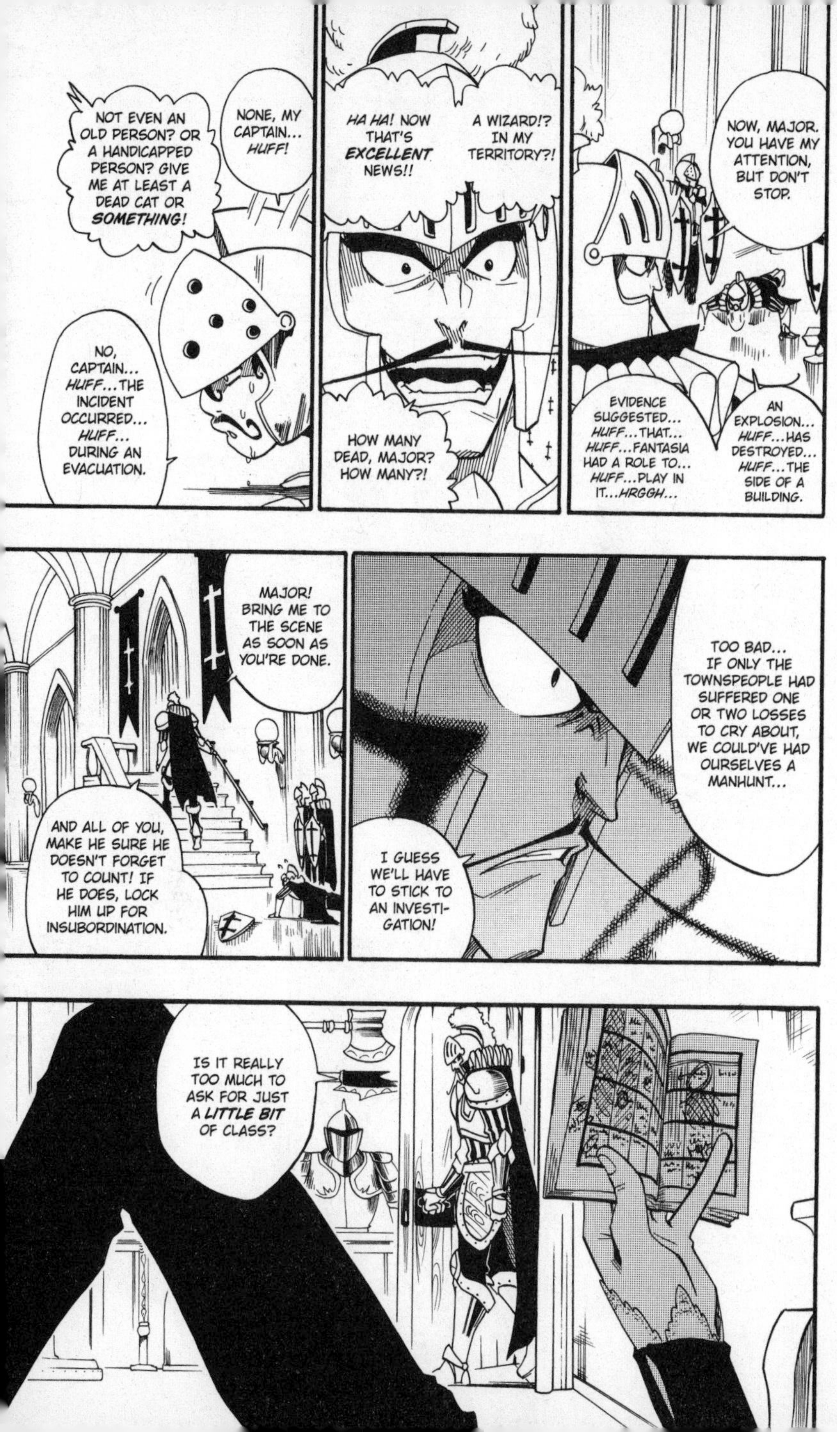

NOW, MAJOR. YOU HAVE MY ATTENTION, BUT DON'T STOP.
AN EXPLOSION... *HUFF*...HAS DESTROYED... *HUFF*...THE SIDE OF A BUILDING.
EVIDENCE SUGGESTED... *HUFF*...THAT... *HUFF*...FANTASIA HAD A ROLE TO... *HUFF*...PLAY IN IT...*HRGGH*...
A WIZARD!? IN MY TERRITORY?!
HA HA! NOW THAT'S ***EXCELLENT*** NEWS!!
HOW MANY DEAD, MAJOR? HOW MANY?!
NONE, MY CAPTAIN... *HUFF!*
NOT EVEN AN OLD PERSON? OR A HANDICAPPED PERSON? GIVE ME AT LEAST A DEAD CAT OR ***SOMETHING!***
NO, CAPTAIN... *HUFF*...THE INCIDENT OCCURRED... *HUFF*... DURING AN EVACUATION.
TOO BAD... IF ONLY THE TOWNSPEOPLE HAD SUFFERED ONE OR TWO LOSSES TO CRY ABOUT, WE COULD'VE HAD OURSELVES A MANHUNT...
I GUESS WE'LL HAVE TO STICK TO AN INVESTI-GATION!
MAJOR! BRING ME TO THE SCENE AS SOON AS YOU'RE DONE.
AND ALL OF YOU, MAKE HE SURE HE DOESN'T FORGET TO COUNT! IF HE DOES, LOCK HIM UP FOR INSUBORDINATION.
IS IT REALLY TOO MUCH TO ASK FOR JUST A ***LITTLE BIT*** OF CLASS?

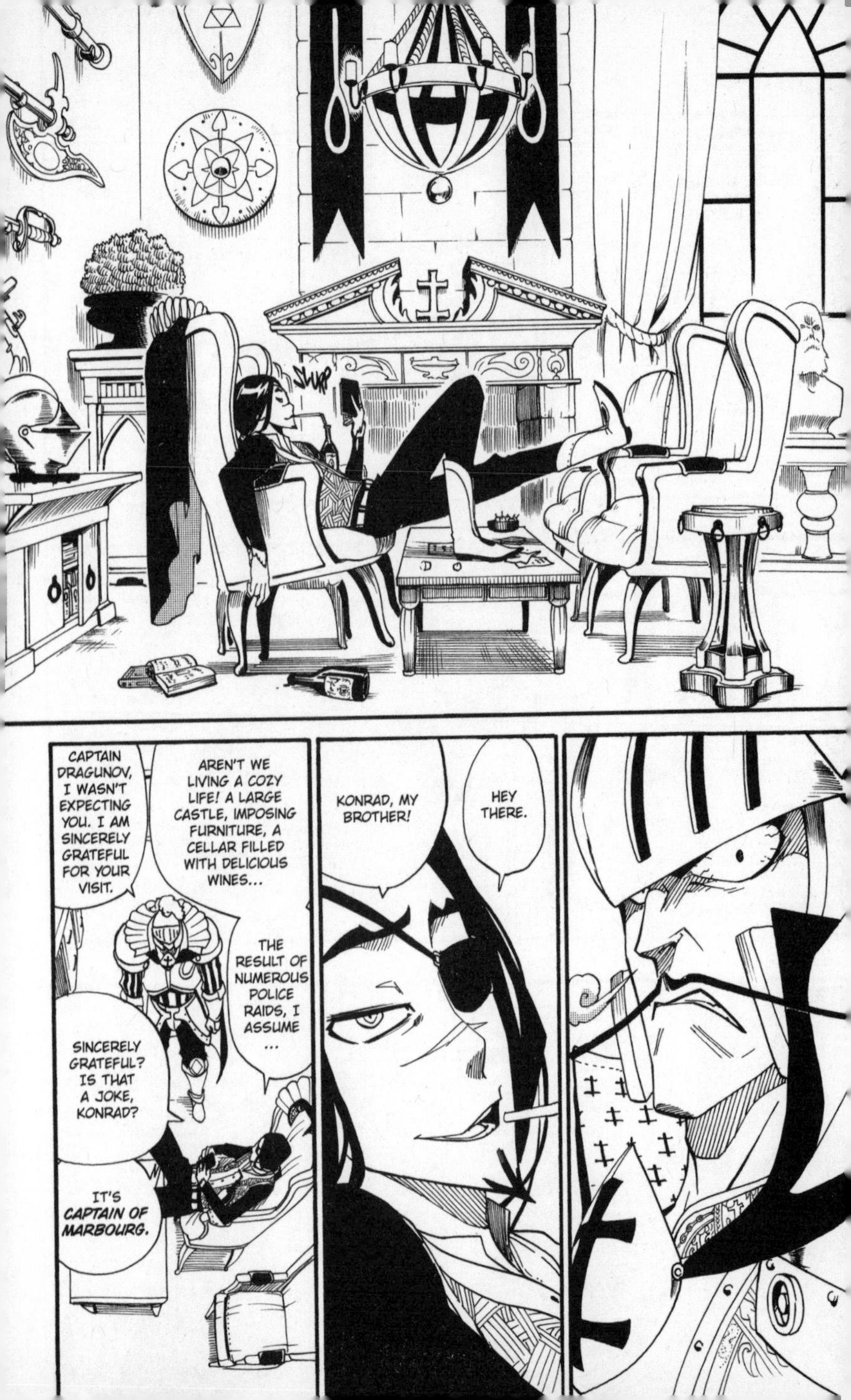
SLURP
HEY THERE.
KONRAD, MY BROTHER!
AREN'T WE LIVING A COZY LIFE! A LARGE CASTLE, IMPOSING FURNITURE, A CELLAR FILLED WITH DELICIOUS WINES...
CAPTAIN DRAGUNOV, I WASN'T EXPECTING YOU. I AM SINCERELY GRATEFUL FOR YOUR VISIT.
THE RESULT OF NUMEROUS POLICE RAIDS, I ASSUME...
SINCERELY GRATEFUL? IS THAT A JOKE, KONRAD?
IT'S CAPTAIN OF MARBOURG.

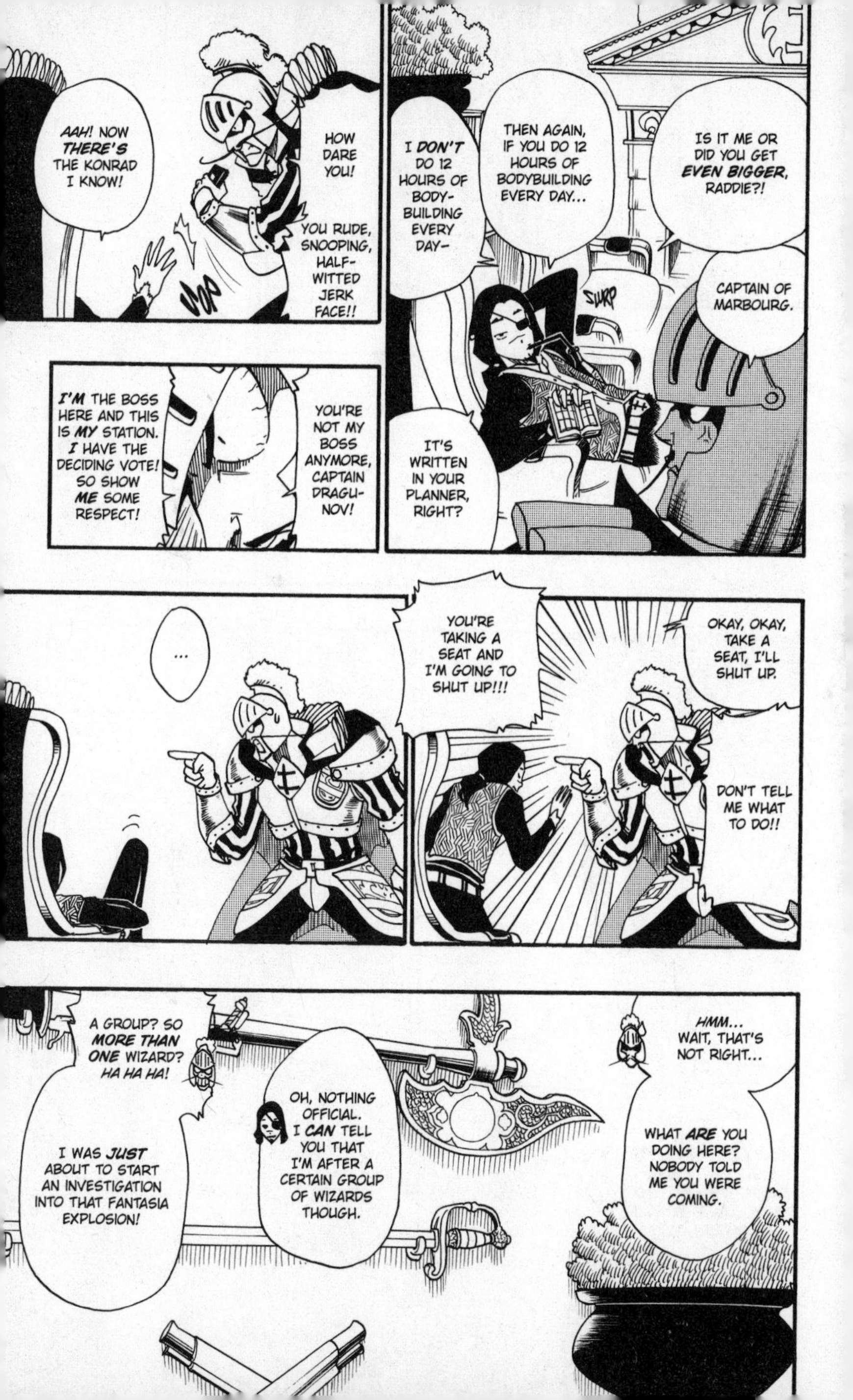
IS IT ME OR DID YOU GET *EVEN BIGGER*, RADDIE?!
CAPTAIN OF MARBOURG.
THEN AGAIN, IF YOU DO 12 HOURS OF BODYBUILDING EVERY DAY...
SLURP
I *DON'T* DO 12 HOURS OF BODY-BUILDING EVERY DAY-
IT'S WRITTEN IN YOUR PLANNER, RIGHT?
HOW DARE YOU!
YOU RUDE, SNOOPING, HALF-WITTED JERK FACE!!
AAH! NOW *THERE'S* THE KONRAD I KNOW!
YOU'RE NOT MY BOSS ANYMORE, CAPTAIN DRAGUNOV!
I'M THE BOSS HERE AND THIS IS *MY* STATION. *I* HAVE THE DECIDING VOTE! SO SHOW *ME* SOME RESPECT!
OKAY, OKAY, TAKE A SEAT, I'LL SHUT UP.
DON'T TELL ME WHAT TO DO!!
YOU'RE TAKING A SEAT AND I'M GOING TO SHUT UP!!!
...
HMM... WAIT, THAT'S NOT RIGHT...
WHAT *ARE* YOU DOING HERE? NOBODY TOLD ME YOU WERE COMING.
OH, NOTHING OFFICIAL. I *CAN* TELL YOU THAT I'M AFTER A CERTAIN GROUP OF WIZARDS THOUGH.
A GROUP? SO *MORE THAN ONE* WIZARD? *HA HA HA!*
I WAS *JUST* ABOUT TO START AN INVESTIGATION INTO THAT FANTASIA EXPLOSION!

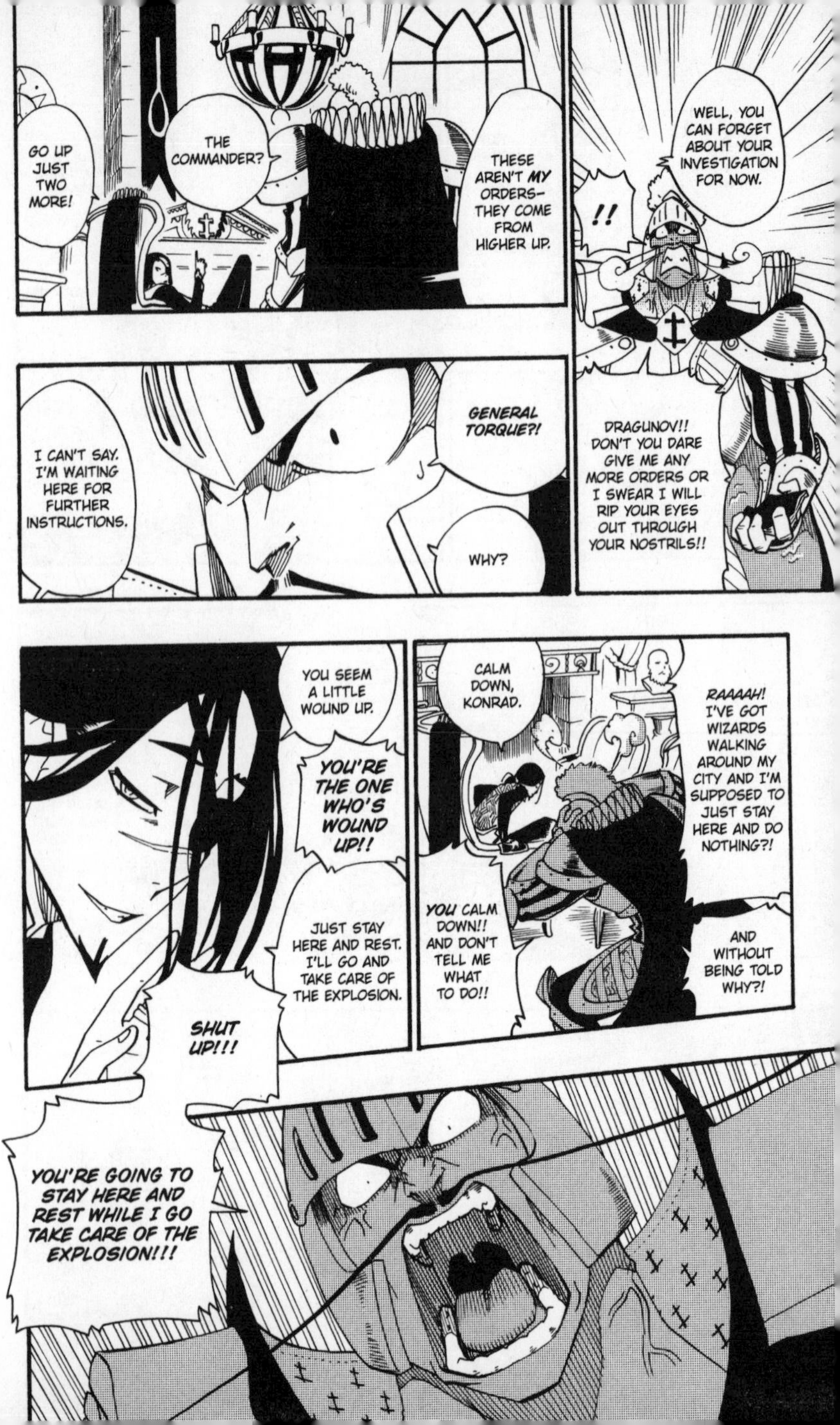
WELL, YOU CAN FORGET ABOUT YOUR INVESTIGATION FOR NOW.
!!
DRAGUNOV!! DON'T YOU DARE GIVE ME ANY MORE ORDERS OR I SWEAR I WILL RIP YOUR EYES OUT THROUGH YOUR NOSTRILS!!
THESE AREN'T *MY* ORDERS— THEY COME FROM HIGHER UP.
THE COMMANDER?
GO UP JUST TWO MORE!
GENERAL TORQUE?!
WHY?
I CAN'T SAY. I'M WAITING HERE FOR FURTHER INSTRUCTIONS.
RAAAAH! I'VE GOT WIZARDS WALKING AROUND MY CITY AND I'M SUPPOSED TO JUST STAY HERE AND DO NOTHING?!
CALM DOWN, KONRAD.
AND WITHOUT BEING TOLD WHY?!
YOU CALM DOWN!! AND DON'T TELL ME WHAT TO DO!!
YOU SEEM A LITTLE WOUND UP.
YOU'RE THE ONE WHO'S WOUND UP!!
JUST STAY HERE AND REST. I'LL GO AND TAKE CARE OF THE EXPLOSION.
SHUT UP!!!
YOU'RE GOING TO STAY HERE AND REST WHILE I GO TAKE CARE OF THE EXPLOSION!!!

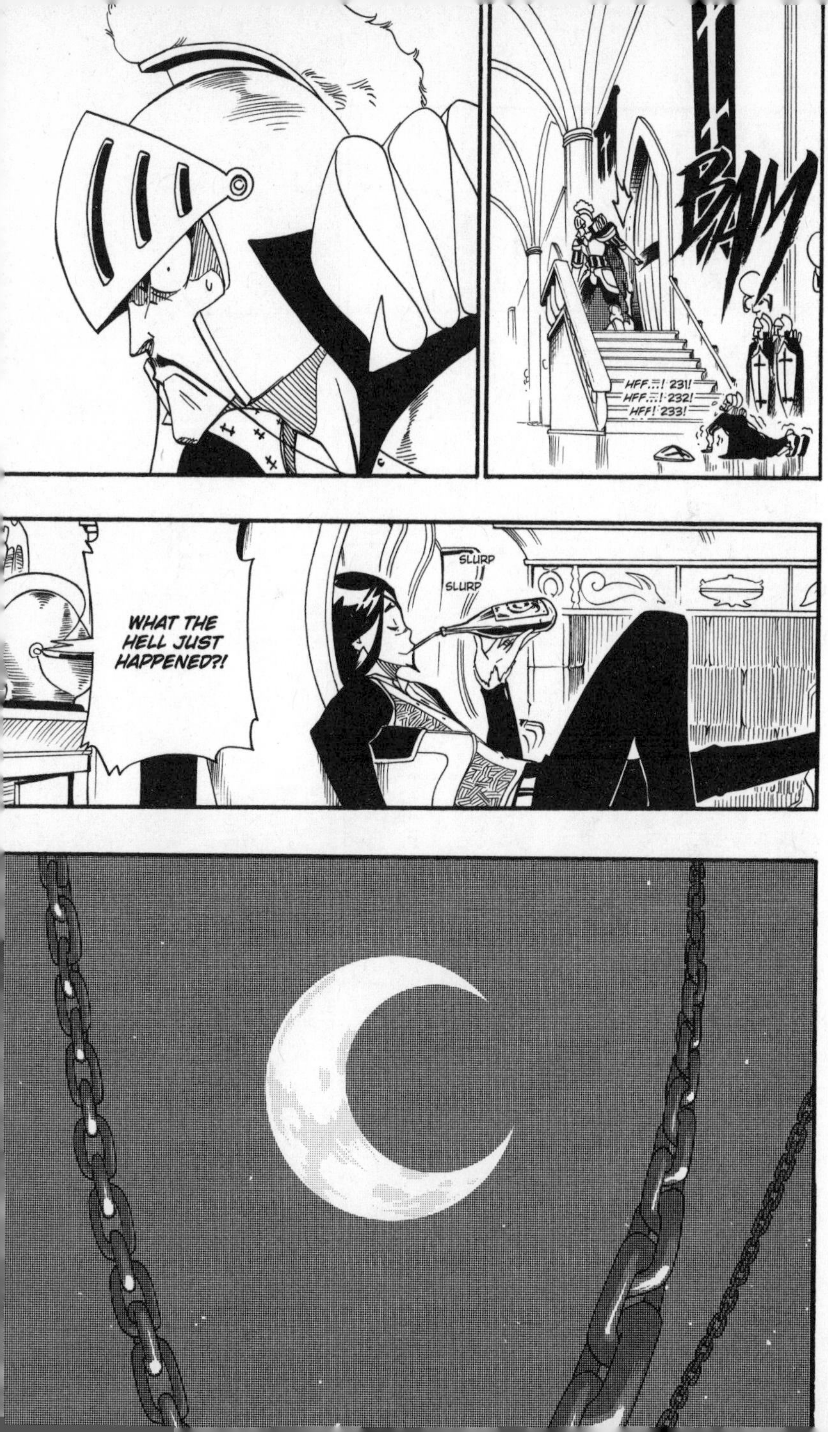
BAM
HFF...! 231!
HFF...! 232!
HFF! 233!
SLURP
SLURP
WHAT THE HELL JUST HAPPENED?!

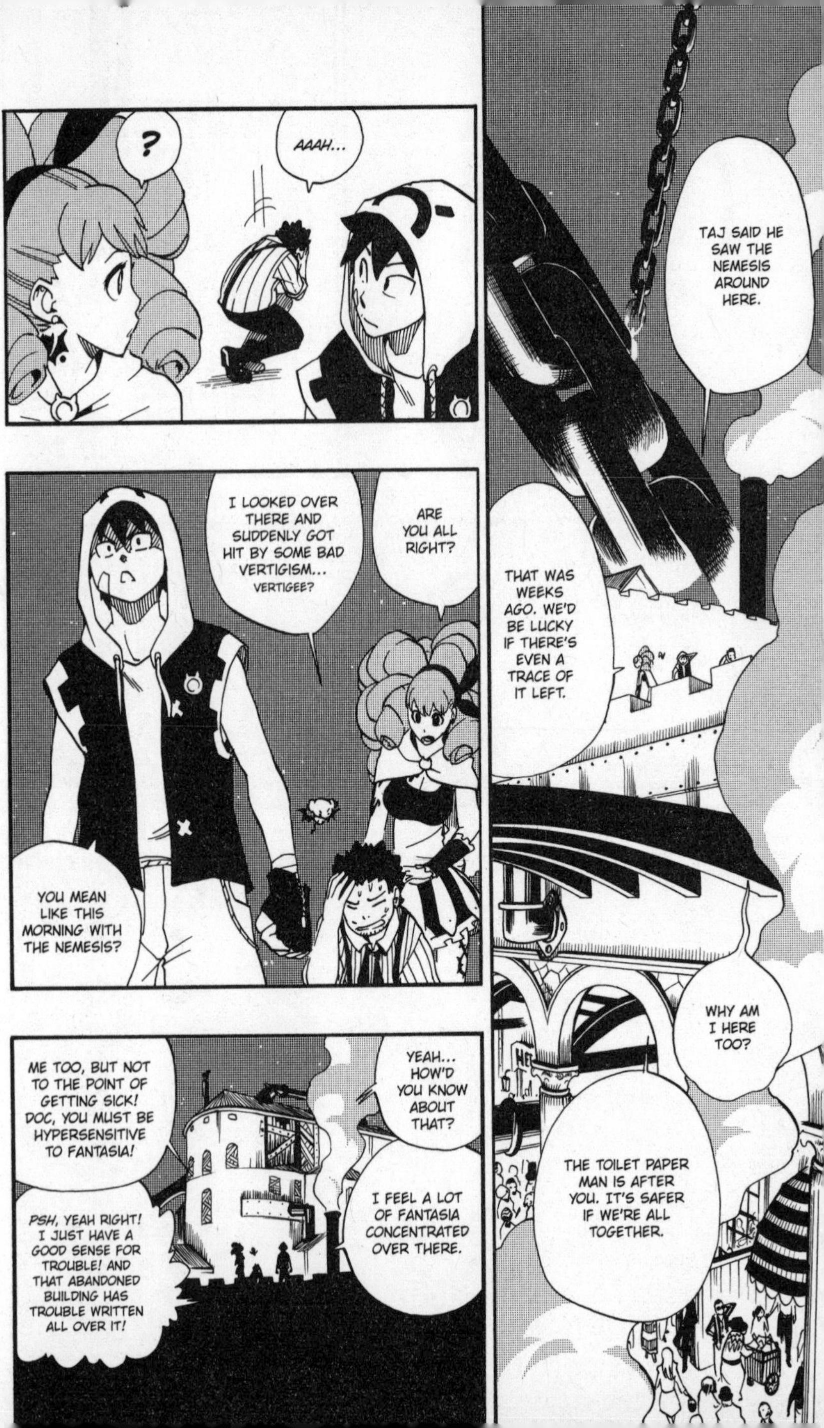
TAJ SAID HE SAW THE NEMESIS AROUND HERE.
THAT WAS WEEKS AGO. WE'D BE LUCKY IF THERE'S EVEN A TRACE OF IT LEFT.
WHY AM I HERE TOO?
THE TOILET PAPER MAN IS AFTER YOU. IT'S SAFER IF WE'RE ALL TOGETHER.
AAAH...
?
ARE YOU ALL RIGHT?
I LOOKED OVER THERE AND SUDDENLY GOT HIT BY SOME BAD VERTIGISM... VERTIGEE?
YOU MEAN LIKE THIS MORNING WITH THE NEMESIS?
YEAH... HOW'D YOU KNOW ABOUT THAT?
I FEEL A LOT OF FANTASIA CONCENTRATED OVER THERE.
ME TOO, BUT NOT TO THE POINT OF GETTING SICK! DOC, YOU MUST BE HYPERSENSITIVE TO FANTASIA!
PSH, YEAH RIGHT! I JUST HAVE A GOOD SENSE FOR TROUBLE! AND THAT ABANDONED BUILDING HAS TROUBLE WRITTEN ALL OVER IT!

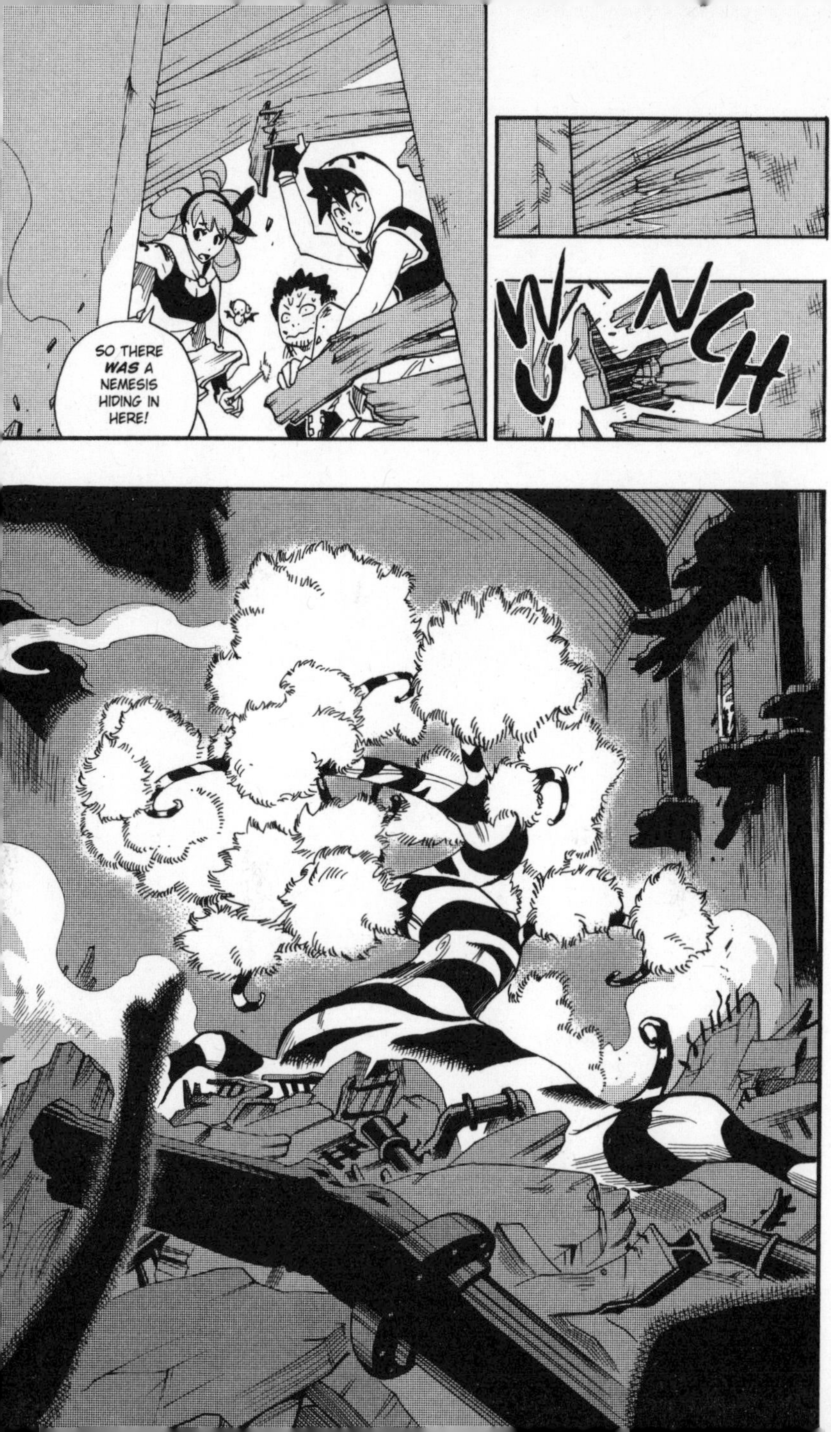
WUNCH
SO THERE *WAS* A NEMESIS HIDING IN HERE!

A TEN-METER-LONG DUCK...

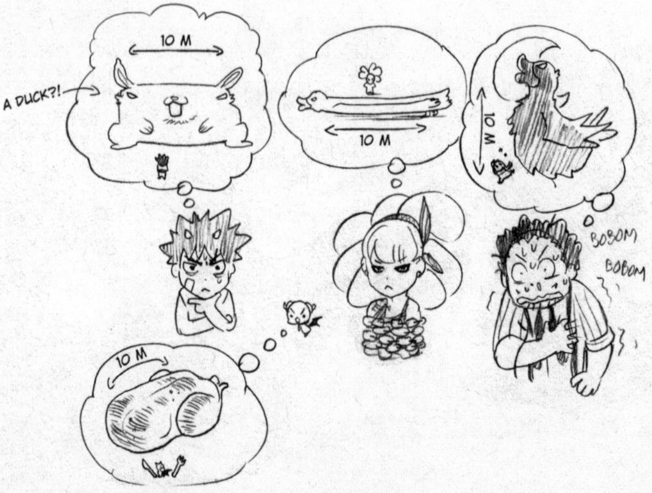
10 M
BOBOM
BOBOM
10 M
10 M
A DUCK?!
10 M

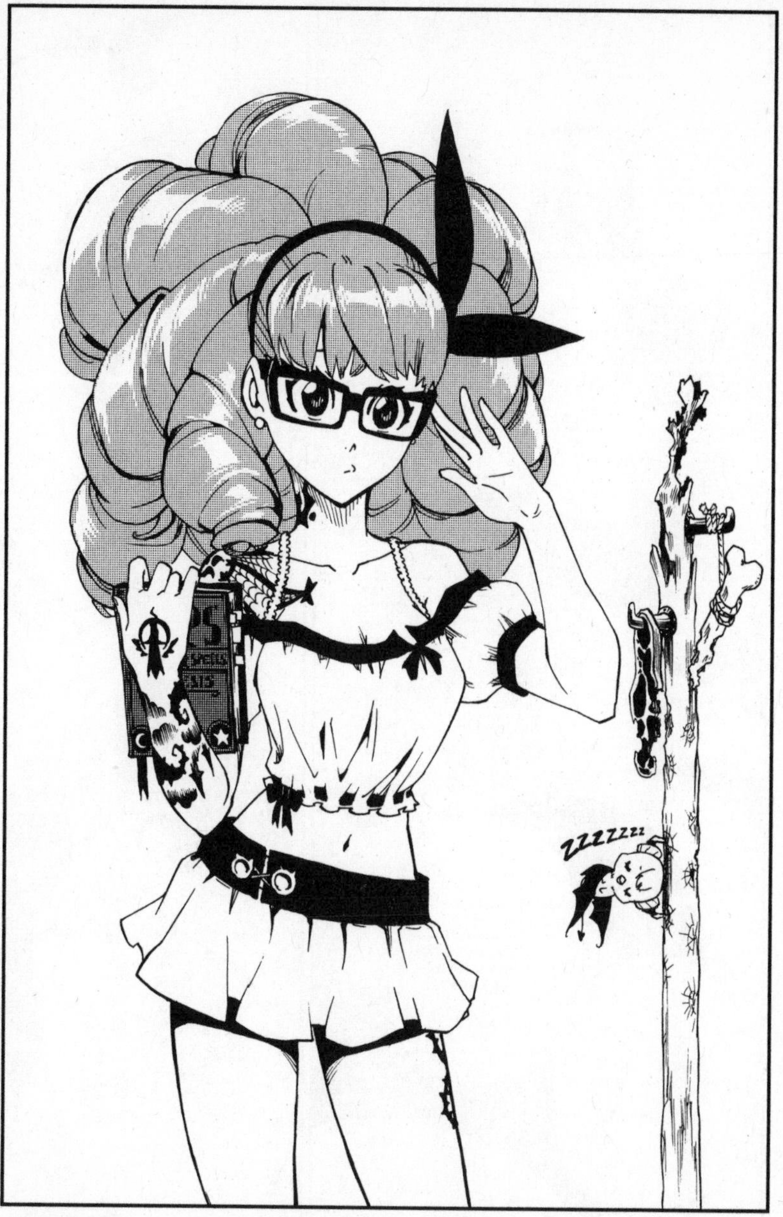
ZZZZZZZ

Chapter 9

A Theater Piece

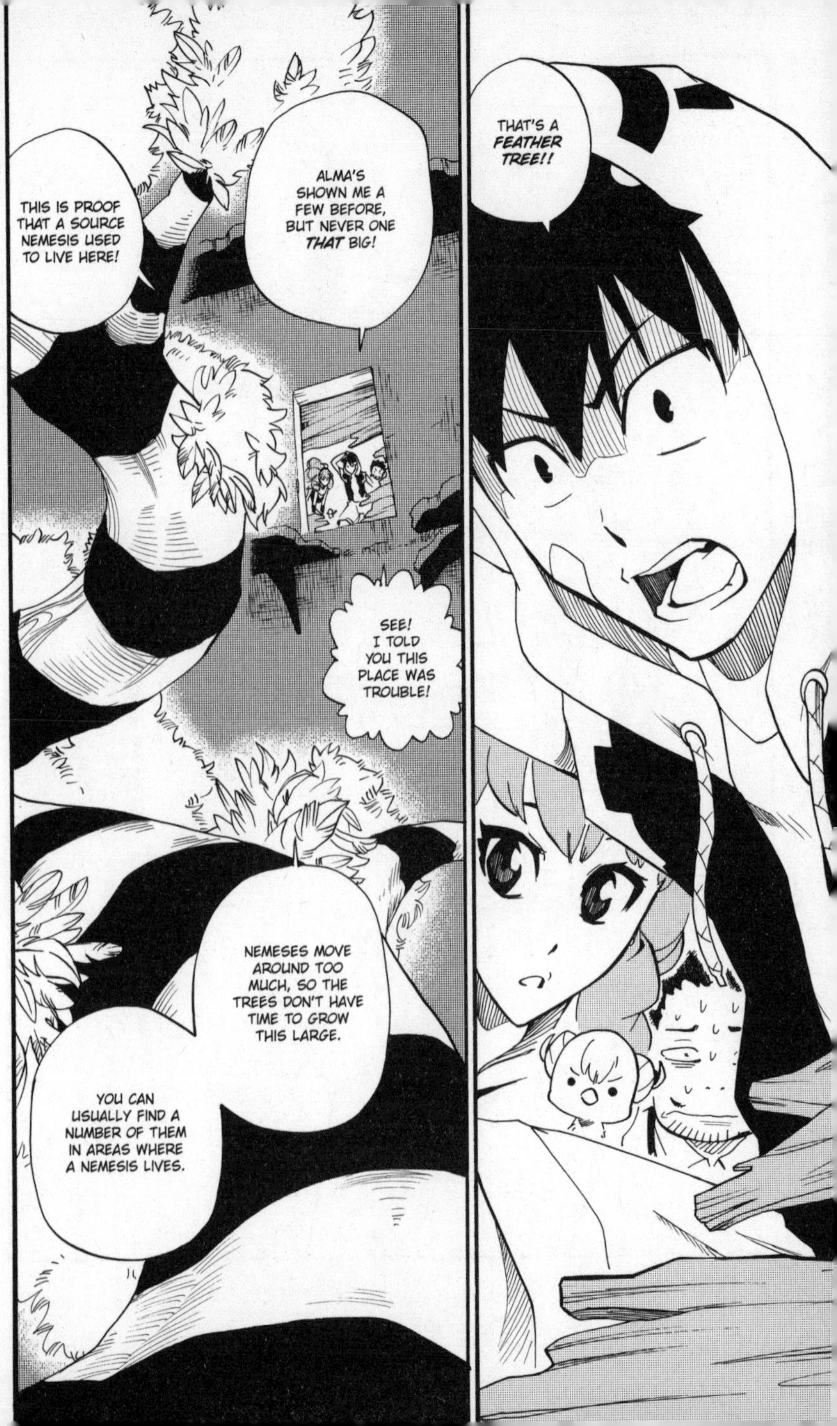
THAT'S A *FEATHER TREE!!*
ALMA'S SHOWN ME A FEW BEFORE, BUT NEVER ONE *THAT* BIG!
THIS IS PROOF THAT A SOURCE NEMESIS USED TO LIVE HERE!
SEE! I TOLD YOU THIS PLACE WAS TROUBLE!
NEMESES MOVE AROUND TOO MUCH, SO THE TREES DON'T HAVE TIME TO GROW THIS LARGE.
YOU CAN USUALLY FIND A NUMBER OF THEM IN AREAS WHERE A NEMESIS LIVES.

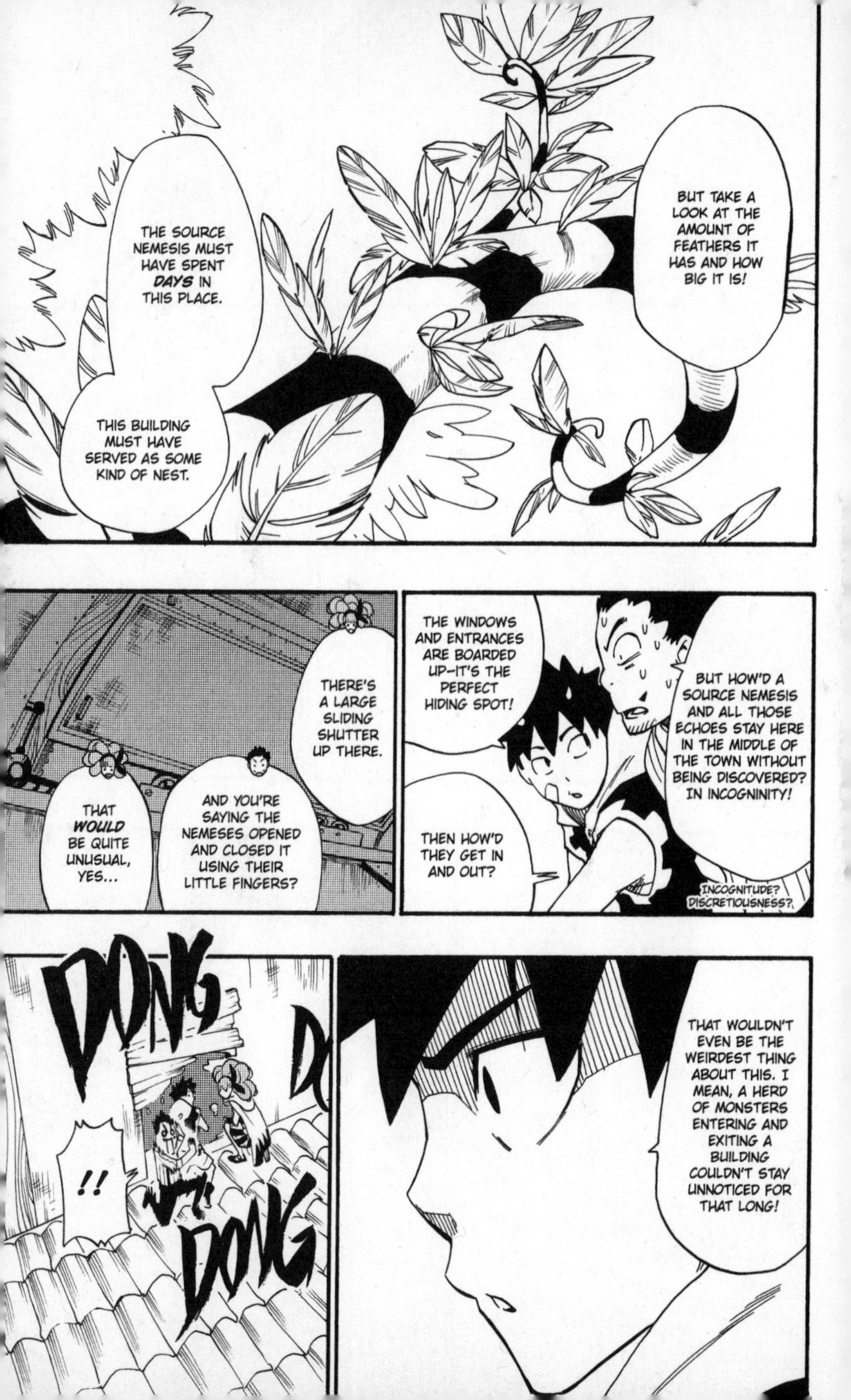
BUT TAKE A LOOK AT THE AMOUNT OF FEATHERS IT HAS AND HOW BIG IT IS!
THE SOURCE NEMESIS MUST HAVE SPENT DAYS IN THIS PLACE.
THIS BUILDING MUST HAVE SERVED AS SOME KIND OF NEST.
BUT HOW'D A SOURCE NEMESIS AND ALL THOSE ECHOES STAY HERE IN THE MIDDLE OF THE TOWN WITHOUT BEING DISCOVERED? IN INCOGNINITY!
INCOGNITUDE? DISCRETIOUSNESS?
THE WINDOWS AND ENTRANCES ARE BOARDED UP—IT'S THE PERFECT HIDING SPOT!
THEN HOW'D THEY GET IN AND OUT?
THERE'S A LARGE SLIDING SHUTTER UP THERE.
AND YOU'RE SAYING THE NEMESES OPENED AND CLOSED IT USING THEIR LITTLE FINGERS?
THAT WOULD BE QUITE UNUSUAL, YES...
THAT WOULDN'T EVEN BE THE WEIRDEST THING ABOUT THIS. I MEAN, A HERD OF MONSTERS ENTERING AND EXITING A BUILDING COULDN'T STAY UNNOTICED FOR THAT LONG!
DONG
DONG
DONG
!!

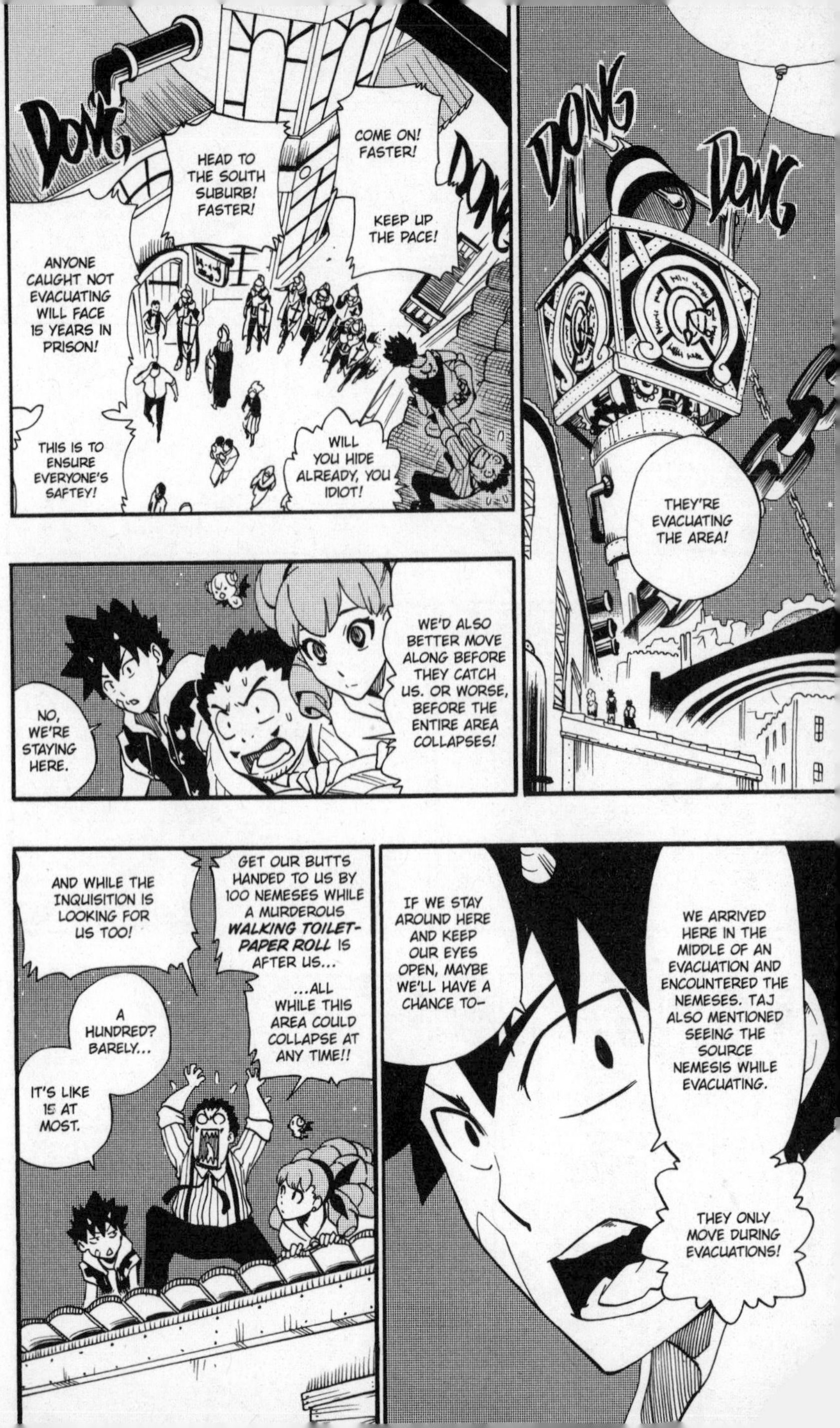
DONG
DONG
THEY'RE EVACUATING THE AREA!
DONG
COME ON! FASTER!
KEEP UP THE PACE!
HEAD TO THE SOUTH SUBURB! FASTER!
DONG,
ANYONE CAUGHT NOT EVACUATING WILL FACE 15 YEARS IN PRISON!
WILL YOU HIDE ALREADY, YOU IDIOT!
THIS IS TO ENSURE EVERYONE'S SAFTEY!
WE'D ALSO BETTER MOVE ALONG BEFORE THEY CATCH US. OR WORSE, BEFORE THE ENTIRE AREA COLLAPSES!
NO, WE'RE STAYING HERE.
WE ARRIVED HERE IN THE MIDDLE OF AN EVACUATION AND ENCOUNTERED THE NEMESES. TAJ ALSO MENTIONED SEEING THE SOURCE NEMESIS WHILE EVACUATING.
IF WE STAY AROUND HERE AND KEEP OUR EYES OPEN, MAYBE WE'LL HAVE A CHANCE TO—
THEY ONLY MOVE DURING EVACUATIONS!
GET OUR BUTTS HANDED TO US BY 100 NEMESES WHILE A MURDEROUS WALKING TOILET-PAPER ROLL IS AFTER US...
AND WHILE THE INQUISITION IS LOOKING FOR US TOO!
...ALL WHILE THIS AREA COULD COLLAPSE AT ANY TIME!!
A HUNDRED? BARELY...
IT'S LIKE 15 AT MOST.

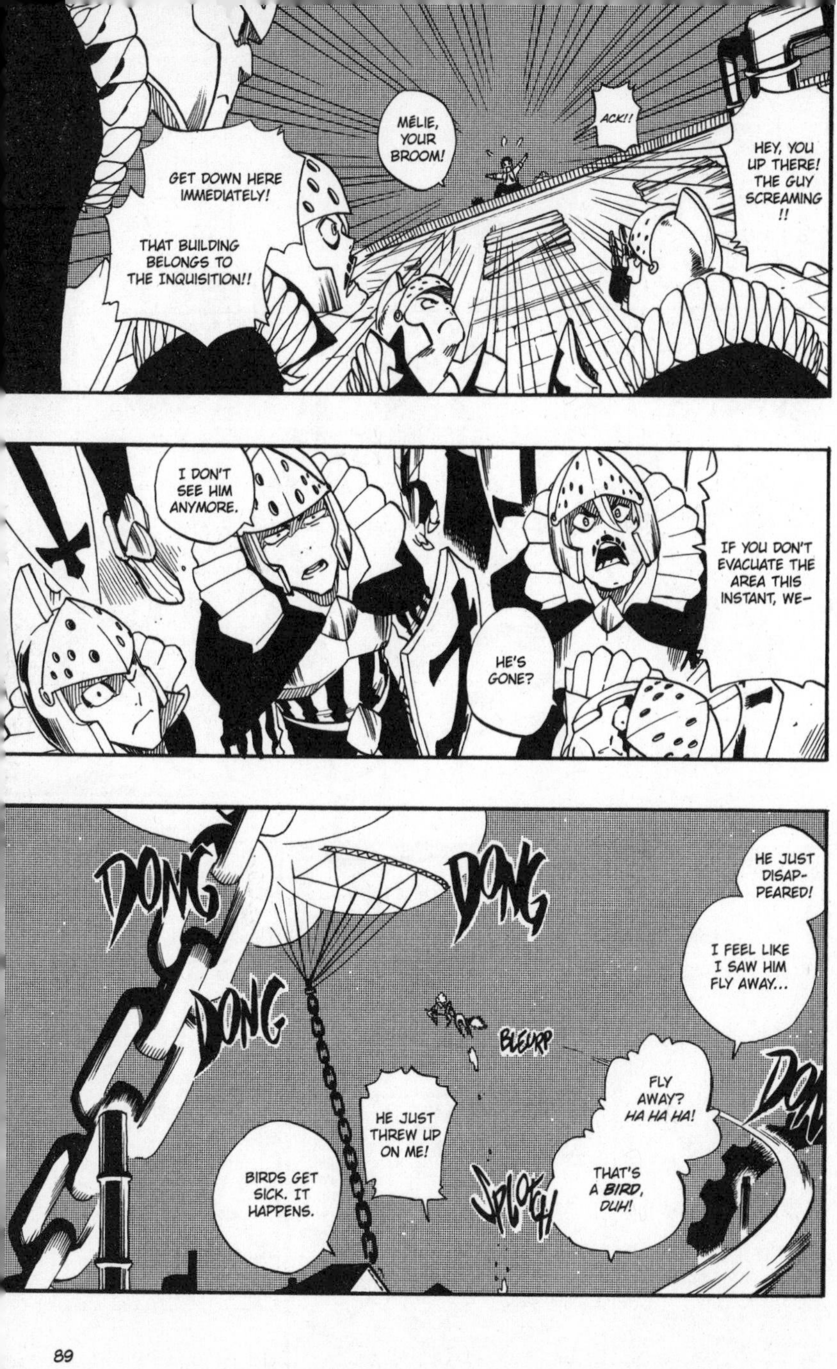
HEY, YOU UP THERE! THE GUY SCREAMING!!
ACK!!
MÉLIE, YOUR BROOM!
GET DOWN HERE IMMEDIATELY!
THAT BUILDING BELONGS TO THE INQUISITION!!
IF YOU DON'T EVACUATE THE AREA THIS INSTANT, WE-
I DON'T SEE HIM ANYMORE.
HE'S GONE?
HE JUST DISAPPEARED!
I FEEL LIKE I SAW HIM FLY AWAY...
DONG
DONG
DONG
BLEURP
FLY AWAY? HA HA HA!
THAT'S A BIRD, DUH!
SPLOTCH
HE JUST THREW UP ON ME!
BIRDS GET SICK. IT HAPPENS.

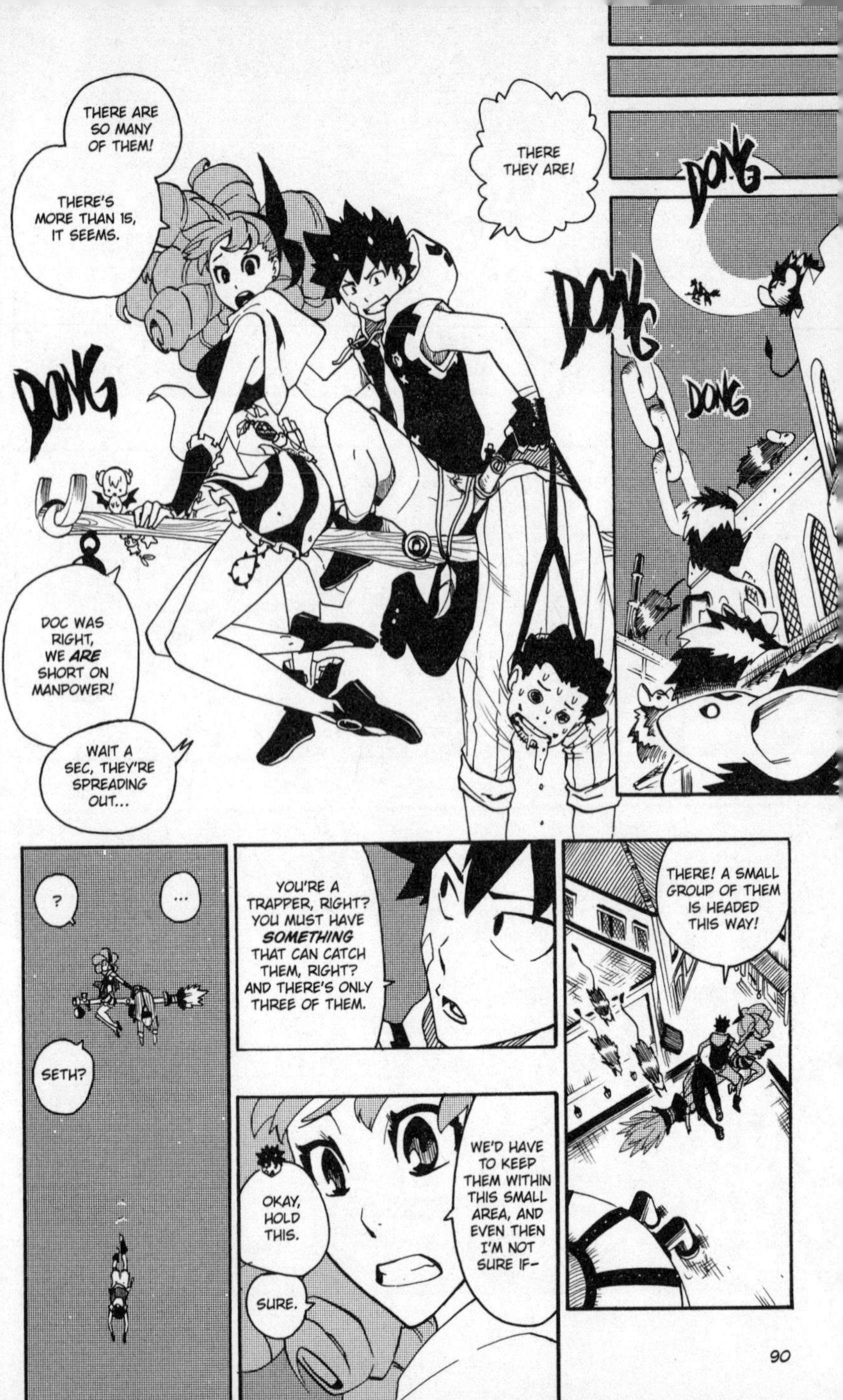
DONG
DONG
DONG
THERE THEY ARE!
THERE ARE SO MANY OF THEM!
THERE'S MORE THAN 15, IT SEEMS.
DONG
DOC WAS RIGHT, WE ***ARE*** SHORT ON MANPOWER!
WAIT A SEC, THEY'RE SPREADING OUT...
THERE! A SMALL GROUP OF THEM IS HEADED THIS WAY!
YOU'RE A TRAPPER, RIGHT? YOU MUST HAVE ***SOMETHING*** THAT CAN CATCH THEM, RIGHT? AND THERE'S ONLY THREE OF THEM.
WE'D HAVE TO KEEP THEM WITHIN THIS SMALL AREA, AND EVEN THEN I'M NOT SURE IF-
OKAY, HOLD THIS.
SURE.
...
?
SETH?

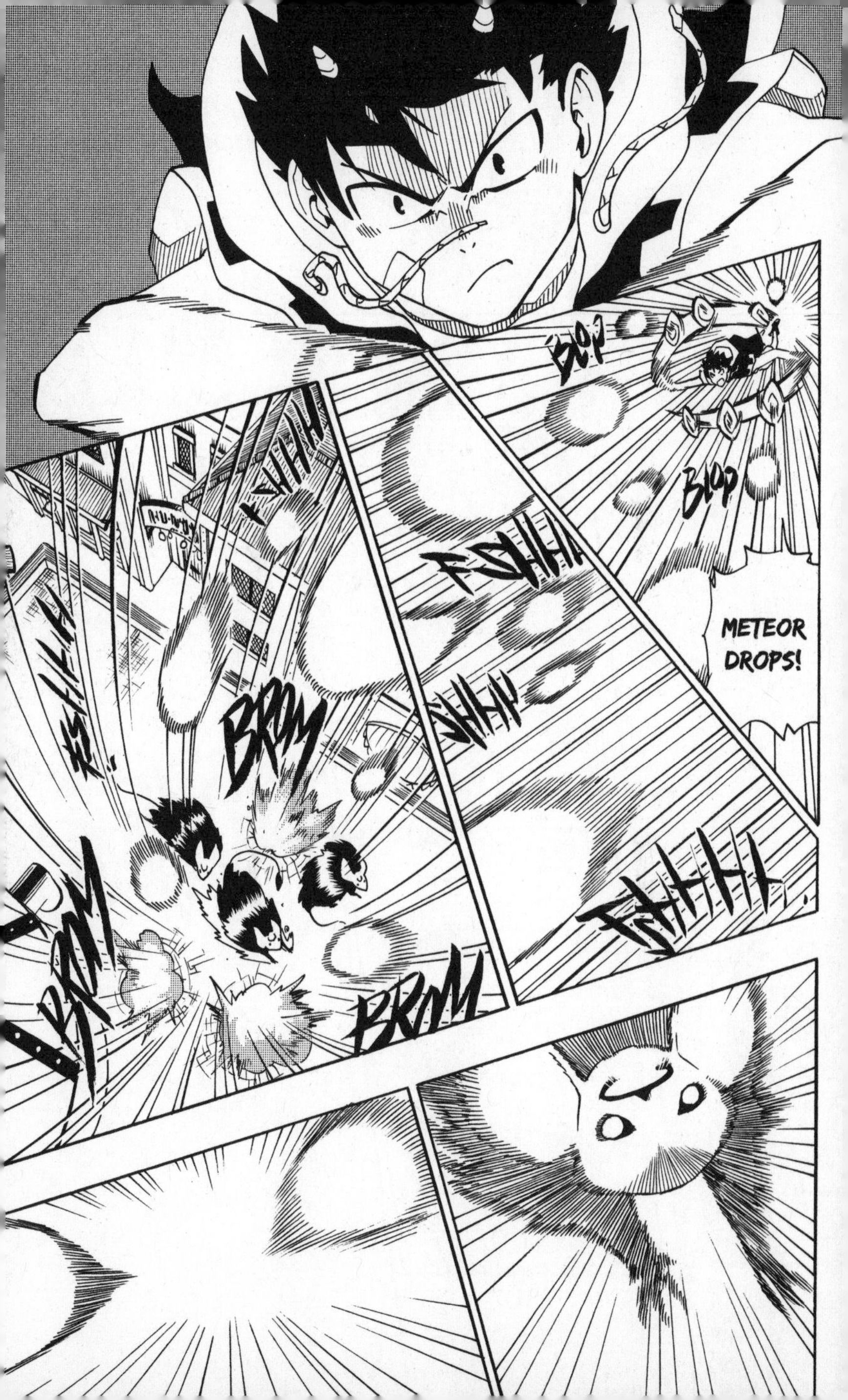
BLOP
BLOP
METEOR DROPS!
BROM
BROM
BROM

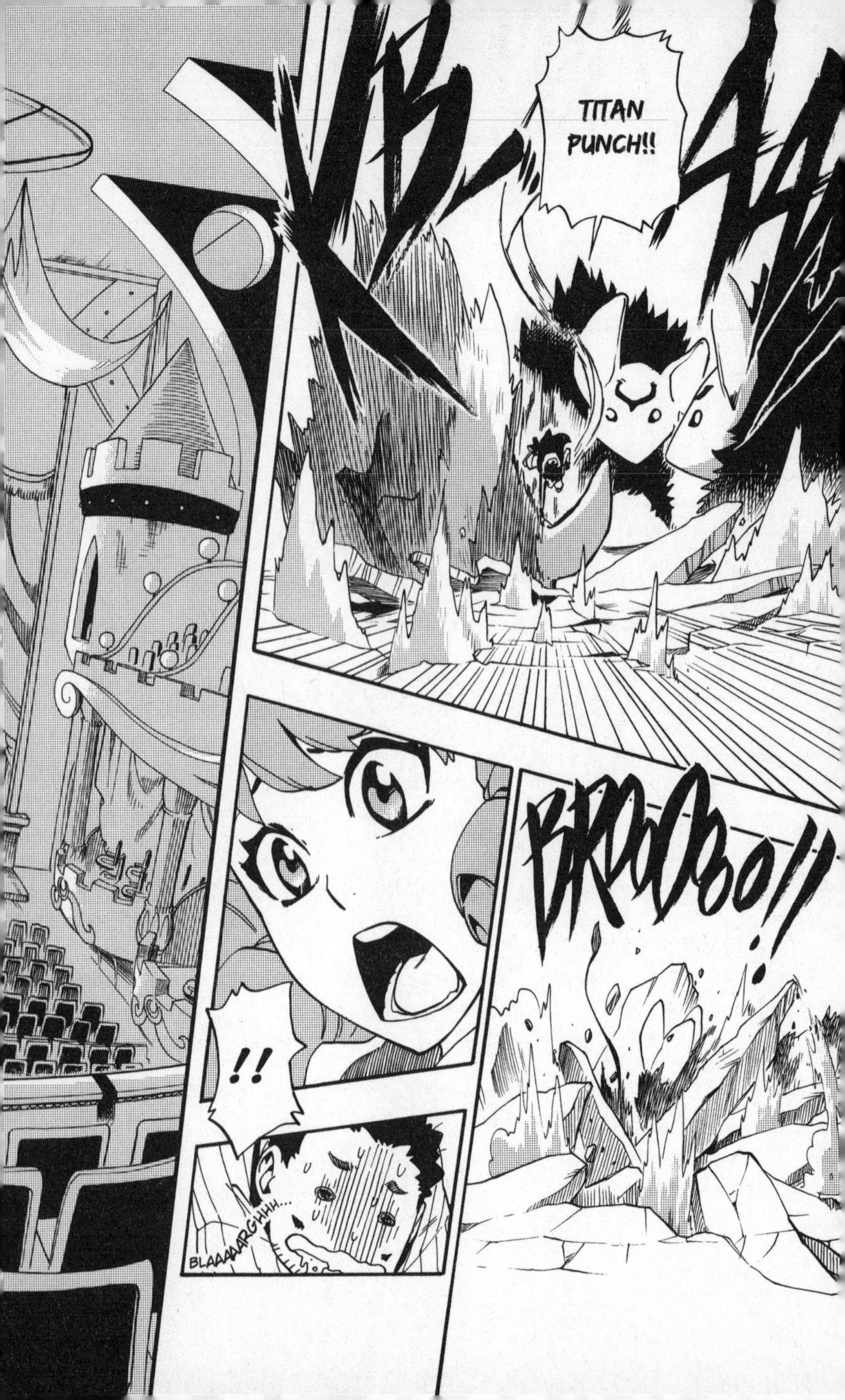
TITAN PUNCH!!
BROOOOO!!
!!
BLAAAARGHHH...

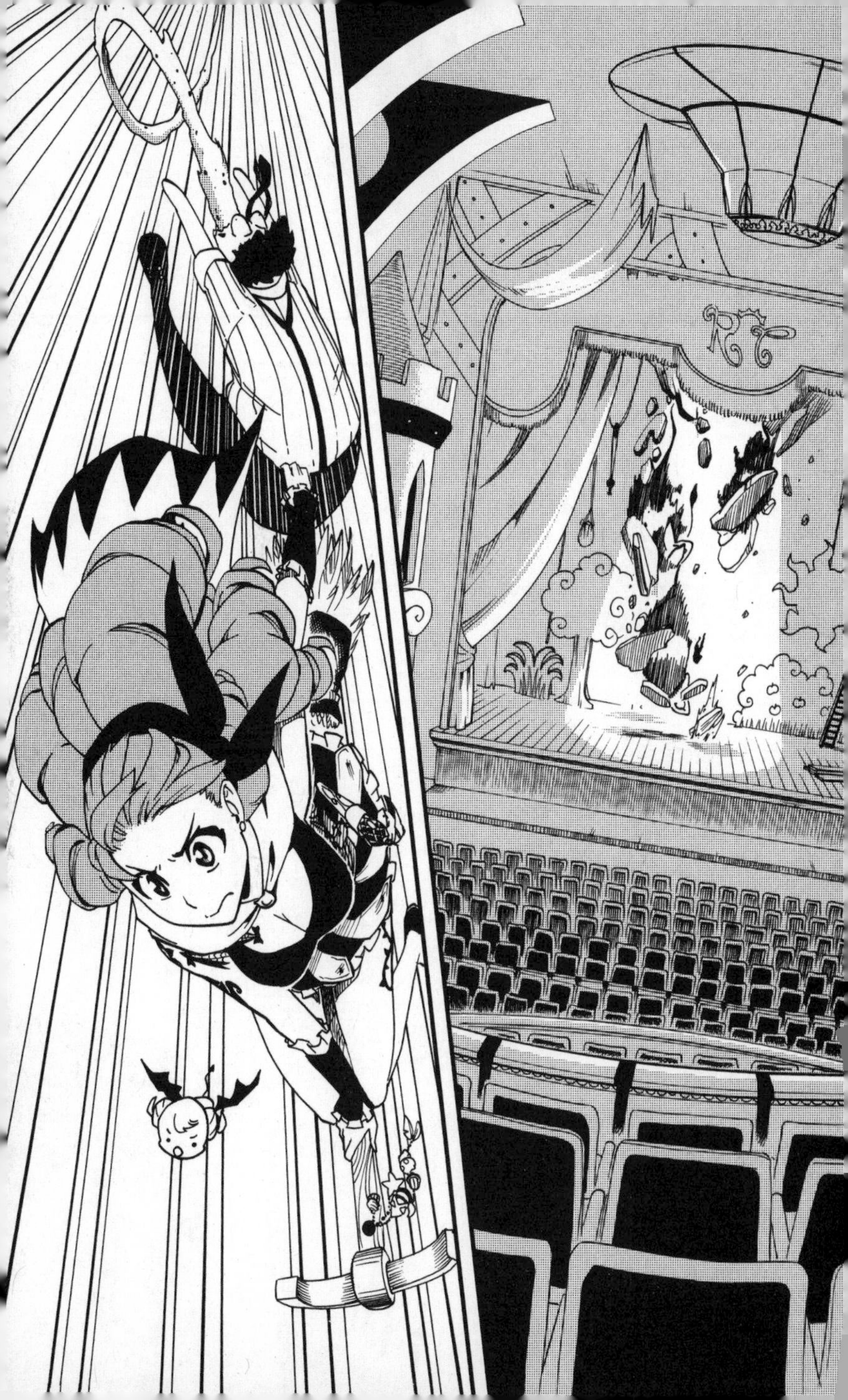

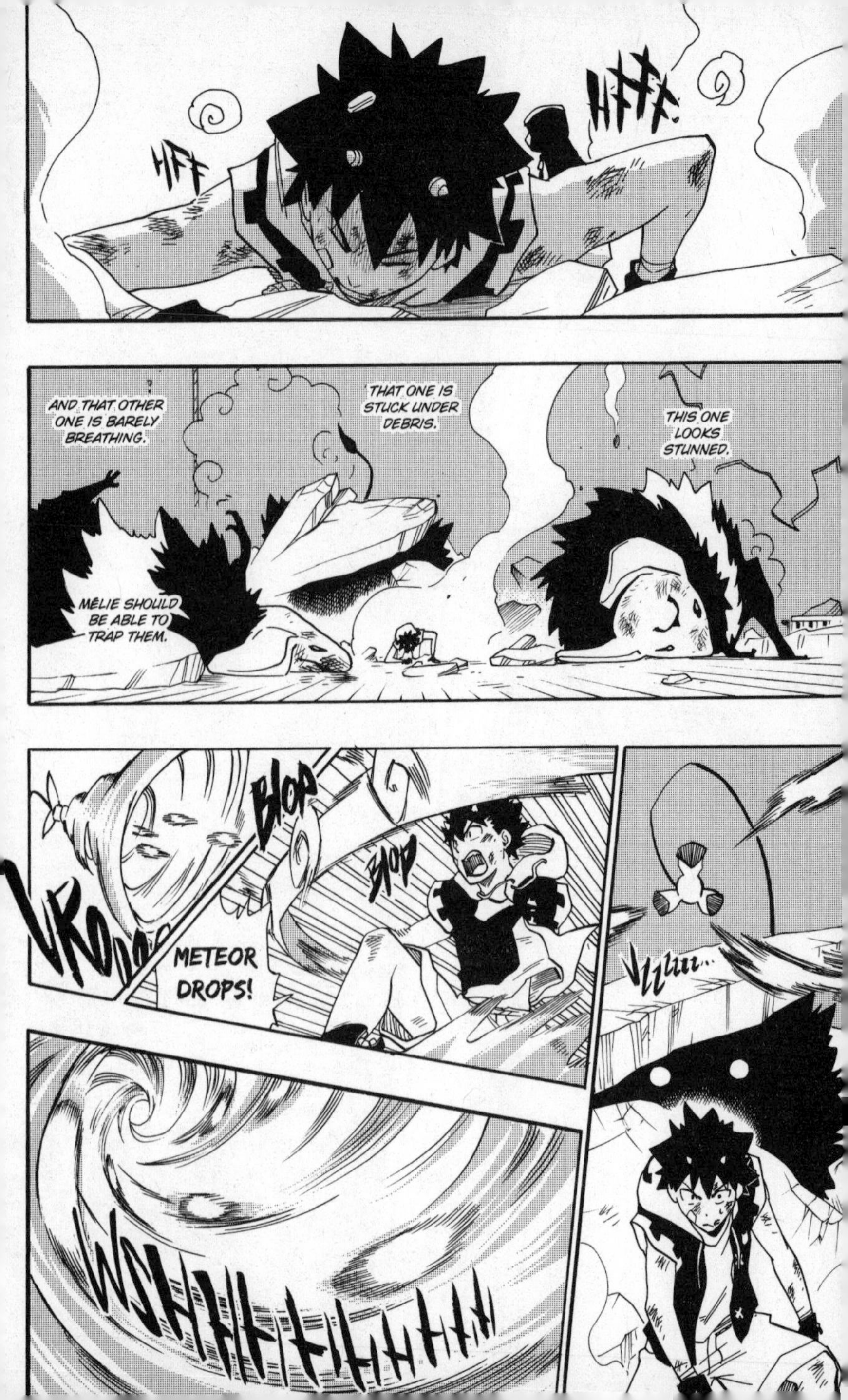

HFFF
HFF
THIS ONE LOOKS STUNNED.
THAT ONE IS STUCK UNDER DEBRIS.
AND THAT OTHER ONE IS BARELY BREATHING.
MÉLIE SHOULD BE ABLE TO TRAP THEM.
VZZZZZ...
BLOP
BLOP
METEOR DROPS!
VROOOO
WSHHHHHHHHHHH

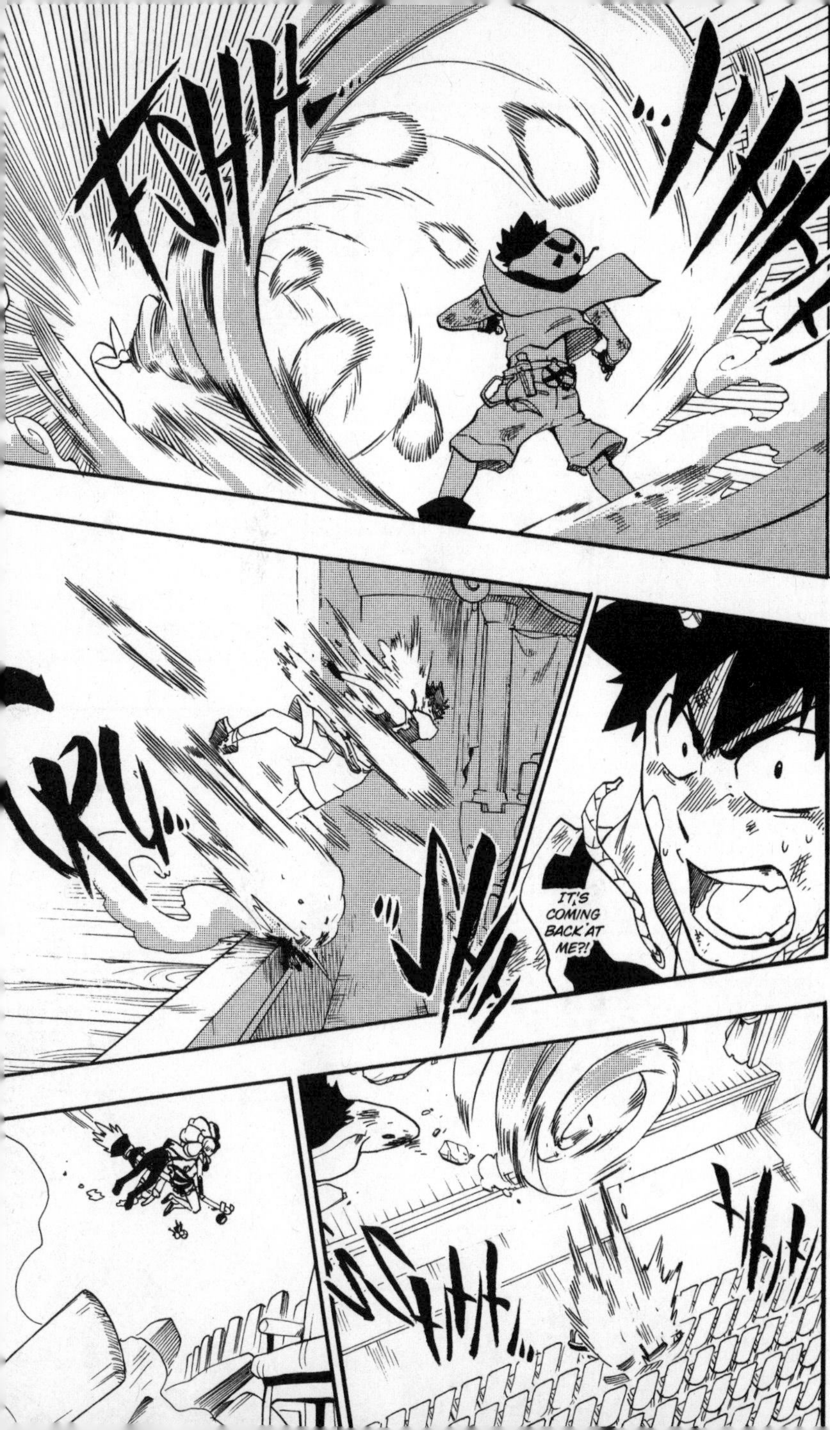
FSHH...
...HHH!!
IT'S COMING BACK AT ME?!
KRU...

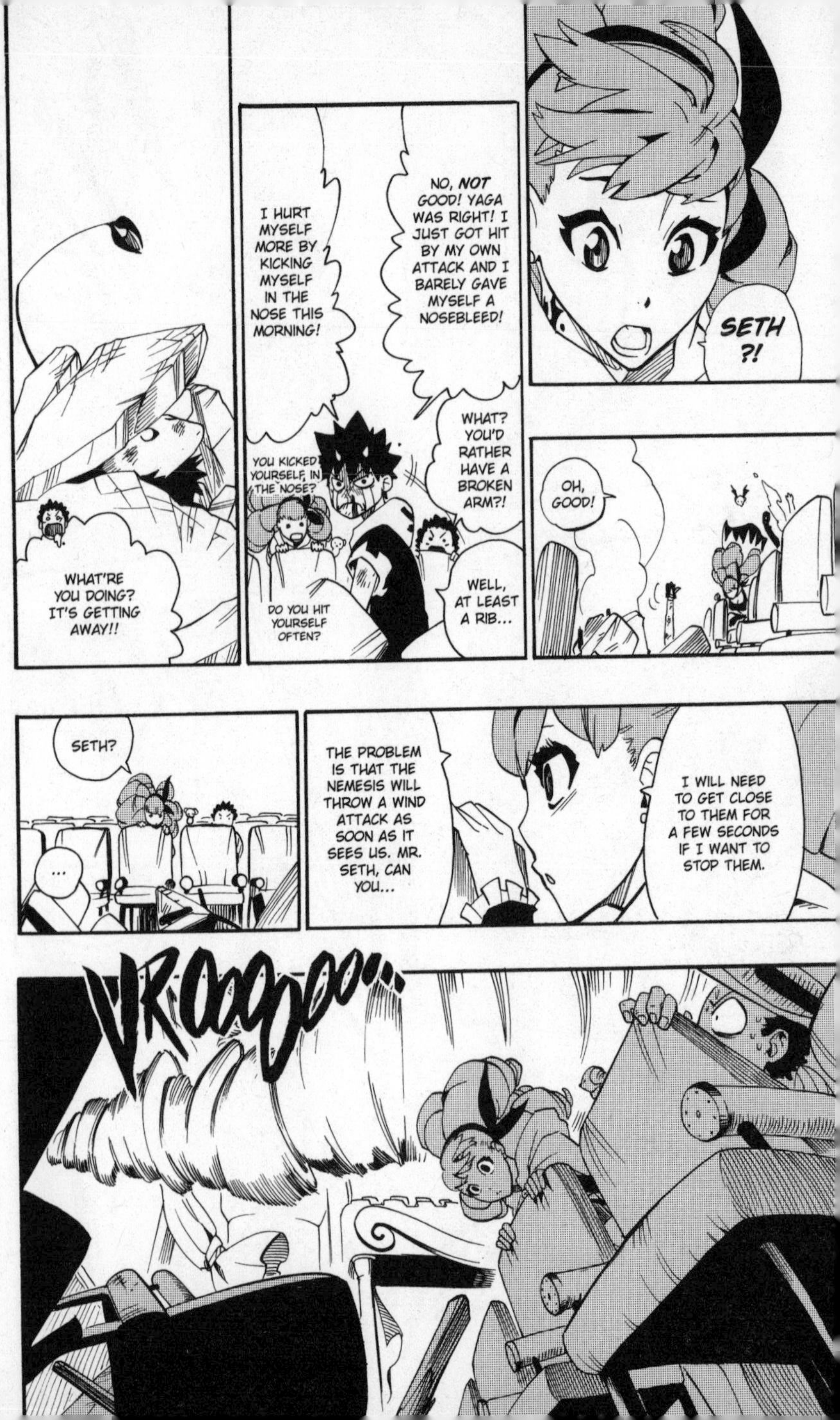
SETH ?!
OH, GOOD!
NO, NOT GOOD! YAGA WAS RIGHT! I JUST GOT HIT BY MY OWN ATTACK AND I BARELY GAVE MYSELF A NOSEBLEED!
I HURT MYSELF MORE BY KICKING MYSELF IN THE NOSE THIS MORNING!
WHAT? YOU'D RATHER HAVE A BROKEN ARM?!
YOU KICKED YOURSELF, IN THE NOSE?
WELL, AT LEAST A RIB...
DO YOU HIT YOURSELF OFTEN?
WHAT'RE YOU DOING? IT'S GETTING AWAY!!
I WILL NEED TO GET CLOSE TO THEM FOR A FEW SECONDS IF I WANT TO STOP THEM.
THE PROBLEM IS THAT THE NEMESIS WILL THROW A WIND ATTACK AS SOON AS IT SEES US. MR. SETH, CAN YOU...
SETH?
...
VROOOOOO...

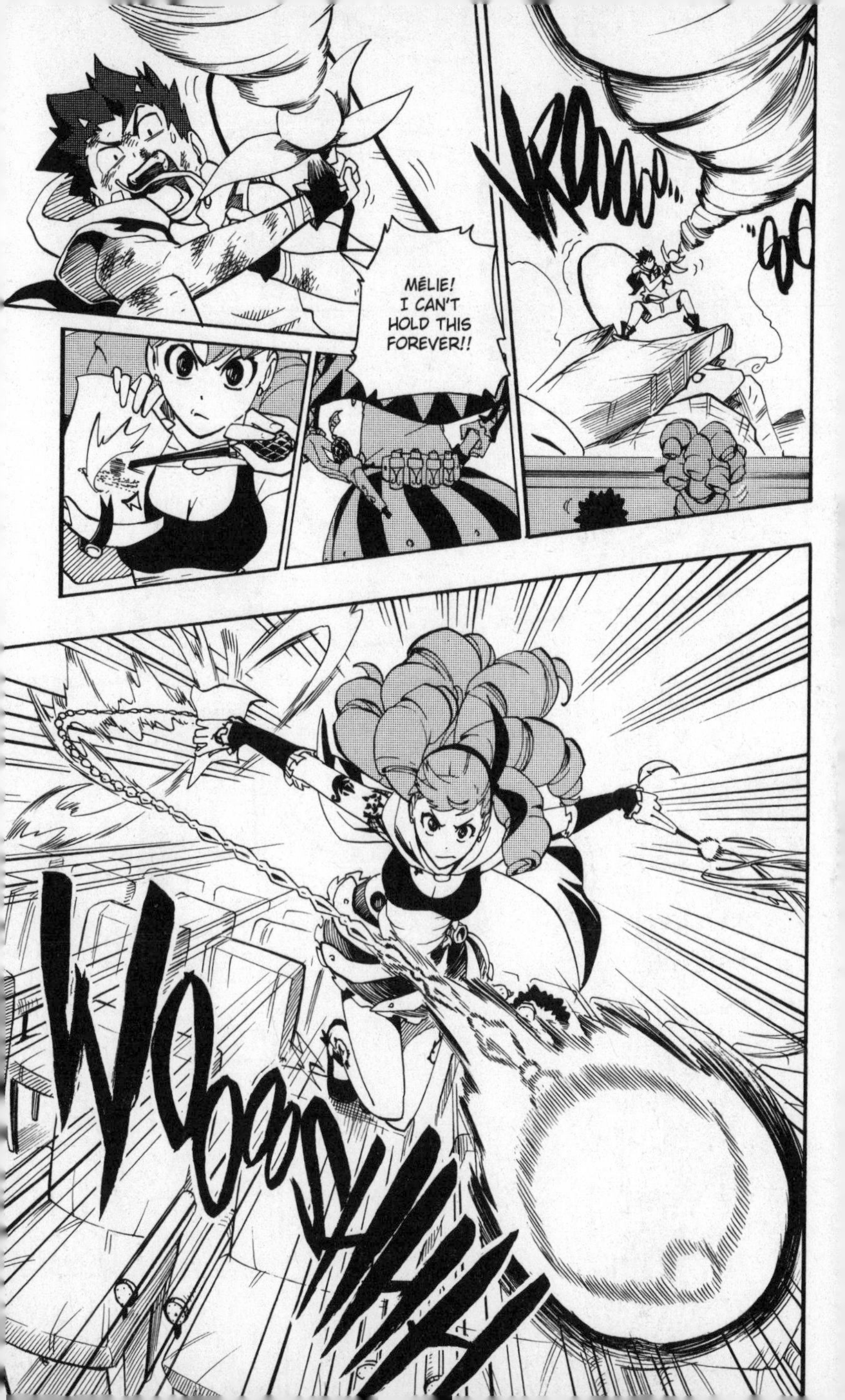
MÉLIE! I CAN'T HOLD THIS FOREVER!!

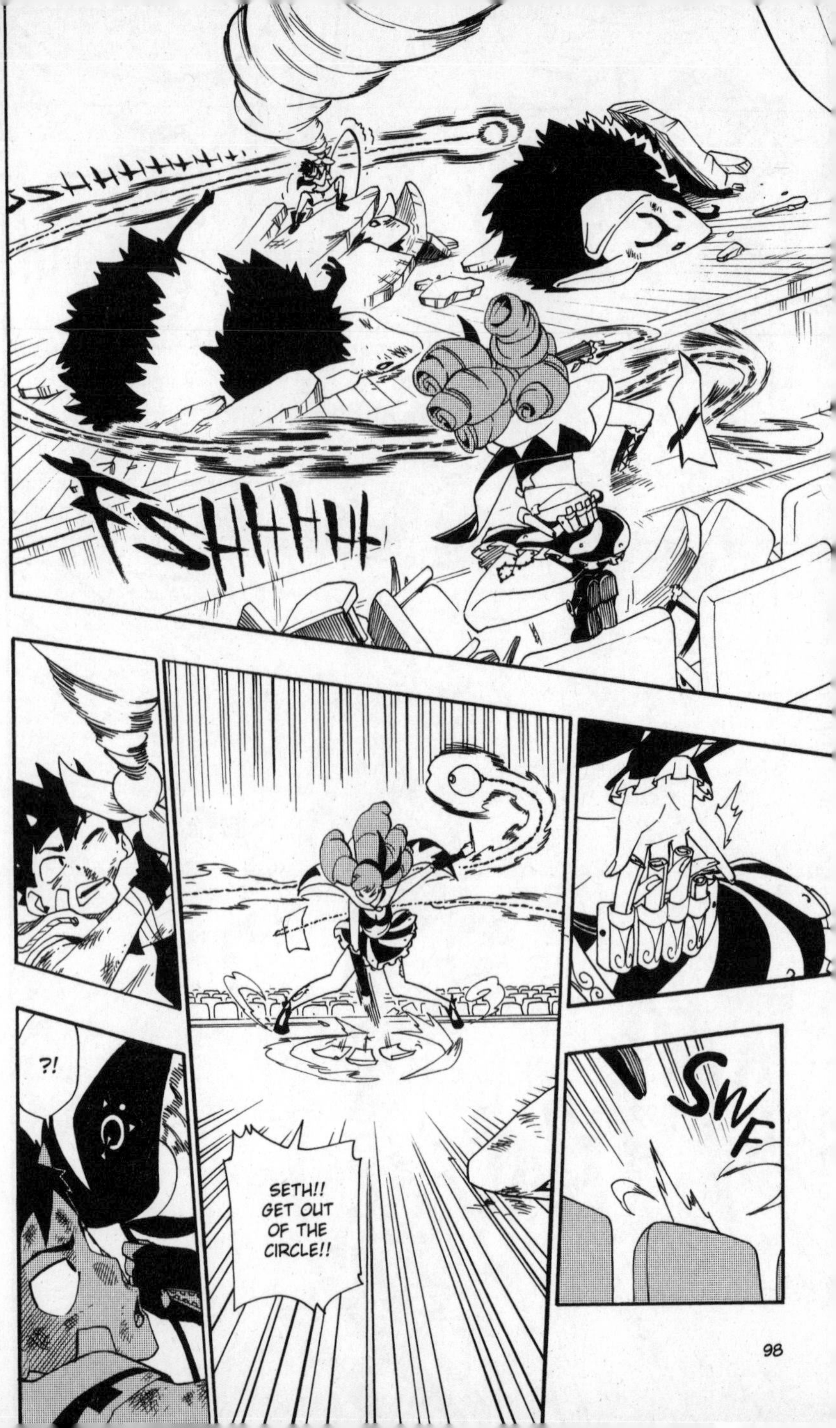
FSHHHH
SWF
SETH!! GET OUT OF THE CIRCLE!!
?!

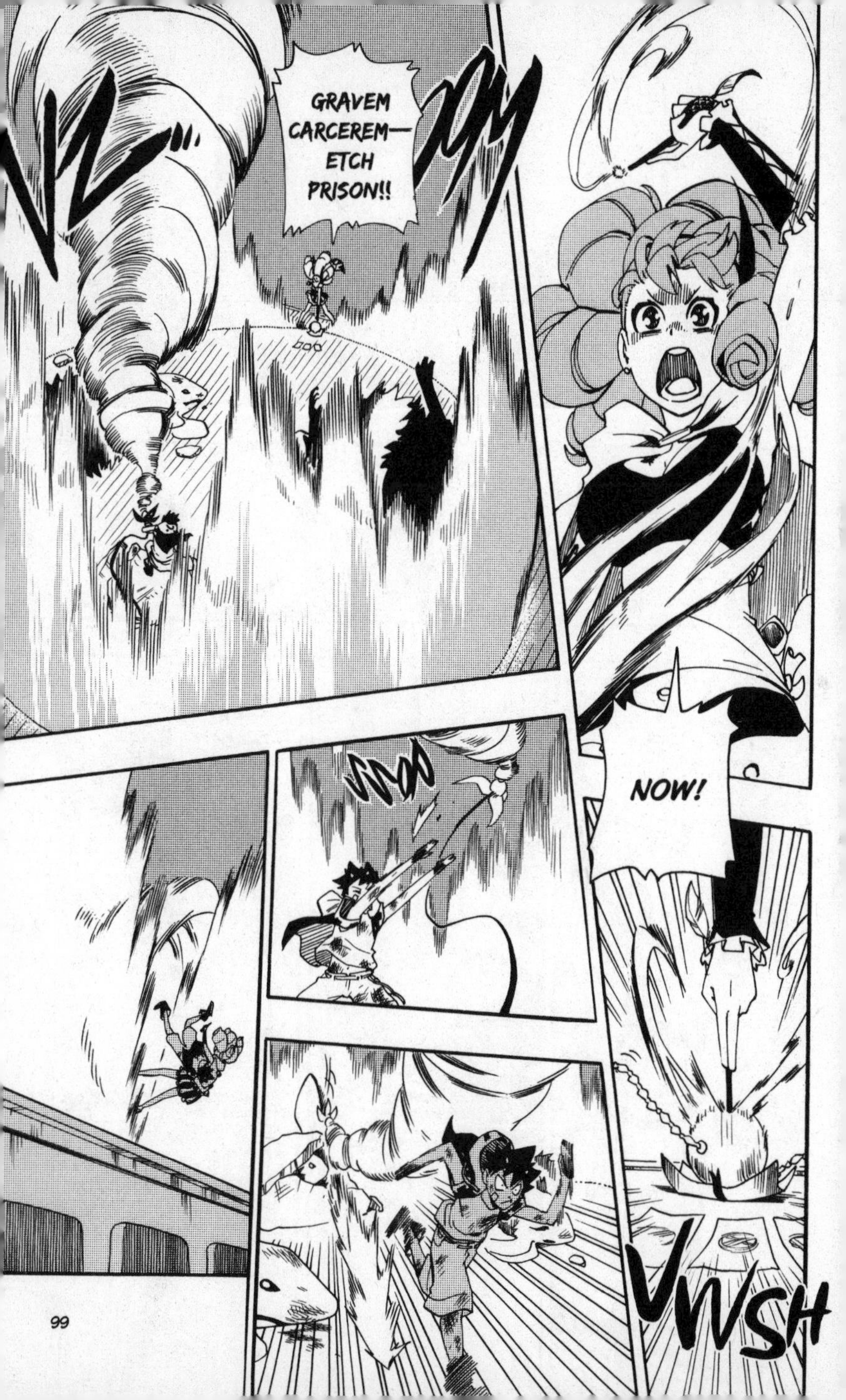
NOW!
GRAVEM CARCEREM—ETCH PRISON!!
VWSH

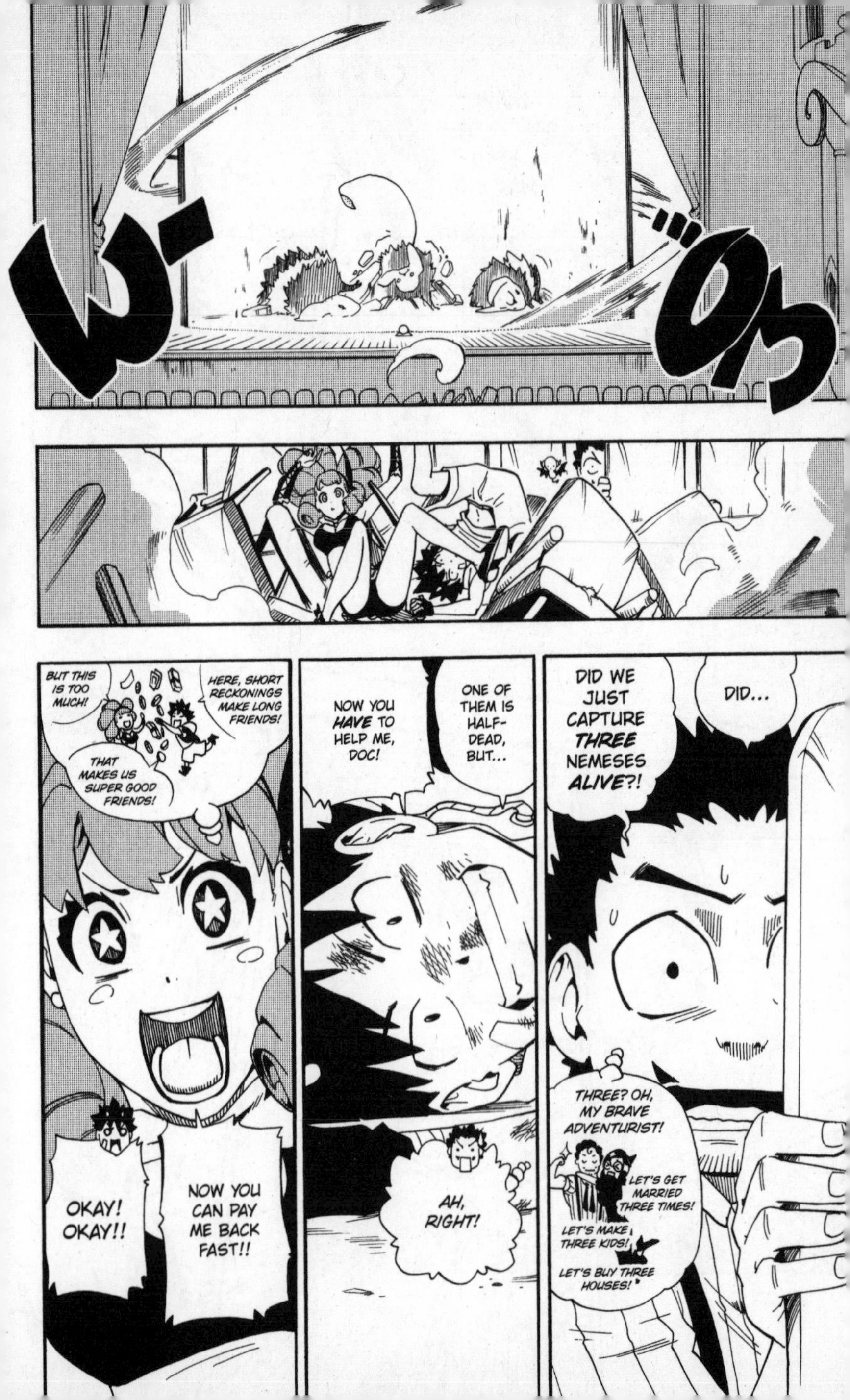
DID...
DID WE JUST CAPTURE THREE NEMESES ALIVE?!
THREE? OH, MY BRAVE ADVENTURIST!
LET'S GET MARRIED THREE TIMES!
LET'S MAKE THREE KIDS!
LET'S BUY THREE HOUSES!
ONE OF THEM IS HALF-DEAD, BUT...
NOW YOU HAVE TO HELP ME, DOC!
AH, RIGHT!
HERE, SHORT RECKONINGS MAKE LONG FRIENDS!
BUT THIS IS TOO MUCH!
THAT MAKES US SUPER GOOD FRIENDS!
NOW YOU CAN PAY ME BACK FAST!!
OKAY! OKAY!!

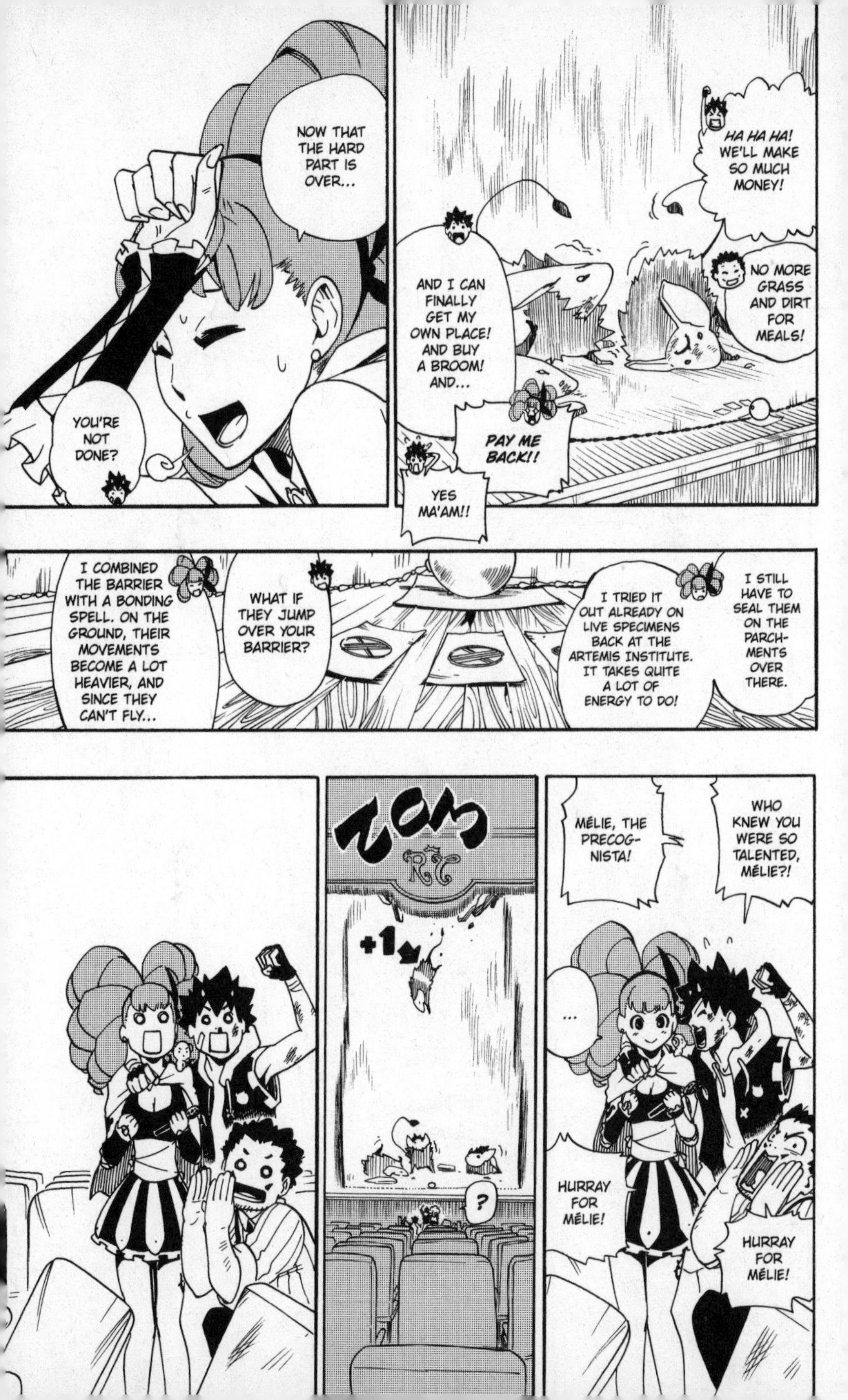
HA HA HA! WE'LL MAKE SO MUCH MONEY!
NO MORE GRASS AND DIRT FOR MEALS!
AND I CAN FINALLY GET MY OWN PLACE! AND BUY A BROOM! AND...
PAY ME BACK!!
YES MA'AM!!
NOW THAT THE HARD PART IS OVER...
YOU'RE NOT DONE?
I STILL HAVE TO SEAL THEM ON THE PARCHMENTS OVER THERE.
I TRIED IT OUT ALREADY ON LIVE SPECIMENS BACK AT THE ARTEMIS INSTITUTE. IT TAKES QUITE A LOT OF ENERGY TO DO!
WHAT IF THEY JUMP OVER YOUR BARRIER?
I COMBINED THE BARRIER WITH A BONDING SPELL. ON THE GROUND, THEIR MOVEMENTS BECOME A LOT HEAVIER, AND SINCE THEY CAN'T FLY...
WHO KNEW YOU WERE SO TALENTED, MÉLIE?!
MÉLIE, THE PRECOG-NISTA!
...
HURRAY FOR MÉLIE!
HURRAY FOR MÉLIE!
ZOM
+1
?

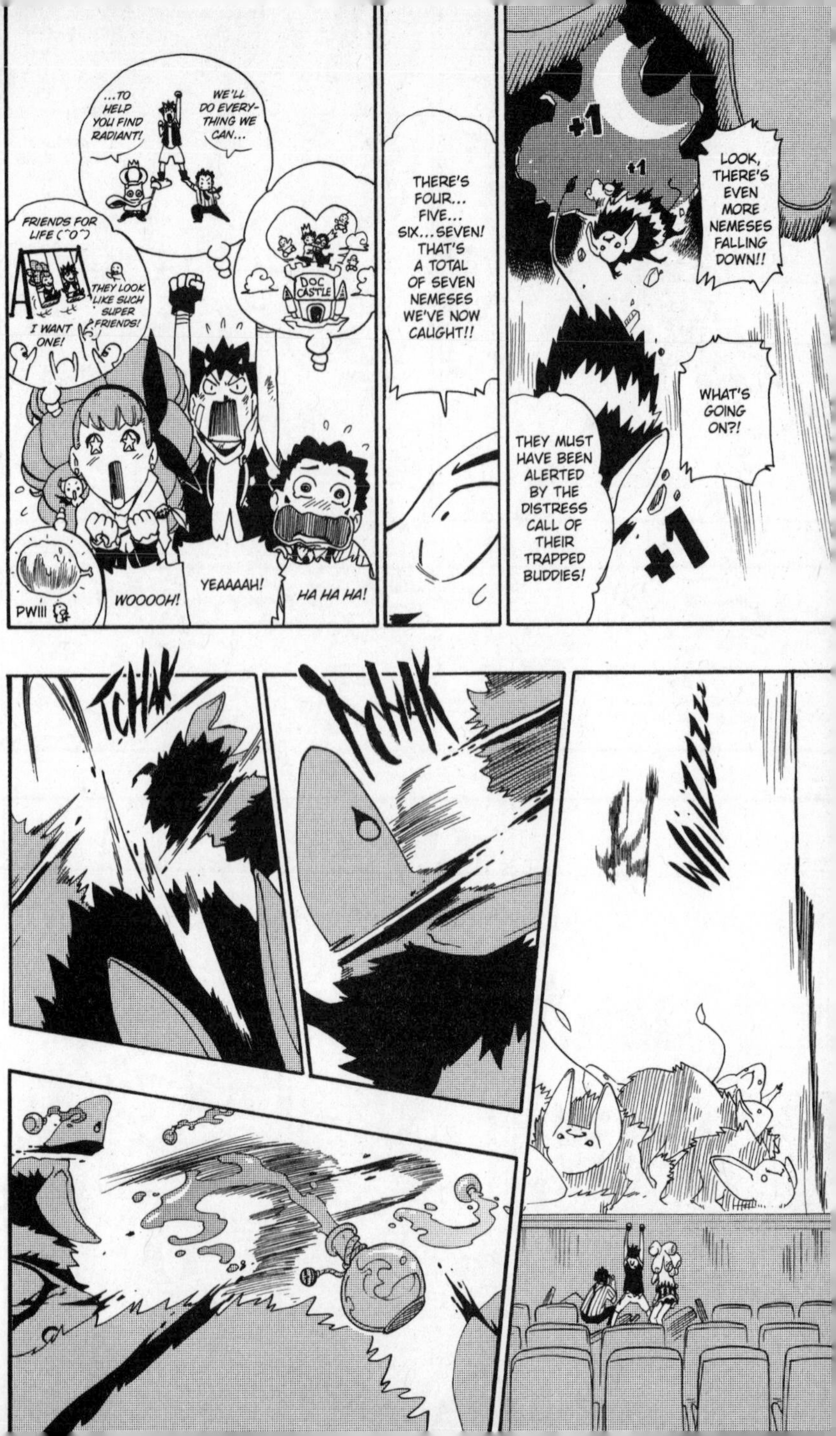

LOOK, THERE'S EVEN MORE NEMESES FALLING DOWN!!
+1
+1
WHAT'S GOING ON?!
THEY MUST HAVE BEEN ALERTED BY THE DISTRESS CALL OF THEIR TRAPPED BUDDIES!
+1
THERE'S FOUR... FIVE... SIX... SEVEN! THAT'S A TOTAL OF SEVEN NEMESES WE'VE NOW CAUGHT!!
WE'LL DO EVERY-THING WE CAN...
...TO HELP YOU FIND RADIANT!
DOC CASTLE
FRIENDS FOR LIFE (^O^)
THEY LOOK LIKE SUCH SUPER FRIENDS!
I WANT ONE!
HA HA HA!
YEAAAAH!
WOOOOH!
PWIII
WHIZZZ
TCHAK
TCHAK

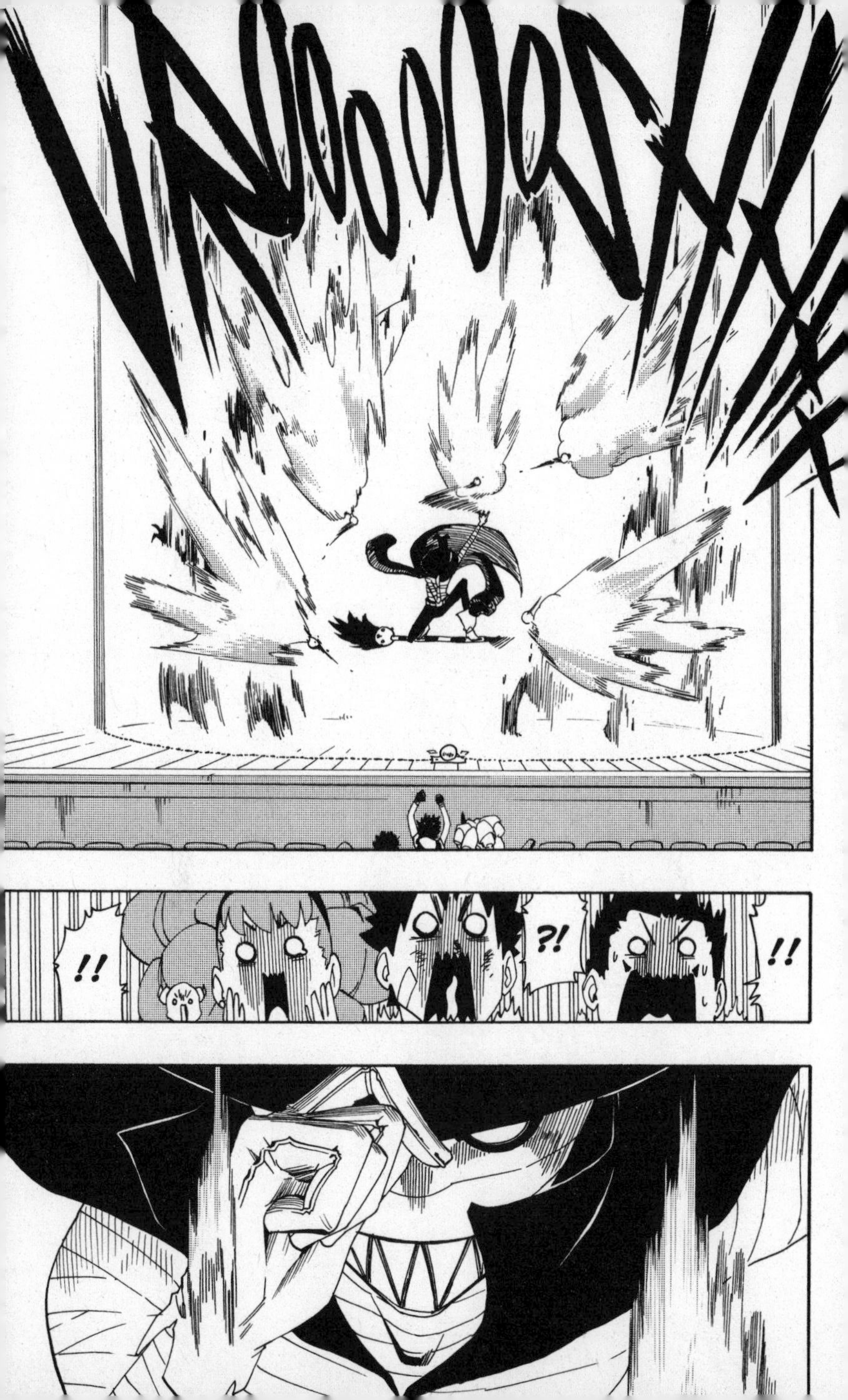
!!
?!
!!

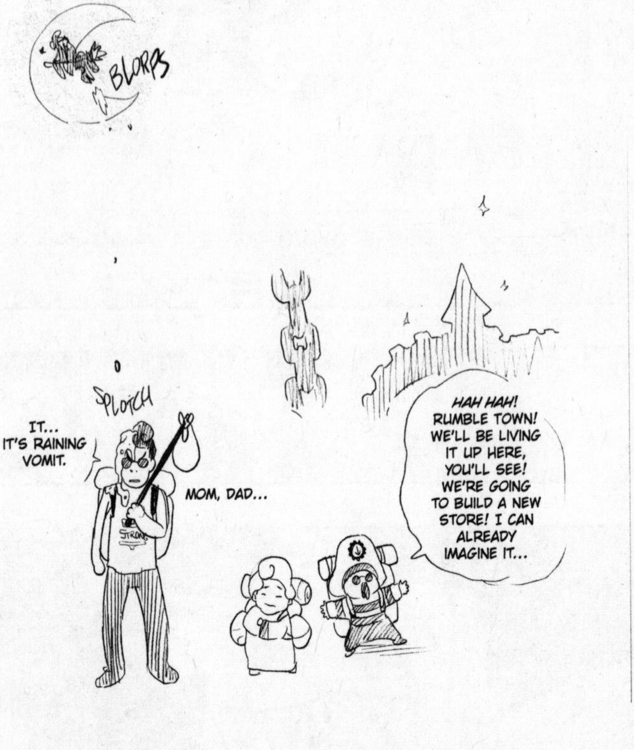
BLORPS
HAH HAH! RUMBLE TOWN! WE'LL BE LIVING IT UP HERE, YOU'LL SEE! WE'RE GOING TO BUILD A NEW STORE! I CAN ALREADY IMAGINE IT...
MOM, DAD...
SPLOTCH
IT... IT'S RAINING VOMIT.
STRONG

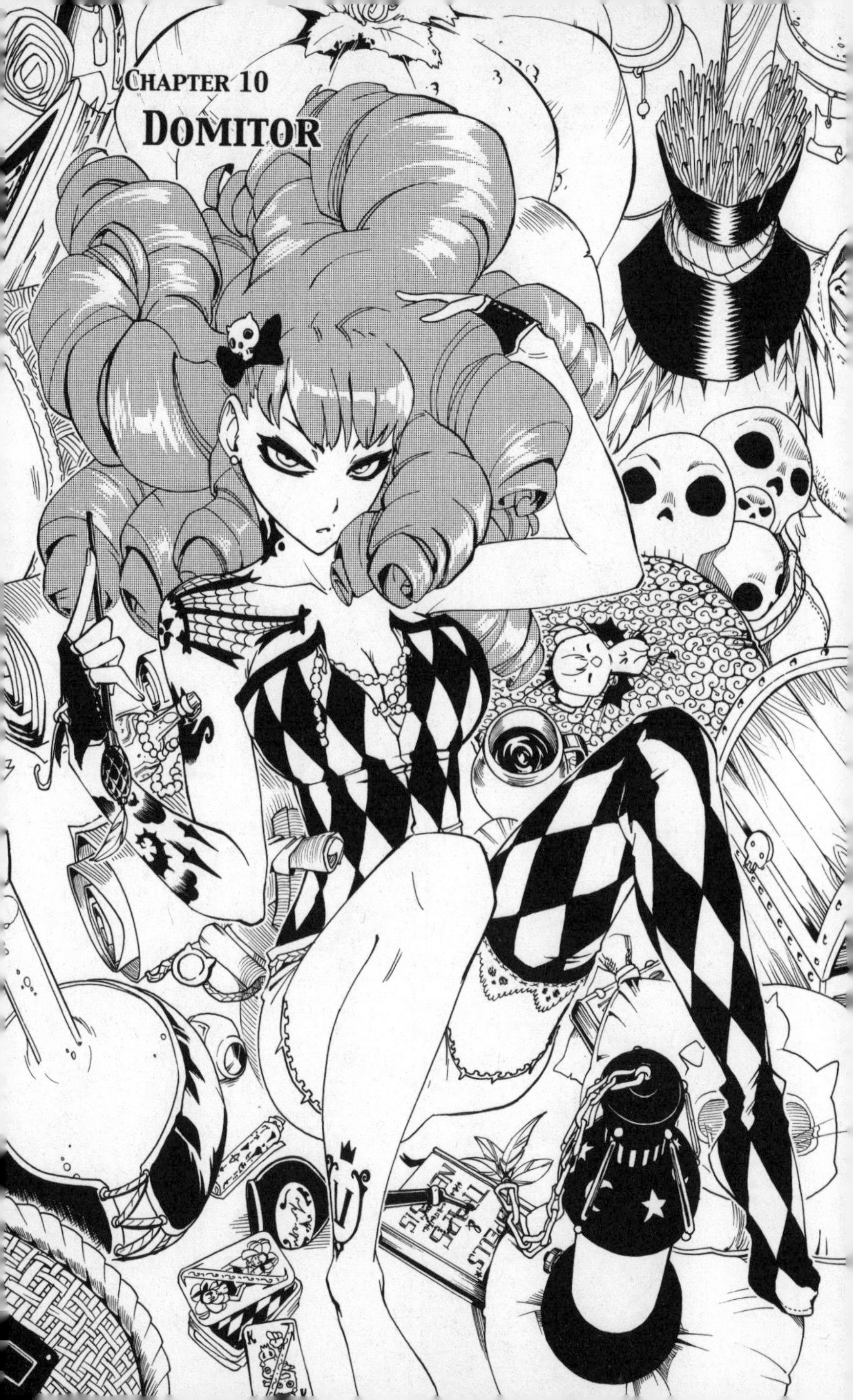
Chapter 10
Domitor

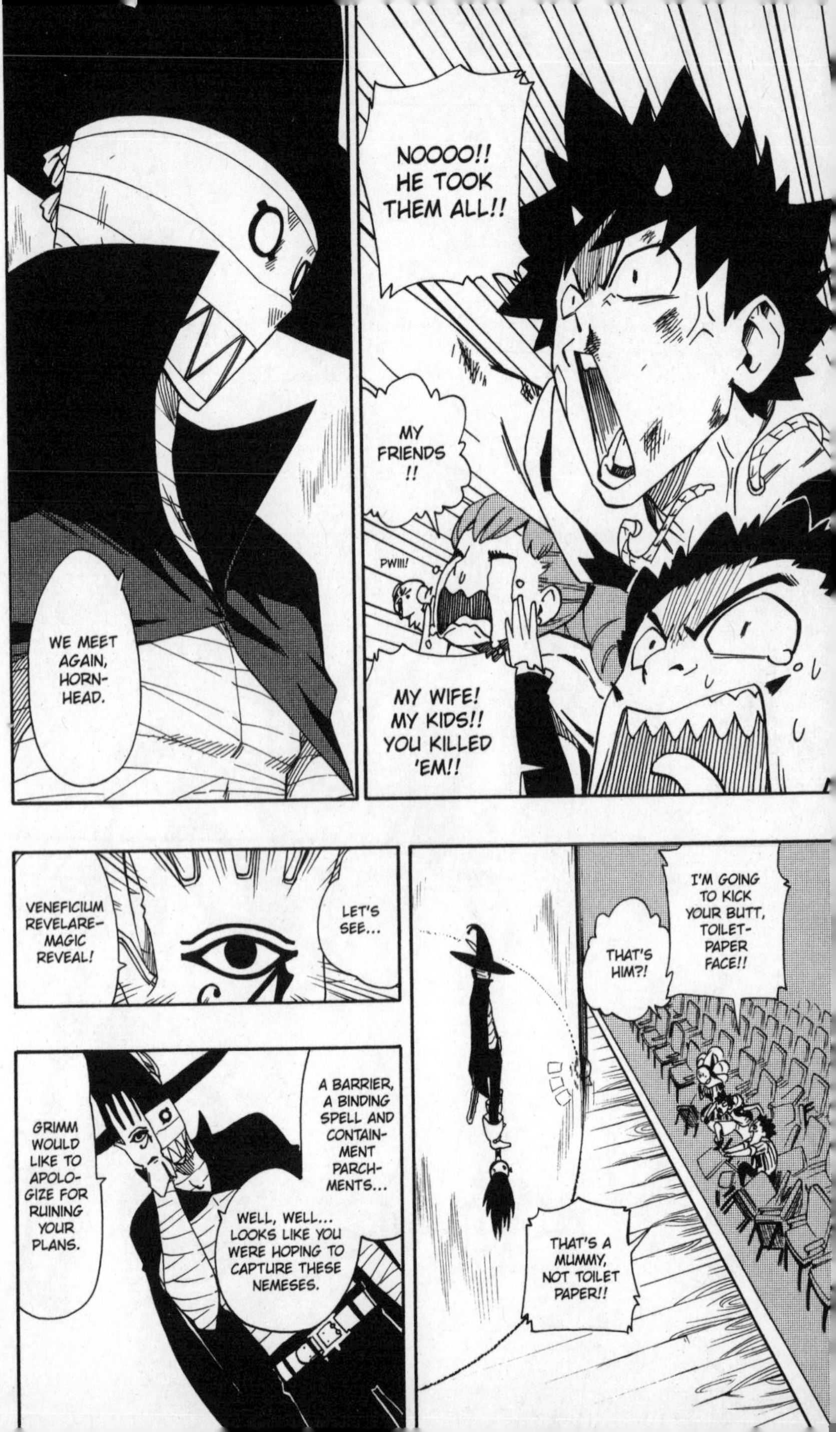
NOOOO!! HE TOOK THEM ALL!!
MY FRIENDS !!
PWIII!
MY WIFE! MY KIDS!! YOU KILLED 'EM!!
WE MEET AGAIN, HORN-HEAD.
I'M GOING TO KICK YOUR BUTT, TOILET-PAPER FACE!!
THAT'S HIM?!
THAT'S A MUMMY, NOT TOILET PAPER!!
LET'S SEE...
VENEFICIUM REVELARE-MAGIC REVEAL!
A BARRIER, A BINDING SPELL AND CONTAIN-MENT PARCH-MENTS...
WELL, WELL... LOOKS LIKE YOU WERE HOPING TO CAPTURE THESE NEMESES.
GRIMM WOULD LIKE TO APOLO-GIZE FOR RUINING YOUR PLANS.

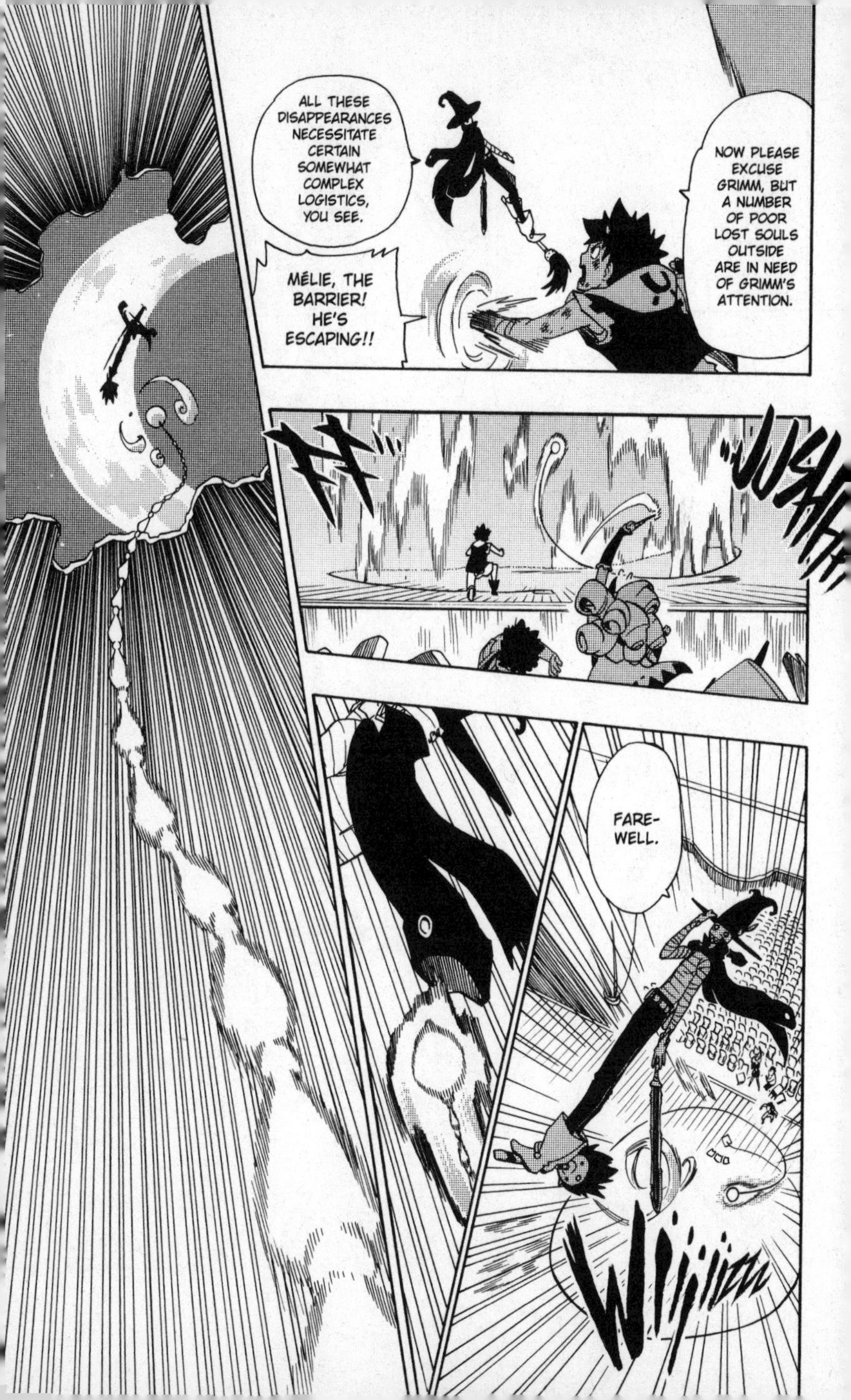
NOW PLEASE EXCUSE GRIMM, BUT A NUMBER OF POOR LOST SOULS OUTSIDE ARE IN NEED OF GRIMM'S ATTENTION.
ALL THESE DISAPPEARANCES NECESSITATE CERTAIN SOMEWHAT COMPLEX LOGISTICS, YOU SEE.
MÉLIE, THE BARRIER! HE'S ESCAPING!!
FARE-WELL.

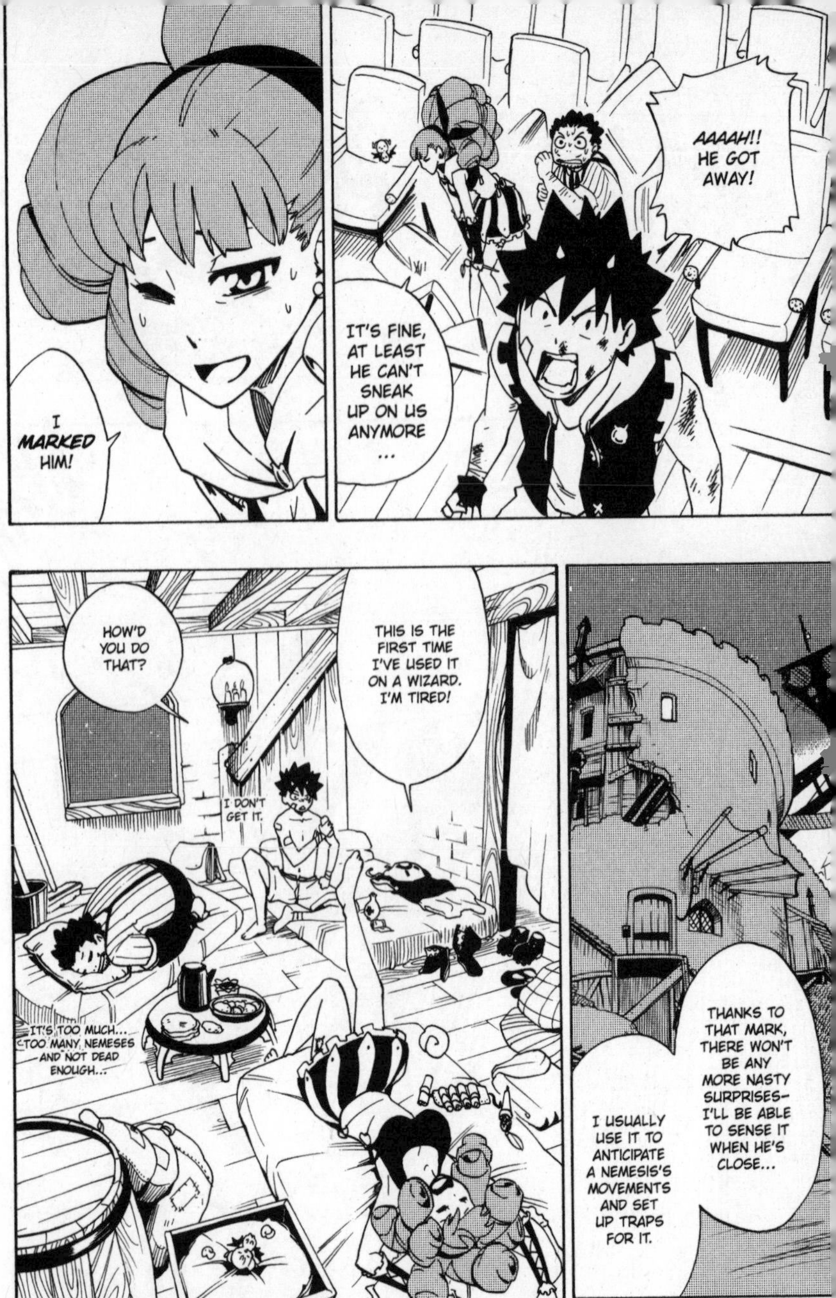
AAAAH!! HE GOT AWAY!
IT'S FINE, AT LEAST HE CAN'T SNEAK UP ON US ANYMORE...
I MARKED HIM!
THANKS TO THAT MARK, THERE WON'T BE ANY MORE NASTY SURPRISES— I'LL BE ABLE TO SENSE IT WHEN HE'S CLOSE...
I USUALLY USE IT TO ANTICIPATE A NEMESIS'S MOVEMENTS AND SET UP TRAPS FOR IT.
THIS IS THE FIRST TIME I'VE USED IT ON A WIZARD. I'M TIRED!
HOW'D YOU DO THAT?
I DON'T GET IT.
IT'S TOO MUCH... TOO MANY NEMESES AND NOT DEAD ENOUGH...

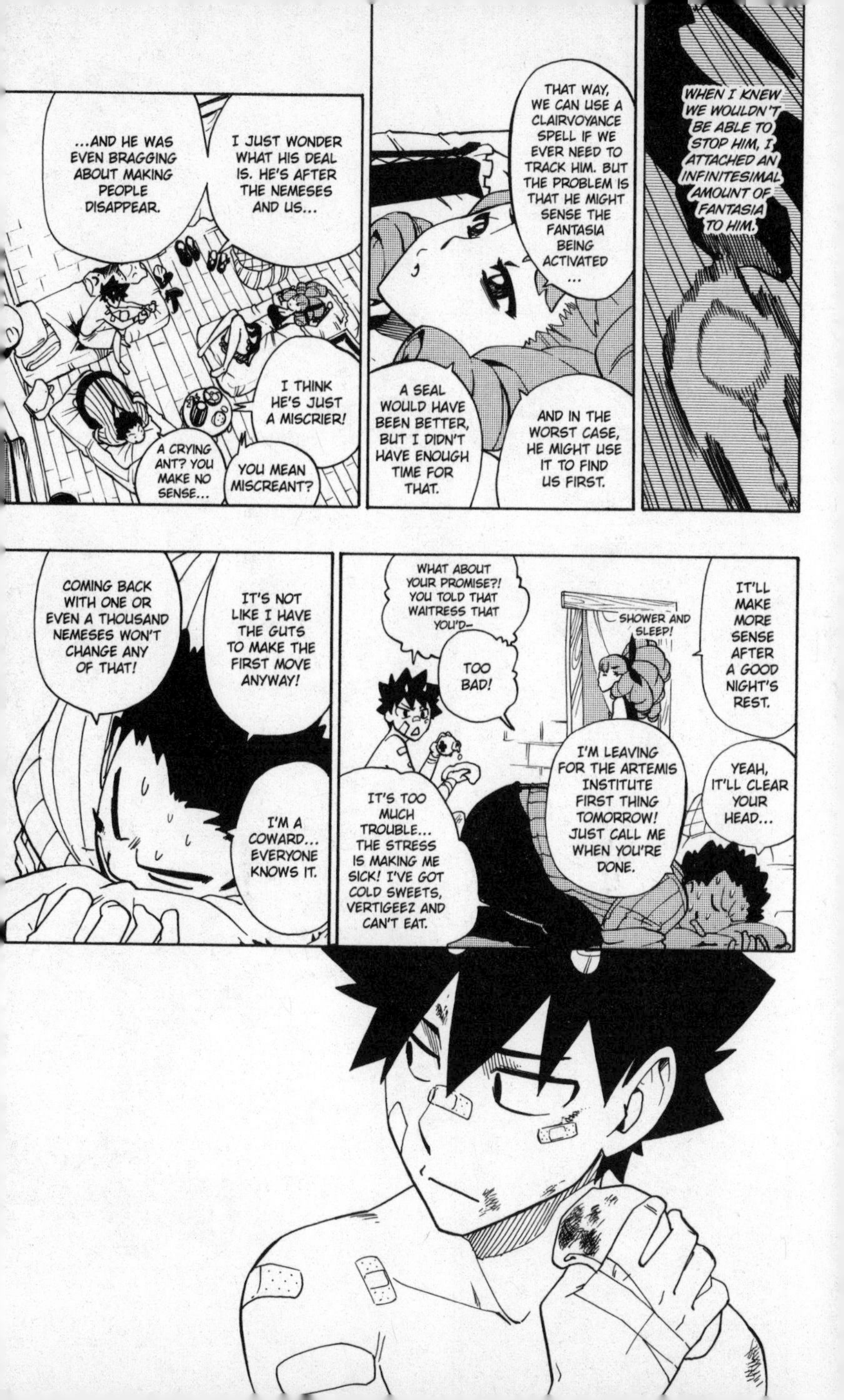
WHEN I KNEW WE WOULDN'T BE ABLE TO STOP HIM, I ATTACHED AN INFINITESIMAL AMOUNT OF FANTASIA TO HIM.
THAT WAY, WE CAN USE A CLAIRVOYANCE SPELL IF WE EVER NEED TO TRACK HIM. BUT THE PROBLEM IS THAT HE MIGHT SENSE THE FANTASIA BEING ACTIVATED ...
AND IN THE WORST CASE, HE MIGHT USE IT TO FIND US FIRST.
A SEAL WOULD HAVE BEEN BETTER, BUT I DIDN'T HAVE ENOUGH TIME FOR THAT.
I JUST WONDER WHAT HIS DEAL IS. HE'S AFTER THE NEMESES AND US...
...AND HE WAS EVEN BRAGGING ABOUT MAKING PEOPLE DISAPPEAR.
I THINK HE'S JUST A MISCRIER!
YOU MEAN MISCREANT?
A CRYING ANT? YOU MAKE NO SENSE...
IT'LL MAKE MORE SENSE AFTER A GOOD NIGHT'S REST.
SHOWER AND SLEEP!
WHAT ABOUT YOUR PROMISE?! YOU TOLD THAT WAITRESS THAT YOU'D—
TOO BAD!
YEAH, IT'LL CLEAR YOUR HEAD...
I'M LEAVING FOR THE ARTEMIS INSTITUTE FIRST THING TOMORROW! JUST CALL ME WHEN YOU'RE DONE.
IT'S TOO MUCH TROUBLE... THE STRESS IS MAKING ME SICK! I'VE GOT COLD SWEETS, VERTIGEEZ AND CAN'T EAT.
IT'S NOT LIKE I HAVE THE GUTS TO MAKE THE FIRST MOVE ANYWAY!
COMING BACK WITH ONE OR EVEN A THOUSAND NEMESES WON'T CHANGE ANY OF THAT!
I'M A COWARD... EVERYONE KNOWS IT.

I DO HOPE YOU'LL EXCUSE GRIMM FOR THIS SLIGHTLY UNCOMFORT-ABLE MODE OF TRANSPOR-TATION.

GNNN!

GNN!

BUT REST ASSURED, THIS IS WHERE THIS TRIP ENDS FOR YOU.

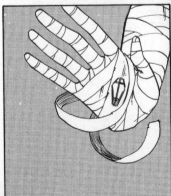

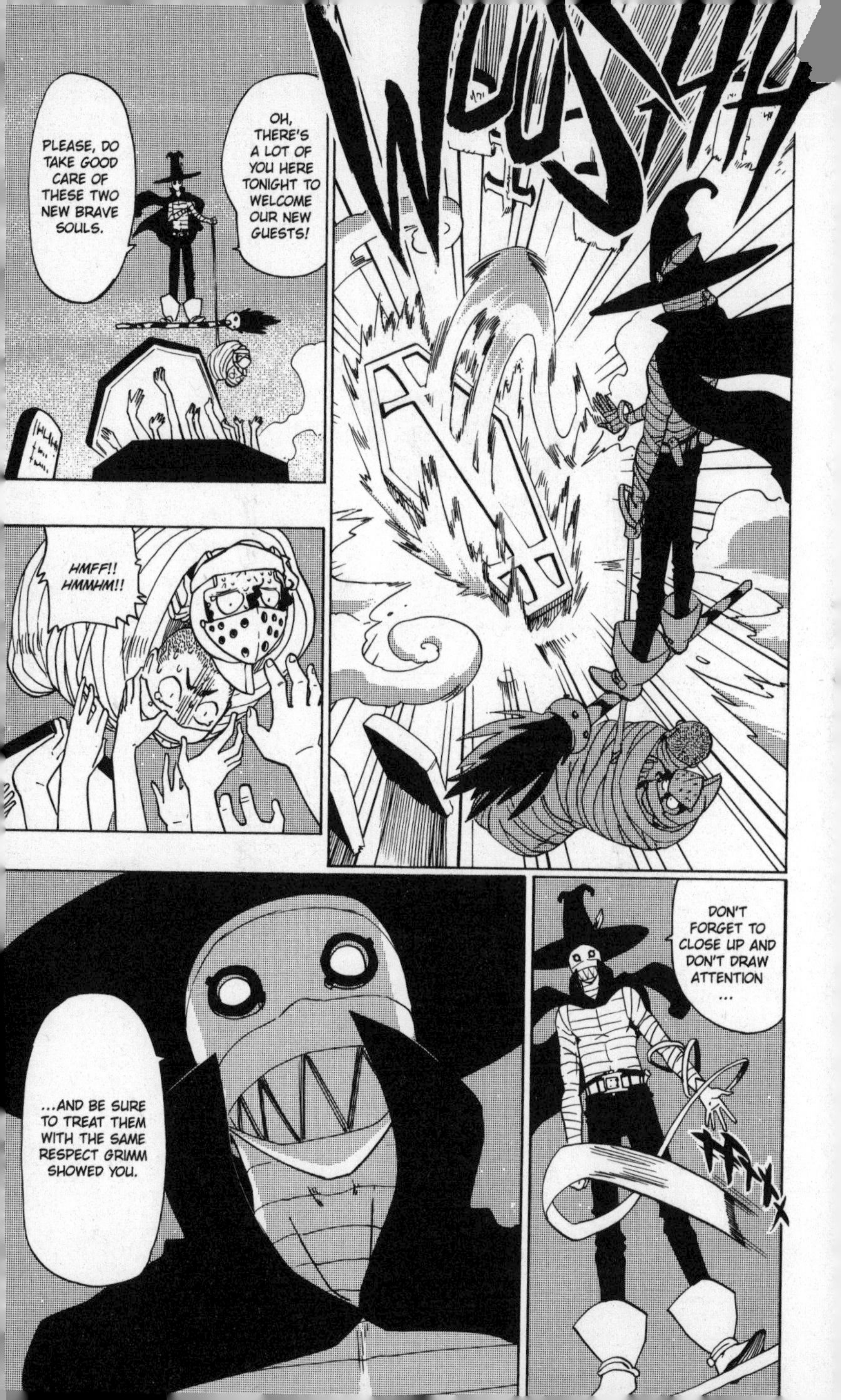
OH, THERE'S A LOT OF YOU HERE TONIGHT TO WELCOME OUR NEW GUESTS!
PLEASE, DO TAKE GOOD CARE OF THESE TWO NEW BRAVE SOULS.
HMFF!! HMMHM!!
DON'T FORGET TO CLOSE UP AND DON'T DRAW ATTENTION ...
...AND BE SURE TO TREAT THEM WITH THE SAME RESPECT GRIMM SHOWED YOU.

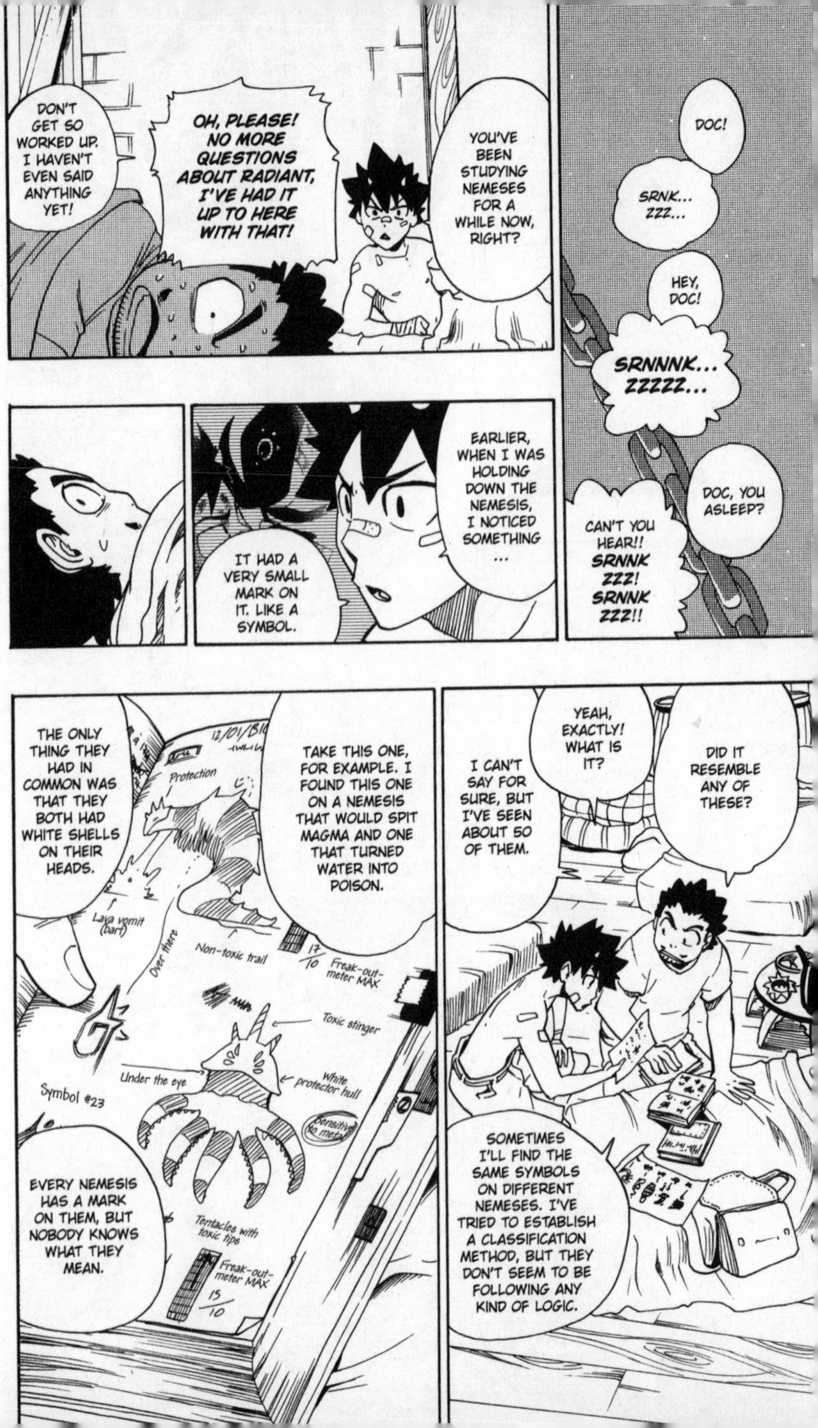
DOC!
SRNK... ZZZ...
HEY, DOC!
SRNNNK... ZZZZZ...
DOC, YOU ASLEEP?
CAN'T YOU HEAR!! SRNNK ZZZ! SRNNK ZZZ!!
YOU'VE BEEN STUDYING NEMESES FOR A WHILE NOW, RIGHT?
OH, PLEASE! NO MORE QUESTIONS ABOUT RADIANT, I'VE HAD IT UP TO HERE WITH THAT!
DON'T GET SO WORKED UP. I HAVEN'T EVEN SAID ANYTHING YET!
EARLIER, WHEN I WAS HOLDING DOWN THE NEMESIS, I NOTICED SOMETHING...
IT HAD A VERY SMALL MARK ON IT. LIKE A SYMBOL.
DID IT RESEMBLE ANY OF THESE?
YEAH, EXACTLY! WHAT IS IT?
I CAN'T SAY FOR SURE, BUT I'VE SEEN ABOUT 50 OF THEM.
SOMETIMES I'LL FIND THE SAME SYMBOLS ON DIFFERENT NEMESES. I'VE TRIED TO ESTABLISH A CLASSIFICATION METHOD, BUT THEY DON'T SEEM TO BE FOLLOWING ANY KIND OF LOGIC.
TAKE THIS ONE, FOR EXAMPLE. I FOUND THIS ONE ON A NEMESIS THAT WOULD SPIT MAGMA AND ONE THAT TURNED WATER INTO POISON.
THE ONLY THING THEY HAD IN COMMON WAS THAT THEY BOTH HAD WHITE SHELLS ON THEIR HEADS.
Protection
Lava vomit (barf)
Over there
Non-toxic trail
17/10
Freak-out-meter MAX
Toxic stinger
Under the eye
white protector hull
Symbol #23
Sensitive to metal
Tentacles with toxic tips
Freak-out-meter MAX
15/10
EVERY NEMESIS HAS A MARK ON THEM, BUT NOBODY KNOWS WHAT THEY MEAN.

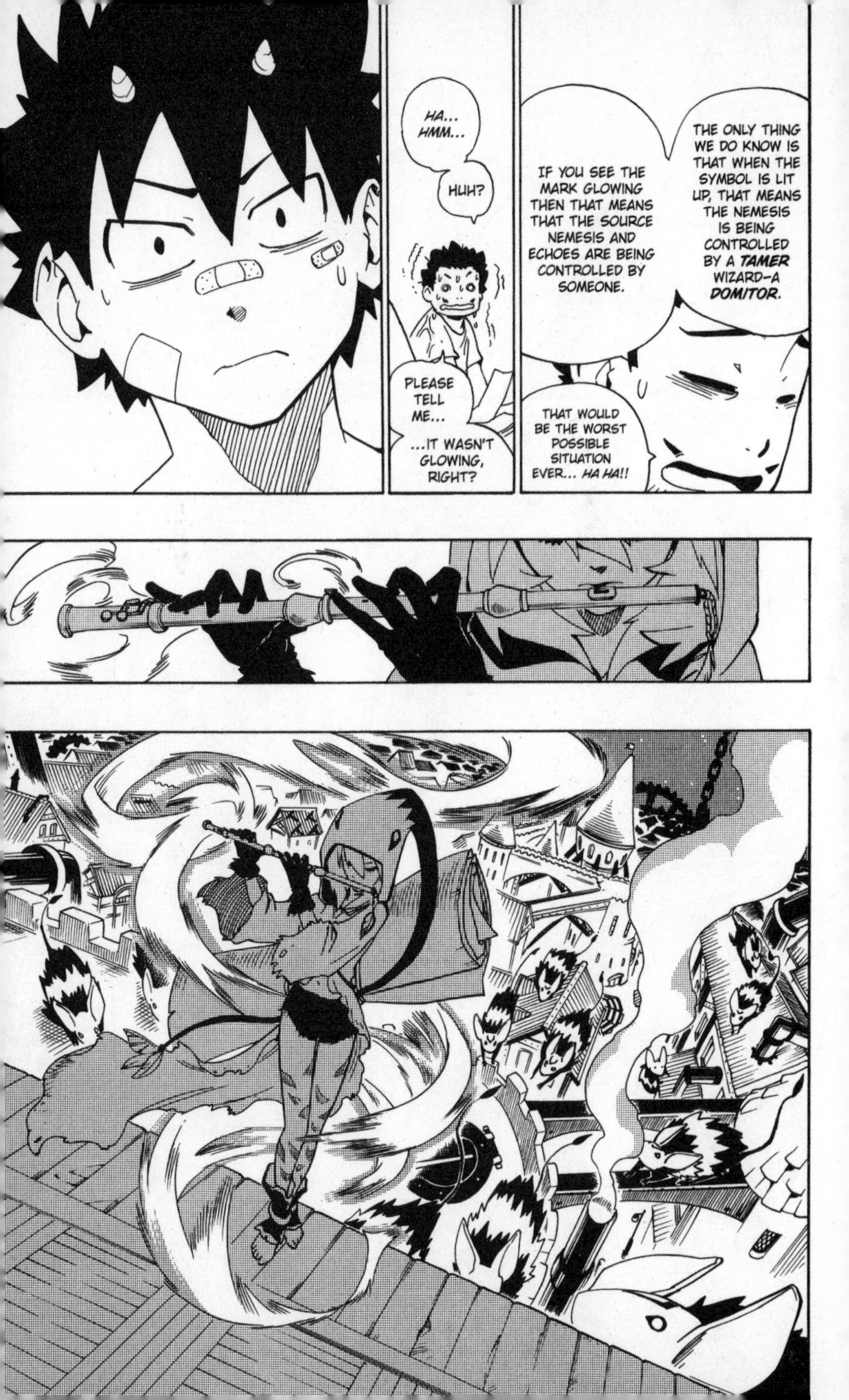
THE ONLY THING WE DO KNOW IS THAT WHEN THE SYMBOL IS LIT UP, THAT MEANS THE NEMESIS IS BEING CONTROLLED BY A ***TAMER*** WIZARD—A ***DOMITOR***.
IF YOU SEE THE MARK GLOWING THEN THAT MEANS THAT THE SOURCE NEMESIS AND ECHOES ARE BEING CONTROLLED BY SOMEONE.
THAT WOULD BE THE WORST POSSIBLE SITUATION EVER... *HA HA!!*
HA... HMM...
HUH?
PLEASE TELL ME...
...IT WASN'T GLOWING, RIGHT?

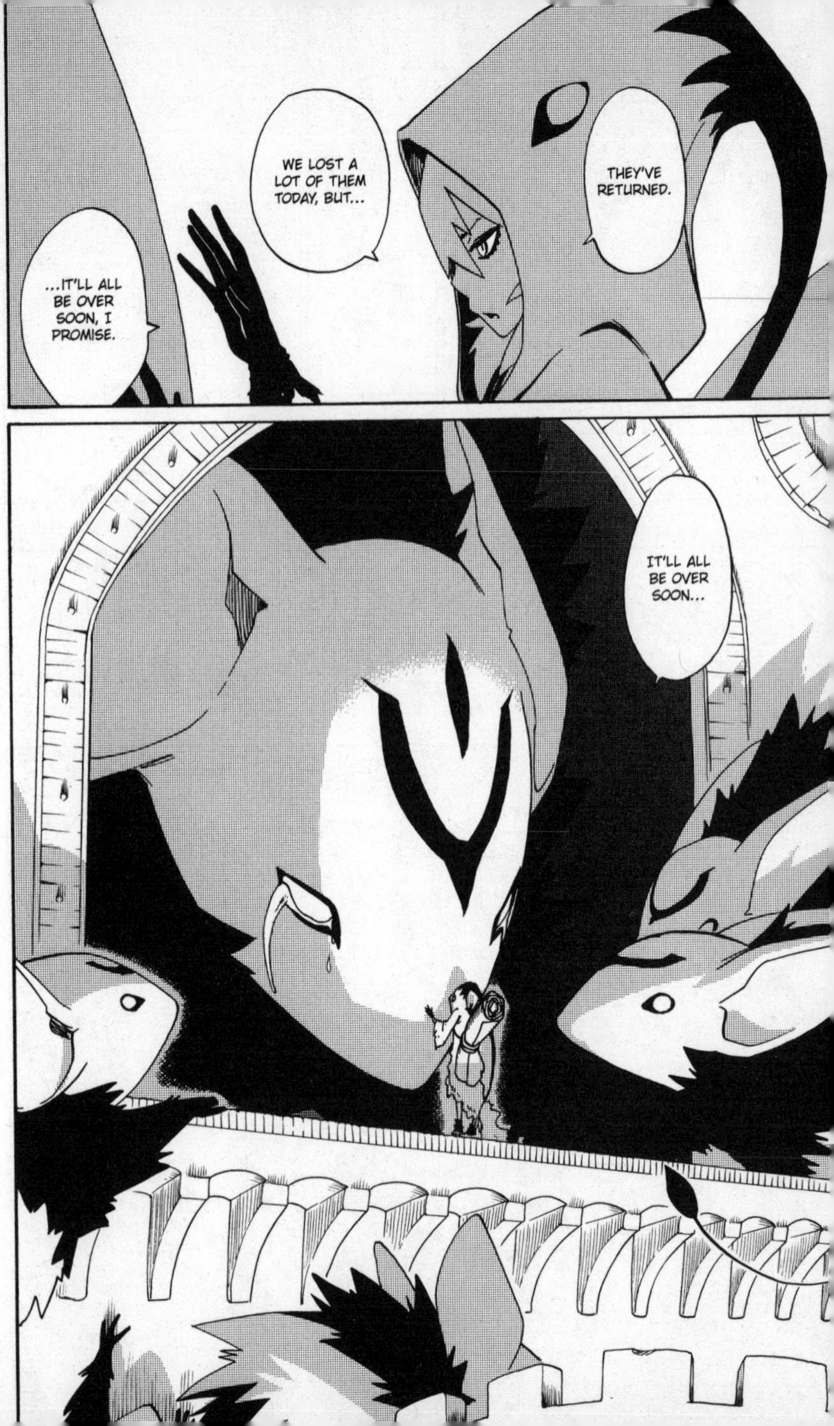
THEY'VE RETURNED.
WE LOST A LOT OF THEM TODAY, BUT...
...IT'LL ALL BE OVER SOON, I PROMISE.
IT'LL ALL BE OVER SOON...

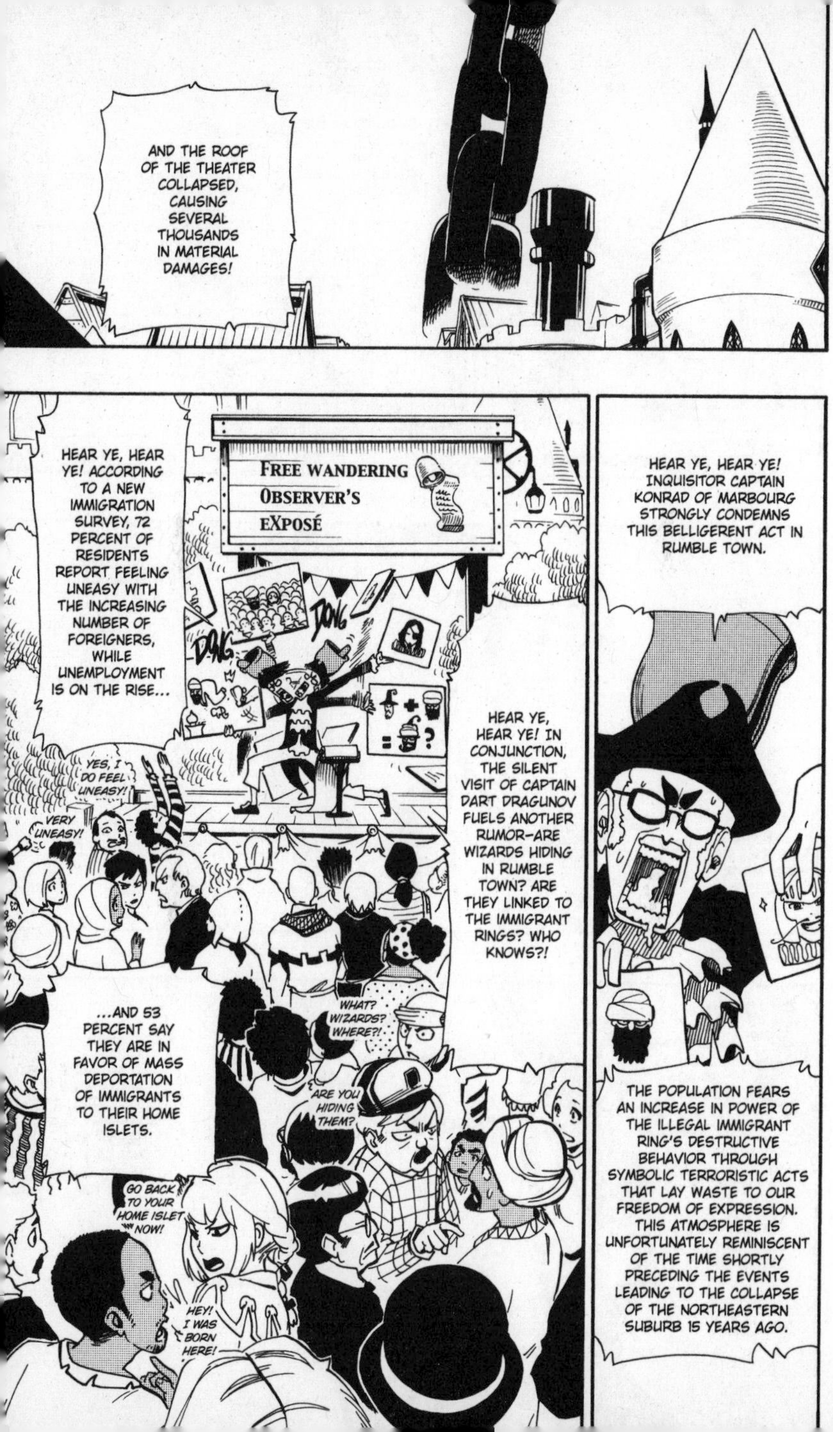
AND THE ROOF OF THE THEATER COLLAPSED, CAUSING SEVERAL THOUSANDS IN MATERIAL DAMAGES!
HEAR YE, HEAR YE! INQUISITOR CAPTAIN KONRAD OF MARBOURG STRONGLY CONDEMNS THIS BELLIGERENT ACT IN RUMBLE TOWN.
THE POPULATION FEARS AN INCREASE IN POWER OF THE ILLEGAL IMMIGRANT RING'S DESTRUCTIVE BEHAVIOR THROUGH SYMBOLIC TERRORISTIC ACTS THAT LAY WASTE TO OUR FREEDOM OF EXPRESSION. THIS ATMOSPHERE IS UNFORTUNATELY REMINISCENT OF THE TIME SHORTLY PRECEDING THE EVENTS LEADING TO THE COLLAPSE OF THE NORTHEASTERN SUBURB 15 YEARS AGO.
FREE WANDERING OBSERVER'S eXPOSÉ
HEAR YE, HEAR YE! ACCORDING TO A NEW IMMIGRATION SURVEY, 72 PERCENT OF RESIDENTS REPORT FEELING UNEASY WITH THE INCREASING NUMBER OF FOREIGNERS, WHILE UNEMPLOYMENT IS ON THE RISE...
DONG
DONG
HEAR YE, HEAR YE! IN CONJUNCTION, THE SILENT VISIT OF CAPTAIN DART DRAGUNOV FUELS ANOTHER RUMOR—ARE WIZARDS HIDING IN RUMBLE TOWN? ARE THEY LINKED TO THE IMMIGRANT RINGS? WHO KNOWS?!
YES, I DO FEEL UNEASY!
VERY UNEASY!
...AND 53 PERCENT SAY THEY ARE IN FAVOR OF MASS DEPORTATION OF IMMIGRANTS TO THEIR HOME ISLETS.
WHAT? WIZARDS? WHERE?!
ARE YOU HIDING THEM?
GO BACK TO YOUR HOME ISLET NOW!
HEY! I WAS BORN HERE!

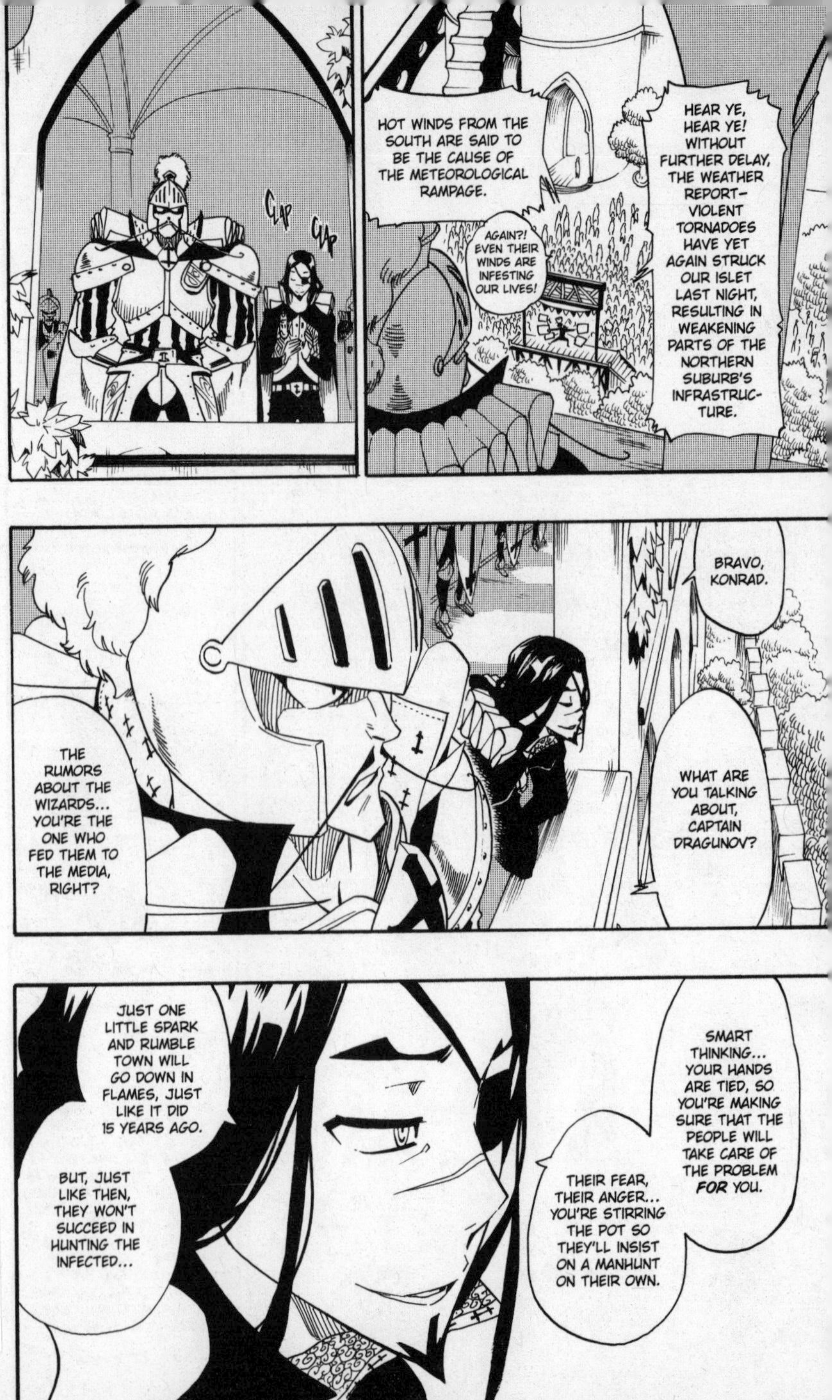
HEAR YE, HEAR YE! WITHOUT FURTHER DELAY, THE WEATHER REPORT— VIOLENT TORNADOES HAVE YET AGAIN STRUCK OUR ISLET LAST NIGHT, RESULTING IN WEAKENING PARTS OF THE NORTHERN SUBURB'S INFRASTRUC-TURE.
HOT WINDS FROM THE SOUTH ARE SAID TO BE THE CAUSE OF THE METEOROLOGICAL RAMPAGE.
AGAIN?! EVEN THEIR WINDS ARE INFESTING OUR LIVES!
CLAP
CLAP
BRAVO, KONRAD.
THE RUMORS ABOUT THE WIZARDS... YOU'RE THE ONE WHO FED THEM TO THE MEDIA, RIGHT?
WHAT ARE YOU TALKING ABOUT, CAPTAIN DRAGUNOV?
SMART THINKING... YOUR HANDS ARE TIED, SO YOU'RE MAKING SURE THAT THE PEOPLE WILL TAKE CARE OF THE PROBLEM FOR YOU.
THEIR FEAR, THEIR ANGER... YOU'RE STIRRING THE POT SO THEY'LL INSIST ON A MANHUNT ON THEIR OWN.
JUST ONE LITTLE SPARK AND RUMBLE TOWN WILL GO DOWN IN FLAMES, JUST LIKE IT DID 15 YEARS AGO.
BUT, JUST LIKE THEN, THEY WON'T SUCCEED IN HUNTING THE INFECTED...

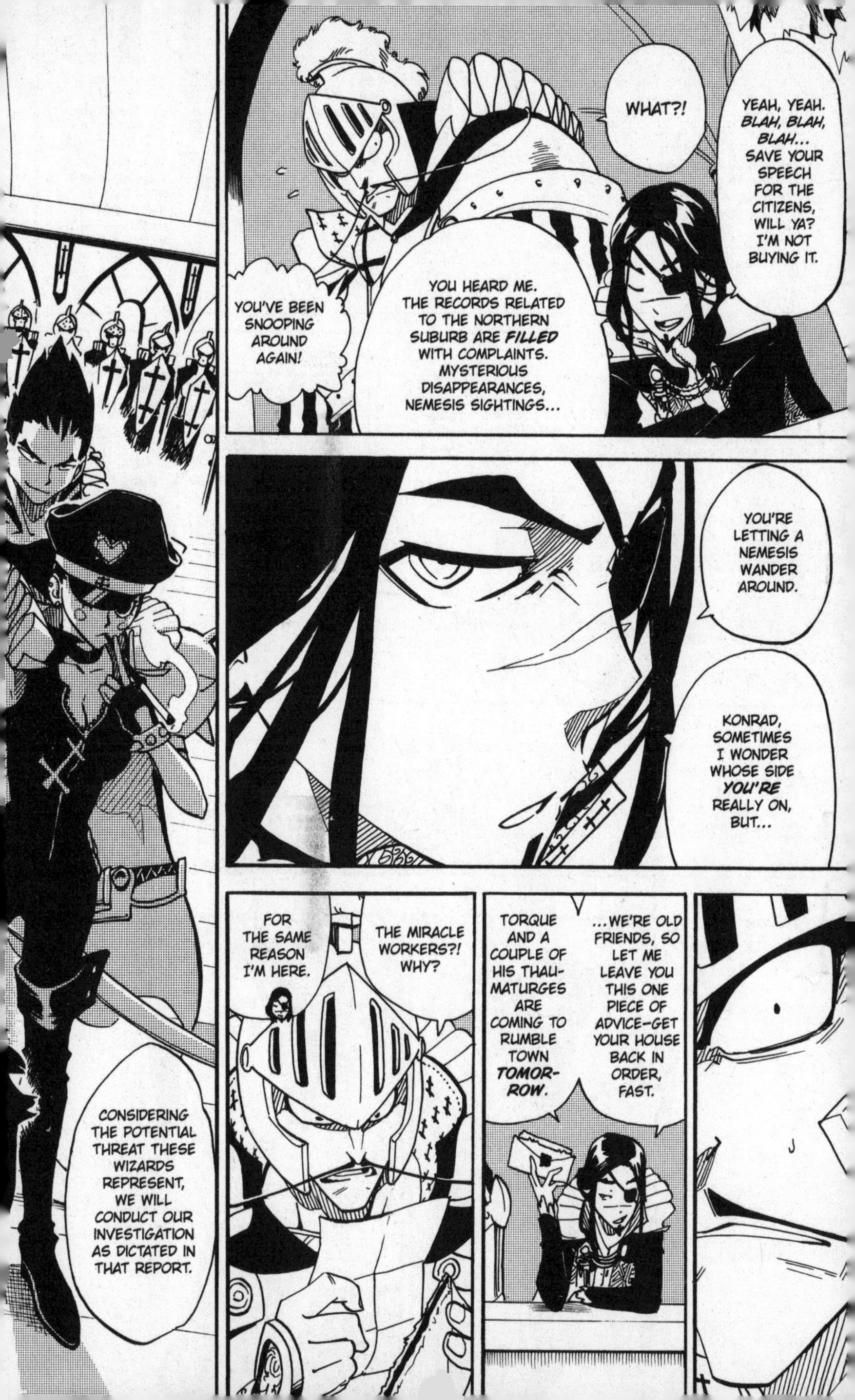
YEAH, YEAH. *BLAH, BLAH, BLAH...* SAVE YOUR SPEECH FOR THE CITIZENS, WILL YA? I'M NOT BUYING IT.
WHAT?!
YOU HEARD ME. THE RECORDS RELATED TO THE NORTHERN SUBURB ARE *FILLED* WITH COMPLAINTS. MYSTERIOUS DISAPPEARANCES, NEMESIS SIGHTINGS...
YOU'VE BEEN SNOOPING AROUND AGAIN!
YOU'RE LETTING A NEMESIS WANDER AROUND.
KONRAD, SOMETIMES I WONDER WHOSE SIDE *YOU'RE* REALLY ON, BUT...
...WE'RE OLD FRIENDS, SO LET ME LEAVE YOU THIS ONE PIECE OF ADVICE–GET YOUR HOUSE BACK IN ORDER, FAST.
TORQUE AND A COUPLE OF HIS THAUMATURGES ARE COMING TO RUMBLE TOWN *TOMORROW*.
THE MIRACLE WORKERS?! WHY?
FOR THE SAME REASON I'M HERE.
CONSIDERING THE POTENTIAL THREAT THESE WIZARDS REPRESENT, WE WILL CONDUCT OUR INVESTIGATION AS DICTATED IN THAT REPORT.

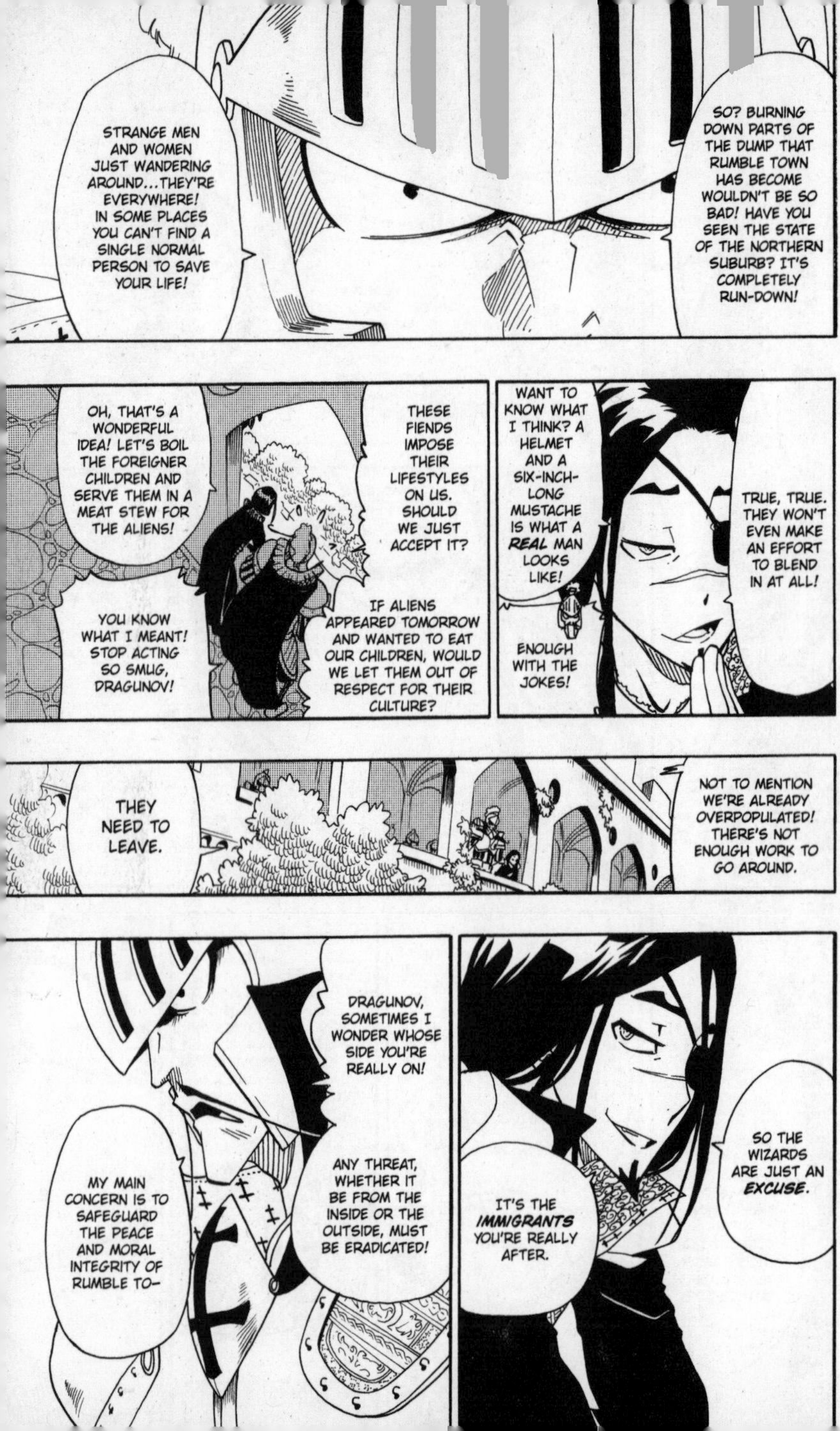
SO? BURNING DOWN PARTS OF THE DUMP THAT RUMBLE TOWN HAS BECOME WOULDN'T BE SO BAD! HAVE YOU SEEN THE STATE OF THE NORTHERN SUBURB? IT'S COMPLETELY RUN-DOWN!
STRANGE MEN AND WOMEN JUST WANDERING AROUND...THEY'RE EVERYWHERE! IN SOME PLACES YOU CAN'T FIND A SINGLE NORMAL PERSON TO SAVE YOUR LIFE!
TRUE, TRUE. THEY WON'T EVEN MAKE AN EFFORT TO BLEND IN AT ALL!
WANT TO KNOW WHAT I THINK? A HELMET AND A SIX-INCH-LONG MUSTACHE IS WHAT A *REAL* MAN LOOKS LIKE!
ENOUGH WITH THE JOKES!
THESE FIENDS IMPOSE THEIR LIFESTYLES ON US. SHOULD WE JUST ACCEPT IT?
IF ALIENS APPEARED TOMORROW AND WANTED TO EAT OUR CHILDREN, WOULD WE LET THEM OUT OF RESPECT FOR THEIR CULTURE?
OH, THAT'S A WONDERFUL IDEA! LET'S BOIL THE FOREIGNER CHILDREN AND SERVE THEM IN A MEAT STEW FOR THE ALIENS!
YOU KNOW WHAT I MEANT! STOP ACTING SO SMUG, DRAGUNOV!
NOT TO MENTION WE'RE ALREADY OVERPOPULATED! THERE'S NOT ENOUGH WORK TO GO AROUND.
THEY NEED TO LEAVE.
SO THE WIZARDS ARE JUST AN ***EXCUSE***.
IT'S THE ***IMMIGRANTS*** YOU'RE REALLY AFTER.
DRAGUNOV, SOMETIMES I WONDER WHOSE SIDE YOU'RE REALLY ON!
ANY THREAT, WHETHER IT BE FROM THE INSIDE OR THE OUTSIDE, MUST BE ERADICATED!
MY MAIN CONCERN IS TO SAFEGUARD THE PEACE AND MORAL INTEGRITY OF RUMBLE TO-

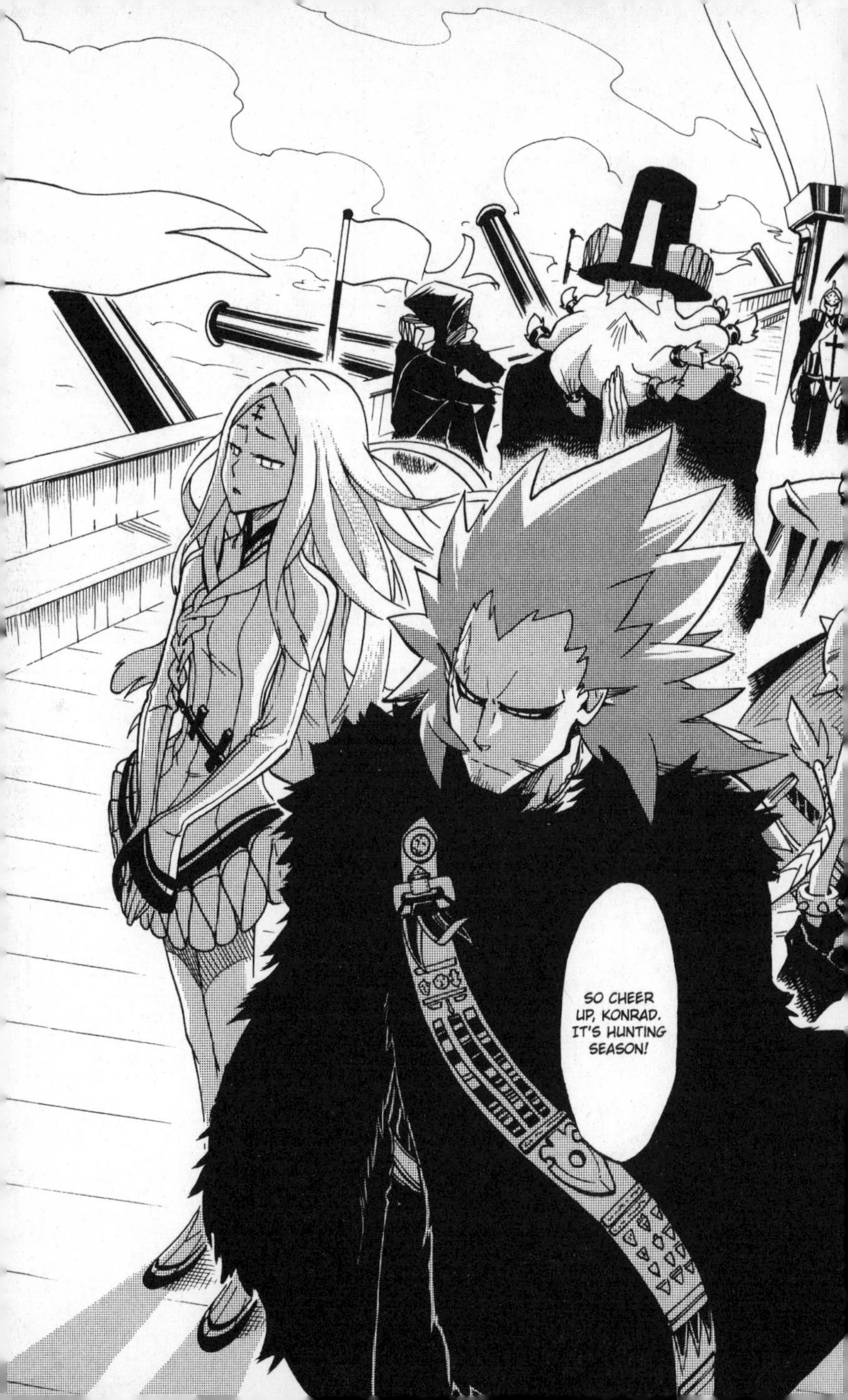
SO CHEER UP, KONRAD. IT'S HUNTING SEASON!

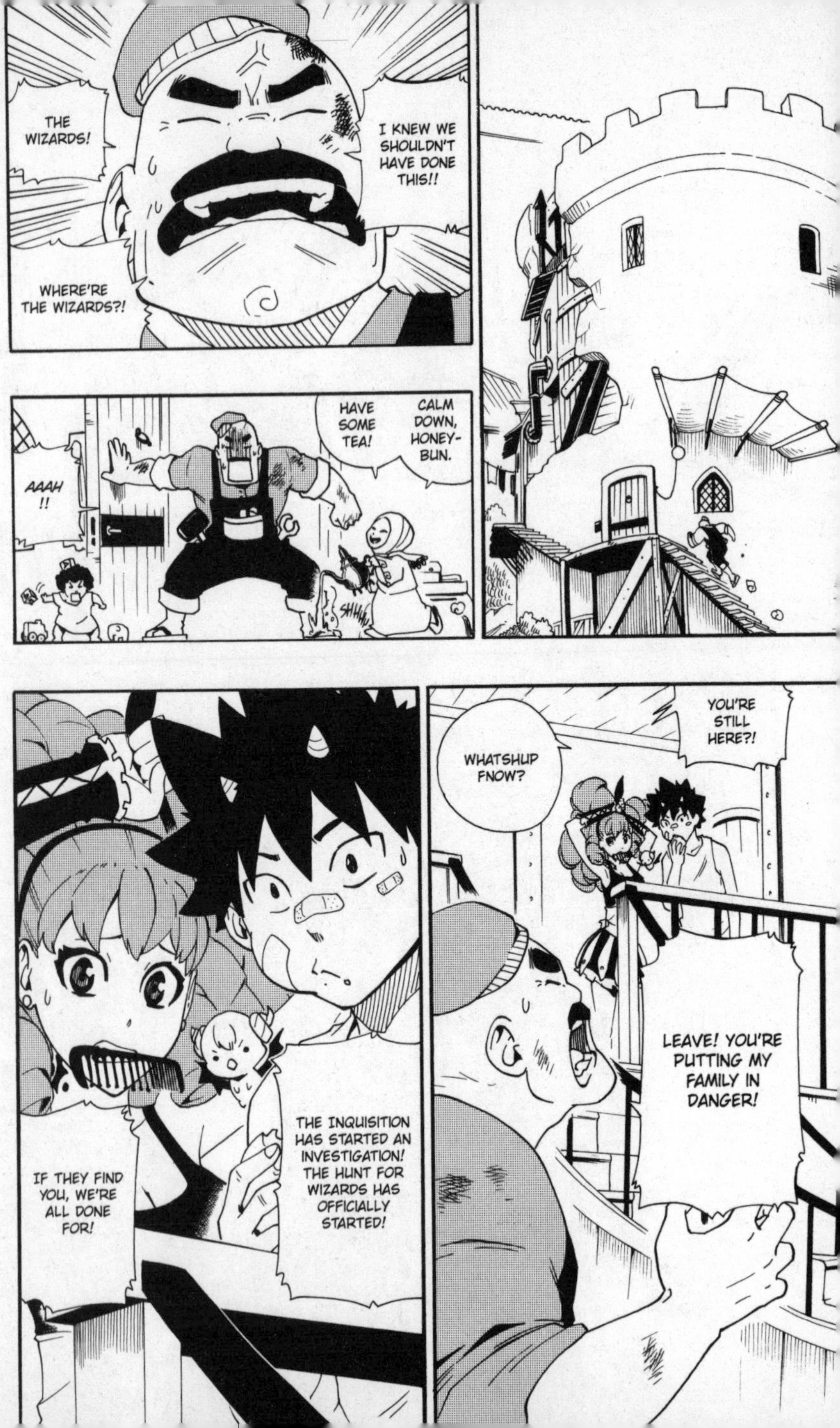
I KNEW WE SHOULDN'T HAVE DONE THIS!!
THE WIZARDS!
WHERE'RE THE WIZARDS?!
CALM DOWN, HONEY-BUN.
HAVE SOME TEA!
AAAH !!
YOU'RE STILL HERE?!
WHATSHUP FNOW?
LEAVE! YOU'RE PUTTING MY FAMILY IN DANGER!
THE INQUISITION HAS STARTED AN INVESTIGATION! THE HUNT FOR WIZARDS HAS OFFICIALLY STARTED!
IF THEY FIND YOU, WE'RE ALL DONE FOR!

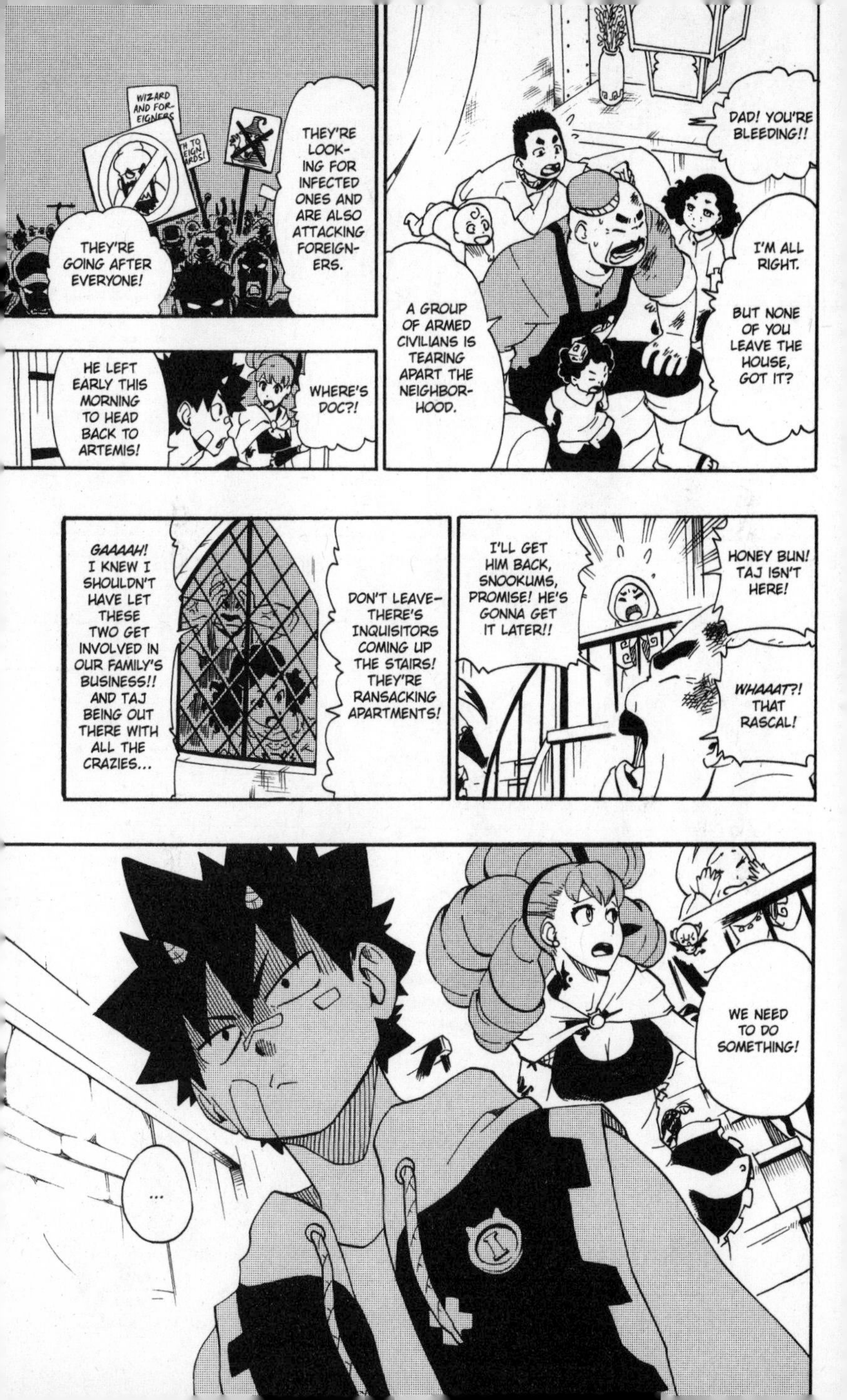
DAD! YOU'RE BLEEDING!!
I'M ALL RIGHT.
BUT NONE OF YOU LEAVE THE HOUSE, GOT IT?
A GROUP OF ARMED CIVILIANS IS TEARING APART THE NEIGHBORHOOD.
THEY'RE LOOKING FOR INFECTED ONES AND ARE ALSO ATTACKING FOREIGNERS.
THEY'RE GOING AFTER EVERYONE!
WHERE'S DOC?!
HE LEFT EARLY THIS MORNING TO HEAD BACK TO ARTEMIS!
HONEY BUN! TAJ ISN'T HERE!
WHAAAT?! THAT RASCAL!
I'LL GET HIM BACK, SNOOKUMS, PROMISE! HE'S GONNA GET IT LATER!!
DON'T LEAVE—THERE'S INQUISITORS COMING UP THE STAIRS! THEY'RE RANSACKING APARTMENTS!
GAAAAH! I KNEW I SHOULDN'T HAVE LET THESE TWO GET INVOLVED IN OUR FAMILY'S BUSINESS!! AND TAJ BEING OUT THERE WITH ALL THE CRAZIES...
WE NEED TO DO SOMETHING!
...

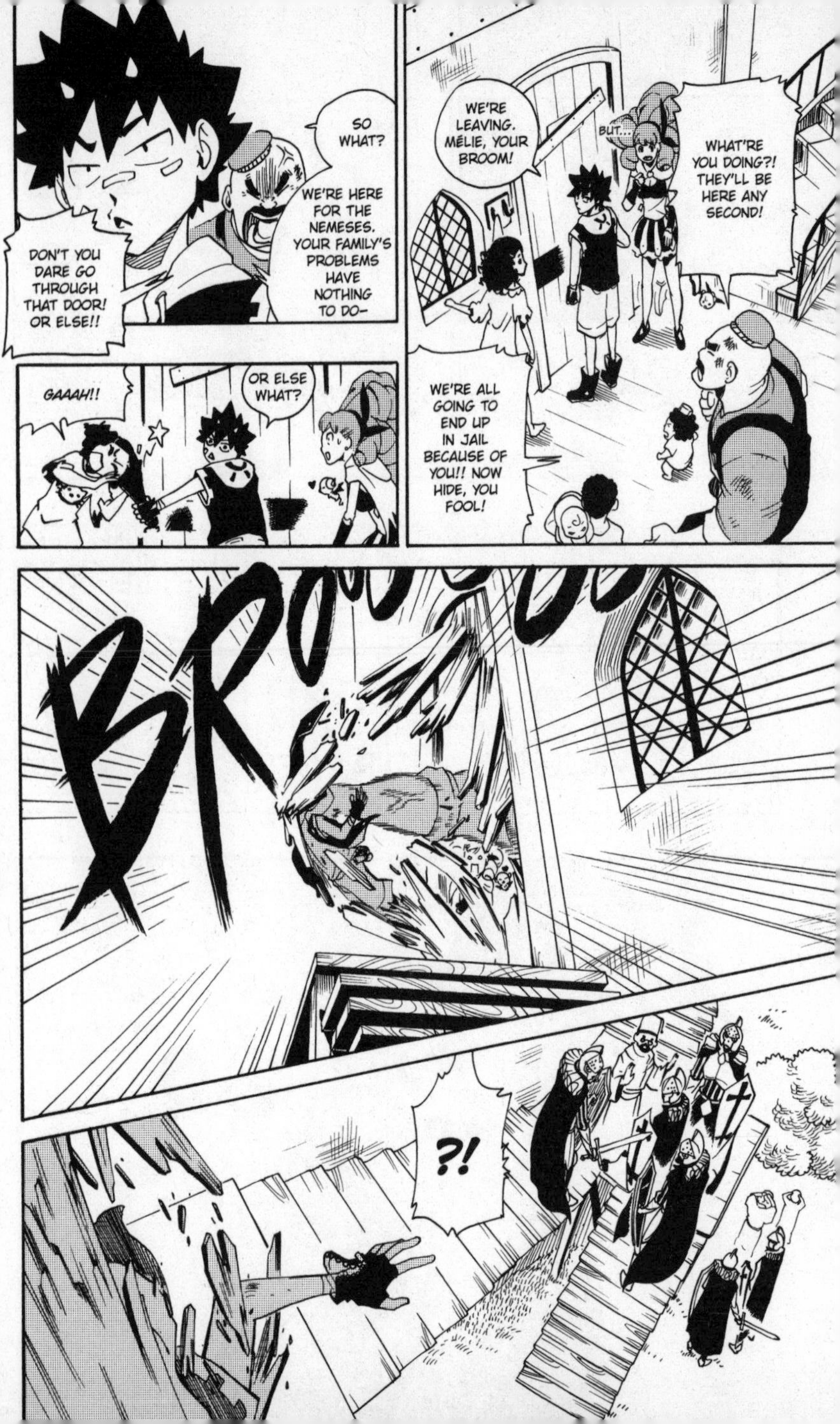
WHAT'RE YOU DOING?! THEY'LL BE HERE ANY SECOND!
BUT...
WE'RE LEAVING. MÉLIE, YOUR BROOM!
WE'RE ALL GOING TO END UP IN JAIL BECAUSE OF YOU!! NOW HIDE, YOU FOOL!
SO WHAT?
WE'RE HERE FOR THE NEMESES. YOUR FAMILY'S PROBLEMS HAVE NOTHING TO DO-
DON'T YOU DARE GO THROUGH THAT DOOR! OR ELSE!!
OR ELSE WHAT?
GAAAH!!
BROOOOOO
?!

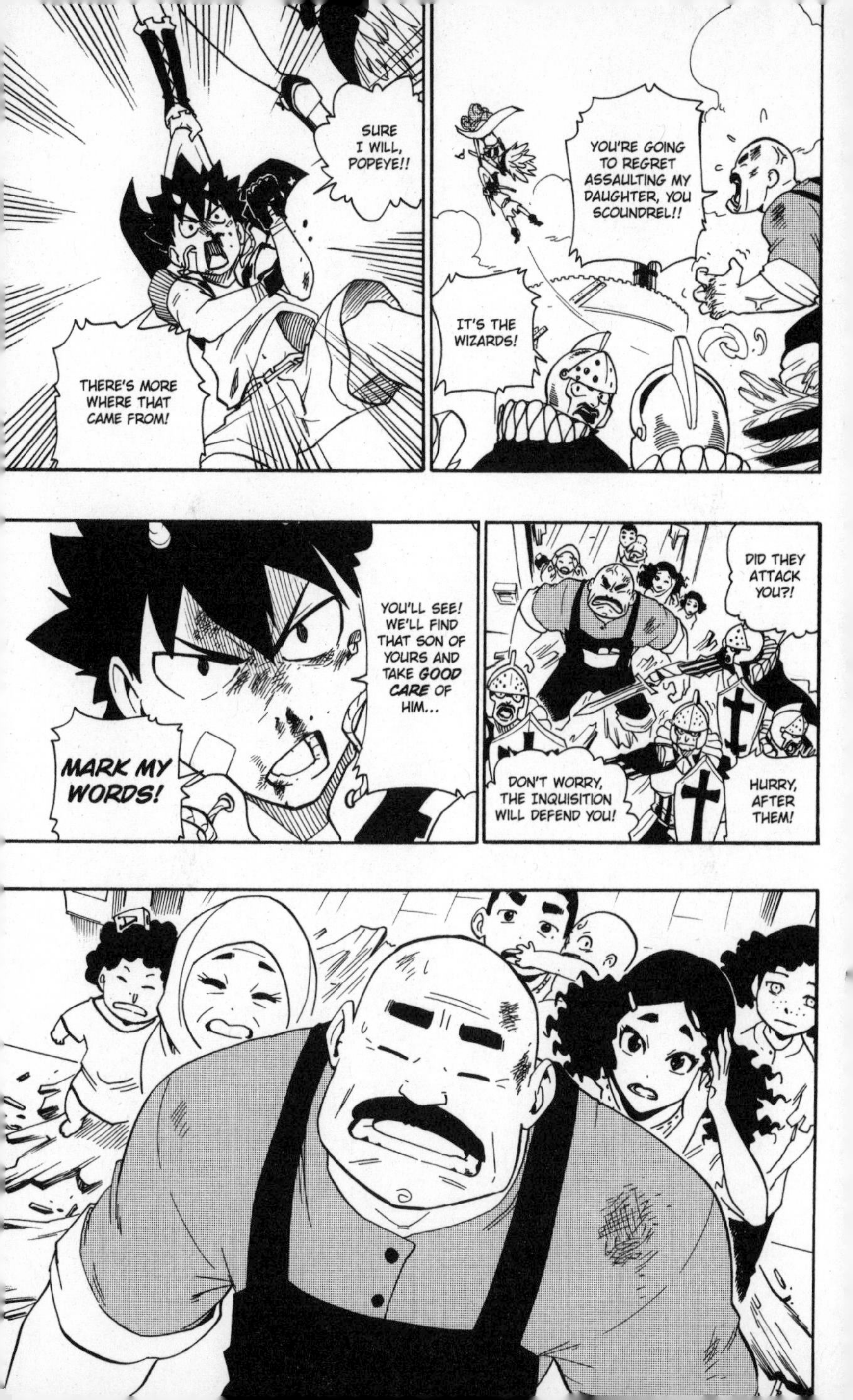
YOU'RE GOING TO REGRET ASSAULTING MY DAUGHTER, YOU SCOUNDREL!!
IT'S THE WIZARDS!
SURE I WILL, POPEYE!!
THERE'S MORE WHERE THAT CAME FROM!
DID THEY ATTACK YOU?!
HURRY, AFTER THEM!
DON'T WORRY, THE INQUISITION WILL DEFEND YOU!
YOU'LL SEE! WE'LL FIND THAT SON OF YOURS AND TAKE GOOD CARE OF HIM...
MARK MY WORDS!

JUST ANOTHER REGULAR NIGHT AT THE TOWN CRIER'S HOUSE...

Chapter 11

Two loogies and some pee

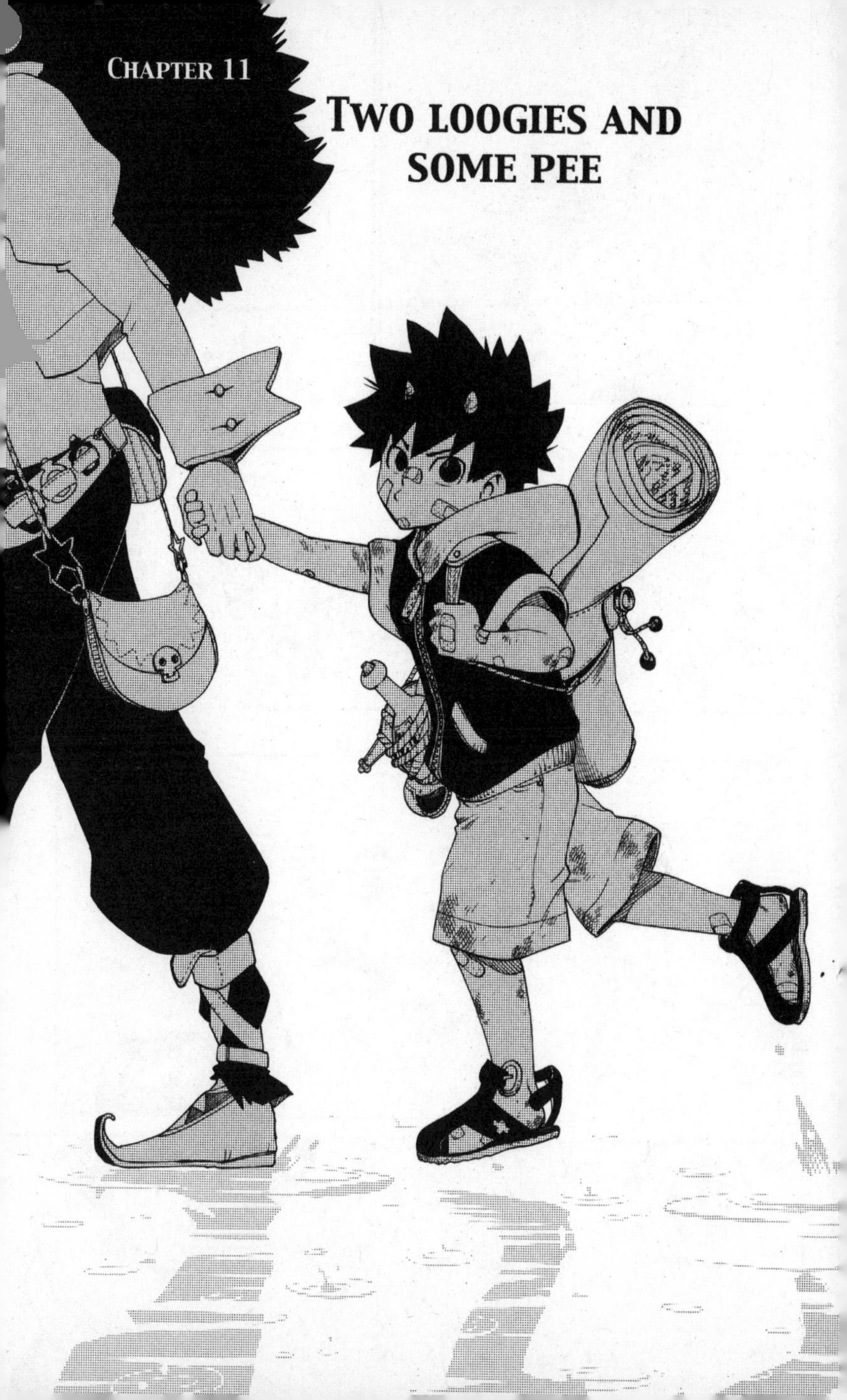

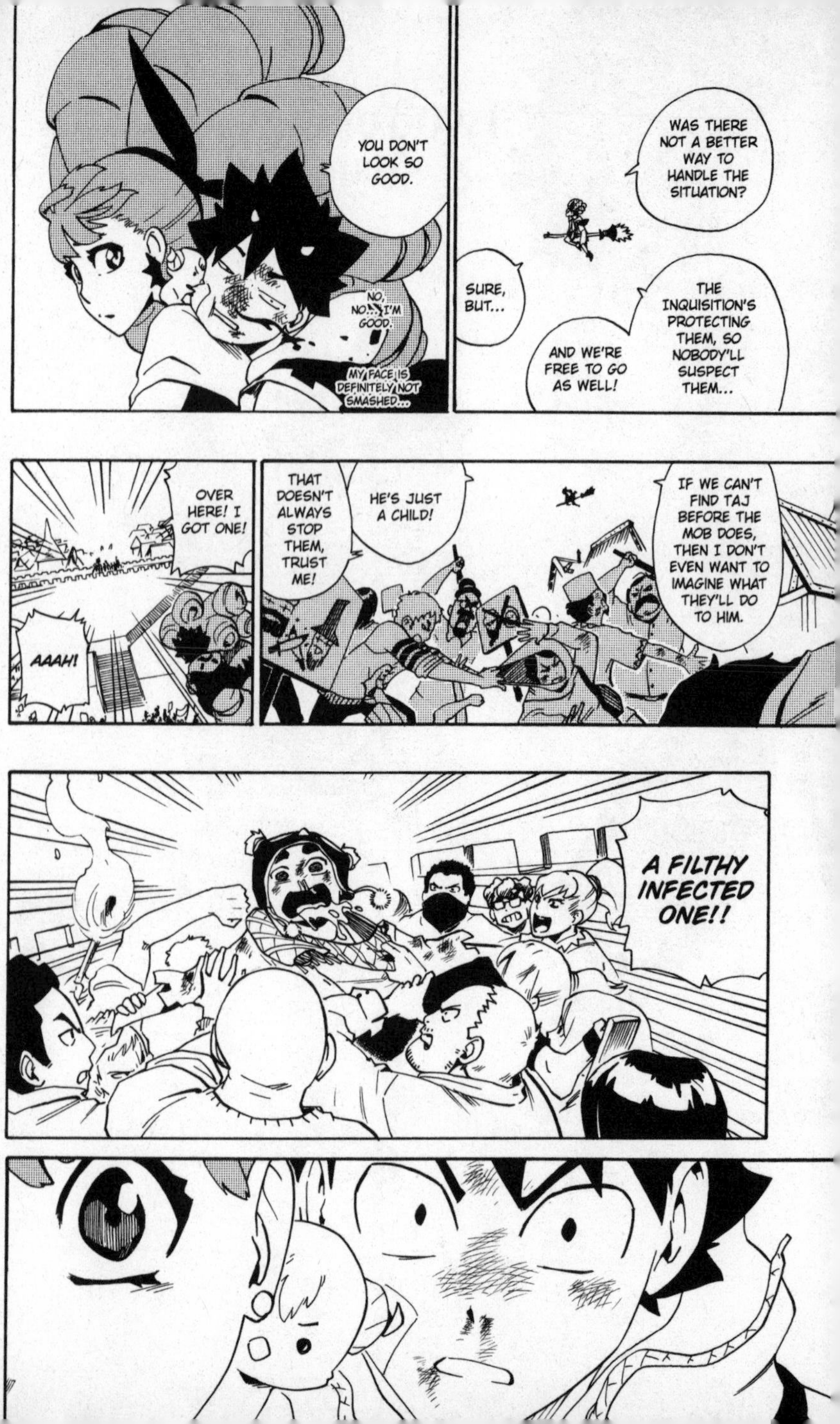
WAS THERE NOT A BETTER WAY TO HANDLE THE SITUATION?
SURE, BUT...
THE INQUISITION'S PROTECTING THEM, SO NOBODY'LL SUSPECT THEM...
AND WE'RE FREE TO GO AS WELL!
YOU DON'T LOOK SO GOOD.
NO, NO... I'M GOOD.
MY FACE IS DEFINITELY NOT SMASHED...
IF WE CAN'T FIND TAJ BEFORE THE MOB DOES, THEN I DON'T EVEN WANT TO IMAGINE WHAT THEY'LL DO TO HIM.
HE'S JUST A CHILD!
THAT DOESN'T ALWAYS STOP THEM, TRUST ME!
OVER HERE! I GOT ONE!
AAAH!
A FILTHY INFECTED ONE!!

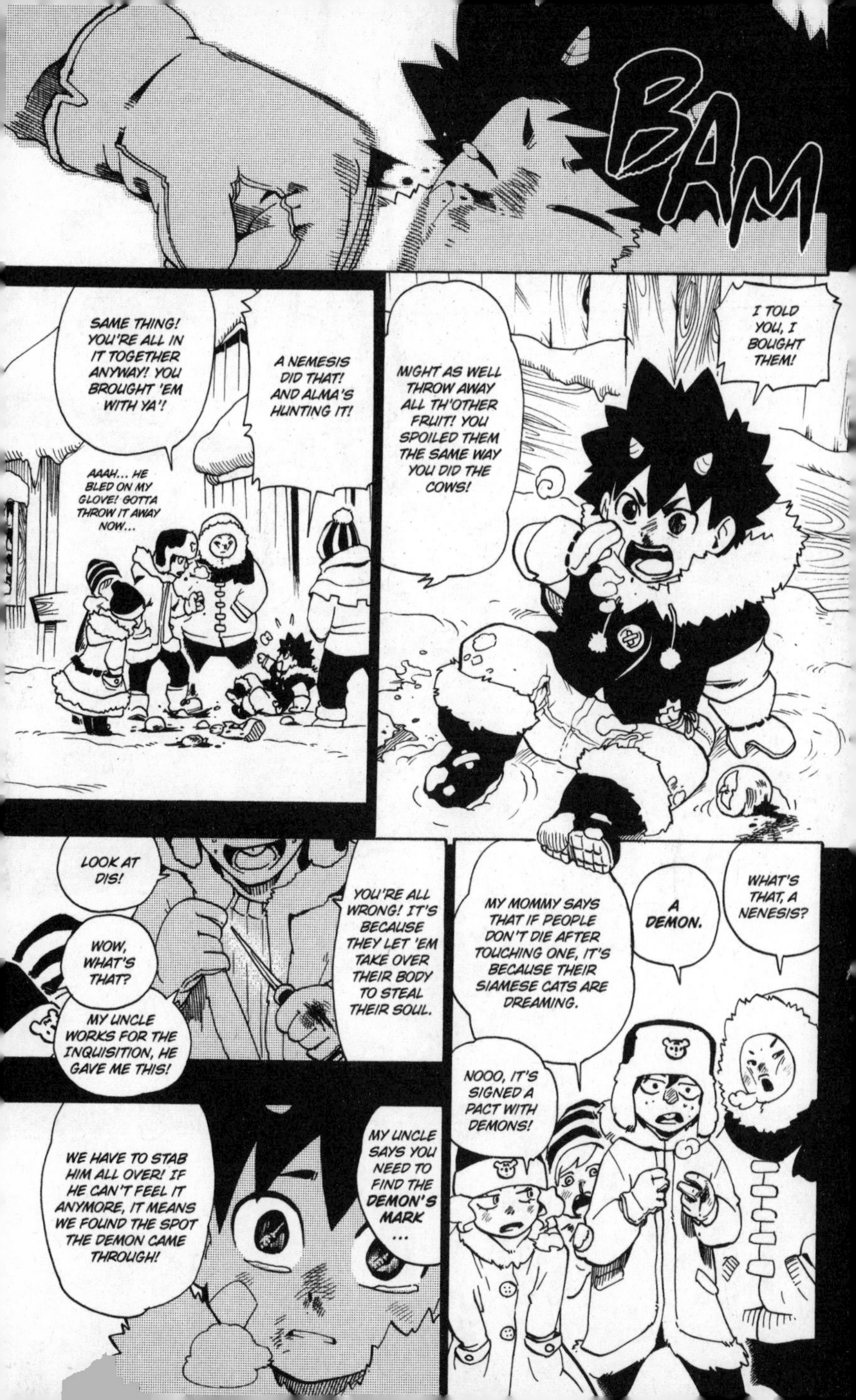
BAM
I TOLD YOU, I BOUGHT THEM!
MIGHT AS WELL THROW AWAY ALL TH'OTHER FRUIT! YOU SPOILED THEM THE SAME WAY YOU DID THE COWS!
A NEMESIS DID THAT! AND ALMA'S HUNTING IT!
SAME THING! YOU'RE ALL IN IT TOGETHER ANYWAY! YOU BROUGHT 'EM WITH YA'!
AAAH... HE BLED ON MY GLOVE! GOTTA THROW IT AWAY NOW...
WHAT'S THAT, A NENESIS?
A DEMON.
MY MOMMY SAYS THAT IF PEOPLE DON'T DIE AFTER TOUCHING ONE, IT'S BECAUSE THEIR SIAMESE CATS ARE DREAMING.
NOOO, IT'S SIGNED A PACT WITH DEMONS!
YOU'RE ALL WRONG! IT'S BECAUSE THEY LET 'EM TAKE OVER THEIR BODY TO STEAL THEIR SOUL.
LOOK AT DIS!
WOW, WHAT'S THAT?
MY UNCLE WORKS FOR THE INQUISITION, HE GAVE ME THIS!
MY UNCLE SAYS YOU NEED TO FIND THE DEMON'S MARK...
WE HAVE TO STAB HIM ALL OVER! IF HE CAN'T FEEL IT ANYMORE, IT MEANS WE FOUND THE SPOT THE DEMON CAME THROUGH!

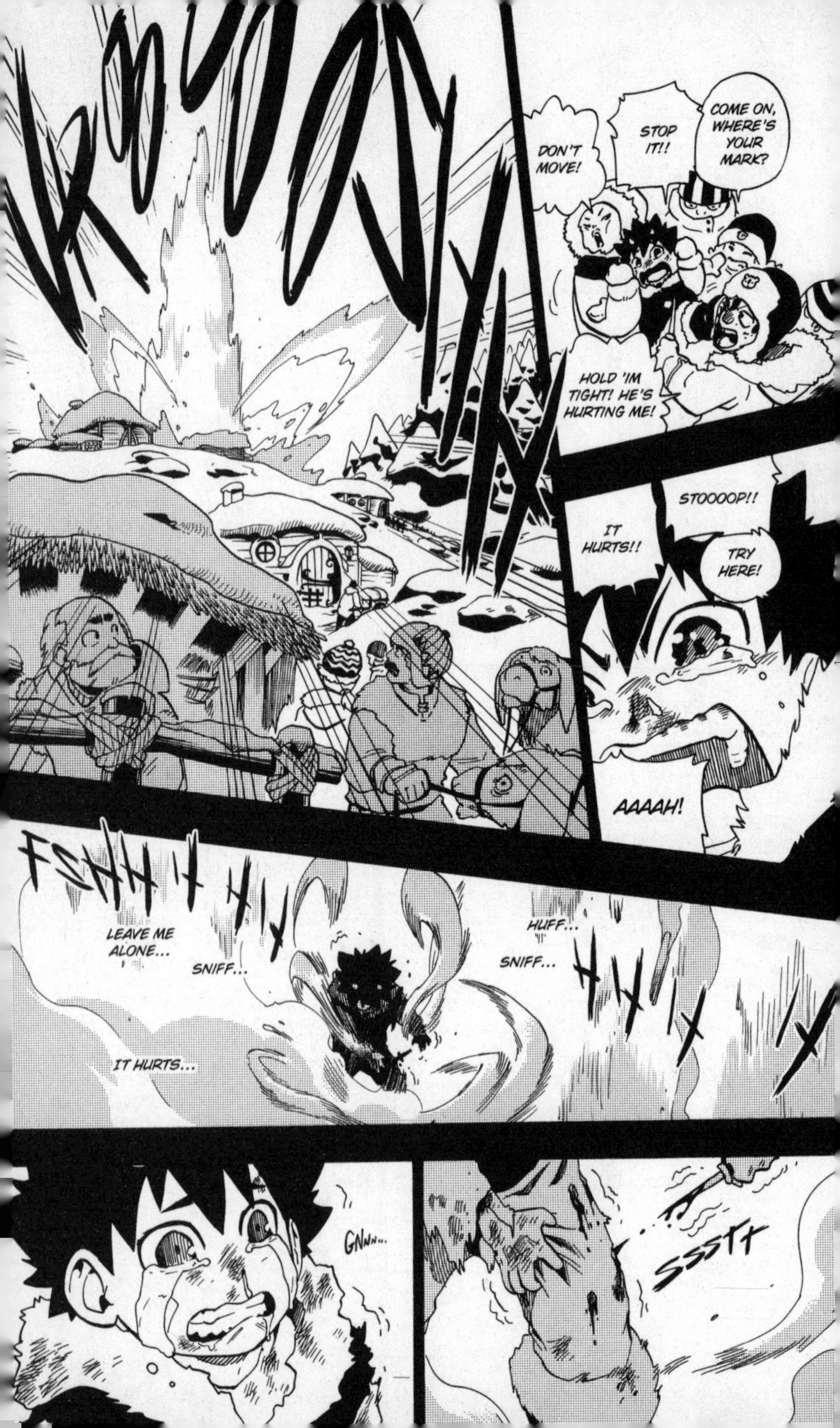
COME ON, WHERE'S YOUR MARK?
STOP IT!!
DON'T MOVE!
HOLD 'IM TIGHT! HE'S HURTING ME!
STOOOOP!!
TRY HERE!
IT HURTS!!
AAAAH!
FSHHH
HUFF...
SNIFF...
LEAVE ME ALONE...
SNIFF...
IT HURTS...
SSSTT
GNNN...

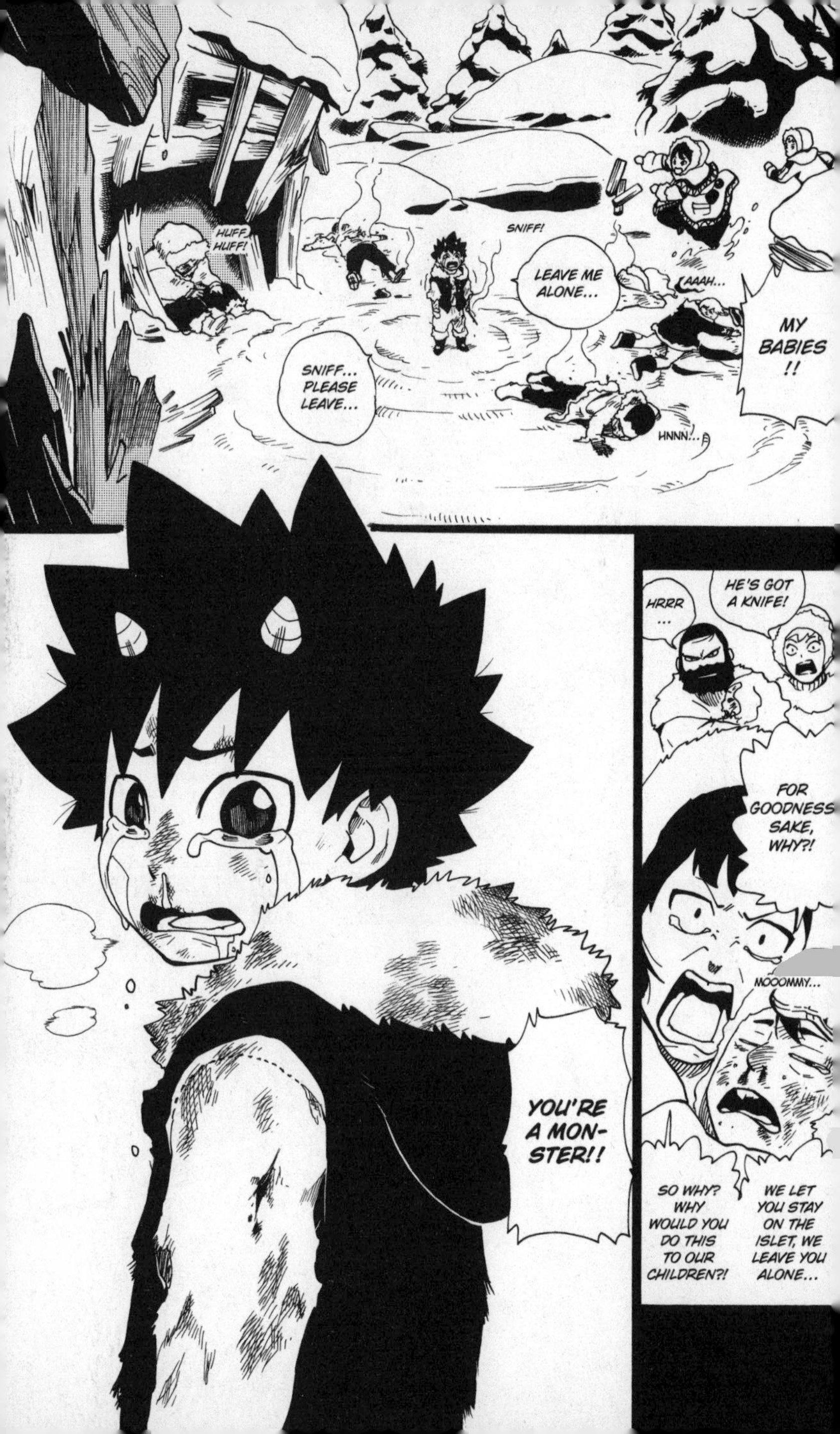
MY BABIES !!
SNIFF!
AAAH...
LEAVE ME ALONE...
HUFF HUFF!
HNNN...
SNIFF... PLEASE LEAVE...
HE'S GOT A KNIFE!
HRRR ...
FOR GOODNESS SAKE, WHY?!
MOOOMMY...
WE LET YOU STAY ON THE ISLET, WE LEAVE YOU ALONE...
SO WHY? WHY WOULD YOU DO THIS TO OUR CHILDREN?!
YOU'RE A MON-STER!!

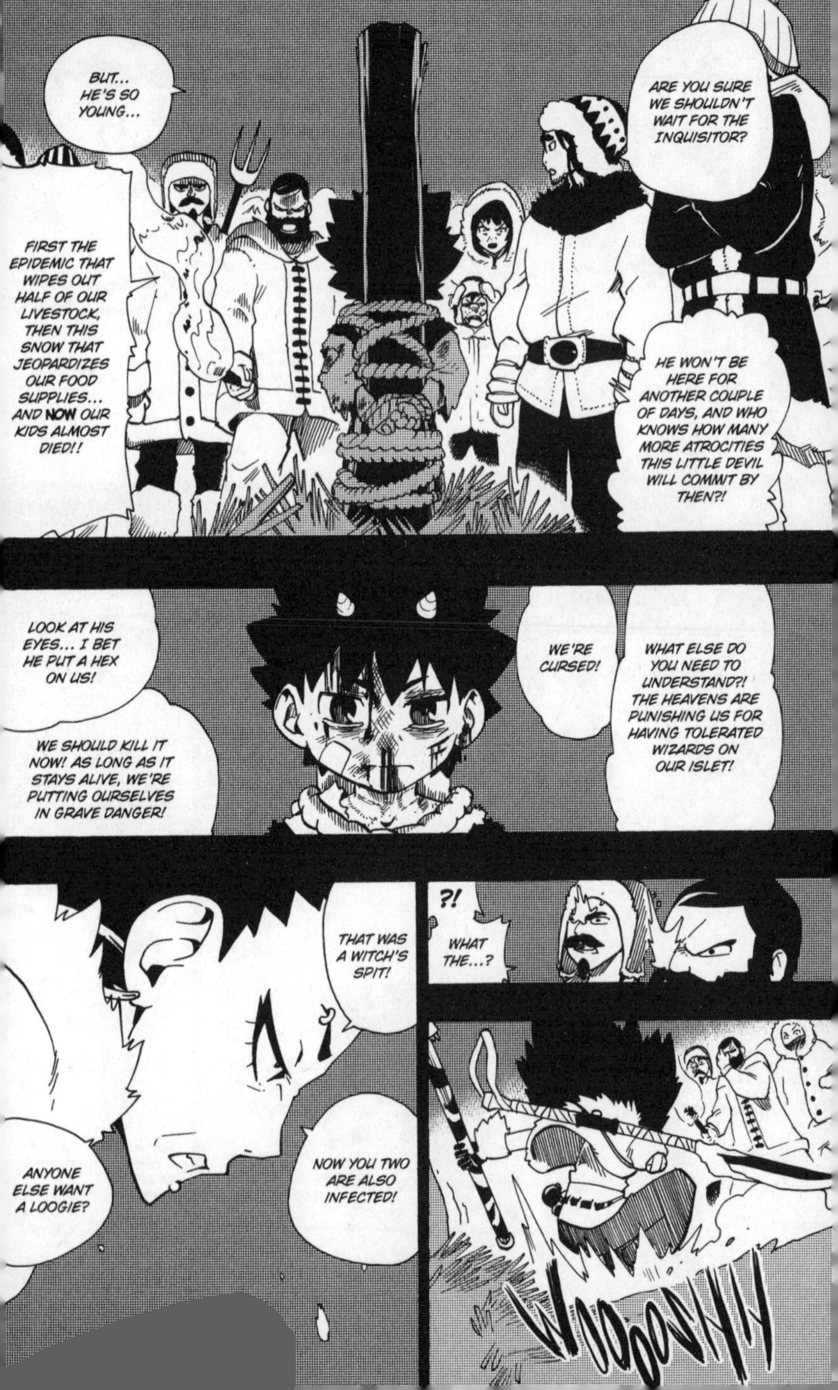
ARE YOU SURE WE SHOULDN'T WAIT FOR THE INQUISITOR?
BUT... HE'S SO YOUNG...
HE WON'T BE HERE FOR ANOTHER COUPLE OF DAYS, AND WHO KNOWS HOW MANY MORE ATROCITIES THIS LITTLE DEVIL WILL COMMIT BY THEN?!
FIRST THE EPIDEMIC THAT WIPES OUT HALF OF OUR LIVESTOCK, THEN THIS SNOW THAT JEOPARDIZES OUR FOOD SUPPLIES... AND **NOW** OUR KIDS ALMOST DIED!!
WHAT ELSE DO YOU NEED TO UNDERSTAND?! THE HEAVENS ARE PUNISHING US FOR HAVING TOLERATED WIZARDS ON OUR ISLET!
WE'RE CURSED!
LOOK AT HIS EYES... I BET HE PUT A HEX ON US!
WE SHOULD KILL IT NOW! AS LONG AS IT STAYS ALIVE, WE'RE PUTTING OURSELVES IN GRAVE DANGER!
?!
WHAT THE...?
THAT WAS A WITCH'S SPIT!
NOW YOU TWO ARE ALSO INFECTED!
ANYONE ELSE WANT A LOOGIE?

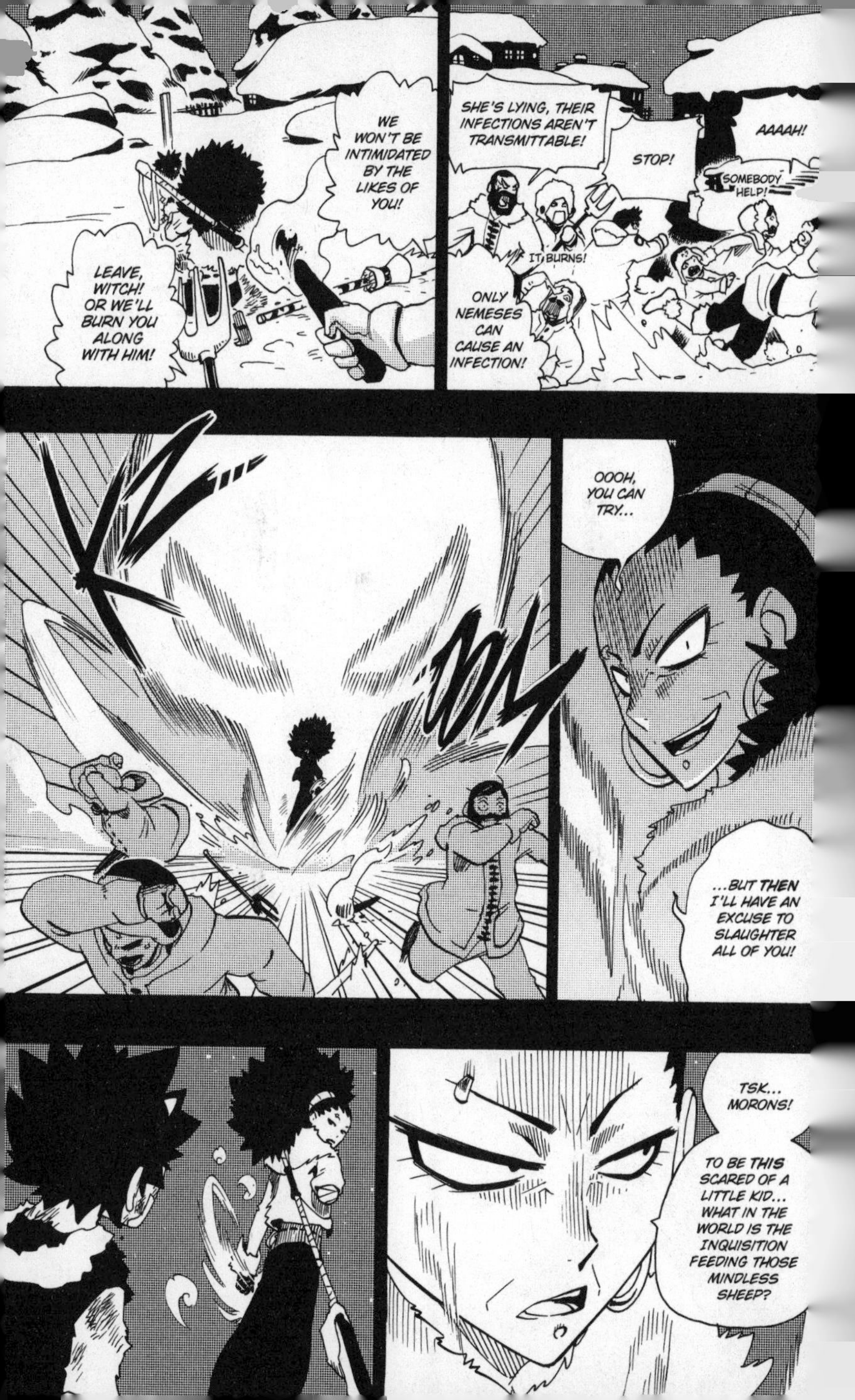
SHE'S LYING, THEIR INFECTIONS AREN'T TRANSMITTABLE!
AAAAH!
STOP!
SOMEBODY HELP!
IT BURNS!
ONLY NEMESES CAN CAUSE AN INFECTION!
WE WON'T BE INTIMIDATED BY THE LIKES OF YOU!
LEAVE, WITCH! OR WE'LL BURN YOU ALONG WITH HIM!
OOOH, YOU CAN TRY...
...BUT THEN I'LL HAVE AN EXCUSE TO SLAUGHTER ALL OF YOU!
TSK... MORONS!
TO BE THIS SCARED OF A LITTLE KID... WHAT IN THE WORLD IS THE INQUISITION FEEDING THOSE MINDLESS SHEEP?

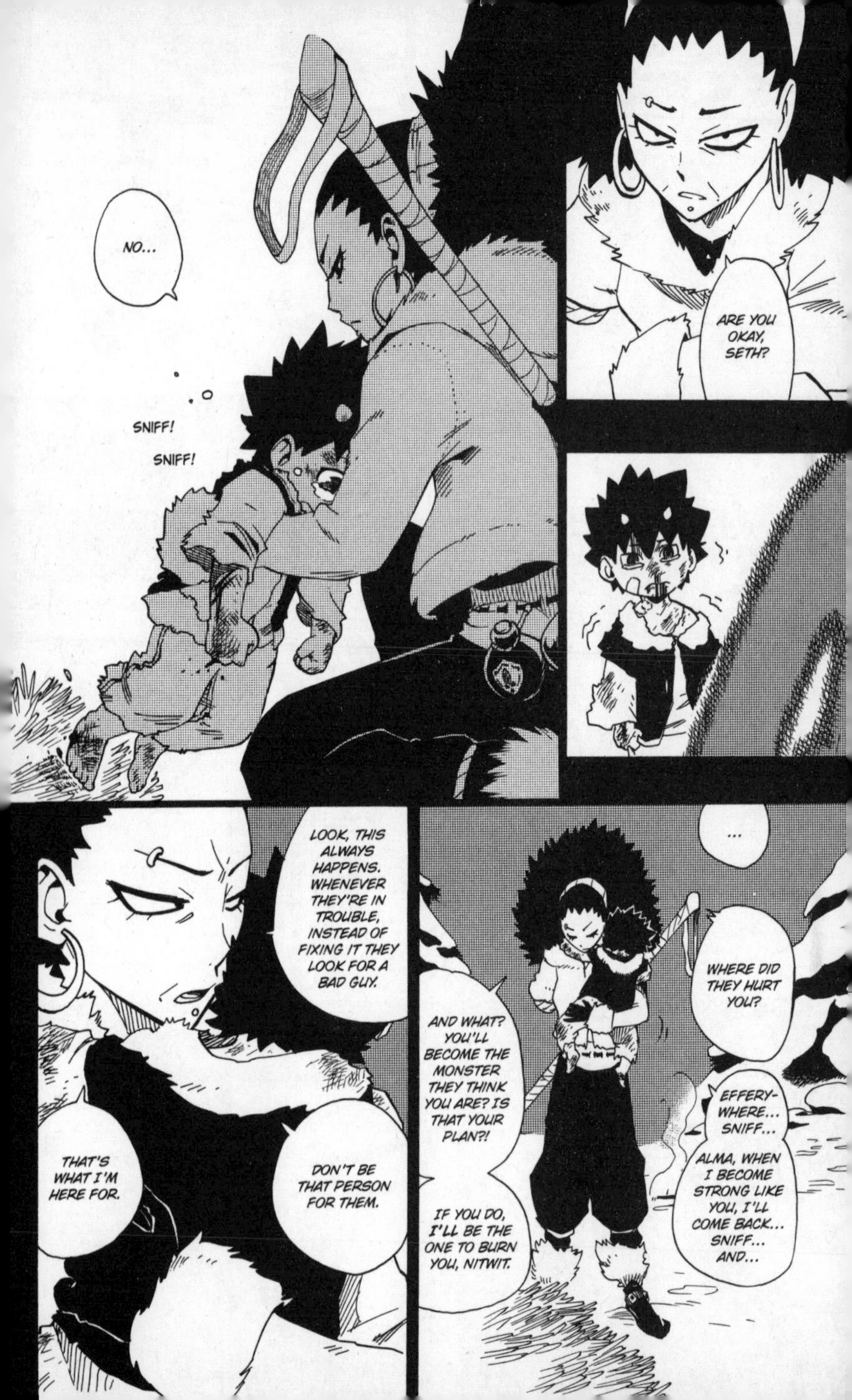
ARE YOU OKAY, SETH?
NO...
SNIFF!
SNIFF!
...
WHERE DID THEY HURT YOU?
EFFERY-WHERE... SNIFF...
ALMA, WHEN I BECOME STRONG LIKE YOU, I'LL COME BACK... SNIFF... AND...
AND WHAT? YOU'LL BECOME THE MONSTER THEY THINK YOU ARE? IS THAT YOUR PLAN?!
IF YOU DO, I'LL BE THE ONE TO BURN YOU, NITWIT.
LOOK, THIS ALWAYS HAPPENS. WHENEVER THEY'RE IN TROUBLE, INSTEAD OF FIXING IT THEY LOOK FOR A BAD GUY.
DON'T BE THAT PERSON FOR THEM.
THAT'S WHAT I'M HERE FOR.

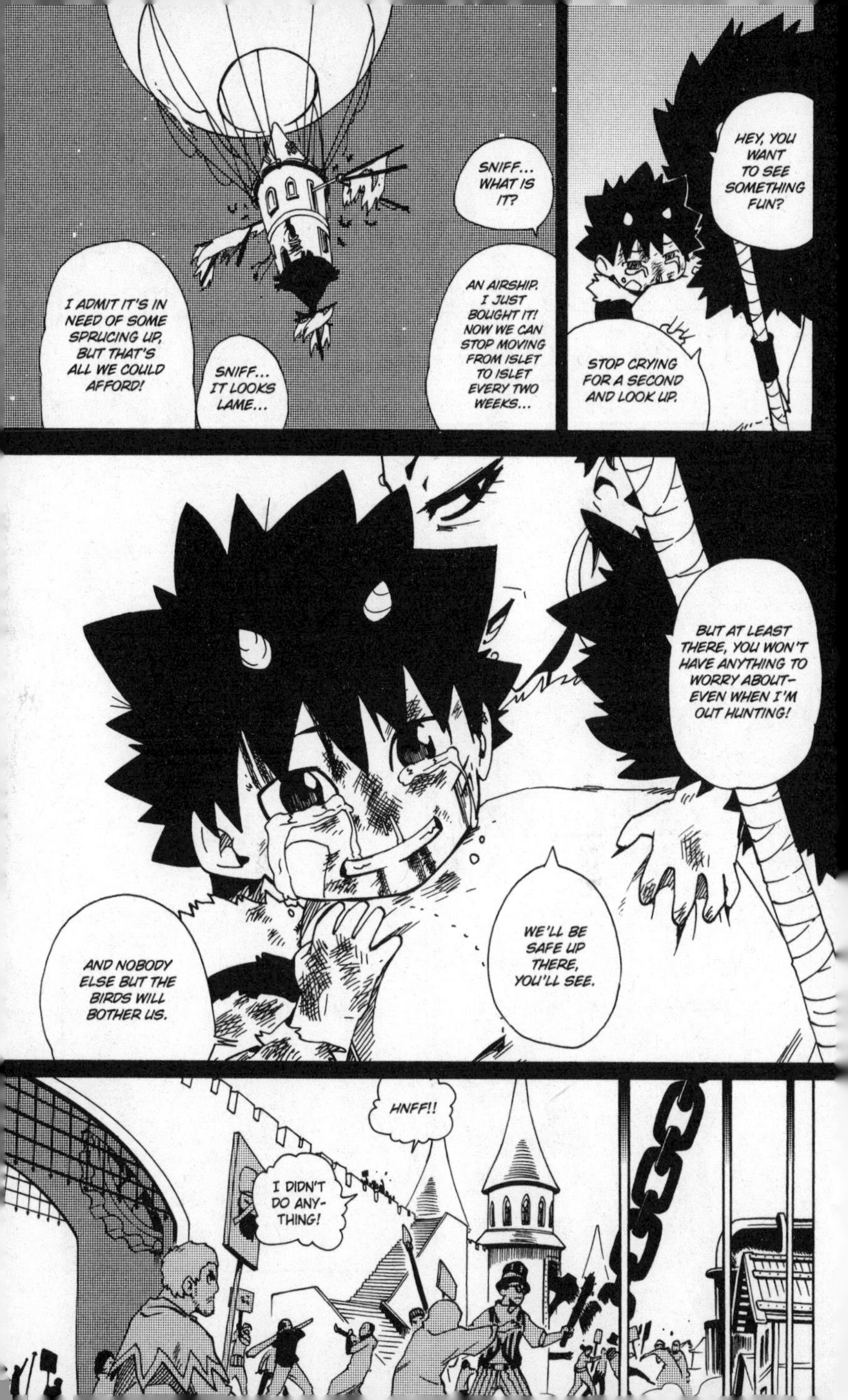
HEY, YOU WANT TO SEE SOMETHING FUN?
STOP CRYING FOR A SECOND AND LOOK UP.
SNIFF... WHAT IS IT?
AN AIRSHIP. I JUST BOUGHT IT! NOW WE CAN STOP MOVING FROM ISLET TO ISLET EVERY TWO WEEKS...
SNIFF... IT LOOKS LAME...
I ADMIT IT'S IN NEED OF SOME SPRUCING UP, BUT THAT'S ALL WE COULD AFFORD!
BUT AT LEAST THERE, YOU WON'T HAVE ANYTHING TO WORRY ABOUT— EVEN WHEN I'M OUT HUNTING!
WE'LL BE SAFE UP THERE, YOU'LL SEE.
AND NOBODY ELSE BUT THE BIRDS WILL BOTHER US.
HNFF!!
I DIDN'T DO ANY-THING!

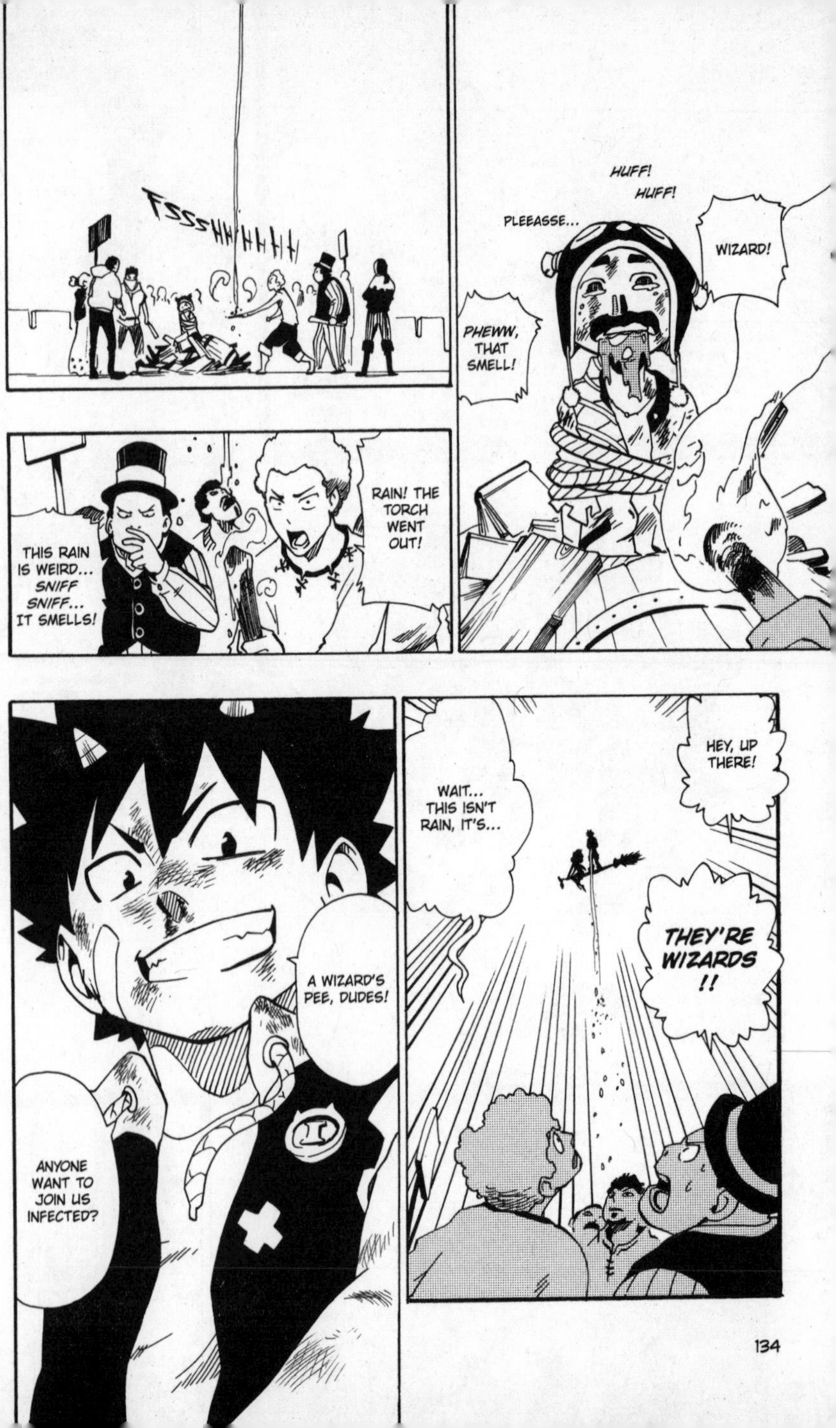
WIZARD!
HUFF!
HUFF!
PLEEASSE...
PHEWW, THAT SMELL!
FSSSHHHHHHH
RAIN! THE TORCH WENT OUT!
THIS RAIN IS WEIRD... SNIFF SNIFF... IT SMELLS!
HEY, UP THERE!
WAIT... THIS ISN'T RAIN, IT'S...
THEY'RE WIZARDS !!
A WIZARD'S PEE, DUDES!
ANYONE WANT TO JOIN US INFECTED?

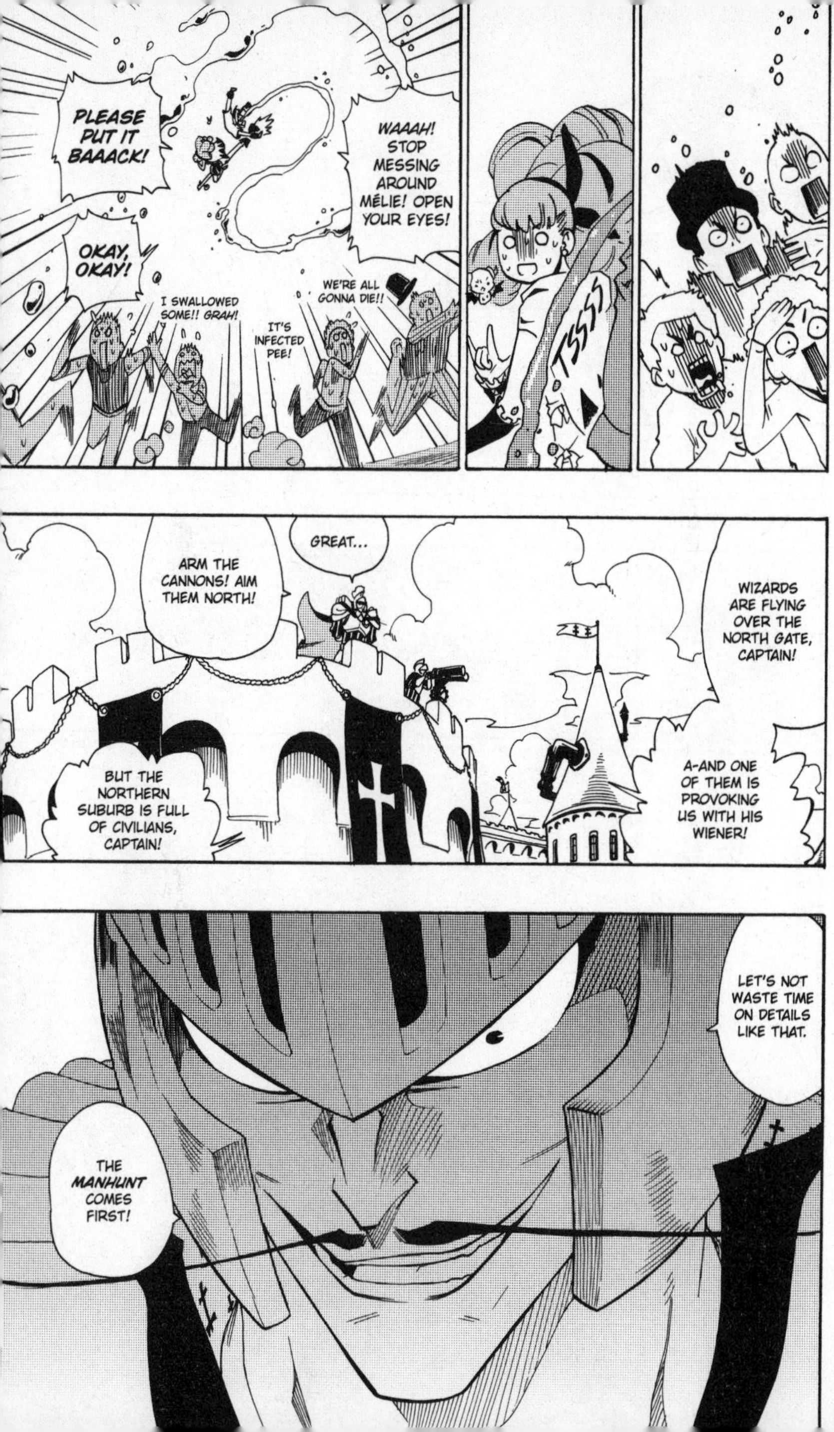
TSSSS
WAAAH! STOP MESSING AROUND MÉLIE! OPEN YOUR EYES!
PLEASE PUT IT BAAACK!
WE'RE ALL GONNA DIE!!
IT'S INFECTED PEE!
I SWALLOWED SOME!! GRAH!
OKAY, OKAY!
WIZARDS ARE FLYING OVER THE NORTH GATE, CAPTAIN!
A-AND ONE OF THEM IS PROVOKING US WITH HIS WIENER!
GREAT...
ARM THE CANNONS! AIM THEM NORTH!
BUT THE NORTHERN SUBURB IS FULL OF CIVILIANS, CAPTAIN!
LET'S NOT WASTE TIME ON DETAILS LIKE THAT.
THE *MANHUNT* COMES FIRST!

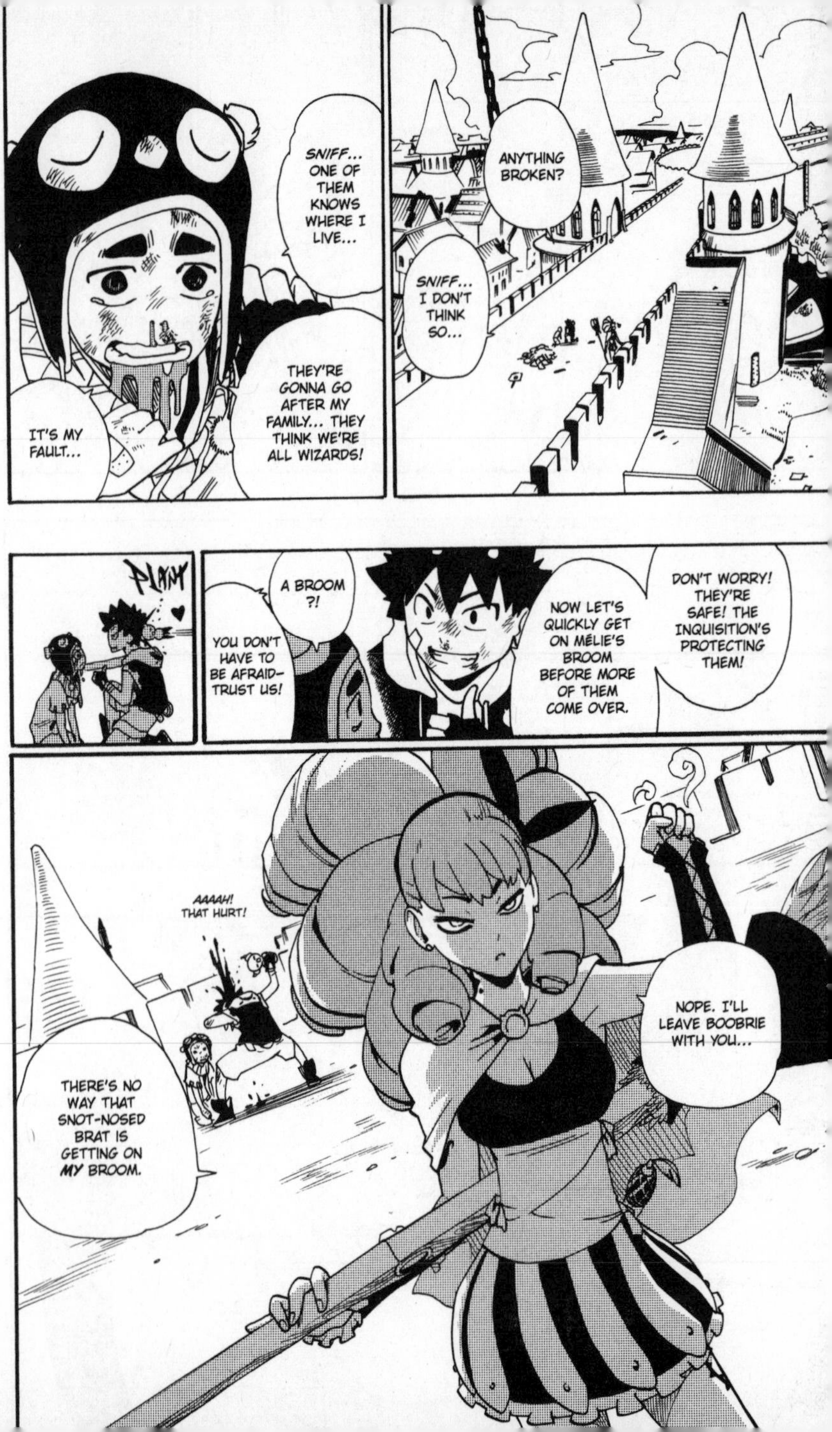
ANYTHING BROKEN?
SNIFF... I DON'T THINK SO...
SNIFF... ONE OF THEM KNOWS WHERE I LIVE...
THEY'RE GONNA GO AFTER MY FAMILY... THEY THINK WE'RE ALL WIZARDS!
IT'S MY FAULT...
DON'T WORRY! THEY'RE SAFE! THE INQUISITION'S PROTECTING THEM!
NOW LET'S QUICKLY GET ON MÉLIE'S BROOM BEFORE MORE OF THEM COME OVER.
A BROOM ?!
YOU DON'T HAVE TO BE AFRAID—TRUST US!
PLANK
NOPE. I'LL LEAVE BOOBRIE WITH YOU...
AAAAH! THAT HURT!
THERE'S NO WAY THAT SNOT-NOSED BRAT IS GETTING ON **MY** BROOM.

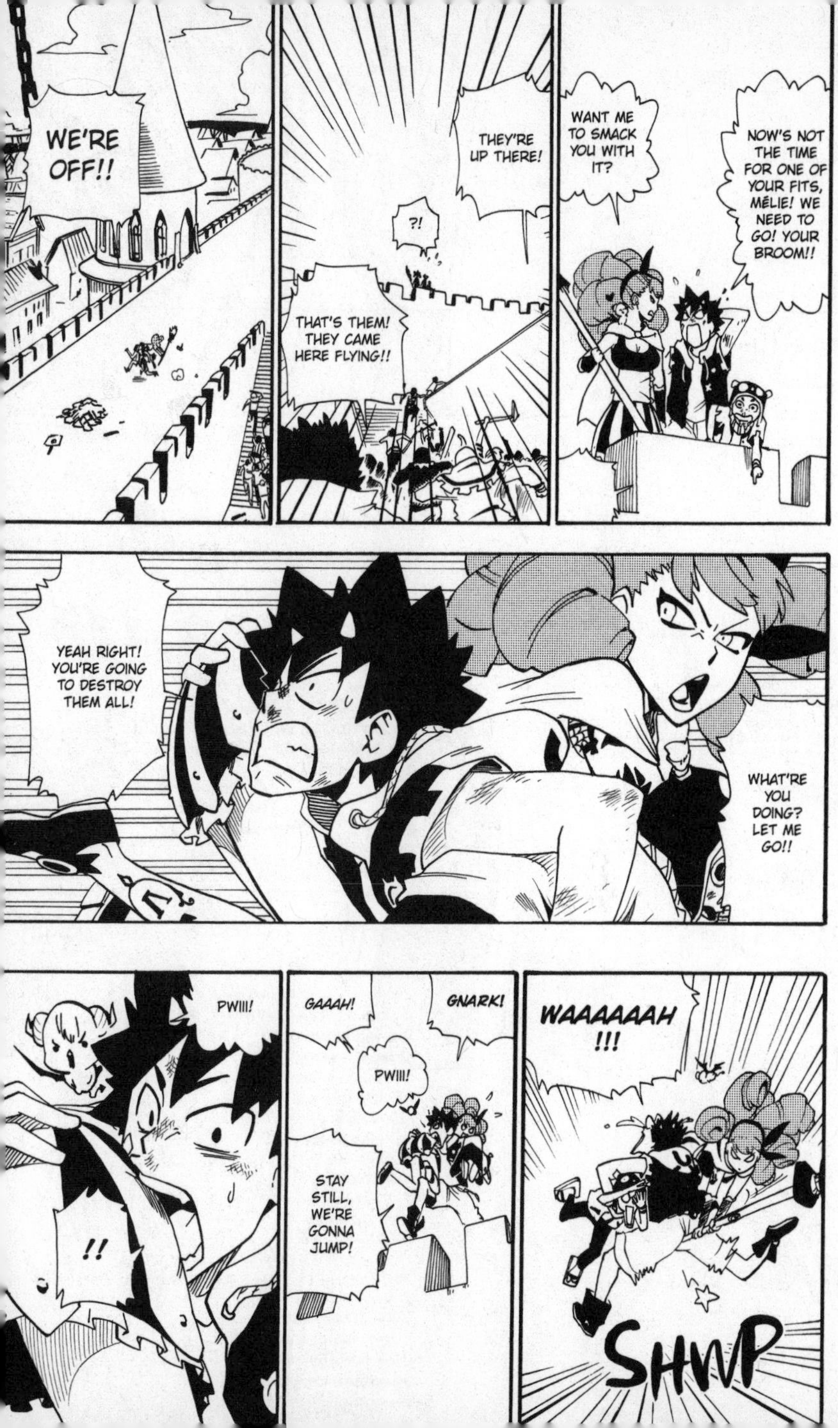
NOW'S NOT THE TIME FOR ONE OF YOUR FITS, MÉLIE! WE NEED TO GO! YOUR BROOM!!
WANT ME TO SMACK YOU WITH IT?
THEY'RE UP THERE!
?!
THAT'S THEM! THEY CAME HERE FLYING!!
WE'RE OFF!!
YEAH RIGHT! YOU'RE GOING TO DESTROY THEM ALL!
WHAT'RE YOU DOING? LET ME GO!!
WAAAAAAH !!!
SHWP
GNARK!
GAAAH!
PWIII!
STAY STILL, WE'RE GONNA JUMP!
PWIII!
!!

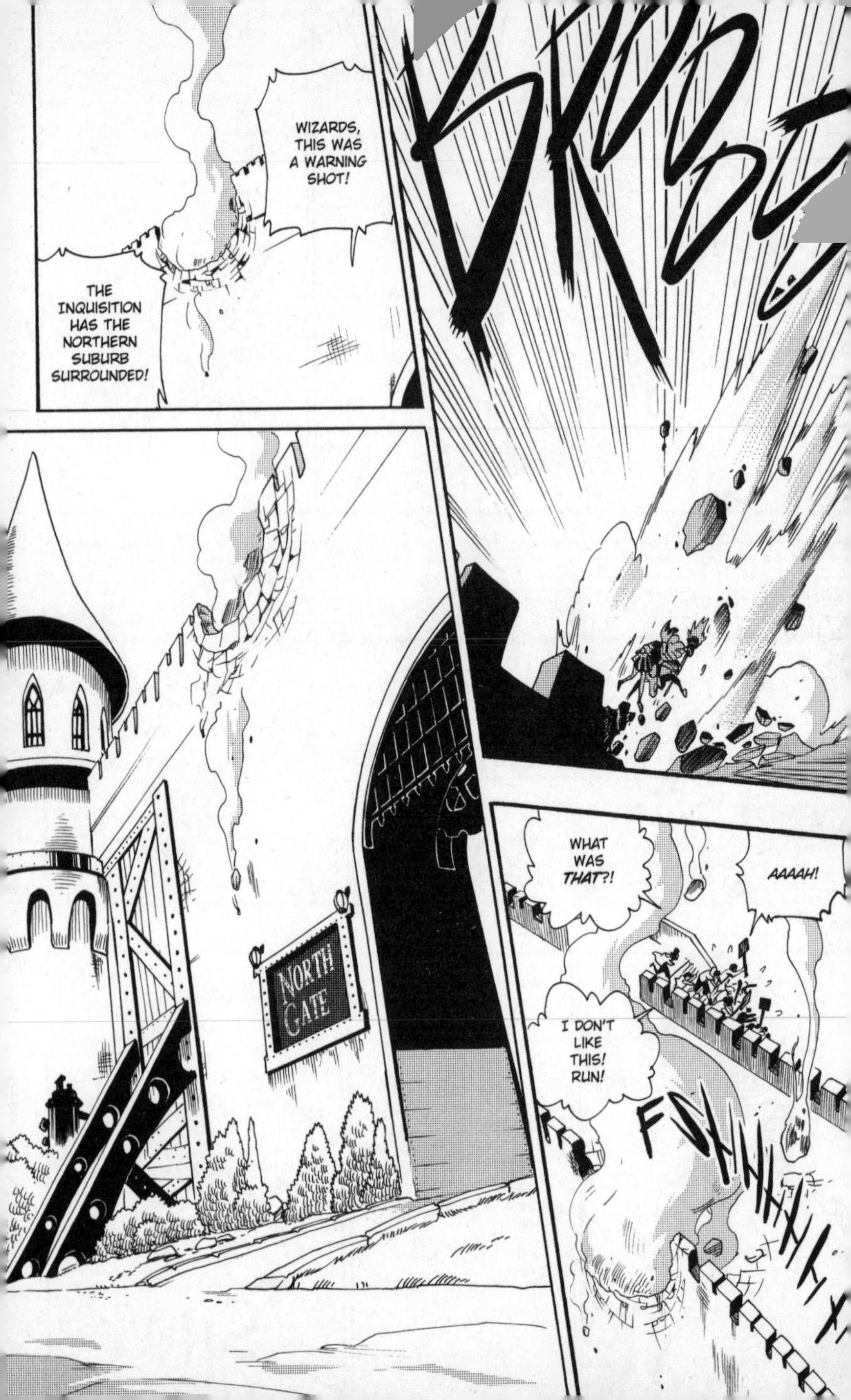
WIZARDS, THIS WAS A WARNING SHOT!
THE INQUISITION HAS THE NORTHERN SUBURB SURROUNDED!
AAAAH!
WHAT WAS *THAT*?!
I DON'T LIKE THIS! RUN!
NORTH GATE

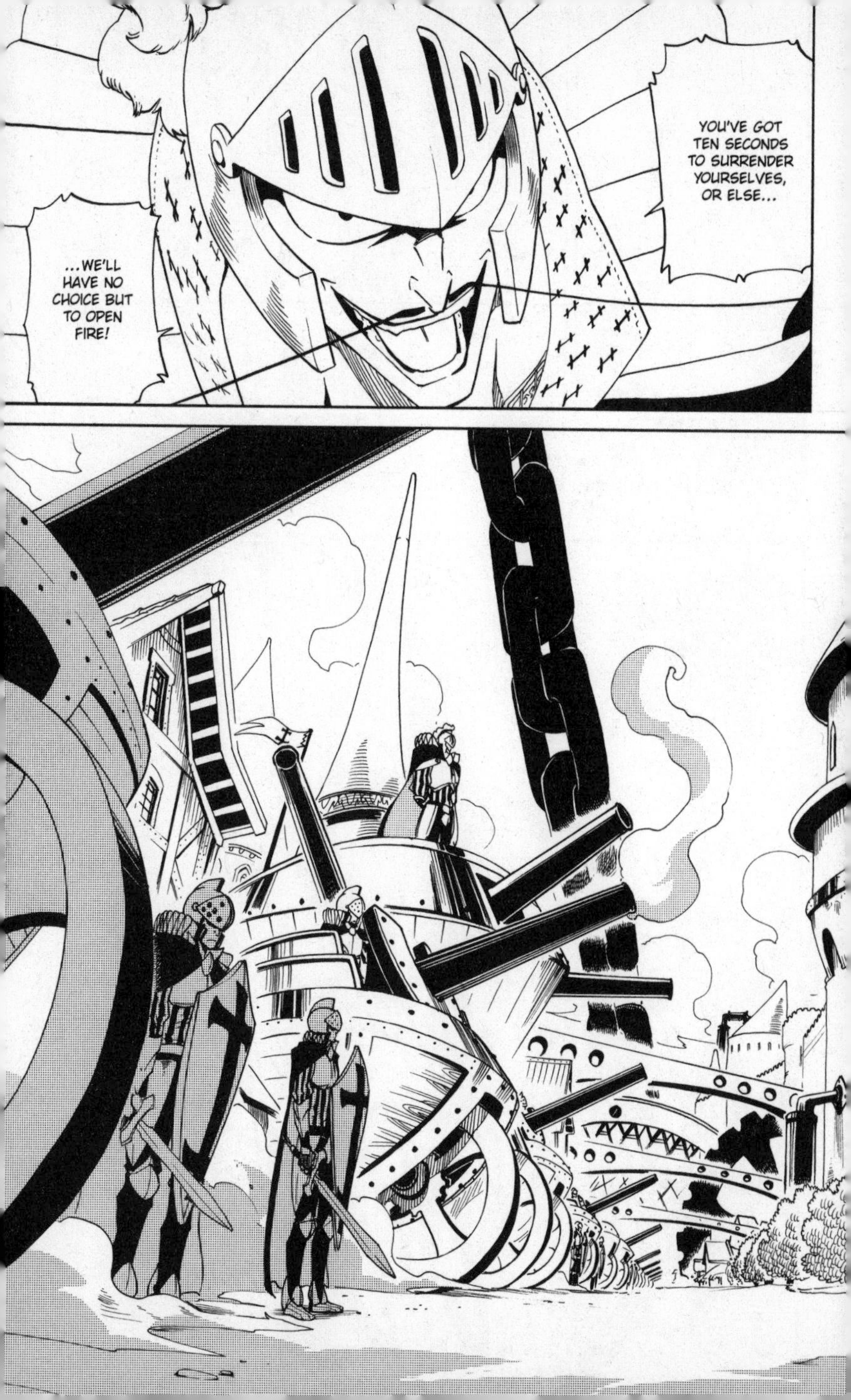
YOU'VE GOT TEN SECONDS TO SURRENDER YOURSELVES, OR ELSE...
...WE'LL HAVE NO CHOICE BUT TO OPEN FIRE!

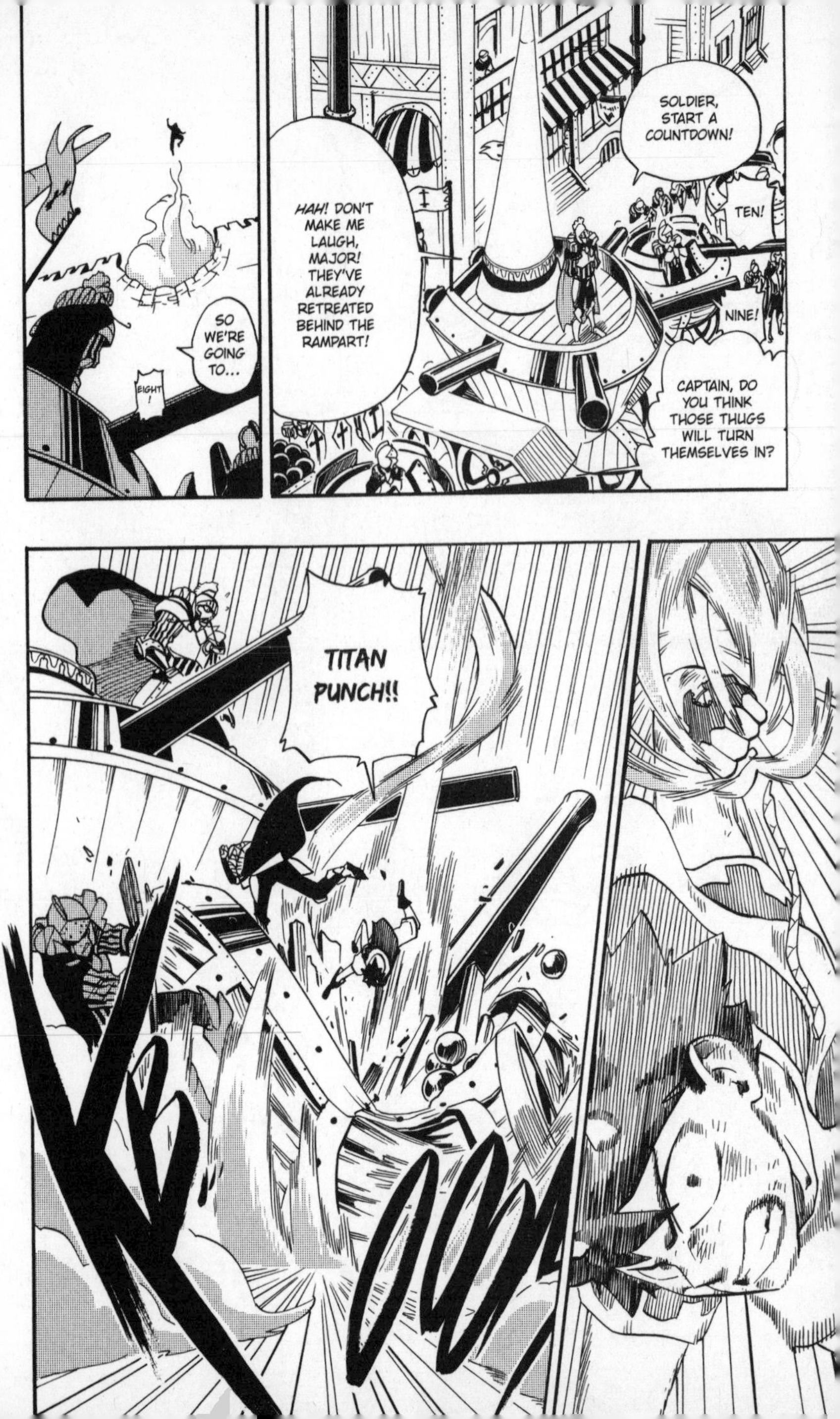
SOLDIER, START A COUNTDOWN!
TEN!
NINE!
CAPTAIN, DO YOU THINK THOSE THUGS WILL TURN THEMSELVES IN?
HAH! DON'T MAKE ME LAUGH, MAJOR! THEY'VE ALREADY RETREATED BEHIND THE RAMPART!
SO WE'RE GOING TO...
EIGHT!
TITAN PUNCH!!

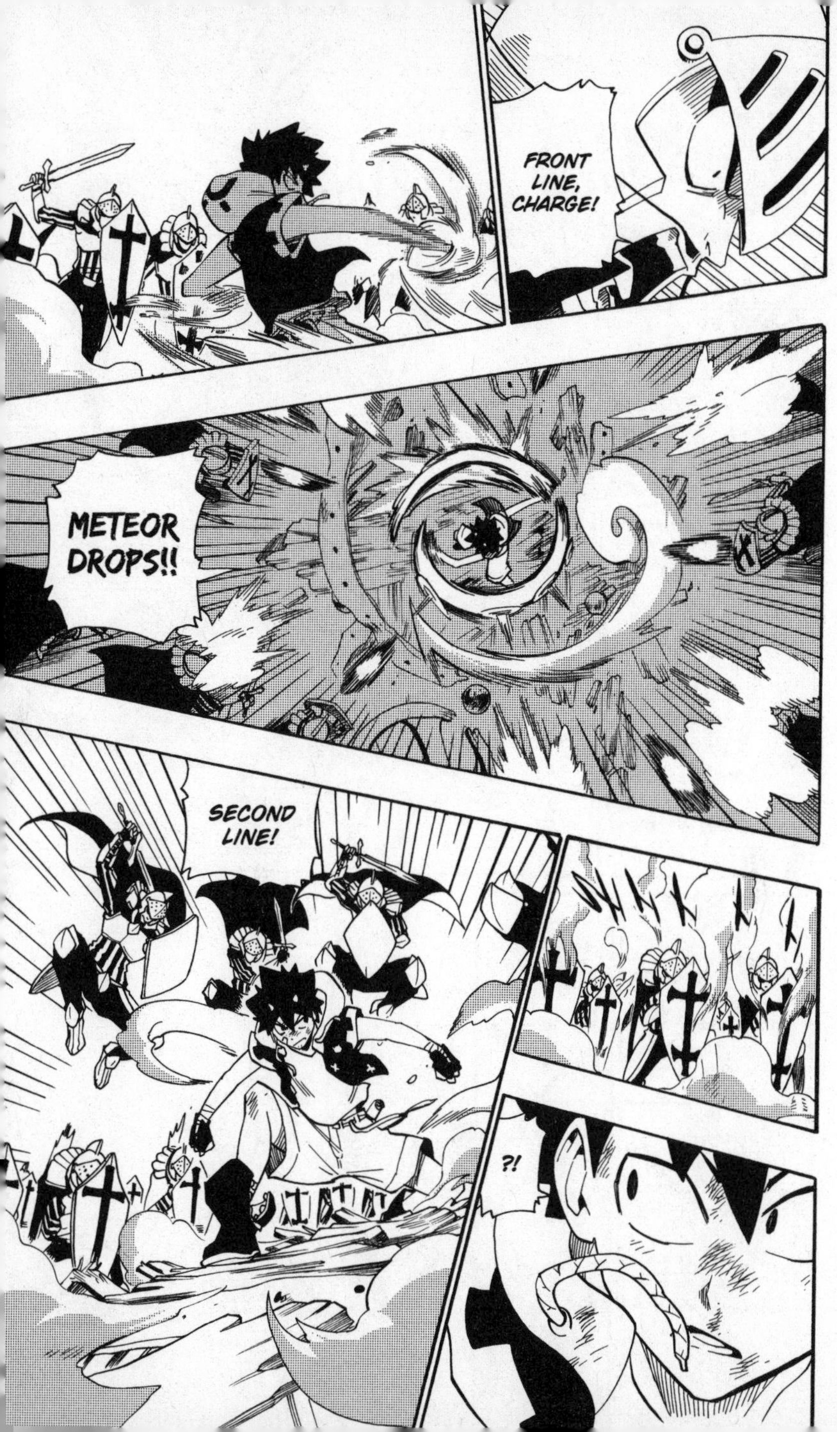
FRONT LINE, CHARGE!
METEOR DROPS!!
SECOND LINE!
?!

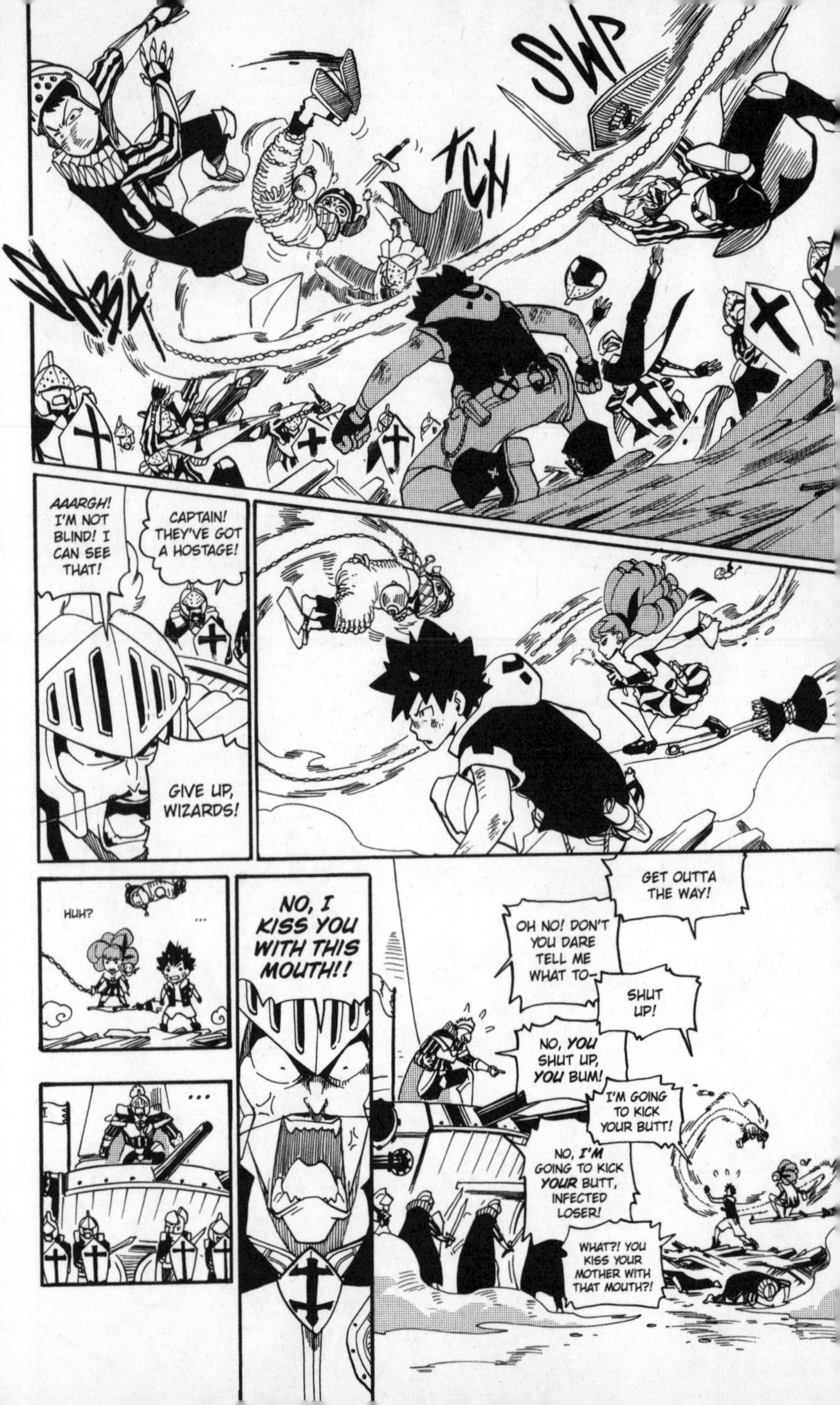
SWP
TCH
CAPTAIN! THEY'VE GOT A HOSTAGE!
AAARGH! I'M NOT BLIND! I CAN SEE THAT!
GIVE UP, WIZARDS!
GET OUTTA THE WAY!
OH NO! DON'T YOU DARE TELL ME WHAT TO—
SHUT UP!
NO, *YOU* SHUT UP, *YOU* BUM!
I'M GOING TO KICK YOUR BUTT!
NO, *I'M* GOING TO KICK *YOUR* BUTT, INFECTED LOSER!
WHAT?! YOU KISS YOUR MOTHER WITH THAT MOUTH?!
NO, I KISS YOU WITH THIS MOUTH!!
...
HUH?
...

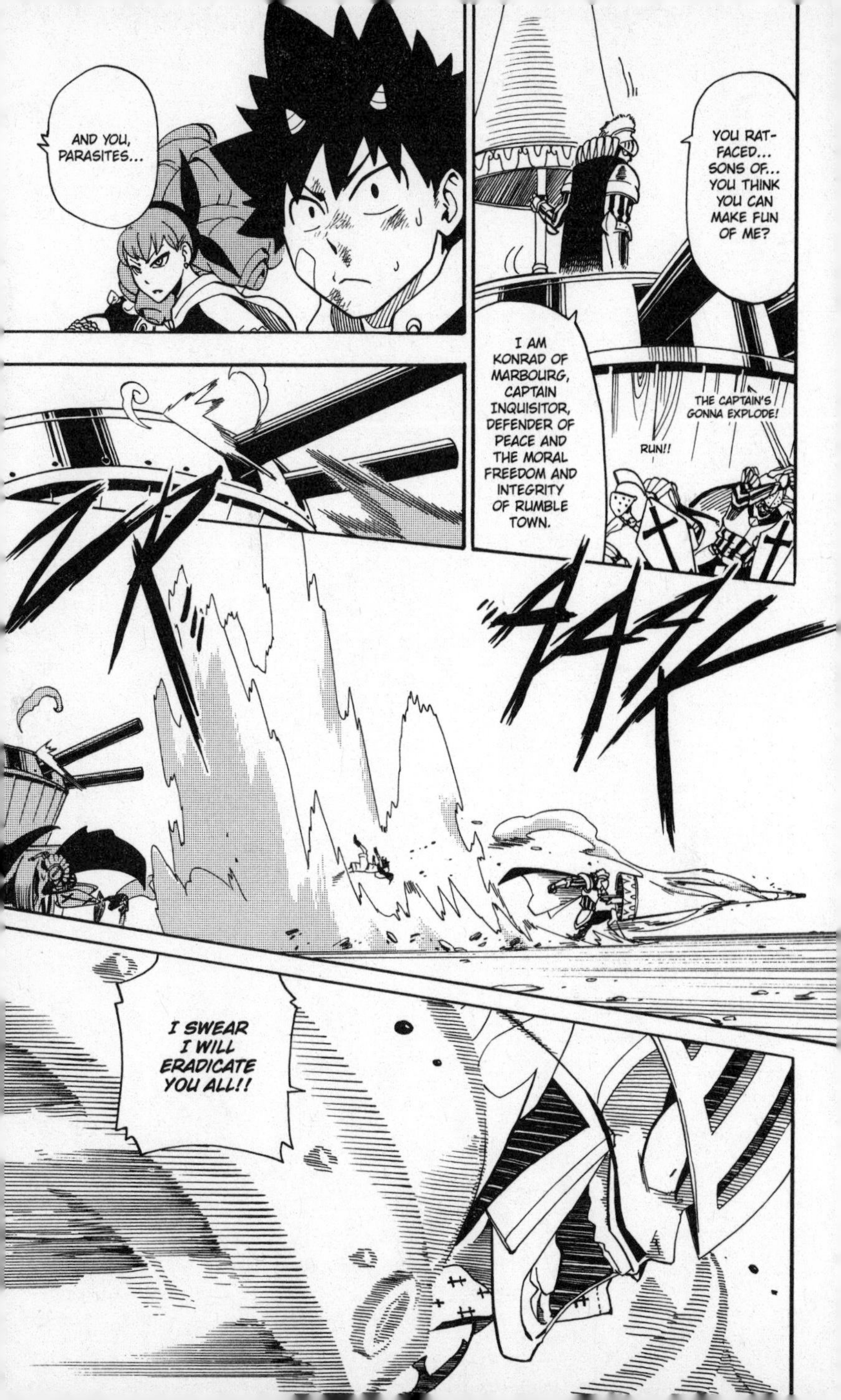
YOU RAT-FACED... SONS OF... YOU THINK YOU CAN MAKE FUN OF ME?
AND YOU, PARASITES...
I AM KONRAD OF MARBOURG, CAPTAIN INQUISITOR, DEFENDER OF PEACE AND THE MORAL FREEDOM AND INTEGRITY OF RUMBLE TOWN.
THE CAPTAIN'S GONNA EXPLODE!
RUN!!
I SWEAR I WILL ERADICATE YOU ALL!!

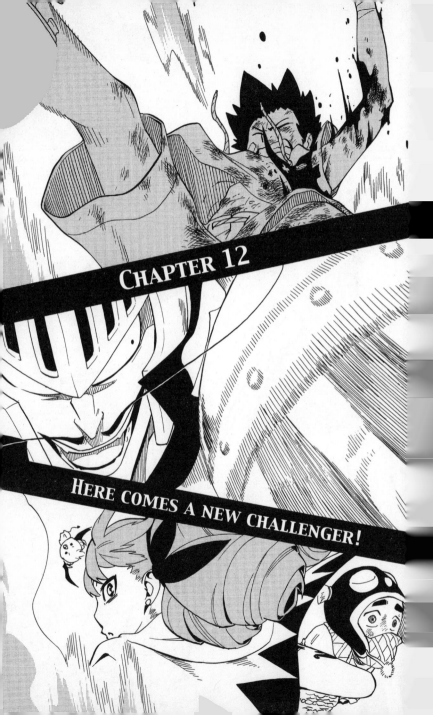

CHAPTER 12

HERE COMES A NEW CHALLENGER!

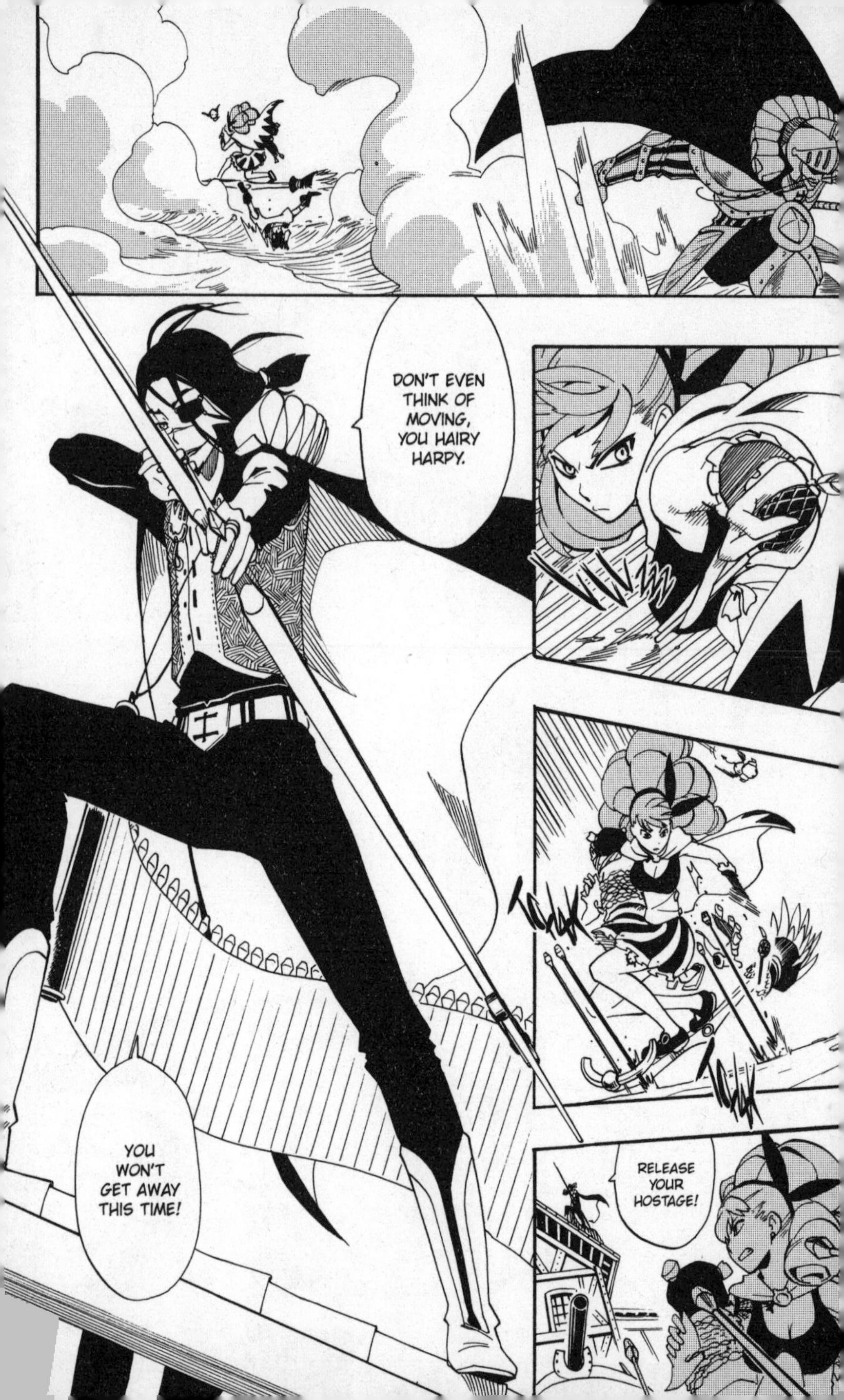
RELEASE YOUR HOSTAGE!
DON'T EVEN THINK OF MOVING, YOU HAIRY HARPY.
YOU WON'T GET AWAY THIS TIME!

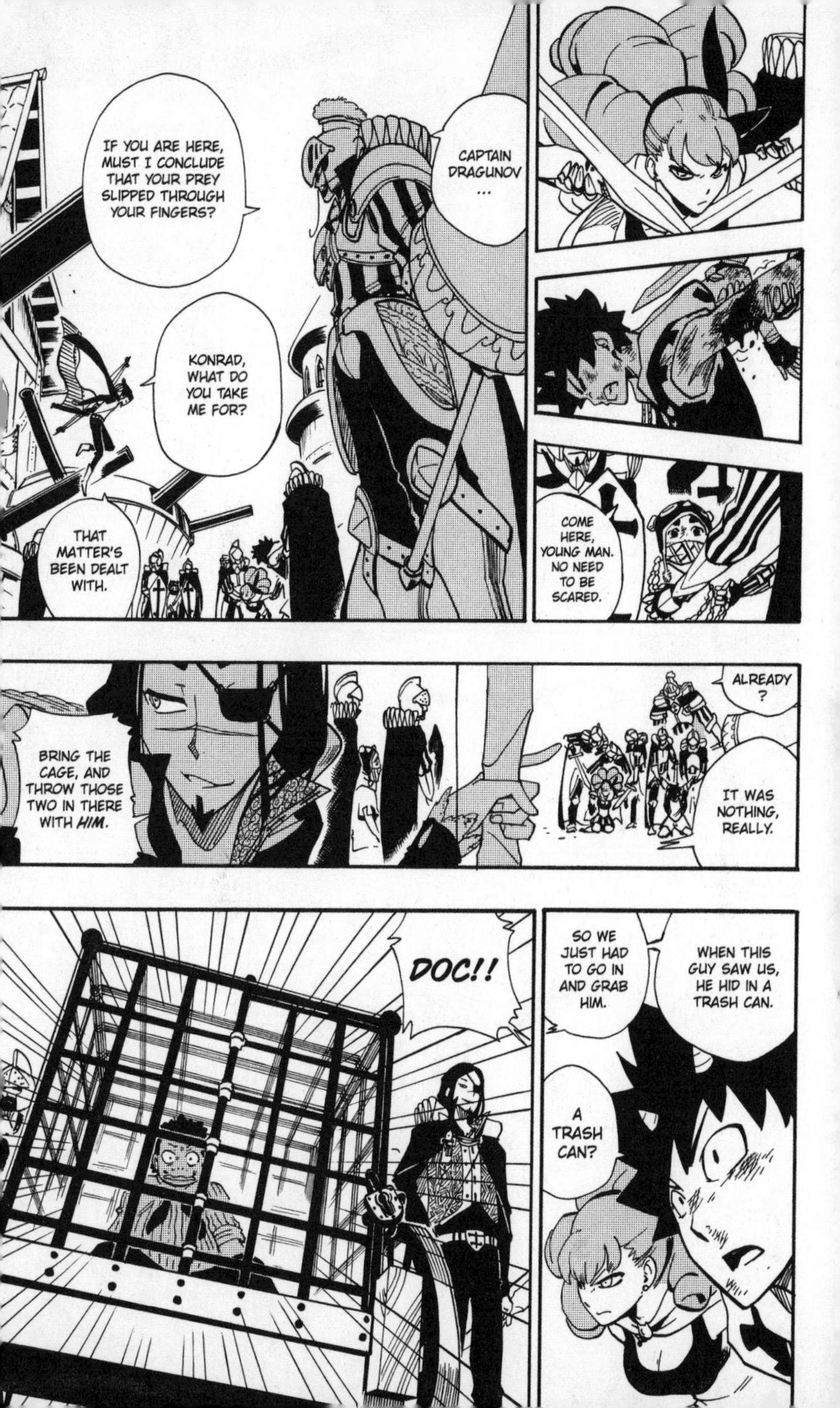
COME HERE, YOUNG MAN. NO NEED TO BE SCARED.
CAPTAIN DRAGUNOV...
IF YOU ARE HERE, MUST I CONCLUDE THAT YOUR PREY SLIPPED THROUGH YOUR FINGERS?
KONRAD, WHAT DO YOU TAKE ME FOR?
THAT MATTER'S BEEN DEALT WITH.
ALREADY?
IT WAS NOTHING, REALLY.
BRING THE CAGE, AND THROW THOSE TWO IN THERE WITH *HIM*.
WHEN THIS GUY SAW US, HE HID IN A TRASH CAN.
SO WE JUST HAD TO GO IN AND GRAB HIM.
A TRASH CAN?
DOC!!

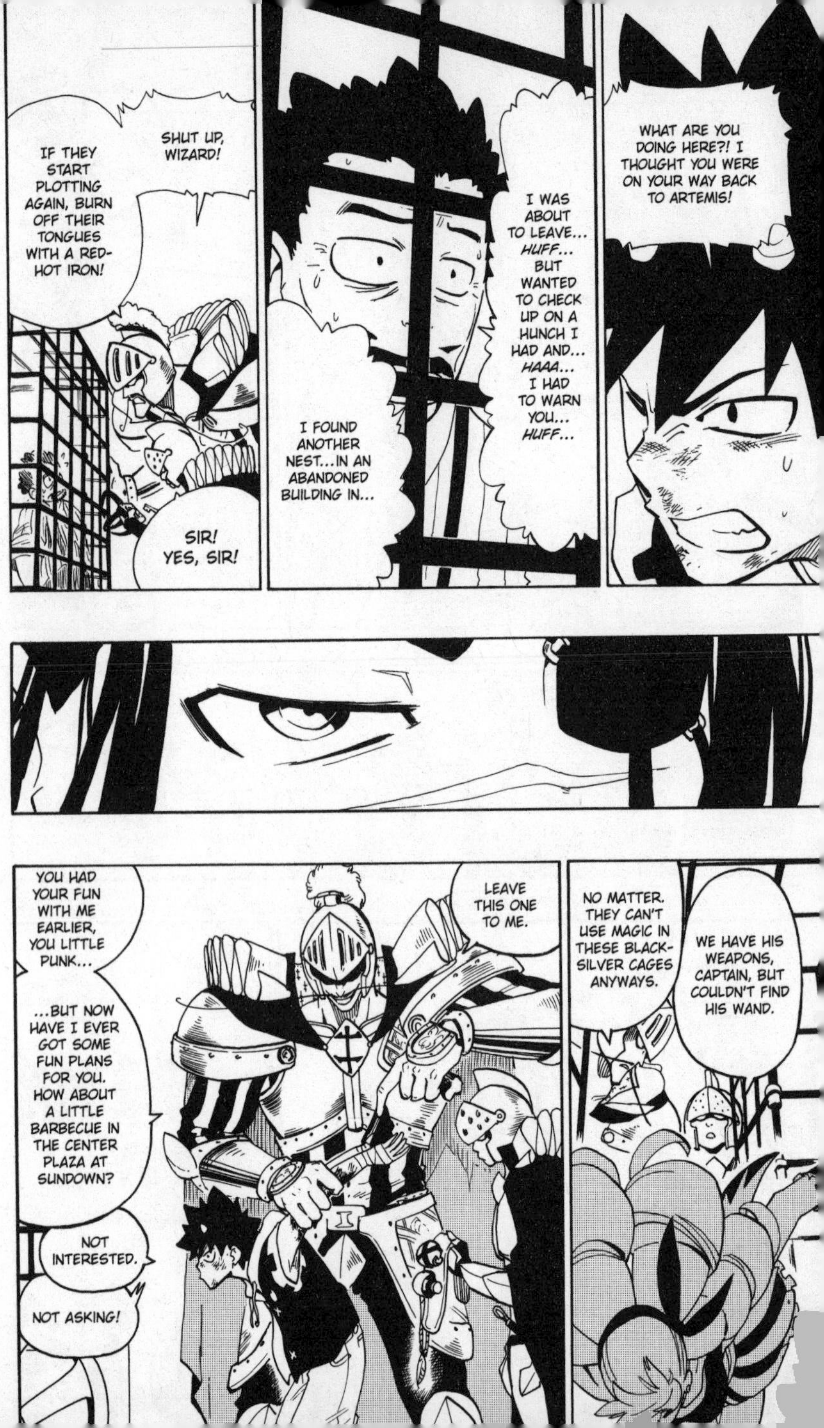
WHAT ARE YOU DOING HERE?! I THOUGHT YOU WERE ON YOUR WAY BACK TO ARTEMIS!
I WAS ABOUT TO LEAVE... *HUFF*... BUT WANTED TO CHECK UP ON A HUNCH I HAD AND... *HAAA*... I HAD TO WARN YOU... *HUFF*...
I FOUND ANOTHER NEST...IN AN ABANDONED BUILDING IN...
SHUT UP, WIZARD!
IF THEY START PLOTTING AGAIN, BURN OFF THEIR TONGUES WITH A RED-HOT IRON!
SIR! YES, SIR!
WE HAVE HIS WEAPONS, CAPTAIN, BUT COULDN'T FIND HIS WAND.
NO MATTER. THEY CAN'T USE MAGIC IN THESE BLACK-SILVER CAGES ANYWAYS.
LEAVE THIS ONE TO ME.
YOU HAD YOUR FUN WITH ME EARLIER, YOU LITTLE PUNK...
...BUT NOW HAVE I EVER GOT SOME FUN PLANS FOR YOU. HOW ABOUT A LITTLE BARBECUE IN THE CENTER PLAZA AT SUNDOWN?
NOT INTERESTED.
NOT ASKING!

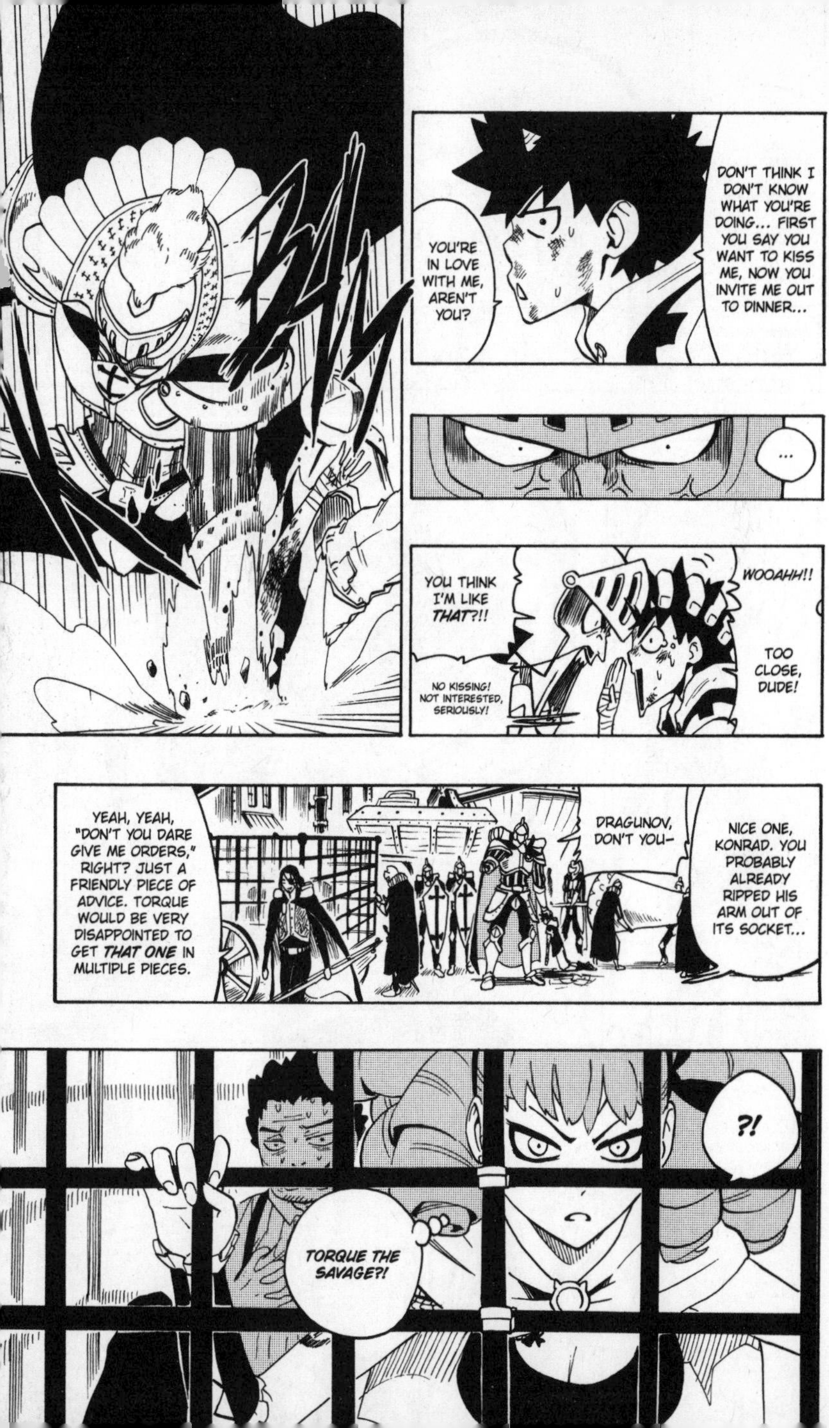
DON'T THINK I DON'T KNOW WHAT YOU'RE DOING... FIRST YOU SAY YOU WANT TO KISS ME, NOW YOU INVITE ME OUT TO DINNER...
YOU'RE IN LOVE WITH ME, AREN'T YOU?
...
WOOAHH!!
TOO CLOSE, DUDE!
YOU THINK I'M LIKE *THAT*?!!
NO KISSING! NOT INTERESTED, SERIOUSLY!
NICE ONE, KONRAD. YOU PROBABLY ALREADY RIPPED HIS ARM OUT OF ITS SOCKET...
DRAGUNOV, DON'T YOU-
YEAH, YEAH, "DON'T YOU DARE GIVE ME ORDERS," RIGHT? JUST A FRIENDLY PIECE OF ADVICE. TORQUE WOULD BE VERY DISAPPOINTED TO GET *THAT ONE* IN MULTIPLE PIECES.
?!
TORQUE THE SAVAGE?!

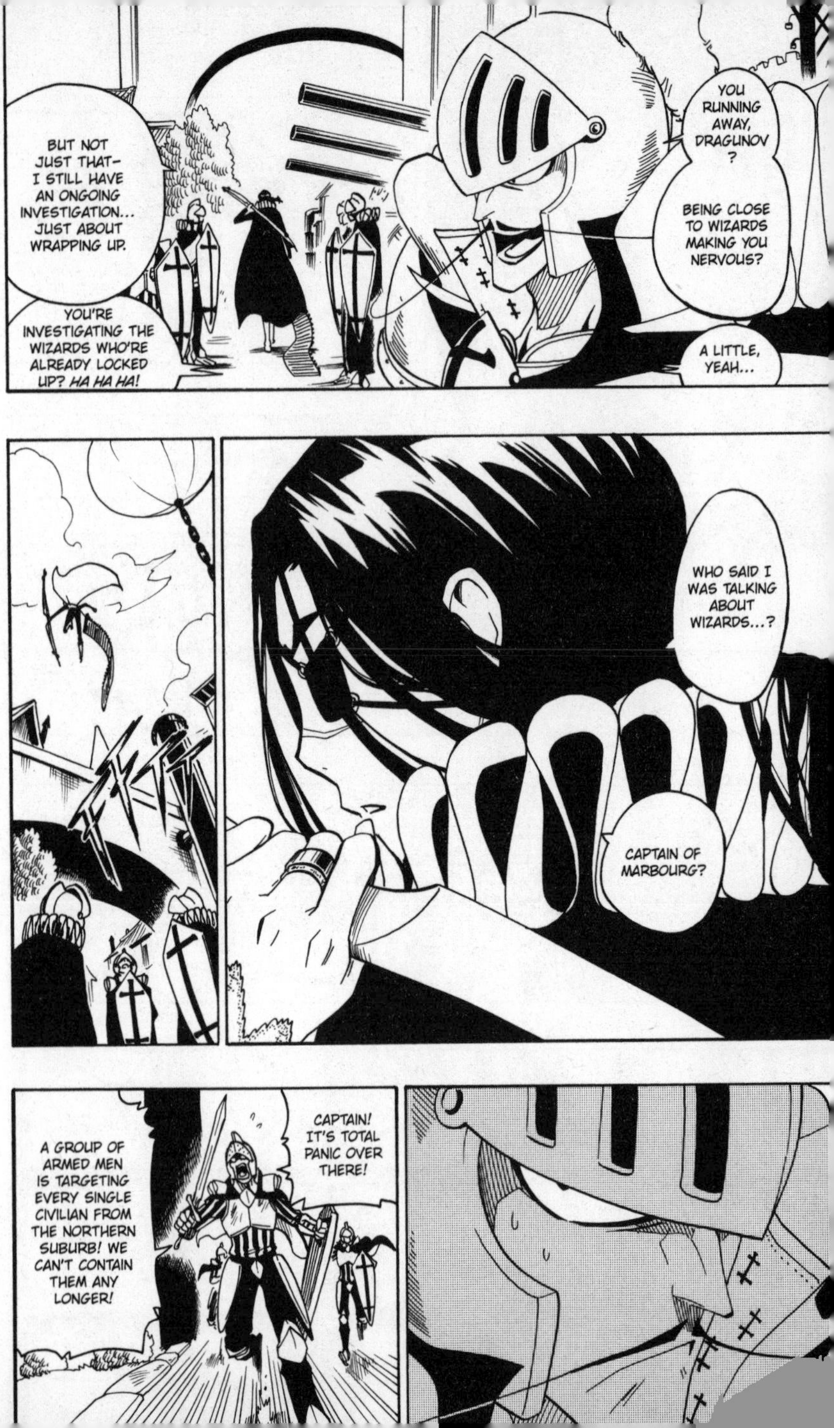
YOU RUNNING AWAY, DRAGUNOV?
BEING CLOSE TO WIZARDS MAKING YOU NERVOUS?
A LITTLE, YEAH...
BUT NOT JUST THAT— I STILL HAVE AN ONGOING INVESTIGATION... JUST ABOUT WRAPPING UP.
YOU'RE INVESTIGATING THE WIZARDS WHO'RE ALREADY LOCKED UP? *HA HA HA!*
WHO SAID I WAS TALKING ABOUT WIZARDS...?
CAPTAIN OF MARBOURG?
CAPTAIN! IT'S TOTAL PANIC OVER THERE!
A GROUP OF ARMED MEN IS TARGETING EVERY SINGLE CIVILIAN FROM THE NORTHERN SUBURB! WE CAN'T CONTAIN THEM ANY LONGER!

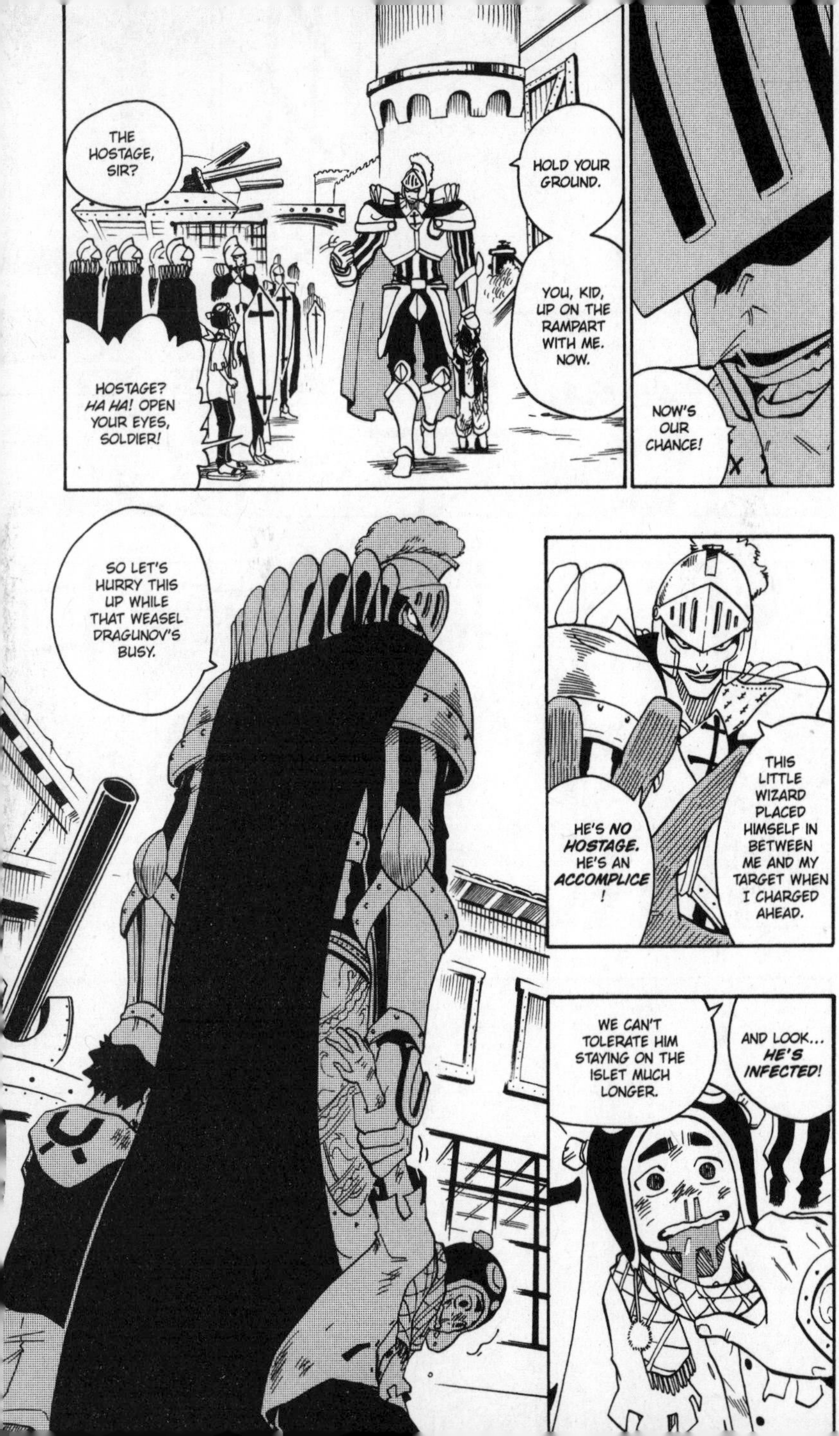
NOW'S OUR CHANCE!
THE HOSTAGE, SIR?
HOLD YOUR GROUND.
YOU, KID, UP ON THE RAMPART WITH ME. NOW.
HOSTAGE? *HA HA!* OPEN YOUR EYES, SOLDIER!
THIS LITTLE WIZARD PLACED HIMSELF IN BETWEEN ME AND MY TARGET WHEN I CHARGED AHEAD.
HE'S ***NO HOSTAGE.*** HE'S AN ***ACCOMPLICE!***
AND LOOK... ***HE'S INFECTED!***
WE CAN'T TOLERATE HIM STAYING ON THE ISLET MUCH LONGER.
SO LET'S HURRY THIS UP WHILE THAT WEASEL DRAGUNOV'S BUSY.

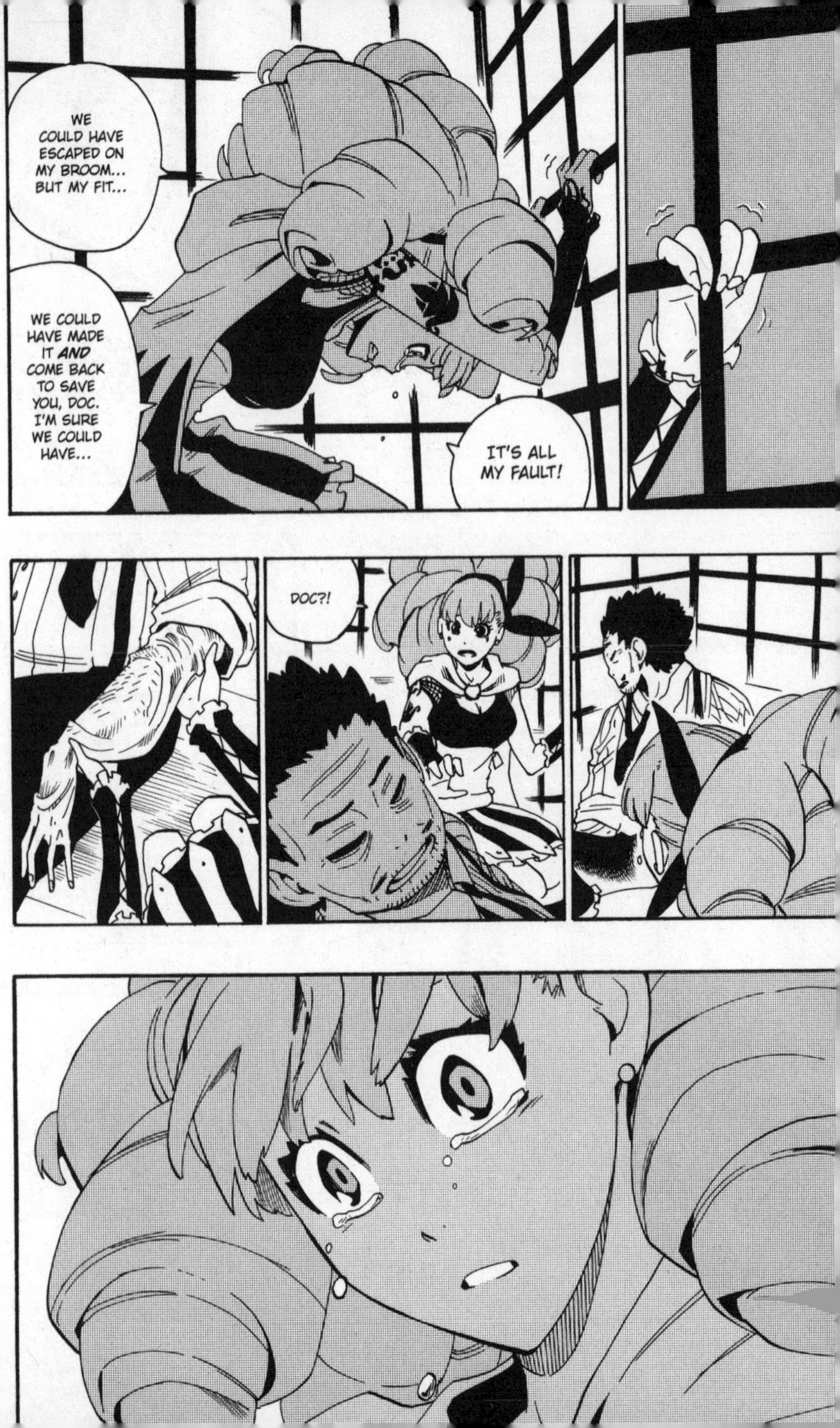
WE COULD HAVE ESCAPED ON MY BROOM... BUT MY FIT...
WE COULD HAVE MADE IT *AND* COME BACK TO SAVE YOU, DOC. I'M SURE WE COULD HAVE...
IT'S ALL MY FAULT!
DOC?!

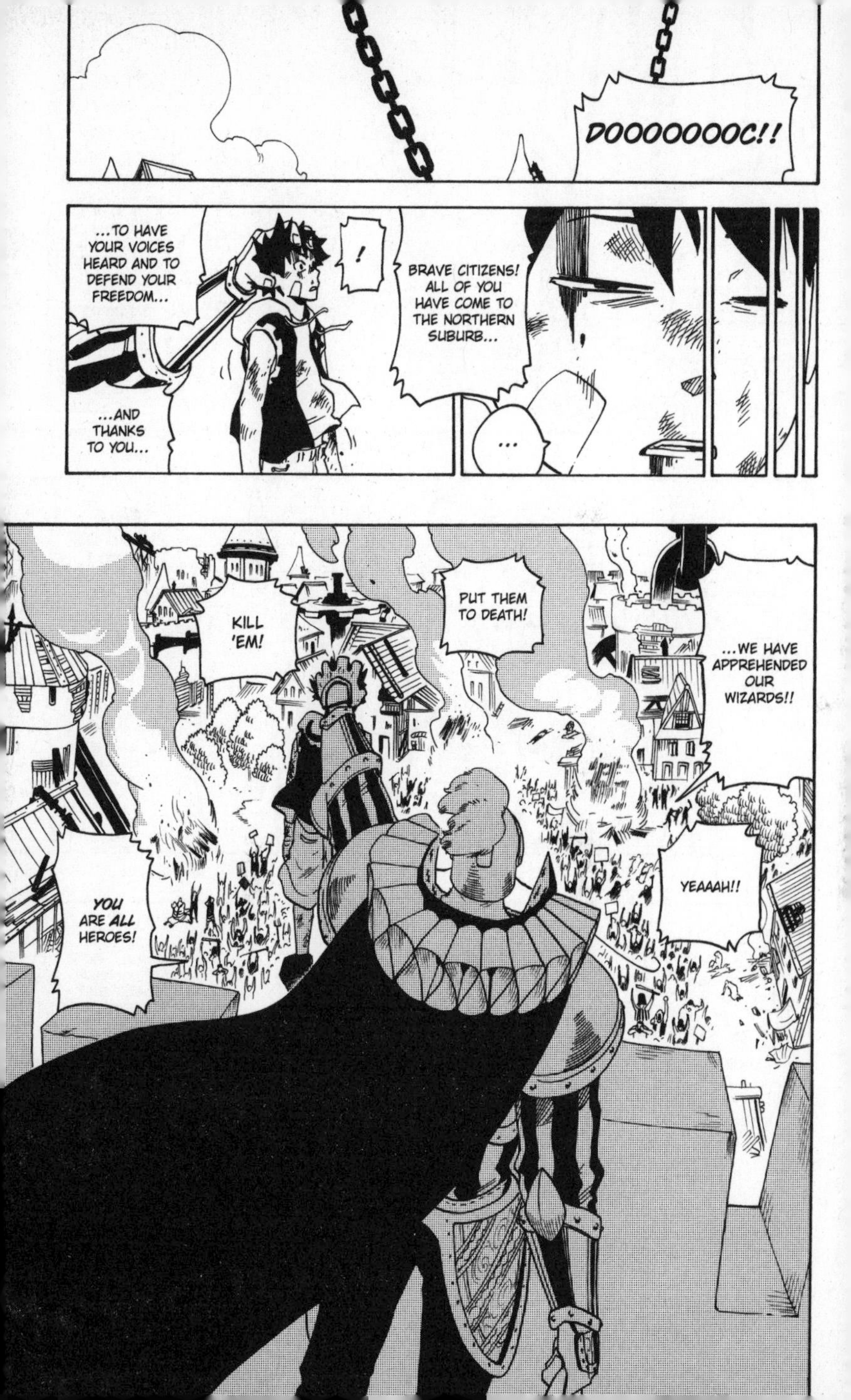
DOOOOOOOC!!
BRAVE CITIZENS! ALL OF YOU HAVE COME TO THE NORTHERN SUBURB...
...
!
...TO HAVE YOUR VOICES HEARD AND TO DEFEND YOUR FREEDOM...
...AND THANKS TO YOU...
...WE HAVE APPREHENDED OUR WIZARDS!!
PUT THEM TO DEATH!
KILL 'EM!
YEAAAH!!
YOU ARE ALL HEROES!

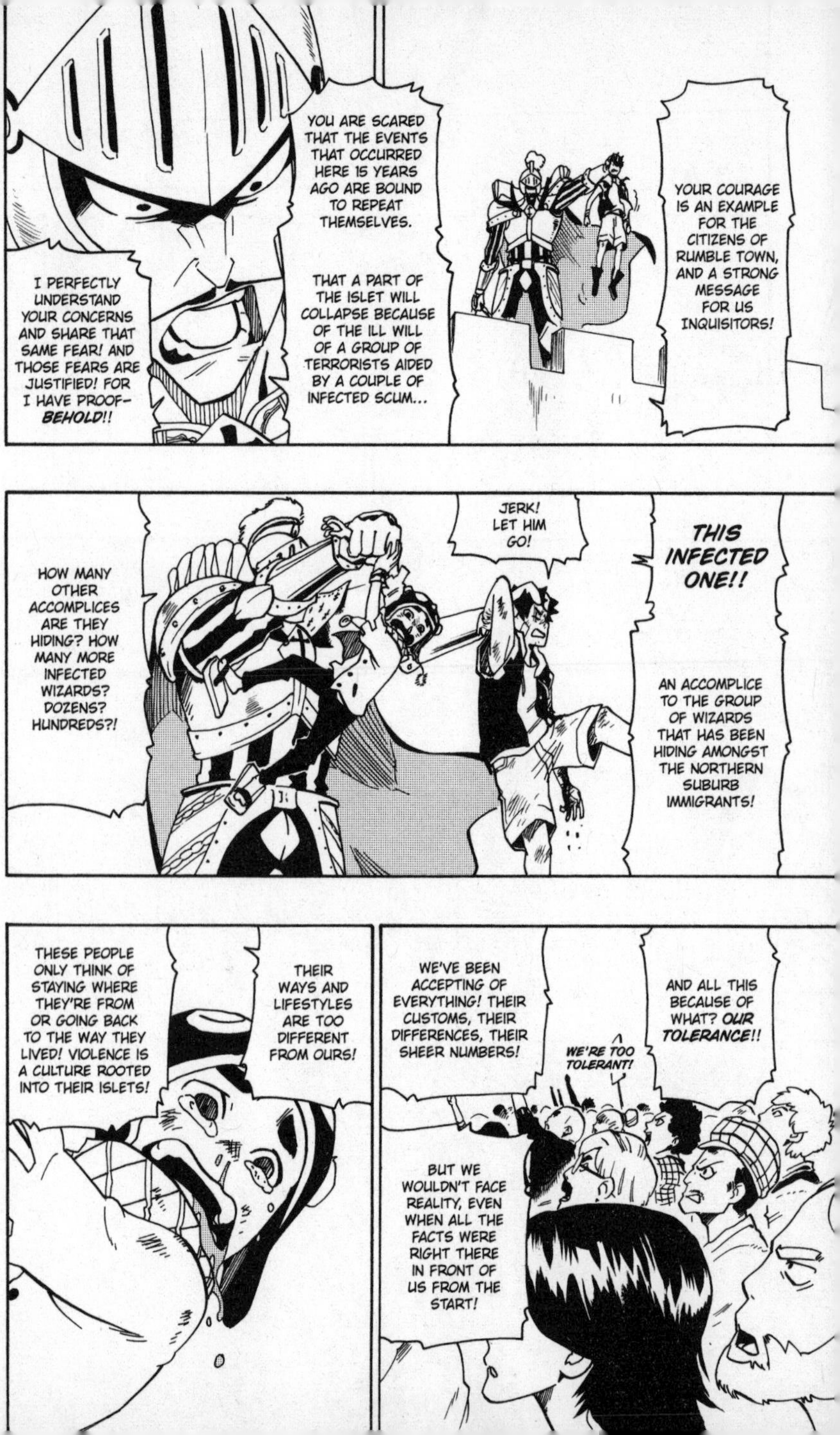
YOUR COURAGE IS AN EXAMPLE FOR THE CITIZENS OF RUMBLE TOWN, AND A STRONG MESSAGE FOR US INQUISITORS!
YOU ARE SCARED THAT THE EVENTS THAT OCCURRED HERE 15 YEARS AGO ARE BOUND TO REPEAT THEMSELVES.
THAT A PART OF THE ISLET WILL COLLAPSE BECAUSE OF THE ILL WILL OF A GROUP OF TERRORISTS AIDED BY A COUPLE OF INFECTED SCUM...
I PERFECTLY UNDERSTAND YOUR CONCERNS AND SHARE THAT SAME FEAR! AND THOSE FEARS ARE JUSTIFIED! FOR I HAVE PROOF-*BEHOLD*!!
THIS INFECTED ONE!!
AN ACCOMPLICE TO THE GROUP OF WIZARDS THAT HAS BEEN HIDING AMONGST THE NORTHERN SUBURB IMMIGRANTS!
JERK! LET HIM GO!
HOW MANY OTHER ACCOMPLICES ARE THEY HIDING? HOW MANY MORE INFECTED WIZARDS? DOZENS? HUNDREDS?!
AND ALL THIS BECAUSE OF WHAT? *OUR TOLERANCE*!!
WE'RE TOO TOLERANT!
WE'VE BEEN ACCEPTING OF EVERYTHING! THEIR CUSTOMS, THEIR DIFFERENCES, THEIR SHEER NUMBERS!
BUT WE WOULDN'T FACE REALITY, EVEN WHEN ALL THE FACTS WERE RIGHT THERE IN FRONT OF US FROM THE START!
THEIR WAYS AND LIFESTYLES ARE TOO DIFFERENT FROM OURS!
THESE PEOPLE ONLY THINK OF STAYING WHERE THEY'RE FROM OR GOING BACK TO THE WAY THEY LIVED! VIOLENCE IS A CULTURE ROOTED INTO THEIR ISLETS!

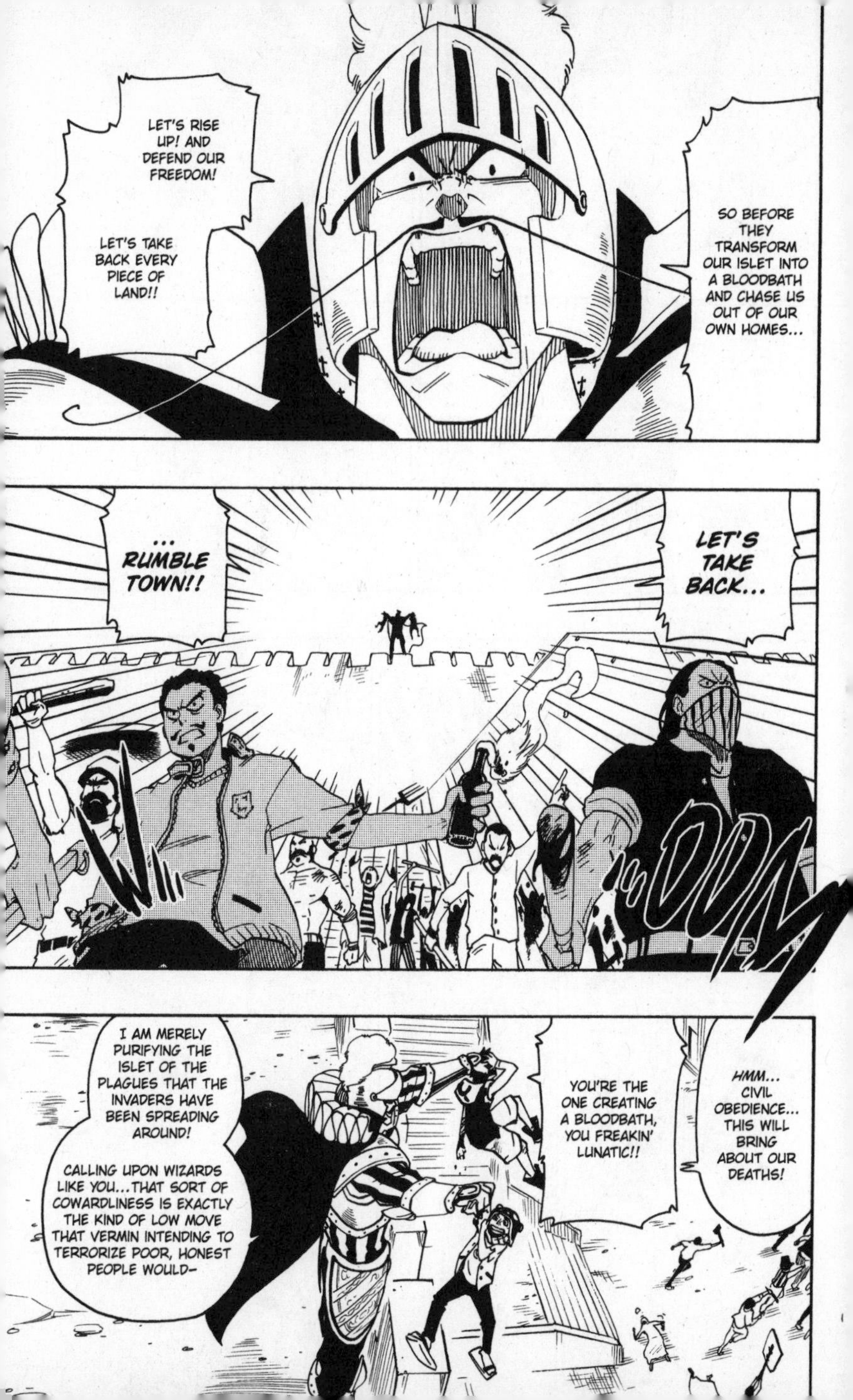
SO BEFORE THEY TRANSFORM OUR ISLET INTO A BLOODBATH AND CHASE US OUT OF OUR OWN HOMES...
LET'S RISE UP! AND DEFEND OUR FREEDOM!
LET'S TAKE BACK EVERY PIECE OF LAND!!
LET'S TAKE BACK...
...RUMBLE TOWN!!
HMM... CIVIL OBEDIENCE... THIS WILL BRING ABOUT OUR DEATHS!
YOU'RE THE ONE CREATING A BLOODBATH, YOU FREAKIN' LUNATIC!!
I AM MERELY PURIFYING THE ISLET OF THE PLAGUES THAT THE INVADERS HAVE BEEN SPREADING AROUND!
CALLING UPON WIZARDS LIKE YOU...THAT SORT OF COWARDLINESS IS EXACTLY THE KIND OF LOW MOVE THAT VERMIN INTENDING TO TERRORIZE POOR, HONEST PEOPLE WOULD-

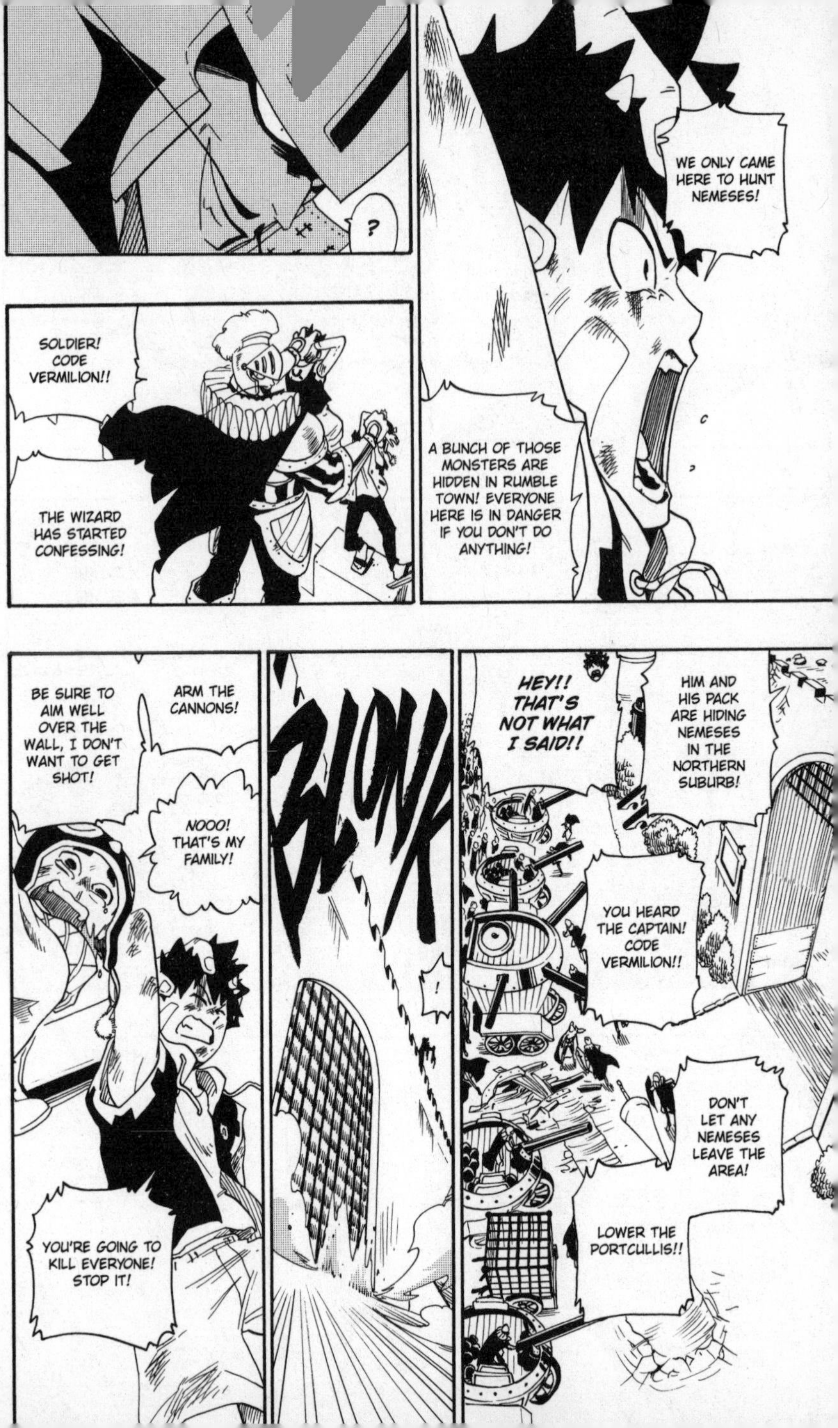
WE ONLY CAME HERE TO HUNT NEMESES!
A BUNCH OF THOSE MONSTERS ARE HIDDEN IN RUMBLE TOWN! EVERYONE HERE IS IN DANGER IF YOU DON'T DO ANYTHING!
?
SOLDIER! CODE VERMILION!!
THE WIZARD HAS STARTED CONFESSING!
HIM AND HIS PACK ARE HIDING NEMESES IN THE NORTHERN SUBURB!
HEY!! THAT'S NOT WHAT I SAID!!
YOU HEARD THE CAPTAIN! CODE VERMILION!!
DON'T LET ANY NEMESES LEAVE THE AREA!
LOWER THE PORTCULLIS!!
BLONK
!
ARM THE CANNONS!
BE SURE TO AIM WELL OVER THE WALL, I DON'T WANT TO GET SHOT!
NOOO! THAT'S MY FAMILY!
YOU'RE GOING TO KILL EVERYONE! STOP IT!

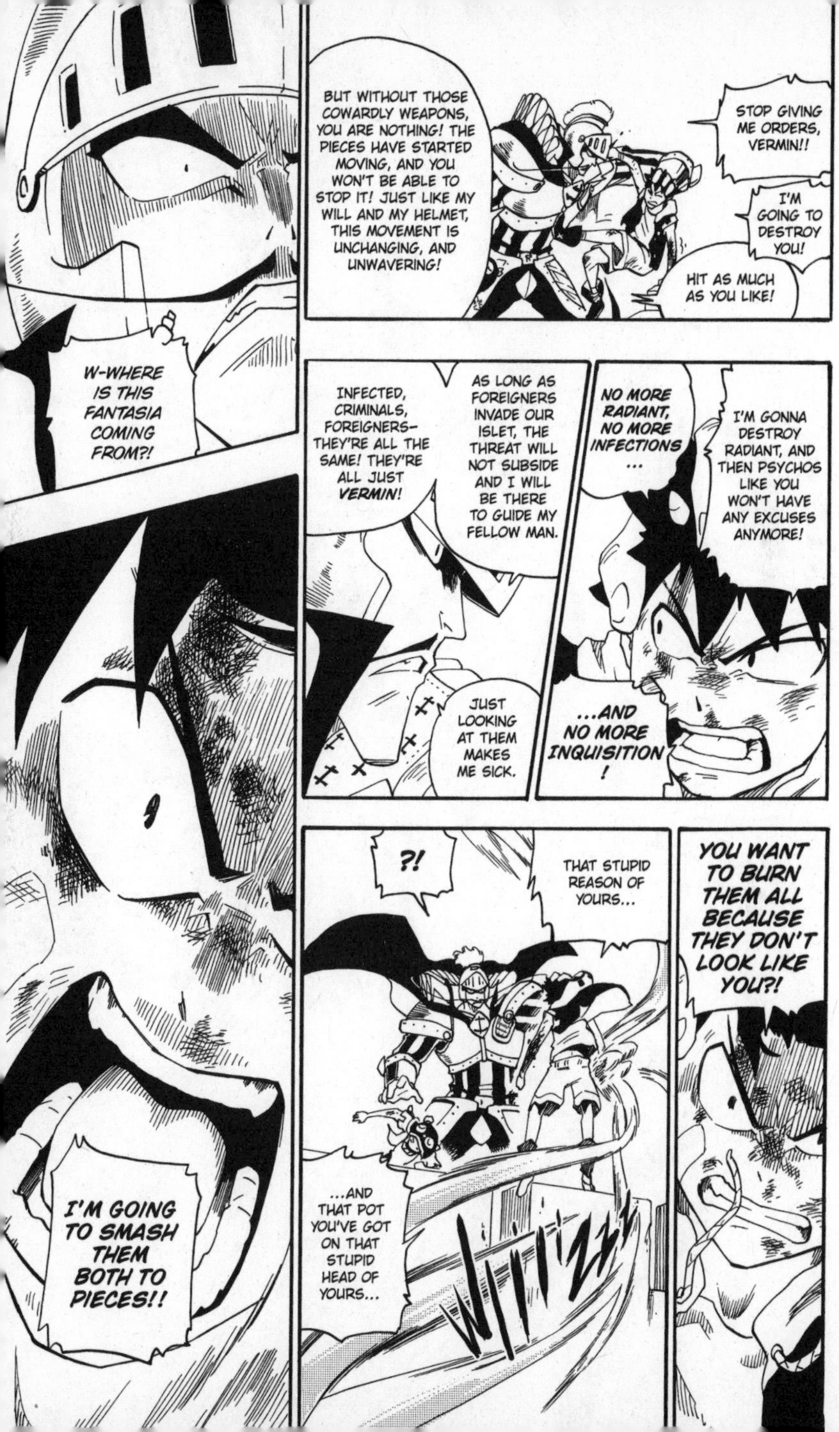
STOP GIVING ME ORDERS, VERMIN!!
I'M GOING TO DESTROY YOU!
HIT AS MUCH AS YOU LIKE!
BUT WITHOUT THOSE COWARDLY WEAPONS, YOU ARE NOTHING! THE PIECES HAVE STARTED MOVING, AND YOU WON'T BE ABLE TO STOP IT! JUST LIKE MY WILL AND MY HELMET, THIS MOVEMENT IS UNCHANGING, AND UNWAVERING!
W-WHERE IS THIS FANTASIA COMING FROM?!
NO MORE RADIANT, NO MORE INFECTIONS...
I'M GONNA DESTROY RADIANT, AND THEN PSYCHOS LIKE YOU WON'T HAVE ANY EXCUSES ANYMORE!
...AND NO MORE INQUISITION!
AS LONG AS FOREIGNERS INVADE OUR ISLET, THE THREAT WILL NOT SUBSIDE AND I WILL BE THERE TO GUIDE MY FELLOW MAN.
INFECTED, CRIMINALS, FOREIGNERS— THEY'RE ALL THE SAME! THEY'RE ALL JUST VERMIN!
JUST LOOKING AT THEM MAKES ME SICK.
YOU WANT TO BURN THEM ALL BECAUSE THEY DON'T LOOK LIKE YOU?!
?!
THAT STUPID REASON OF YOURS...
...AND THAT POT YOU'VE GOT ON THAT STUPID HEAD OF YOURS...
I'M GOING TO SMASH THEM BOTH TO PIECES!!

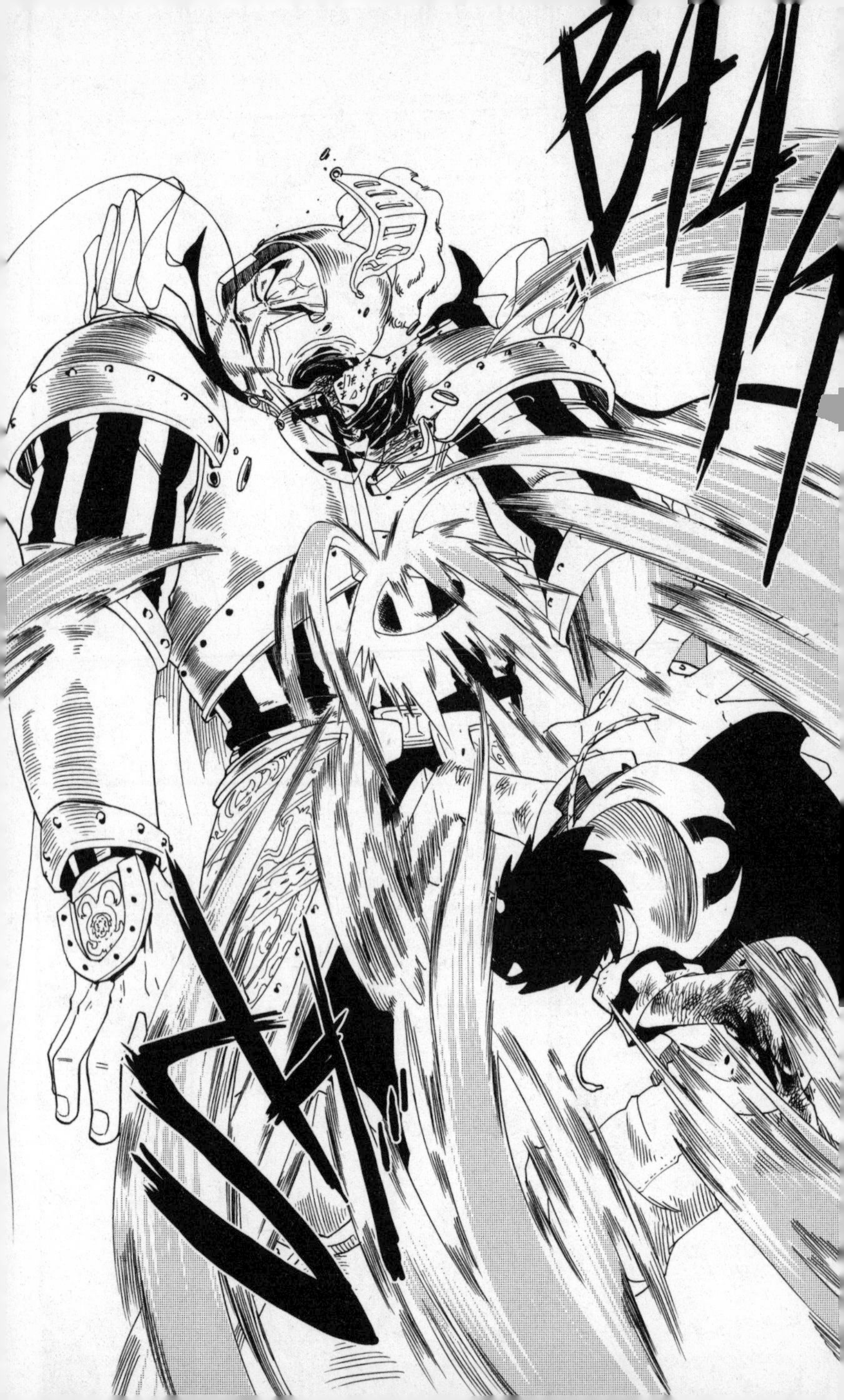

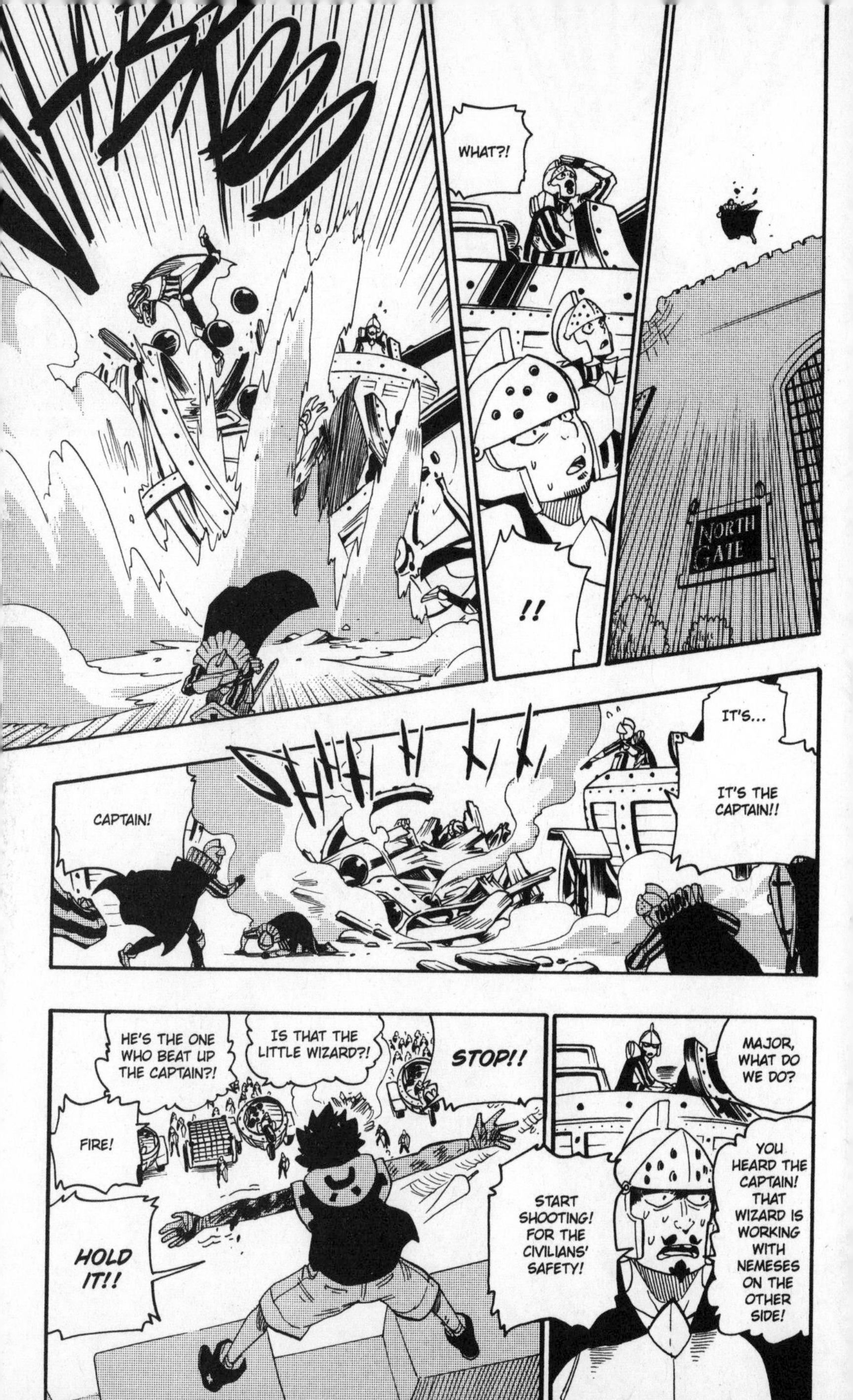

NORTH GATE
WHAT?!
!!
IT'S...
IT'S THE CAPTAIN!!
CAPTAIN!
MAJOR, WHAT DO WE DO?
YOU HEARD THE CAPTAIN! THAT WIZARD IS WORKING WITH NEMESES ON THE OTHER SIDE!
START SHOOTING! FOR THE CIVILIANS' SAFETY!
STOP!!
IS THAT THE LITTLE WIZARD?!
HE'S THE ONE WHO BEAT UP THE CAPTAIN?!
FIRE!
HOLD IT!!

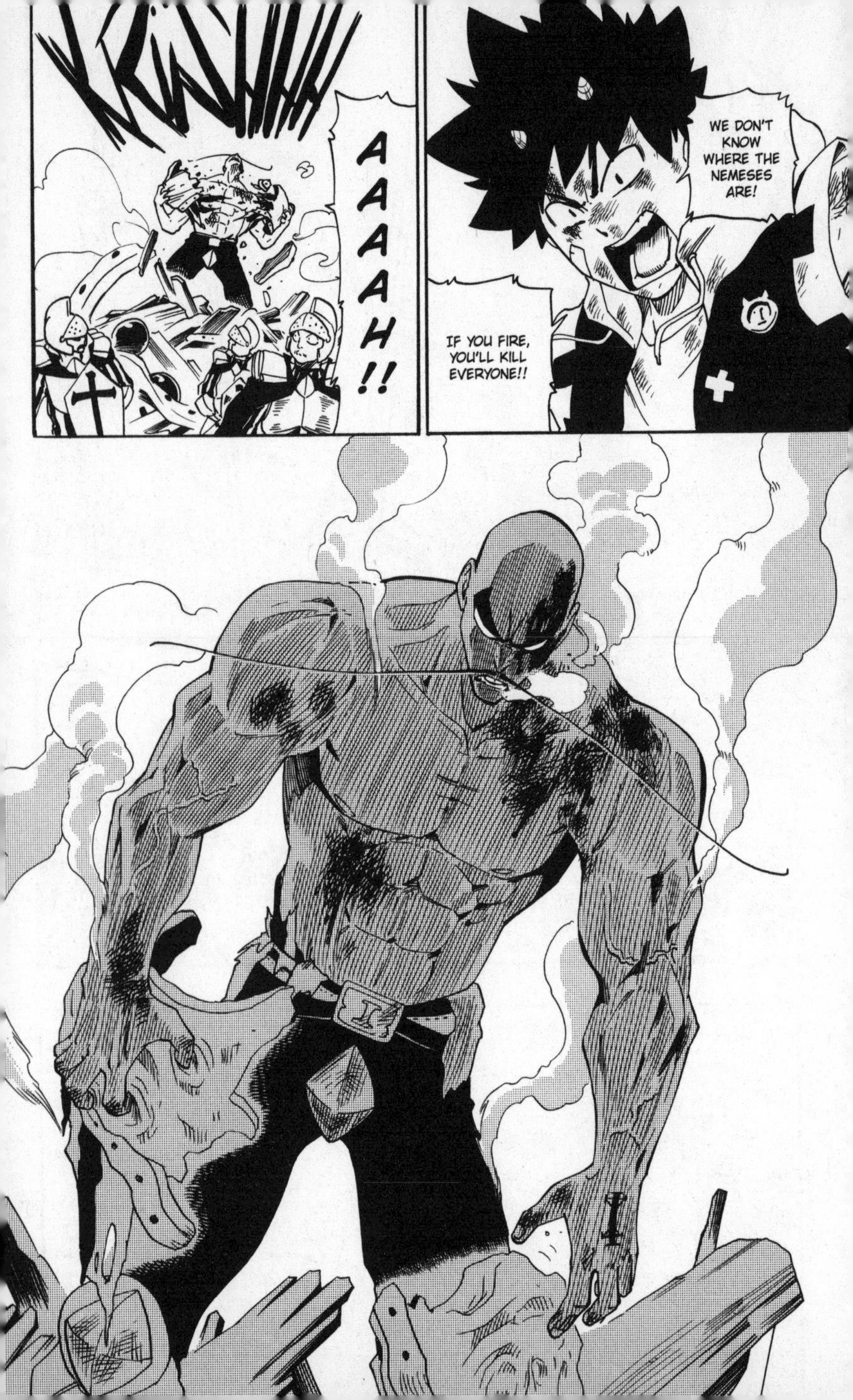
WE DON'T KNOW WHERE THE NEMESES ARE!
IF YOU FIRE, YOU'LL KILL EVERYONE!!
AAAAH!!

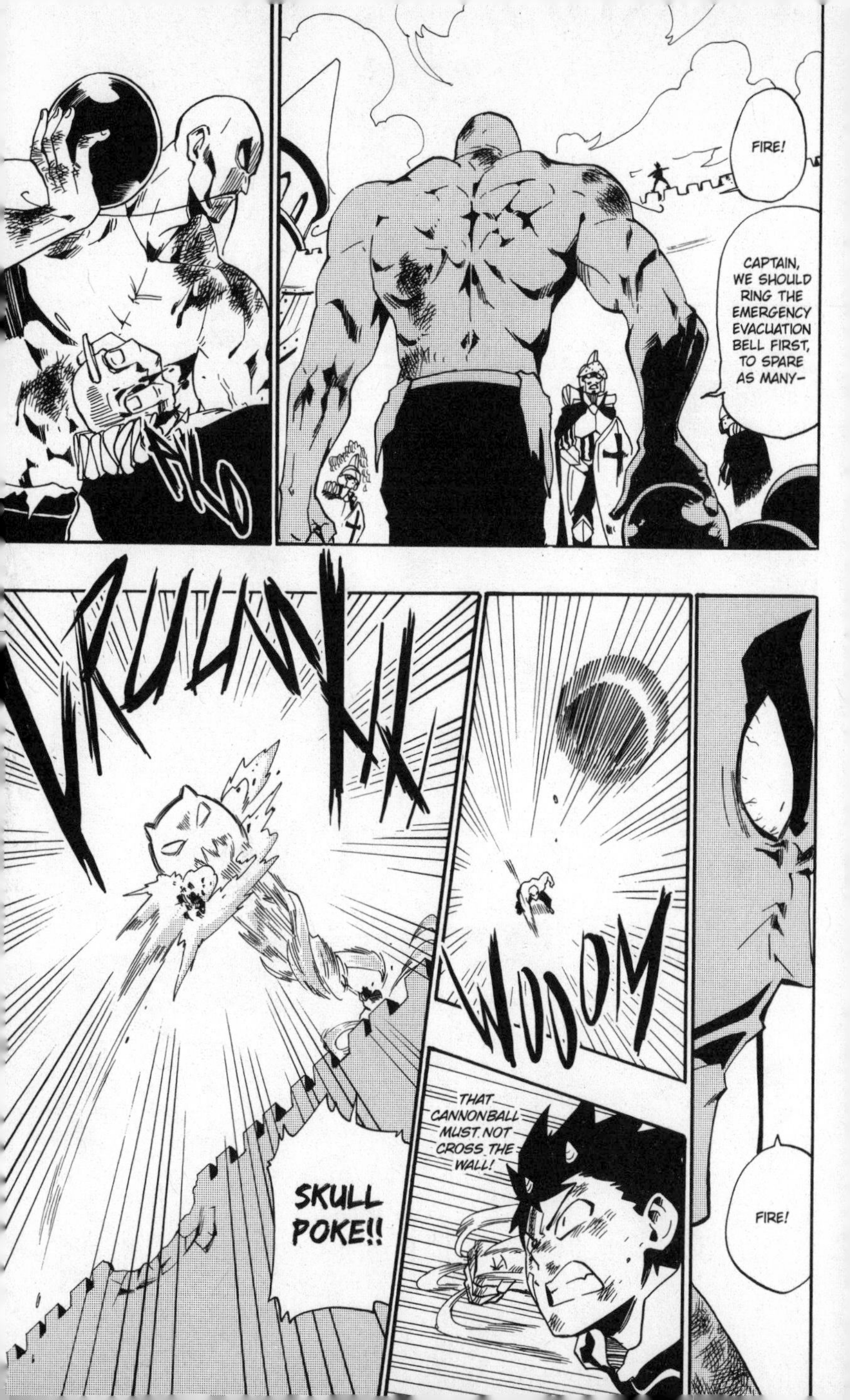
FIRE!
CAPTAIN, WE SHOULD RING THE EMERGENCY EVACUATION BELL FIRST, TO SPARE AS MANY—
FIRE!
WOOOM
THAT CANNONBALL MUST NOT CROSS THE WALL!
SKULL POKE!!

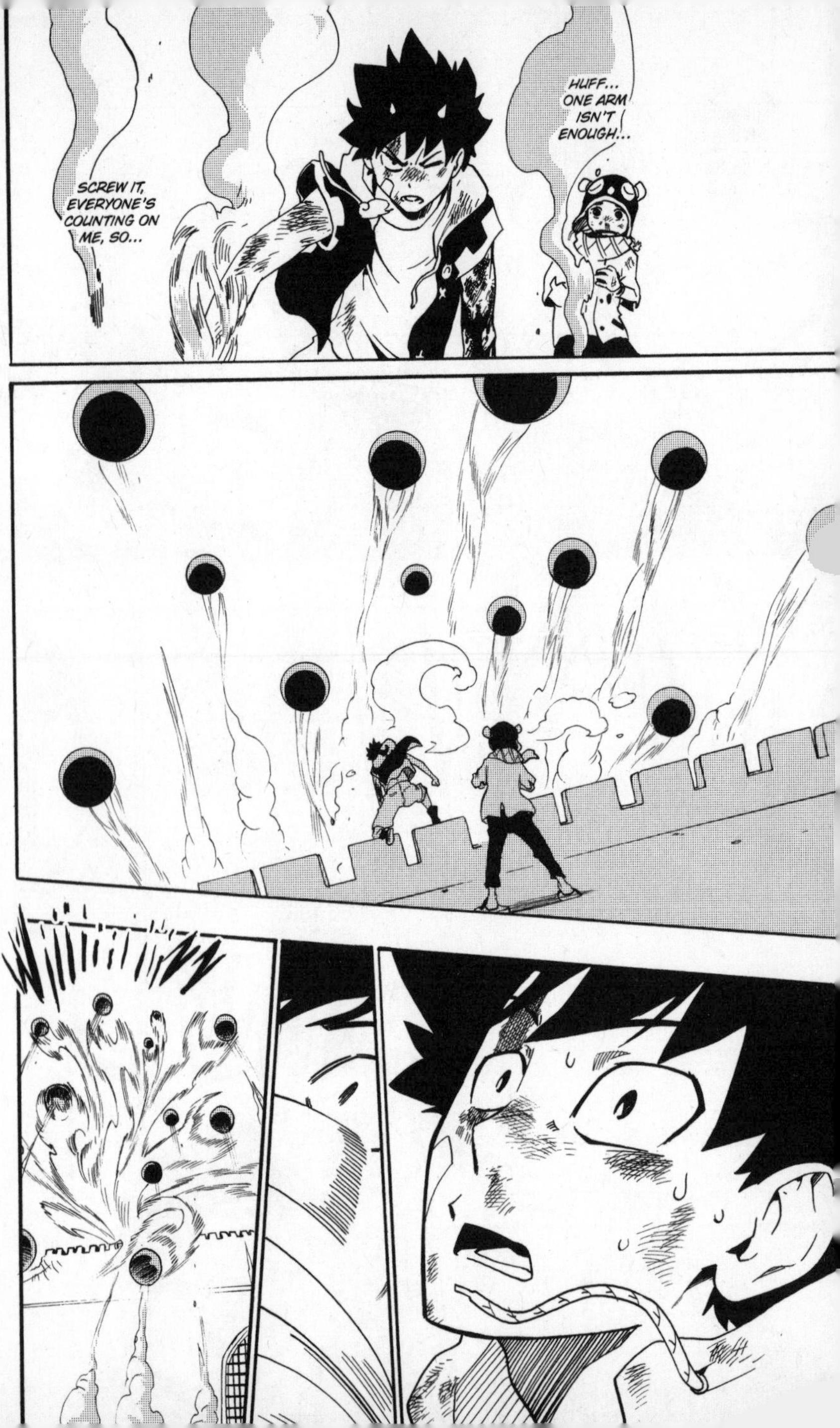
HUFF... ONE ARM ISN'T ENOUGH...
SCREW IT, EVERYONE'S COUNTING ON ME, SO...

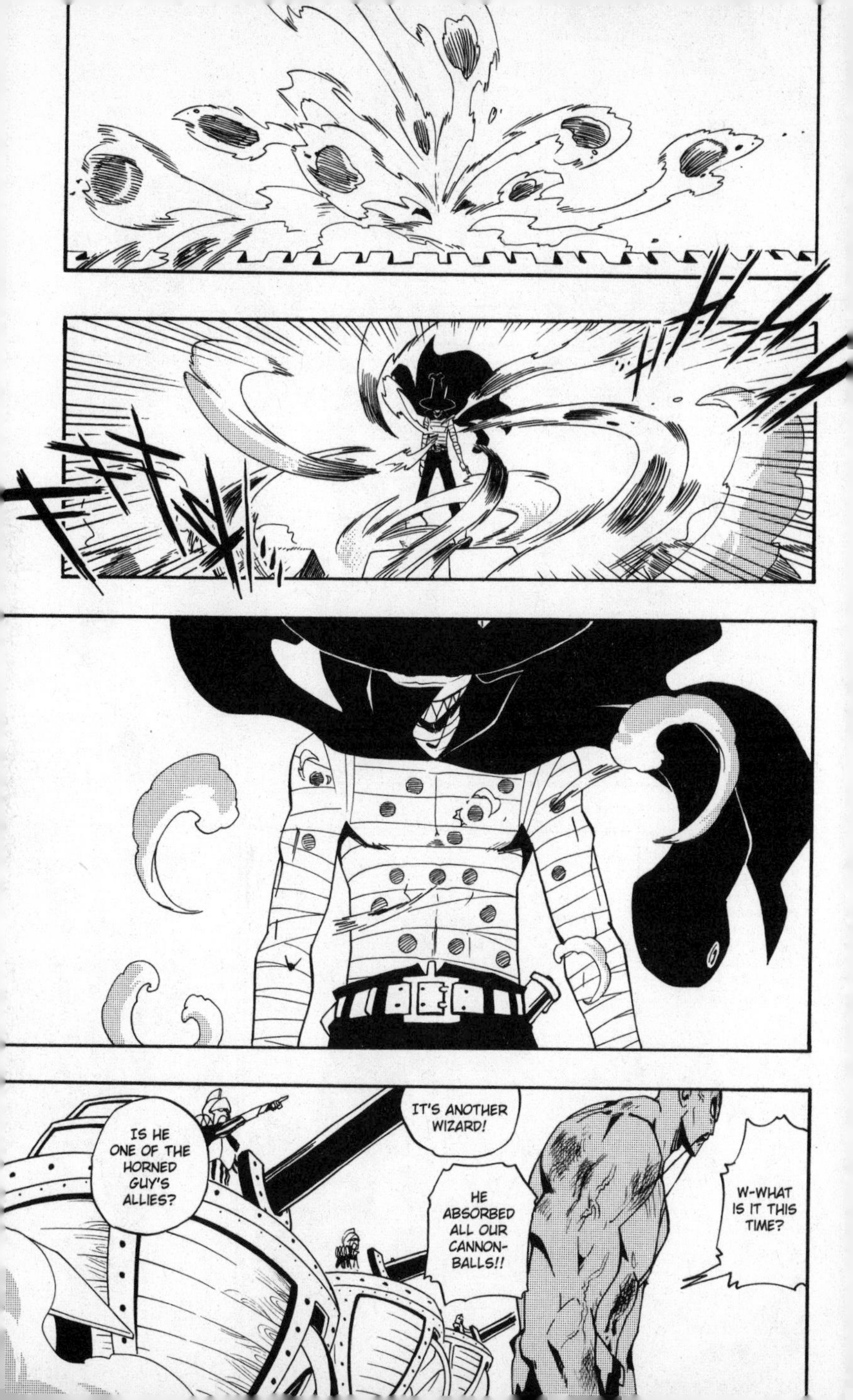
W-WHAT IS IT THIS TIME?
IT'S ANOTHER WIZARD!
HE ABSORBED ALL OUR CANNON-BALLS!!
IS HE ONE OF THE HORNED GUY'S ALLIES?

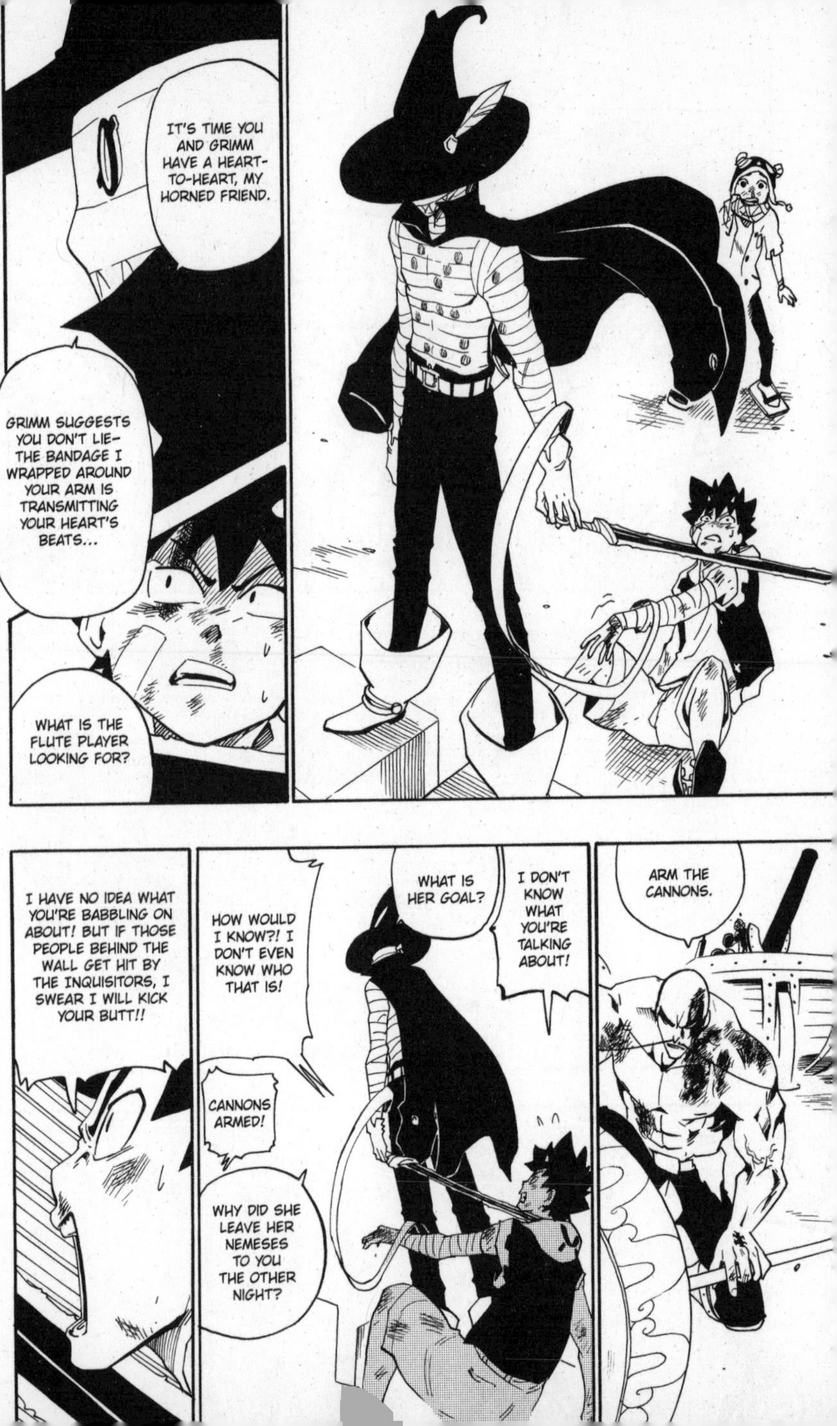
IT'S TIME YOU AND GRIMM HAVE A HEART-TO-HEART, MY HORNED FRIEND.
GRIMM SUGGESTS YOU DON'T LIE–THE BANDAGE I WRAPPED AROUND YOUR ARM IS TRANSMITTING YOUR HEART'S BEATS...
WHAT IS THE FLUTE PLAYER LOOKING FOR?
ARM THE CANNONS.
I DON'T KNOW WHAT YOU'RE TALKING ABOUT!
WHAT IS HER GOAL?
HOW WOULD I KNOW?! I DON'T EVEN KNOW WHO THAT IS!
CANNONS ARMED!
WHY DID SHE LEAVE HER NEMESES TO YOU THE OTHER NIGHT?
I HAVE NO IDEA WHAT YOU'RE BABBLING ON ABOUT! BUT IF THOSE PEOPLE BEHIND THE WALL GET HIT BY THE INQUISITORS, I SWEAR I WILL KICK YOUR BUTT!!

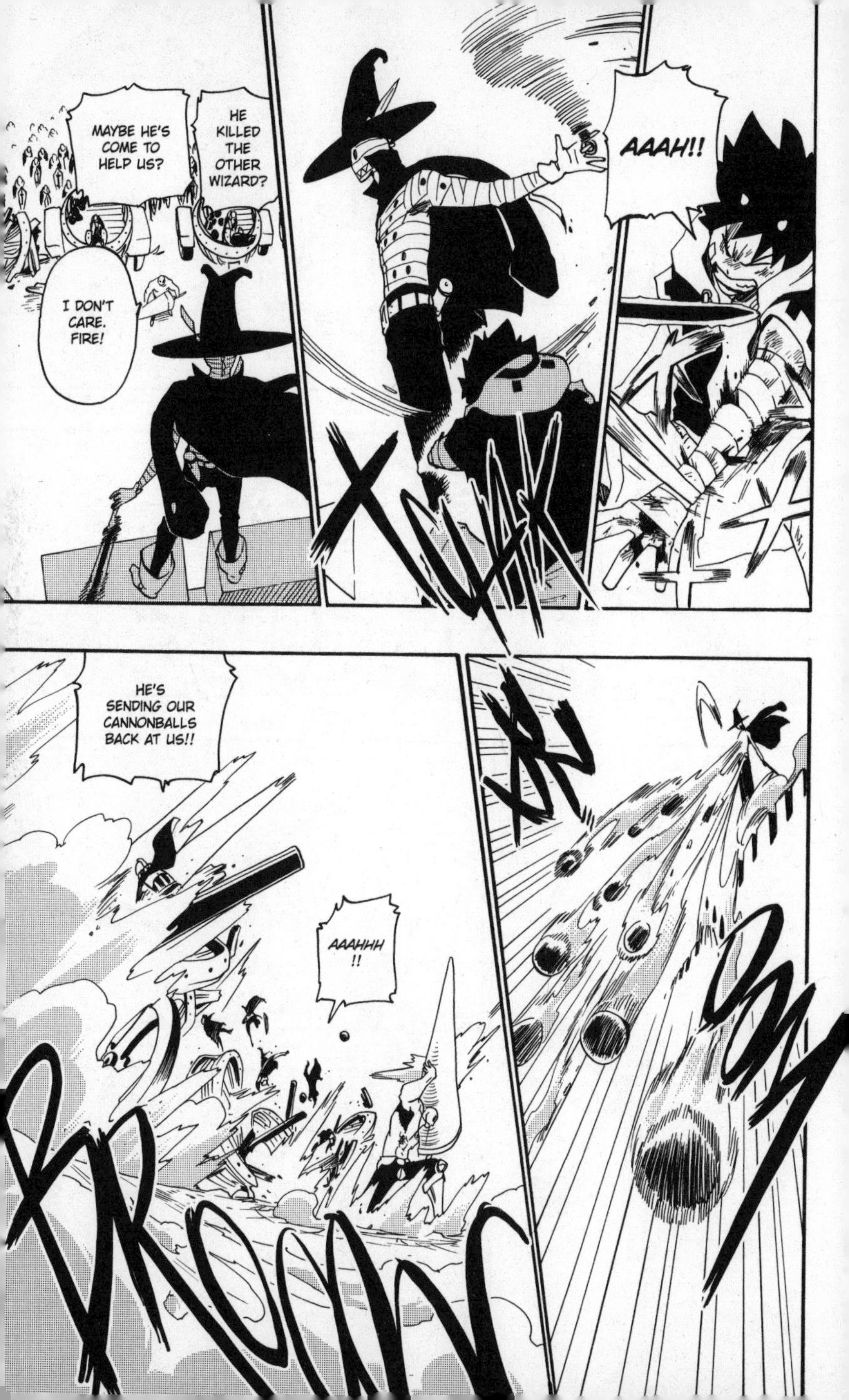
AAAH!!
HE KILLED THE OTHER WIZARD?
MAYBE HE'S COME TO HELP US?
I DON'T CARE. FIRE!
HE'S SENDING OUR CANNONBALLS BACK AT US!!
AAAHHH!!

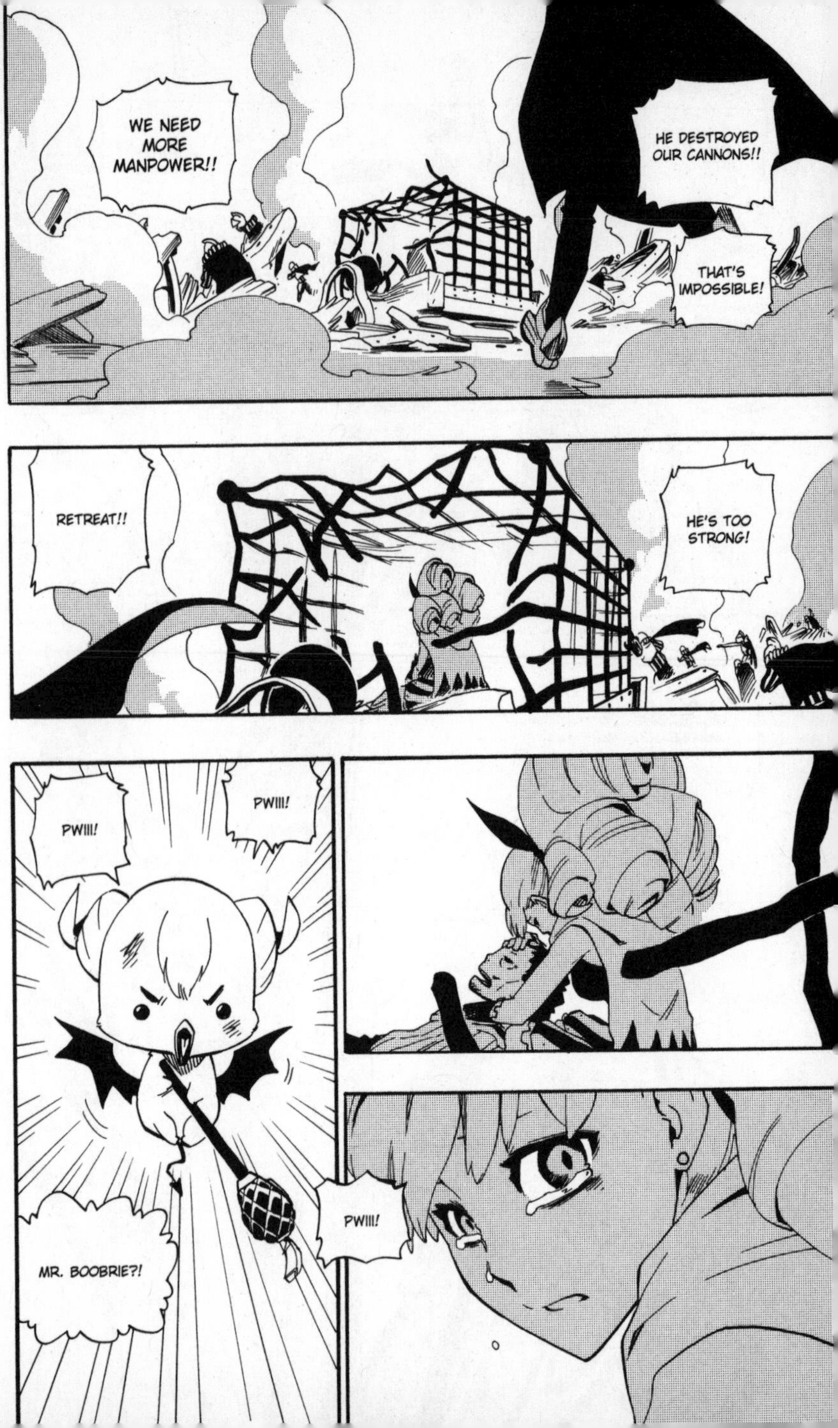
HE DESTROYED OUR CANNONS!!
THAT'S IMPOSSIBLE!
WE NEED MORE MANPOWER!!
HE'S TOO STRONG!
RETREAT!!
PWIII!
PWIII!
PWIII!
MR. BOOBRIE?!

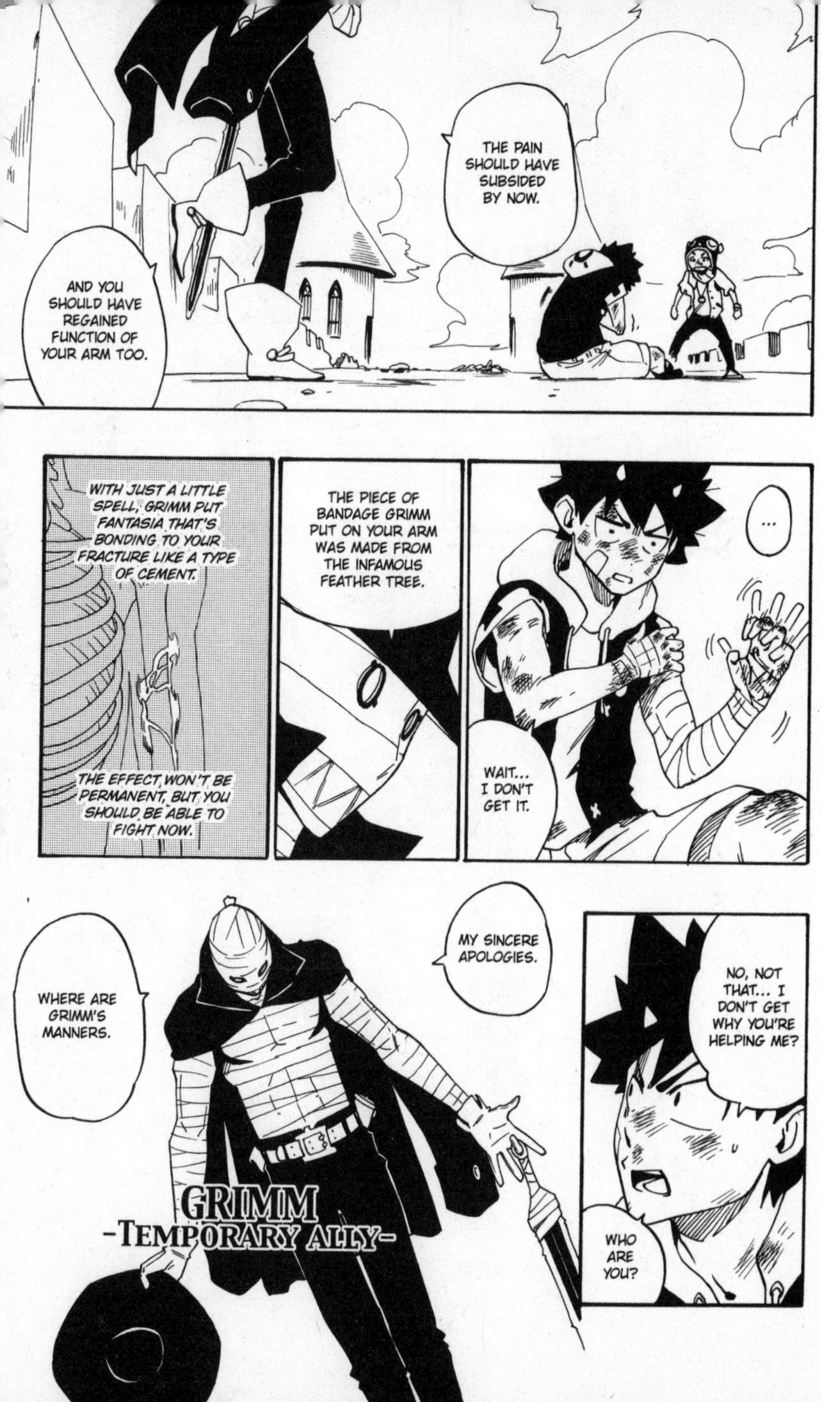
THE PAIN SHOULD HAVE SUBSIDED BY NOW.
AND YOU SHOULD HAVE REGAINED FUNCTION OF YOUR ARM TOO.
...
WAIT... I DON'T GET IT.
THE PIECE OF BANDAGE GRIMM PUT ON YOUR ARM WAS MADE FROM THE INFAMOUS FEATHER TREE.
WITH JUST A LITTLE SPELL, GRIMM PUT FANTASIA THAT'S BONDING TO YOUR FRACTURE LIKE A TYPE OF CEMENT.
THE EFFECT WON'T BE PERMANENT, BUT YOU SHOULD BE ABLE TO FIGHT NOW.
NO, NOT THAT... I DON'T GET WHY YOU'RE HELPING ME?
WHO ARE YOU?
MY SINCERE APOLOGIES.
WHERE ARE GRIMM'S MANNERS.
GRIMM
-TEMPORARY ALLY-

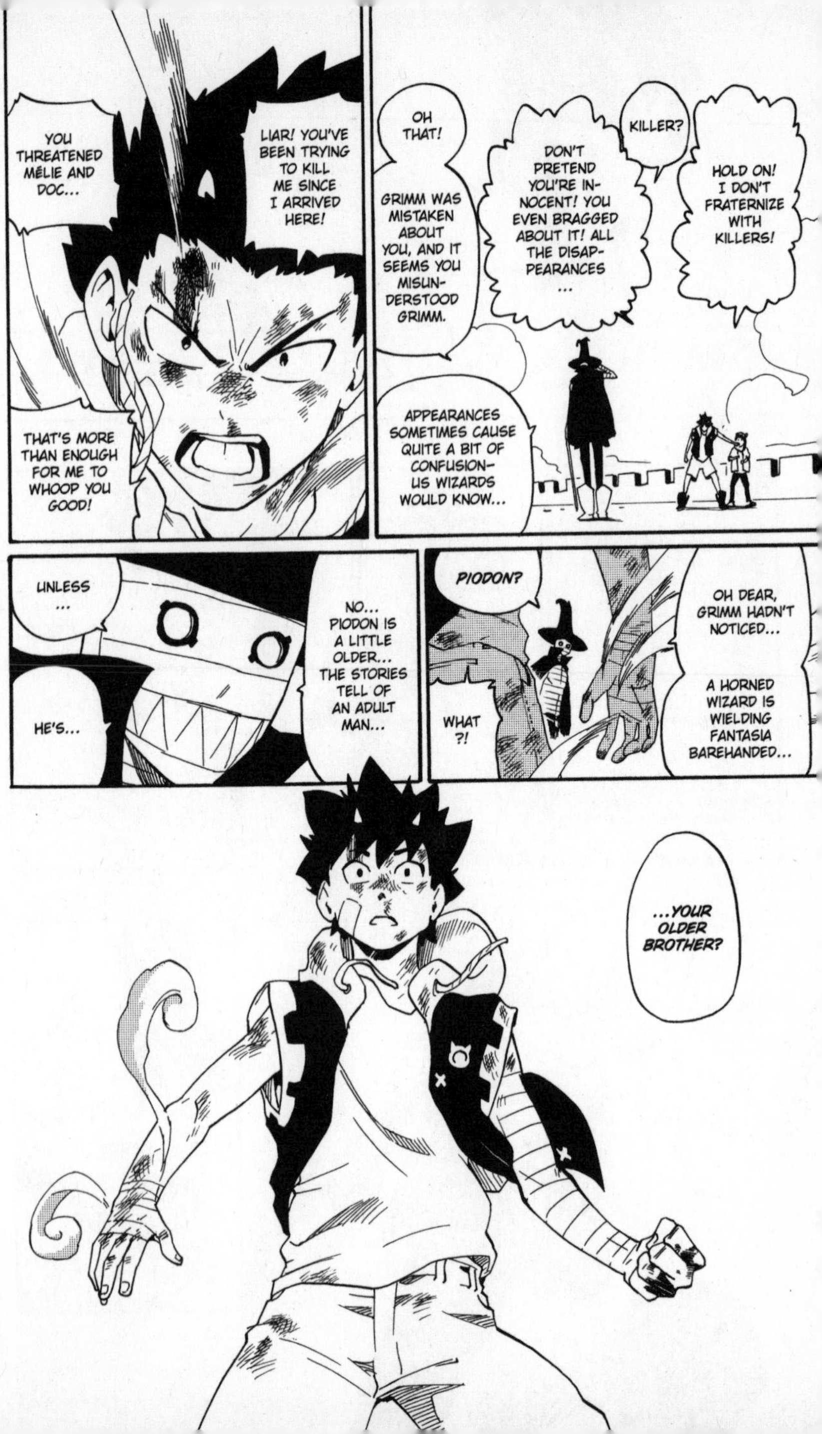
HOLD ON! I DON'T FRATERNIZE WITH KILLERS!
KILLER?
DON'T PRETEND YOU'RE IN-NOCENT! YOU EVEN BRAGGED ABOUT IT! ALL THE DISAP-PEARANCES...
OH THAT!
GRIMM WAS MISTAKEN ABOUT YOU, AND IT SEEMS YOU MISUN-DERSTOOD GRIMM.
APPEARANCES SOMETIMES CAUSE QUITE A BIT OF CONFUSION—US WIZARDS WOULD KNOW...
LIAR! YOU'VE BEEN TRYING TO KILL ME SINCE I ARRIVED HERE!
YOU THREATENED MÉLIE AND DOC...
THAT'S MORE THAN ENOUGH FOR ME TO WHOOP YOU GOOD!
OH DEAR, GRIMM HADN'T NOTICED...
A HORNED WIZARD IS WIELDING FANTASIA BAREHANDED...
PIODON?
WHAT?!
NO... PIODON IS A LITTLE OLDER... THE STORIES TELL OF AN ADULT MAN...
UNLESS...
HE'S...
...YOUR OLDER BROTHER?

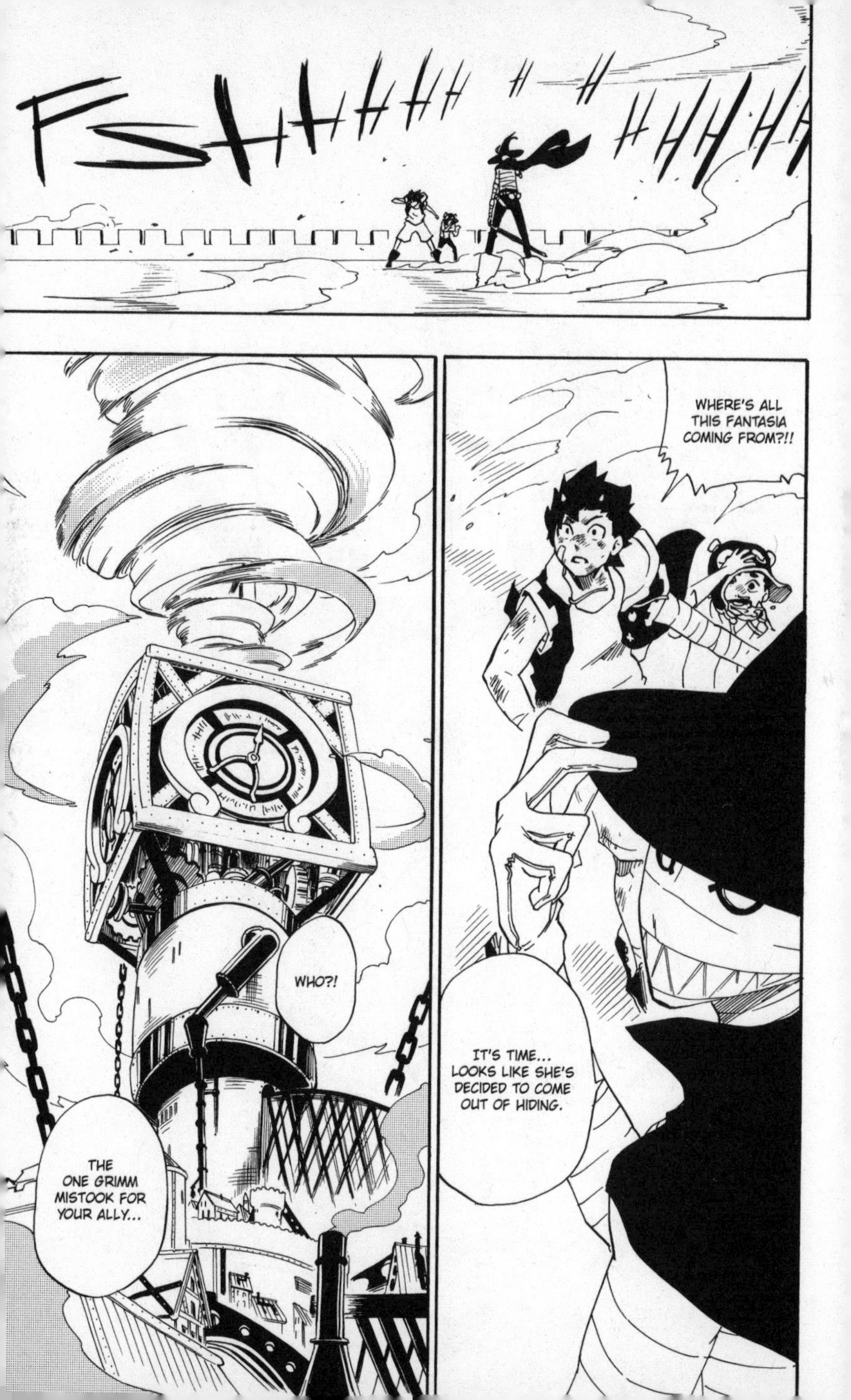
FSHHHHHHHHHHHHHH
WHERE'S ALL THIS FANTASIA COMING FROM?!!
IT'S TIME... LOOKS LIKE SHE'S DECIDED TO COME OUT OF HIDING.
WHO?!
THE ONE GRIMM MISTOOK FOR YOUR ALLY...

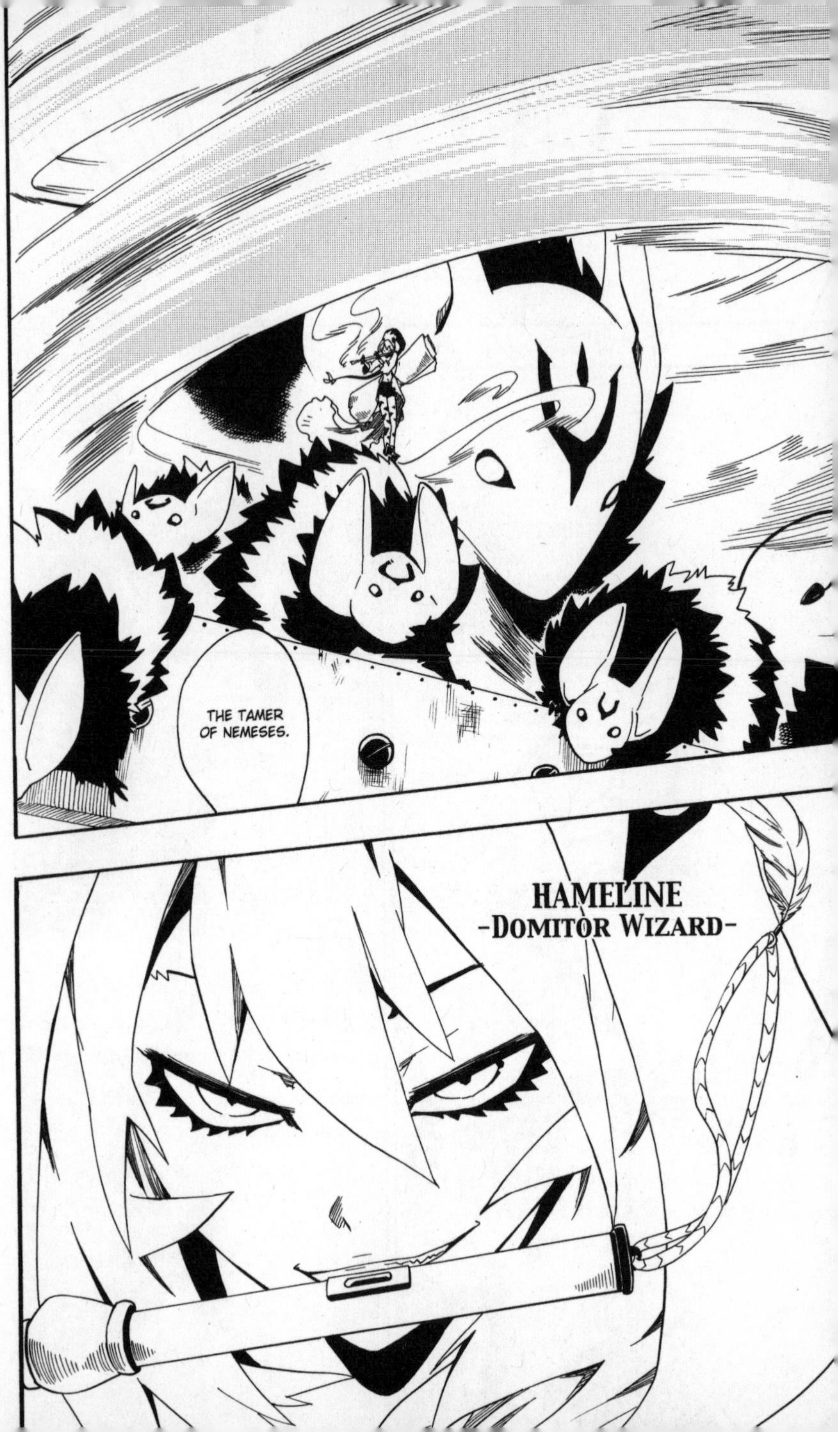
THE TAMER OF NEMESES.
HAMELINE
-DOMITOR WIZARD-

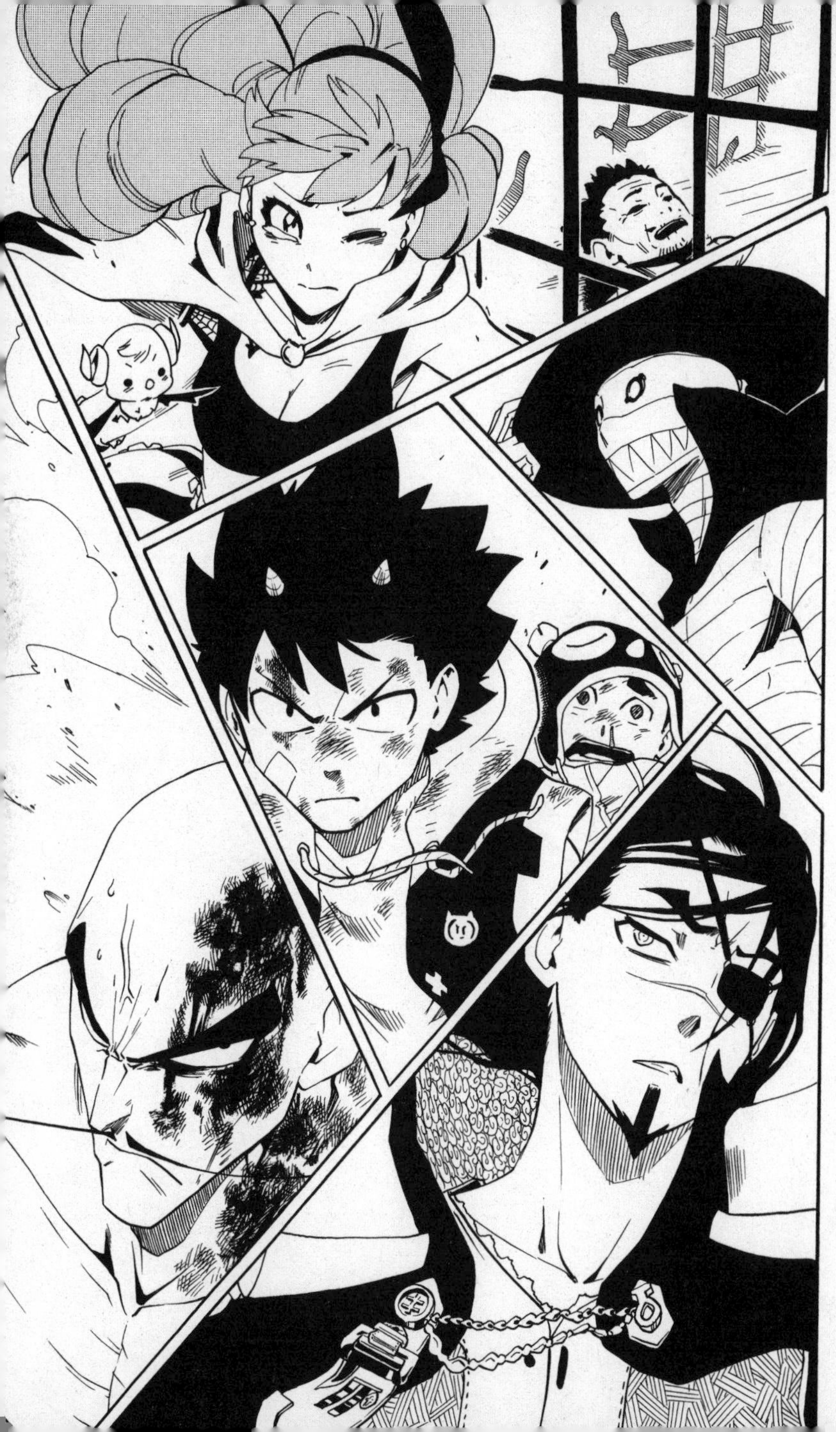

TO BE CONTINUED...

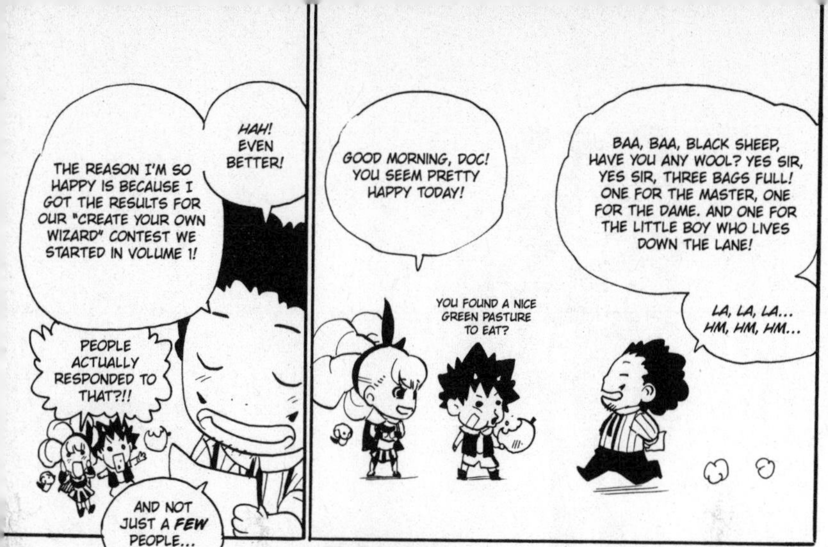
BAA, BAA, BLACK SHEEP, HAVE YOU ANY WOOL? YES SIR, YES SIR, THREE BAGS FULL! ONE FOR THE MASTER, ONE FOR THE DAME. AND ONE FOR THE LITTLE BOY WHO LIVES DOWN THE LANE!
GOOD MORNING, DOC! YOU SEEM PRETTY HAPPY TODAY!
LA, LA, LA... HM, HM, HM...
YOU FOUND A NICE GREEN PASTURE TO EAT?
HAH! EVEN BETTER!
THE REASON I'M SO HAPPY IS BECAUSE I GOT THE RESULTS FOR OUR "CREATE YOUR OWN WIZARD" CONTEST WE STARTED IN VOLUME 1!
PEOPLE ACTUALLY RESPONDED TO THAT?!!
AND NOT JUST A FEW PEOPLE...

BONUS

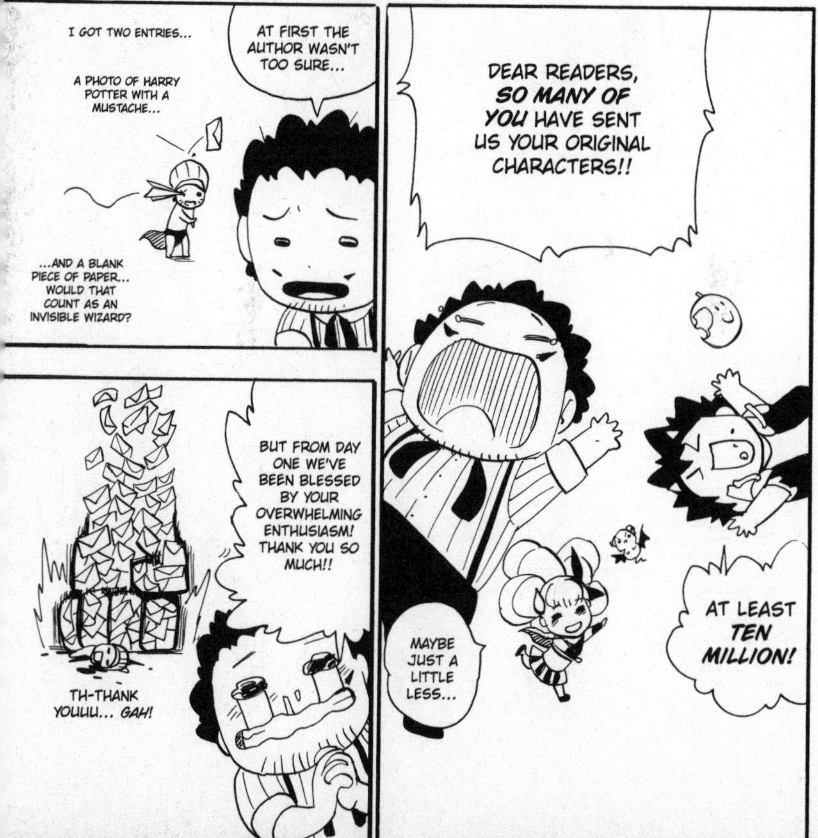
DEAR READERS, SO MANY OF YOU HAVE SENT US YOUR ORIGINAL CHARACTERS!!
AT LEAST TEN MILLION!
MAYBE JUST A LITTLE LESS...
AT FIRST THE AUTHOR WASN'T TOO SURE...
I GOT TWO ENTRIES...
A PHOTO OF HARRY POTTER WITH A MUSTACHE...
...AND A BLANK PIECE OF PAPER... WOULD THAT COUNT AS AN INVISIBLE WIZARD?
BUT FROM DAY ONE WE'VE BEEN BLESSED BY YOUR OVERWHELMING ENTHUSIASM! THANK YOU SO MUCH!!
TH-THANK YOUUU... GAH!

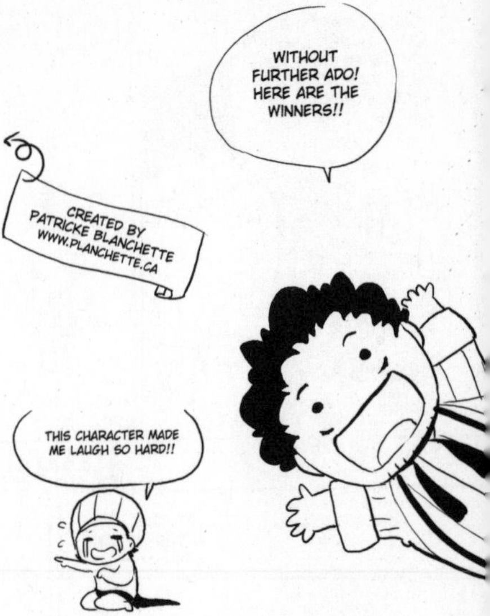
WITHOUT FURTHER ADO! HERE ARE THE WINNERS!!
CREATED BY PATRICKE BLANCHETTE WWW.PLANCHETTE.CA
THIS CHARACTER MADE ME LAUGH SO HARD!!

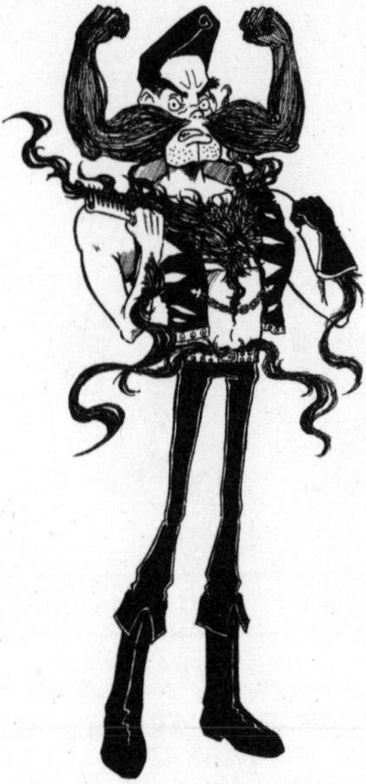

THE WIZARD WITH STRONG FACIAL HAIR!
THE NAME SAYS IT ALL.

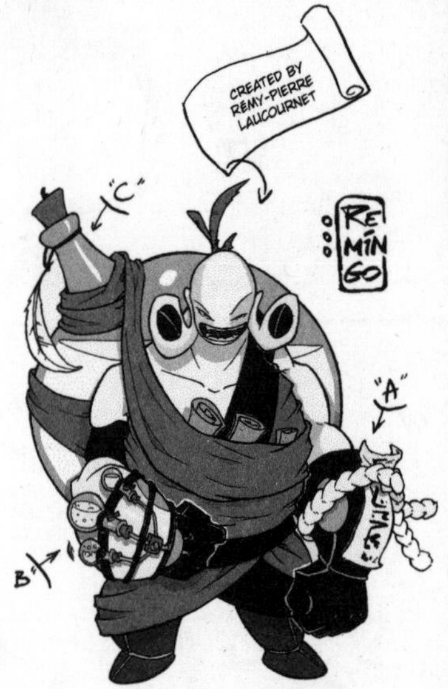
CREATED BY RÉMY-PIERRE LAUCOURNET
"C"
RE MIN GO
"A"
B

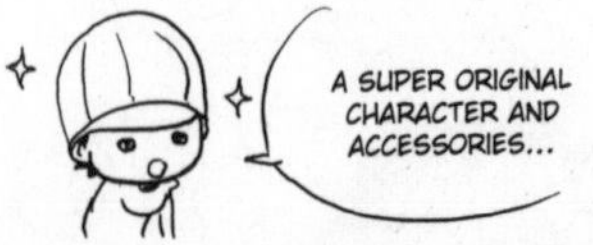
A SUPER ORIGINAL CHARACTER AND ACCESSORIES...

Infection: Disproportionate limbs. This character is 7'7" and weighs 346 lbs.
Specialty: His disproportionate limbs make him a very slow fighter and not very good at magic, but his equipment and powerful attacks more than compensate for these weaknesses.
Accessories:
Ⓐ Protection Spell: Activates a defensive bubble in the case of an enemy attack. Strong point: Doesn't use up Fantasia. Weak point: After activation the spell can't be used again.
Ⓑ Glove with direct injection of Potions into the user's hand. Strong point: Multiplies the effect of any potion. Can create giant flames, ice, etc and hits depending application. Weak point: The potion only allows for three attacks.
Ⓒ Potion Boost: Moving this gigantic body and using these overpowered magic attacks all demand a lot of energy. Weak points: Very addictive and can cause dependence. Users habituated to this must consume an increasing amount to keep up the effect.

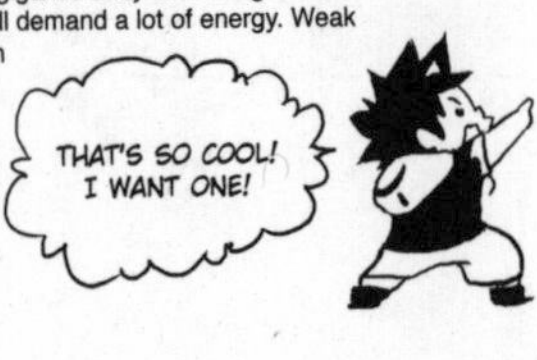
THAT'S SO COOL! I WANT ONE!

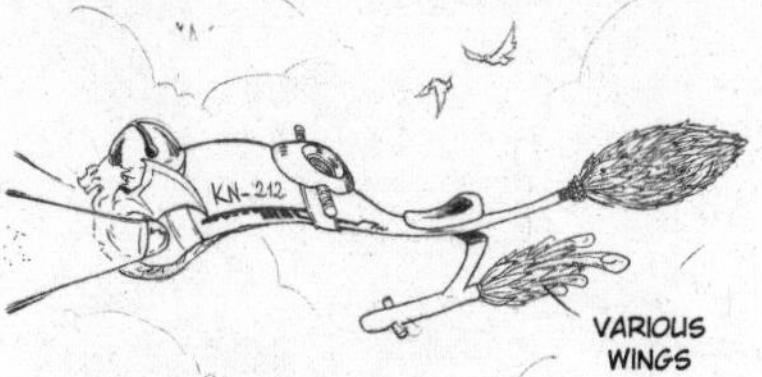
KN-212
VARIOUS WINGS

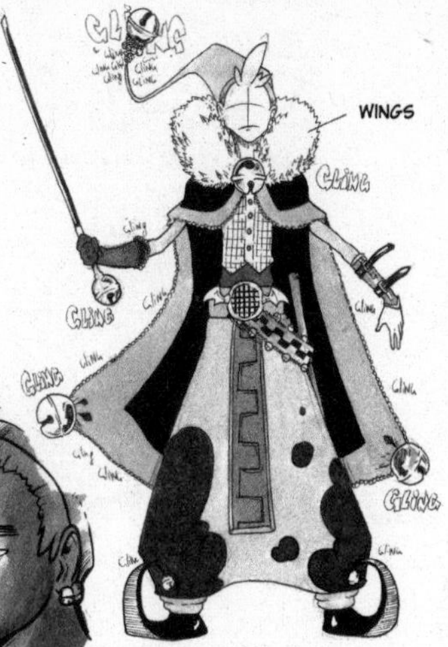
GLING
WINGS
GLING
GLING
GLING
GLING

GLING-GLING.

A MESSENGER WHO TRAVELS ON ONE OF THE FASTEST BROOMS EVER CREATED.
INFECTION: HE FALLS ASLEEP WHENEVER HIS SURROUNDINGS ARE COMPLETELY SILENT.
TO REMEDY THAT, HE'S ATTACHED BELLS TO HIS CLOTHES AND BROOM (THUS HIS NAME).

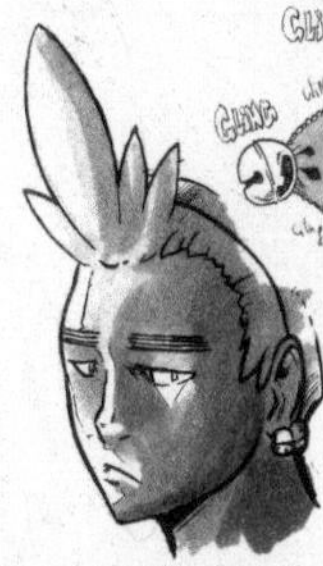

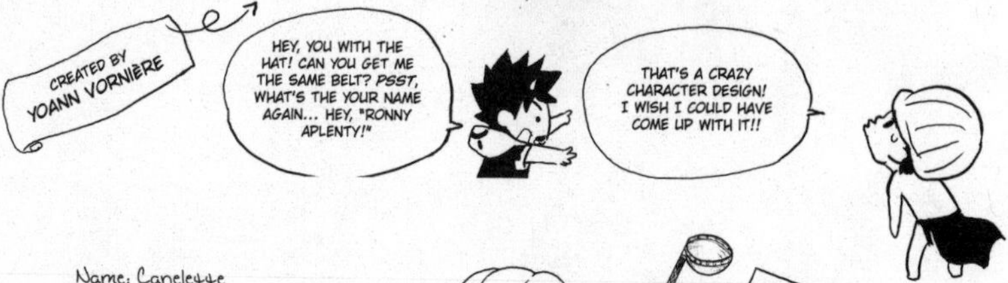
THAT'S A CRAZY CHARACTER DESIGN! I WISH I COULD HAVE COME UP WITH IT!!
HEY, YOU WITH THE HAT! CAN YOU GET ME THE SAME BELT? PSST, WHAT'S THE YOUR NAME AGAIN... HEY, "RONNY APLENTY!"
CREATED BY YOANN VORNIÈRE

Name: Canelette

Healer specialized in potions

Infection: She's entirely consumable, but her body slowly regenerates itself after a certain amount of time. Her blood smells like strawberries, her skin of almond paste, etc.

Useful when the pantry is empty or when you forgot your snacks! Nevertheless, her body is quite small, so her "guests" are never completely full.

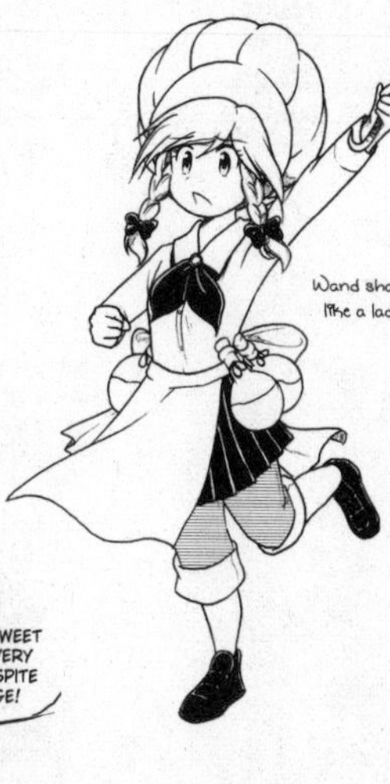
CREATED BY VELKIA
Wand shaped like a ladle.

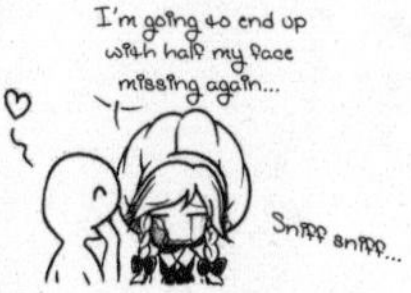
I'm going to end up with half my face missing again...
Sniff sniff...

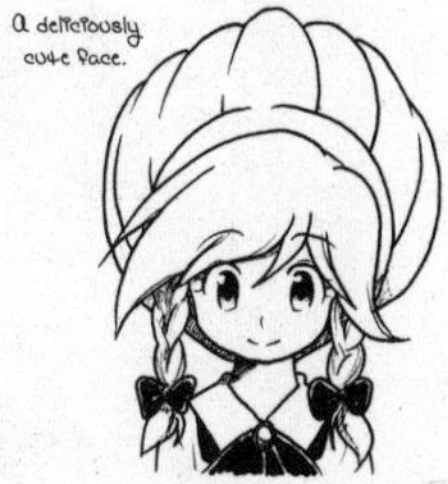
A deliciously cute face.

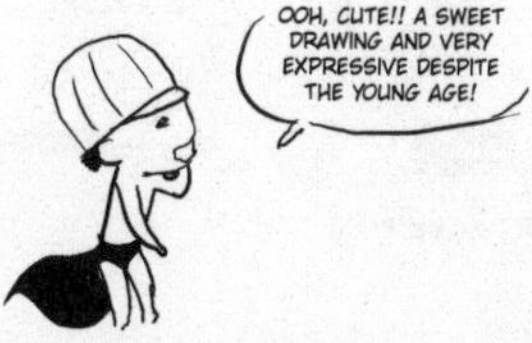
OOH, CUTE!! A SWEET DRAWING AND VERY EXPRESSIVE DESPITE THE YOUNG AGE!

LOCUS

LOCUS IS AN OLD INQUISITION SOLDIER. HIS AIRSHIP AND THE BRIGADE HE WAS IN WERE ERADICATED BY A NEMESIS. HE WAS THE ONLY SURVIVOR. THOUGHT TO BE DEAD, HE QUIT THE INQUISITION AND BECAME A SOLITARY WIZARD.

HIS CONTACT WITH THE NEMESIS MADE HIM LOSE HIS SIGHT.

HE USES HIS MAGIC RAKE TO FLY AROUND, BUT ALSO USES IT AS A WEAPON. HIS MAGIC HELMET ALLOWS HIM TO MORE EASILY PERCEIVE AND SURVEY PEOPLE'S MINDS.

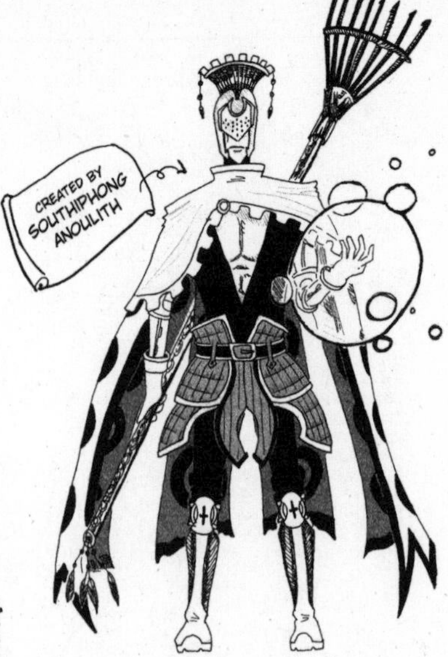
CREATED BY SOUTHIPHONG ANOULITH

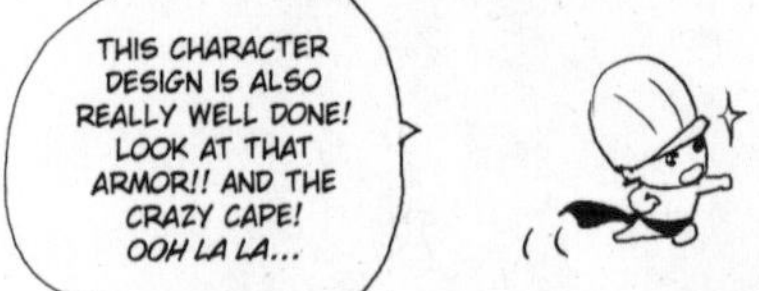
THIS CHARACTER DESIGN IS ALSO REALLY WELL DONE! LOOK AT THAT ARMOR!! AND THE CRAZY CAPE! OOH LA LA...

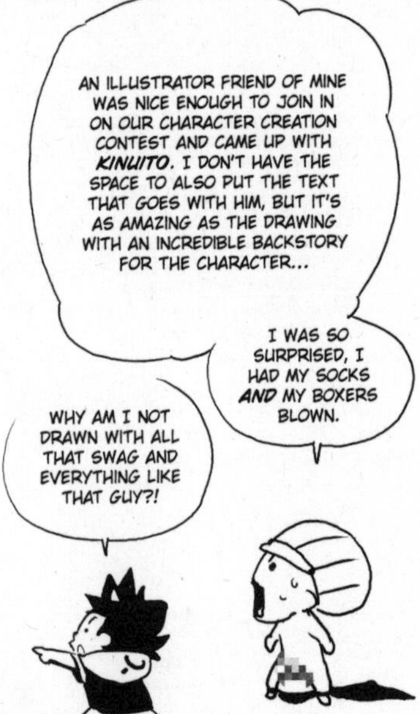
AN ILLUSTRATOR FRIEND OF MINE WAS NICE ENOUGH TO JOIN IN ON OUR CHARACTER CREATION CONTEST AND CAME UP WITH KINUITO. I DON'T HAVE THE SPACE TO ALSO PUT THE TEXT THAT GOES WITH HIM, BUT IT'S AS AMAZING AS THE DRAWING WITH AN INCREDIBLE BACKSTORY FOR THE CHARACTER...
I WAS SO SURPRISED, I HAD MY SOCKS AND MY BOXERS BLOWN.
WHY AM I NOT DRAWN WITH ALL THAT SWAG AND EVERYTHING LIKE THAT GUY?!

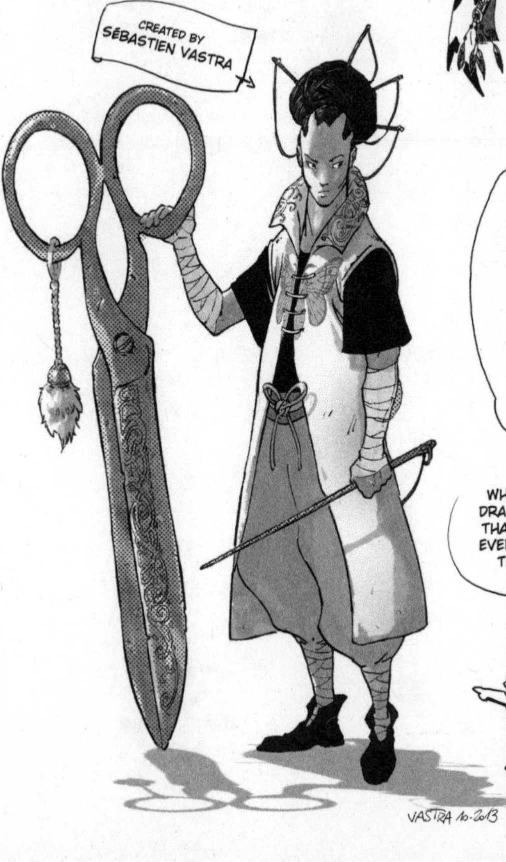
CREATED BY SÉBASTIEN VASTRA
VASTRA 10-2013

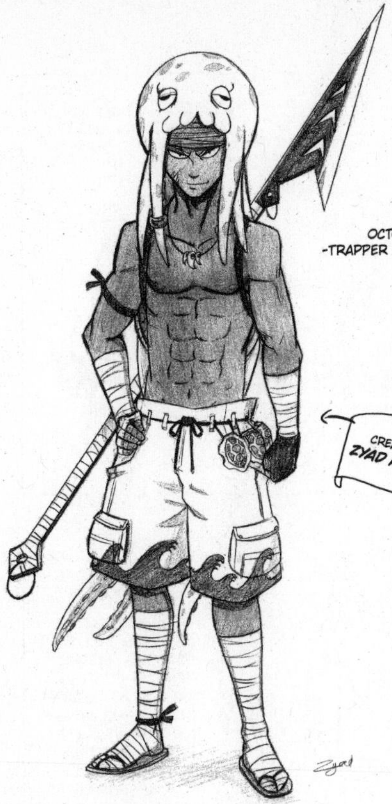

CREATED BY
ZYAD HAMANI

OCTO
-TRAPPER WIZARD-

AND LAST BUT NOT LEAST, THE WINNER: OCTO!!!

LOOK AT THAT POISE! THAT CHARISMA!! AND BEING ABLE TO PULL OFF AN OCTOPUS ON YOUR HEAD—NOW THAT'S QUITE THE FEAT! HERE WE HAVE ANOTHER REALLY ORIGINAL CHARACTER THAT'S VERY UNIFORM AND EXTREMELY EXPRESSIVE. IT REALLY MADE ME WANT TO REDRAW HIM AND THAT DEFIANT LOOK OF HIS.

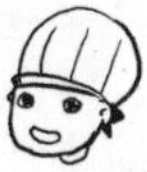

ZYAD WILL RECEIVE THE ORIGINAL COPY OF THE DRAWING PICTURED HERE!

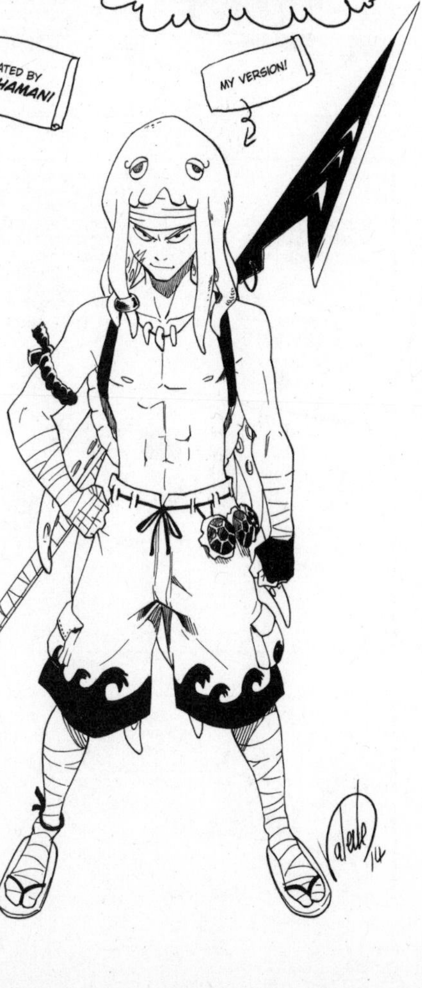

MY VERSION!

History:
Octo is a young man. He's egocentric and a rebellious lone wolf. He's very brave, but just slightly too self-confident. He eats fish all the time and loves sleeping in his hammock.
His favorite hobbies are surfing and fishing. His other hobby is flirting with beautiful young women. Unfortunately, that's when he always loses his confidence and ends up goofing it up when he's in front of them. And his infection doesn't help either: his hair (dreadlocks) was replaced by an octopus! So Octo can't flirt with women while keeping a straight face anymore and keeps on getting tentacles slapped in his face and ink sprayed all over him.

Powers, Equipment:
Octo controls water. He can summon large quantities of water, or even sharks, using his parchments. All of his equipment (parchments, maps etc.) are kept in the turtle shells that he uses as a backpack. Smaller turtle shells are used to hold his potions. He fights Nemeses using spells, his blade and his knuckle-dusters made from shark teeth. He uses his surfboard instead of a magic broom, surfing on top of magic water that floats underneath his surfboard as he moves.

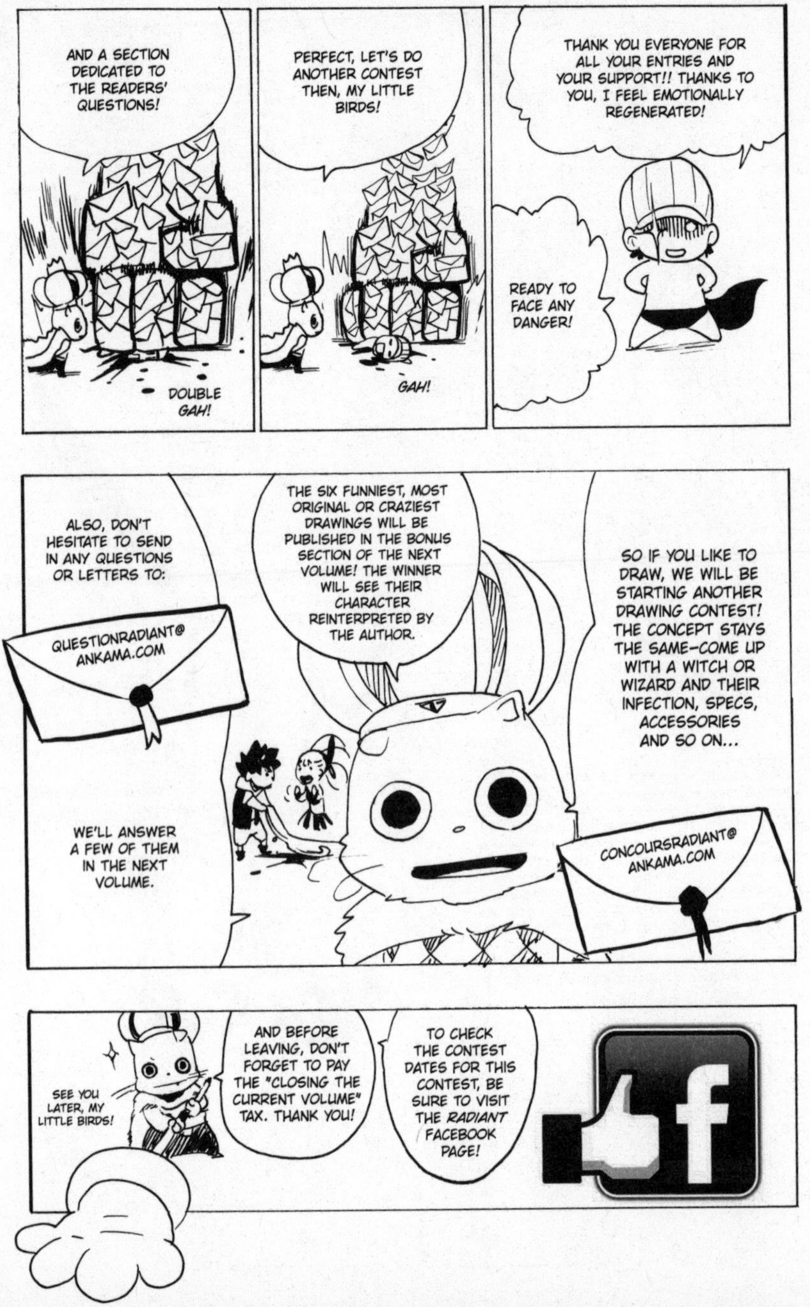
THANK YOU EVERYONE FOR ALL YOUR ENTRIES AND YOUR SUPPORT!! THANKS TO YOU, I FEEL EMOTIONALLY REGENERATED!
READY TO FACE ANY DANGER!
PERFECT, LET'S DO ANOTHER CONTEST THEN, MY LITTLE BIRDS!
GAH!
AND A SECTION DEDICATED TO THE READERS' QUESTIONS!
DOUBLE GAH!
SO IF YOU LIKE TO DRAW, WE WILL BE STARTING ANOTHER DRAWING CONTEST! THE CONCEPT STAYS THE SAME—COME UP WITH A WITCH OR WIZARD AND THEIR INFECTION, SPECS, ACCESSORIES AND SO ON...
CONCOURSRADIANT@ ANKAMA.COM
THE SIX FUNNIEST, MOST ORIGINAL OR CRAZIEST DRAWINGS WILL BE PUBLISHED IN THE BONUS SECTION OF THE NEXT VOLUME! THE WINNER WILL SEE THEIR CHARACTER REINTERPRETED BY THE AUTHOR.
ALSO, DON'T HESITATE TO SEND IN ANY QUESTIONS OR LETTERS TO:
QUESTIONRADIANT@ ANKAMA.COM
WE'LL ANSWER A FEW OF THEM IN THE NEXT VOLUME.
TO CHECK THE CONTEST DATES FOR THIS CONTEST, BE SURE TO VISIT THE *RADIANT* FACEBOOK PAGE!
AND BEFORE LEAVING, DON'T FORGET TO PAY THE "CLOSING THE CURRENT VOLUME" TAX. THANK YOU!
SEE YOU LATER, MY LITTLE BIRDS!

GUEST ARTISTS

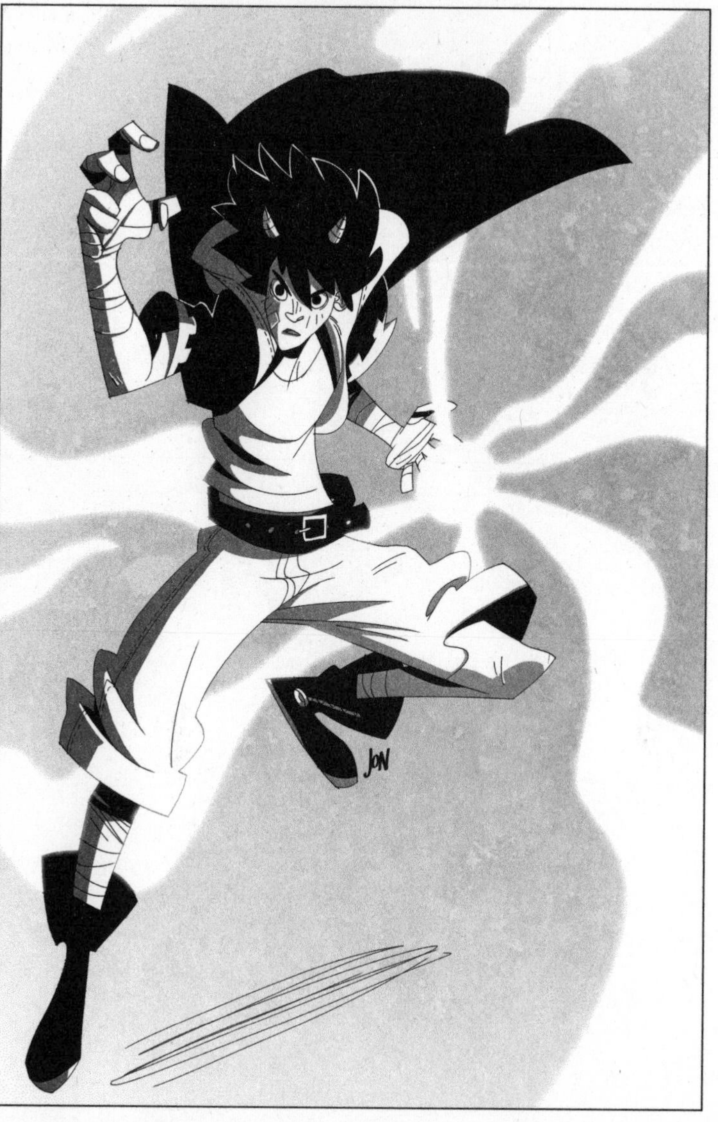
JON

-JON LANKRY-

-POP-

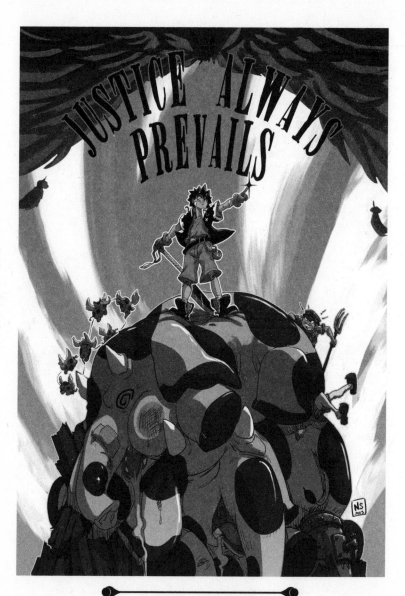

JUSTICE ALWAYS PREVAILS

-NICOLAS SAUGE-

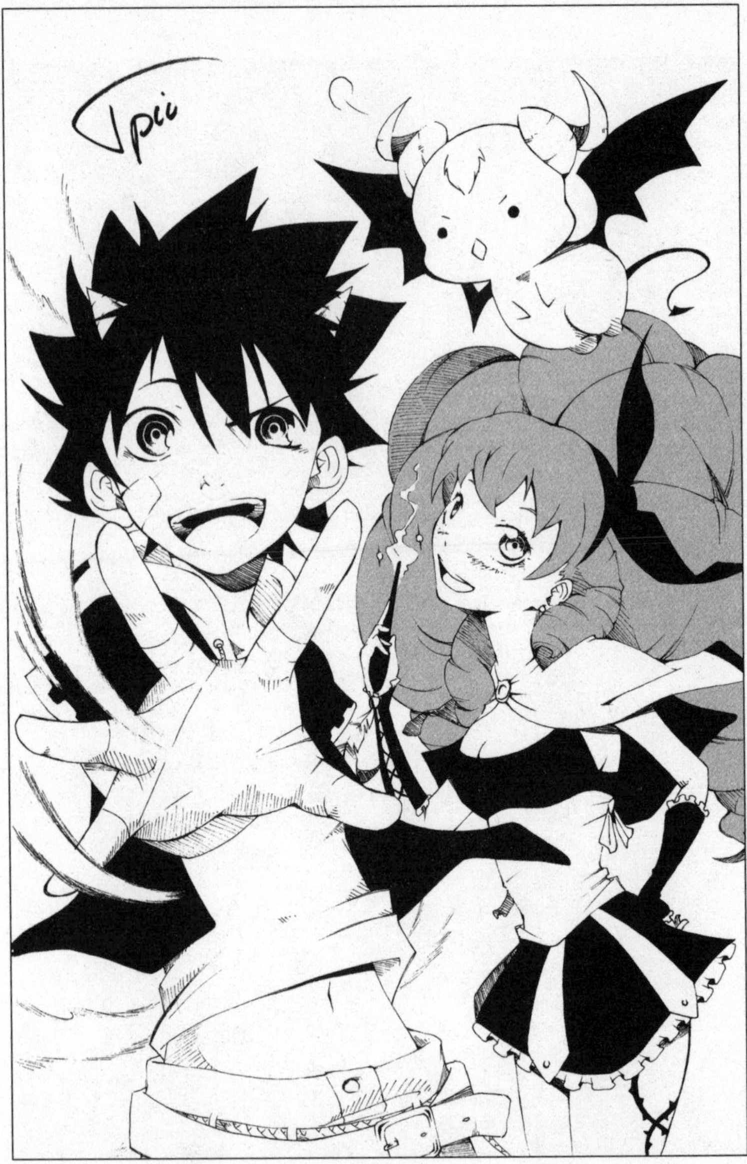
Ipii

-TPIU-

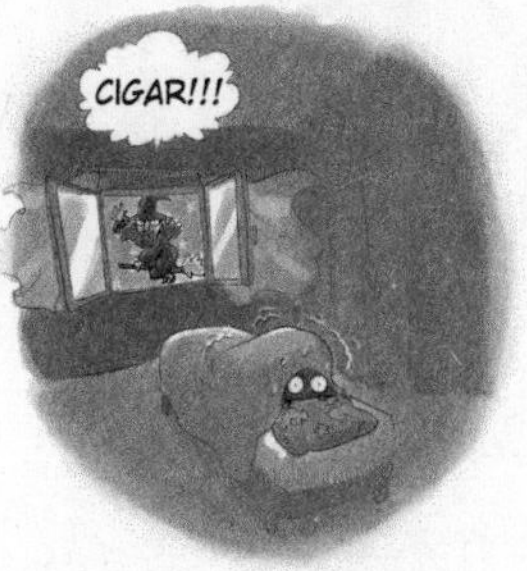
CIGAR!!!

This one time when I was a kid, something strange happened to me. It was late at night and I was in my bed minding my own business when suddenly, the wind violently opened my window! An old woman on a rotten magic broom appeared and I tried to move all "Hngh...!" But nothing happened! She opened her eyes and stared at me. I tried to scream, but nothing came out. She pointed at me, the wind still roaring and the curtain flying in the wind and the windows shattered... She pursed her lips and with her mouth wide open yelled with a resounding voice, "Cigar!!!" I suddenly woke up after that. I have no idea what happened and this dream will forever remain a mystery to me...

—Tony Valente

Tony Valente began working as a comic artist with the series *The Four Princes of Ganahan*, written by Raphael Drommelschlager. He then launched a new three-volume project, *Hana Attori*, after which he produced *S.P.E.E.D. Angels*, a series written by Didier Tarquin and colored by Pop.

In preparation for *Radiant*, he relocated to Canada. Through confronting caribou and grizzlies, he gained the wherewithal to train in obscure manga techniques. Since then, his eating habits have changed, his lifestyle became completely different and even his singing voice has changed a bit!

RADIANT

RADIANT VOL. 2
VIZ MEDIA Manga Edition

STORY AND ART BY **TONY VALENTE**

Translation/**(´・∀・`)ｻｧ?**
Touch-Up Art & Lettering/**Erika Terriquez**
Design/**Julian [JR] Robinson**
Editor/**Marlene First**

Published by arrangement with MEDIATOON LICENSING/Ankama.
RADIANT T02

Printed in the U.S.A.

Published by VIZ Media, LLC
P.O. Box 77010
San Francisco, CA 94107

10 9 8 7 6 5 4 3 2 1
First printing, November 2018

VIZ MEDIA
viz.com

ratings.viz.com RATED T TEEN

PARENTAL ADVISORY
RADIANT is rated T for Teen and is recommended for ages 13 and up. This volume contains fantasy violence.

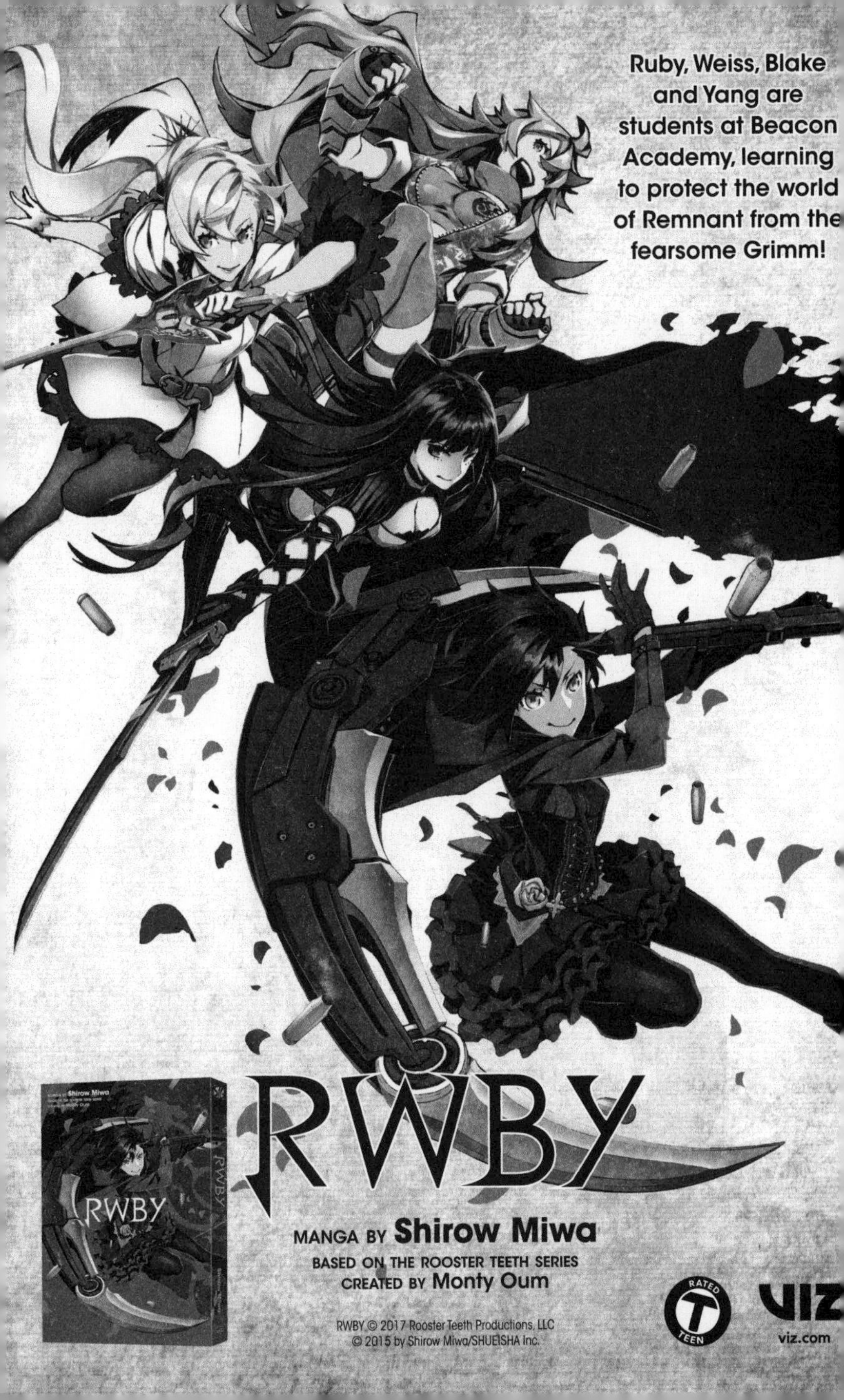

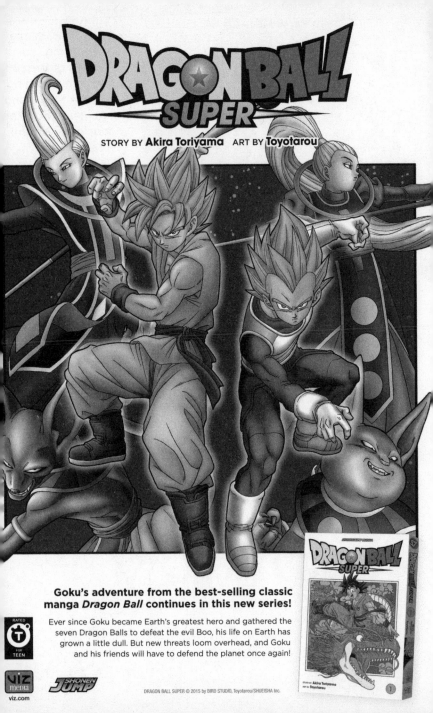

THE ACTION-PACKED SUPERHERO COMEDY ABOUT
ONE MAN'S AMBITION TO BE A HERO FOR FUN!

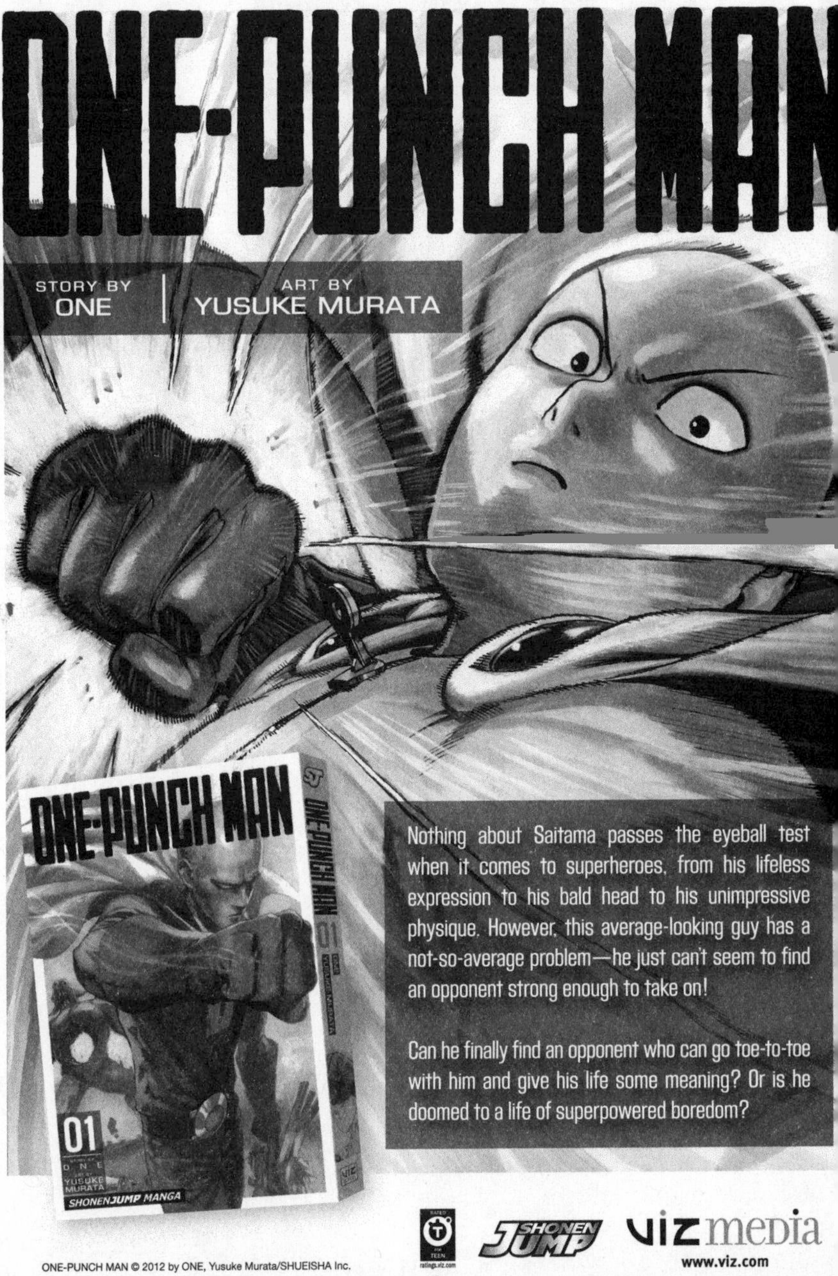
ONE-PUNCH MAN
STORY BY
ONE
ART BY
YUSUKE MURATA
ONE-PUNCH MAN
01
ONE
YUSUKE MURATA
SHONENJUMP MANGA
Nothing about Saitama passes the eyeball test when it comes to superheroes, from his lifeless expression to his bald head to his unimpressive physique. However, this average-looking guy has a not-so-average problem—he just can't seem to find an opponent strong enough to take on!
Can he finally find an opponent who can go toe-to-toe with him and give his life some meaning? Or is he doomed to a life of superpowered boredom?

SHONEN JUMP

VIZ media
www.viz.com